HAMAS

HAMAS

FROM RESISTANCE TO GOVERNMENT

PAOLA CARIDI

Translated by Andrea Teti

Seven Stories Press

NEW YORK

Seven Stories Press
140 Watts Street
New York, NY 10013
www.sevenstories.com

College professors may order examination copies of Seven Stories Press titles for a free six-month trial period. To order, visit http://www.sevenstories.com/textbook or send a fax on school letterhead to (212) 226-1411.

Library of Congress Cataloging-in-Publication Data:
Caridi, P. (Paola)
[Hamas. English]
Hamas : from resistance to government / by Paola Caridi ; translated by Andrea Teti.
    p. cm.
ISBN 978-1-60980-382-7 (pbk.)
1. Harakat al-Muqawamah al-Islamiyah. 2. Palestinian Arabs--Politics and government. 3. Islam and politics--Gaza Strip. 4. Islam and politics--West Bank. 5. Arab-Israeli conflict--1973-1993. 6. Arab-Israeli conflict--1993- I. Title.
JQ1830.A98H373313 2012
324.25695'3082--dc23
956.953   2011051400

Book design by Phoebe Hwang

Printed in the USA

9 8 7 6 5 4 3 2 1

To the memory of my teacher,
Paolo Spriano,
historian and journalist

CONTENTS

UNGA PARTITION PLAN, 1947

PASSIA

Acre
Haifa
Mediterranean
Sea
Nazareth

Jenin

Nablus

Tel Aviv
Jaffa

Ramallah
Jericho
Jerusalem
Bethlehem
Gaza
Hebron
Khan Yunis
Bir Saba

Dead Sea

N e g e v

	Proposed Jewish State
	Proposed Arab State
	Internationally administered 'Corpus Separatum' of Jerusalem

Map: PASSIA, 2002

ARMISTICE LINES, 1949

PASSIA

Acre
Haifa
Mediterranean
Sea
Nazareth

Jenin

Nablus
JORDAN

Tel Aviv
Jaffa

Ramallah
Jericho
Jerusalem
Bethlehem
Gaza
Hebron
Khan Yunis
Bir Saba

Dead Sea

Al-Auja

N e g e v

EGYPT

	Proposed Jewish State
	Arab territory
	Territories seized by Israel beyond the area for the proposed Jewish State

Map: PASSIA, 2002

Gaza, 2009

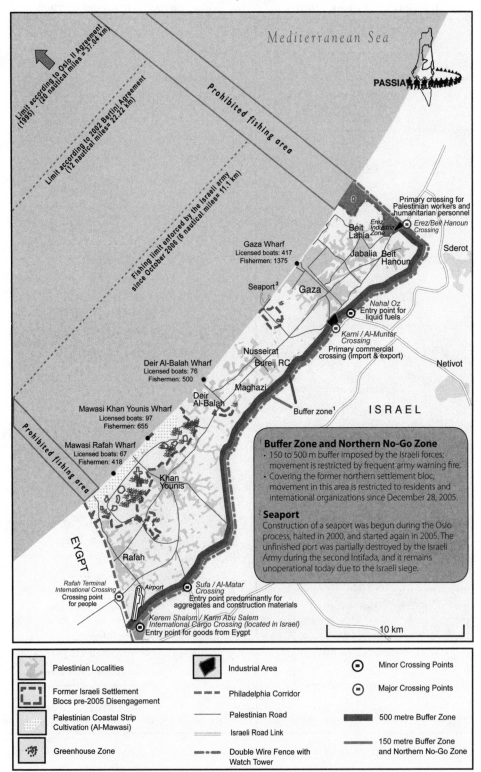

Mediterranean Sea

PASSIA

Limit according to Oslo (I Agreement) (1995) - (20 nautical miles = 37.04 km)

Limit according to 2002 Bertini Agreement (12 nautical miles= 22.22 km)

Fishing limit enforced by the Israeli army since October 2006 (6 nautical miles= 11.1 km)

Prohibited fishing area

Prohibited fishing area

Primary crossing for Palestinian workers and humanitarian personnel

Erez/Beit Hanoun Crossing

Erez Industrial Zone

Beit Lahia

Jabalia

Beit Hanoun

Sderot

Gaza Wharf
Licensed boats: 417
Fishermen: 1375

Seaport²

Gaza

Nahal Oz
Entry point for liquid fuels

Karni / Al-Muntar Crossing
Primary commercial crossing (import & export)

Netivot

Nusseirat

Bureij RC

Deir Al-Balah Wharf
Licensed boats: 76
Fishermen: 500

Maghazi

Deir Al-Balah

Mawasi Khan Younis Wharf
Licensed boats: 97
Fishermen: 655

Buffer zone¹

ISRAEL

Mawasi Rafah Wharf
Licensed boats: 67
Fishermen: 418

Khan Younis

¹ Buffer Zone and Northern No-Go Zone
- 150 to 500 m buffer imposed by the Israeli forces; movement is restricted by frequent army warning fire.
- Covering the former northern settlement bloc, movement in this area is restricted to residents and international organizations since December 28, 2005.

² Seaport
Construction of a seaport was begun during the Oslo process, halted in 2000, and started again in 2005. The unfinished port was partially destroyed by the Israeli Army during the second Intifada, and it remains unoperational today due to the Israeli siege.

EYGPT

Rafah

Rafah Terminal
International Crossing
Crossing point for people

Airport

Sufa / Al-Matar Crossing
Entry point predominantly for aggregates and construction materials

Kerem Shalom / Karm Abu Salem
International Cargo Crossing (located in Israel)
Entry point for goods from Eygpt

10 km

Palestinian Localities	Industrial Area	⊖ Minor Crossing Points
Former Israeli Settlement Blocs pre-2005 Disengagement	- - - Philadelphia Corridor	⊖ Major Crossing Points
Palestinian Coastal Strip Cultivation (Al-Mawasi)	Palestinian Road	500 metre Buffer Zone
Greenhouse Zone	Israeli Road Link	150 metre Buffer Zone and Northern No-Go Zone
	Double Wire Fence with Watch Tower	

ACKNOWLEDGMENTS

A book on Hamas necessarily handles sensitive issues and demands field research that is somehow unique. This is the reason I will not thank individuals by name. Rather, I will thank groups. Groups composed, of course, of individuals who, in different ways and at various periods during my time in the Middle East and North Africa, provided me with keys for interpretation, testimonies, evidences, *insana corporis*, insights, reserved or public information, opinions, and pathos.

There are notable exceptions to this, one being Raf Scelsi in his "institutional" role as editor at the Italian publishing house Feltrinelli, as well as in his capacity as an intellectual and a friend. His was the initial idea for this book, and he encouraged me to bring together my job as a journalist and my training as a historian of political parties. I am grateful to Raf, to his intuition and to his gentle tenacity.

It was Paolo Spriano (1925–1988)—professor of political parties in Rome University's literature faculty, author of the authoritative *History of the Italian Communist Party*, renowned journalist, and not least of all member of the Italian (armed) Resistance against Nazi-Fascism during World War II—who taught me most of what I know.

There are then very specific "groups" in which each of those to whom I am indebted will recognize themselves: friends, journalists, experts, the Pickwick Club, people on the street. I will name neither their gender nor nationality—much less their religious faith.

There are men and women, Israelis and Palestinians, Italians, Europeans and Americans, Arabs, Christians, Jews and Muslims. Despite the fact that this book analyzes a very specific part of Arab political Islam, I do not wish to label anyone because—first and foremost—they are individuals, with all the baggage that naturally comes along with their personal and community identities. To all go my heartfelt thanks, with different nuances that all know.

This English edition, first published in Jerusalem, would not have seen the light had it not been for the decision of Dr. Mahdi Abdul Hadi, chairman of PASSIA (Palestinian Academic Society for the Study of International Affairs), to invest in this book during one of the many delicate, difficult, and demoralizing periods of recent Palestinian history. My deep thanks to him not only for his support, but mainly for his intellectual work and for his role as a facilitator between the different Palestinian political cultures. Special thanks to Andrea Teti, lecturer at the Department of Politics and International Relations at the University of Aberdeen, who decided to jump into the adventure of translating this book with enthusiasm, working between Jerusalem and Aberdeen, Naples and Sydney. My very special and informal thanks to Deniz Altayli, who dedicated her time to edit and review the book with her proverbial rigor and helpfulness, and to Imad Farrah, for his support.

Dan Simon of Seven Stories Press honored me with his choice to publish the American edition of my book, providing support to the idea of reading Middle East political history in all its complexity, without resorting to a simplified, stereotypical, useless picture. Jeanne Thornton for Seven Stories guided the process of updating the American edition with care and dedication. The new edition includes both a full chapter devoted to Hamas's political evolution after Operation Cast Lead and a revised epilogue, both products of my continuing assignment, since 2003, as a journalist in Jerusalem, for which I not only follow the daily evolution of the politics of Hamas and the Palestine people, but also continue to research the stages of Hamas's history. I've also decided to add details here and there throughout the text that I consider important to the understanding of the whole picture.

The last (but not the least) "thank you," the one that stands forever—before, beyond, and after this book—goes to my precious family. Especially for the deep patience that each of its members showed during the long stretch I was researching life and politics in Palestine for this book. With passion.

—PC
Jerusalem
December 2011

TRANSLATOR'S NOTE

The original text was translated with the privilege of close and fruitful collaboration with the author, to whom my thanks must go first and foremost. I am grateful to Paola Caridi for affording me the responsibility and the privilege of translating a book that is certainly timely, informative, and insightful. Accessible to readers of all backgrounds, this book is thoroughly useful to both specialist and nonspecialist audiences. I am also grateful to Dr. Mahdi Abdul Hadi and to PASSIA for generously supporting this undertaking.

In coordination with the author, the original Italian text has been modified in places, changing certain expressions, sentence constructions, and some of the original Italian references for an English-speaking audience.

Terms in Arabic have been rendered either as those best known in English, according to the spelling most commonly in use, or in the case of all others, according to a transliteration that avoids specialist conventions. Names of authors are given as spelled in the publications referred to. All terminology relating to the land occupied by Israel during the 1967 War has been modeled on OCHA (the United Nations Office for the Coordination of Humanitarian Affairs) conventions.

All of the translation's limitations and faults remain entirely my own.

—AT
Aberdeen, UK
January 2010

FOREWORD

The Palestinian case is not an isolated one. It was born and nurtured in a particular cultural environment. Only within this cultural environment do apparently radical political developments, like the electoral victory of Hamas in January 2006, become comprehensible. Indeed, before this development there were many signs suggesting the change: the decline of leftist trends in the 1990s; the retreat of the national pan-Arab awareness because of the absence of charismatic pan-Arab leadership, such as that of Gamal Abdel Nasser; and the very visible American military presence in the Arab region, especially after the 2003 US invasion of Iraq. Consequently, Arab liberals entered their regime's offices and spread the culture of democracy, injecting Arab society with the thoughts of the Western bourgeoisie.

This changing landscape also influenced Palestine, which itself witnessed profound changes in the last decades. The national dream of liberation, independence, sovereignty, and statehood diminished, and the long period of negotiations between the liberal Fatah government on the one hand, and the numerous Israeli governments—Labor or Likud—on the other, came to an unsuccessful end. Socioeconomic development in society stagnated, as did the philosophy of steadfastness and resistance, while domestic political corruption and international political hypocrisy came to the fore. It was in these circumstances that Hamas won its landslide victory in the January 2006 elections. Its electoral success was not merely a result of the confrontation between two political tribes, Fatah and Hamas, but was grounded in the latter's message of "Change and Reform" and its mission to halt the deterioration of society and change the status quo.

The election was more than wake-up call, more than a slap in the face, more than a mere demand for change. Here, the roles and the missions of intellectuals and journalists come in. One of them, Italian writer and historian Paola Caridi, looked at the transition in the political elite and the takeover of authority since the elections. Caridi shows in her book different interpretations, statements, and views on Hamas, as well as the conditions imposed on and offers presented to both the movement and Palestinian society afterward. First and foremost are the International Quartet's three famous demands, the preconditions for Hamas to enter the political arena, share political power, and be recognized and legitimized: (1) recognition of Israel, (2) renouncing terror, and (3) honoring and respecting all previous agreements reached between Israel and the Palestinians. Hamas responded by offering a truce, the acceptance of a Palestinian state on the 1967 borders, and aquiescence to the PLO taking the leading role in negotiations.

The election also had its effect on the Palestinian national identity, as it resulted in an unprecedented geographical and political division and the formation of two separate administrations, governments, and realities in Gaza and the West Bank.

In focusing on Hamas's political agenda and personalities, its battles and relationships, its evolution and prospects, this book is not Islamist in nature but offers a sober insight in the unfolding history of the movement since the beginning of the Muslim Brotherhood, as well as developments in its culture, behavior, and internal discourse. Obviously it is thereby also necessary and unavoidable to underline the Islamic nature and way of life of Hamas members to understand what happened in the last four years in the Palestinian political arena.

Many of Hamas's representatives and leaders have roots in educational and social fields, having worked in welfare institutions, hospitals, clinics, kindergartens, and so on. Politically, they were newcomers, but they learned fast and now perform remarkably, especially in the national dialogue in Cairo. The main question today, however, is how to deal with the doctrine, ideology, and rationale leading to political Islam and to the moral responsibility of representing it. Unlike Fatah and other movements, which developed their doctrine through the national struggle with Israel, Hamas, as the operational movement of the Palestinian Muslim Brotherhood, politicized its faith as reflected in its flag, political language, social discourse, and ideological principles, which, in recent years, have proved very resonant in society. In following its philosophy of "faithful politics," Hamas has not only gained popularity, but support, as well, pushing leftist, nationalist, and pan-Arabist forces aside.

That understood, it should be clear why it is a severe interpretational mistake to reduce Hamas's electoral victory to a protest against corruption and failure in the negotiations, or the absence of Yasser Arafat. Hamas succeeded in using elections as a political tool to move to the political stage as an "alternative," or as Paola Caridi puts it in this book: "The end of suicide bombings within Israeli cities, the substantive end of the Second Intifada, and Hamas's choice in favor of participating in Palestinian electoral politics are interpreted by the Palestinian population as a specific political proposal."

The political agenda of Hamas has developed in different stages since 2006, depending on events on the ground. We've seen the Mecca Agreement, the formation of a national unity government, confrontation and reconciliation talks with Fatah, *hudna* talks with Israel, and internal discourses on the reform of the security apparatuses, the release of prisoners, the reconstruction of the PLO, and on humanitarian needs and reconstruction after Operation Cast Lead.

Today, Palestinian society is divided, angry, and frustrated with the two mediocre regimes that govern in the West Bank and in Gaza. In the West Bank, people are not content with the security and economic performance of the Palestinian National Authority, nor with matters of participation and institution building. In Gaza, the Hamas regime is also increasingly under attack, one issue being the de-democratization of the society and system. Both regimes can be labeled as no more than "big municipalities," and the Palestinian street is calling for reconciliation and unity to overcome the current *nakba*—a term that is increasingly being used these days not in reference to its historical origin, the partition of Palestine and dispossession and forced exile of Palestinians in 1948—but to the situation on the ground and the two political tribes that are jeopardizing Palestine's future by focusing on their own interests and supremacy at the expense of their loyalty to the cause.

—Dr. Mahdi Abdul Hadi

EMOTIONAL PROLOGUE

The Number 19 Bus

"Good luck!" a dear friend said to me, with both affection and concern, when I told him what I was about to do: write a book about Hamas. His words gave me the key for my labors: what else could be said about the most important Palestinian Islamist movement? In Israel there are those who call Hamas militants "animals" or even "cannibals." During Bill Clinton's presidency, the United States placed the movement on its list of terrorist organizations. A few years later, Europe followed the American example. In this context, what can one possibly write? What *should* one write? Should I provide a detailed description of how a suicide belt is built? Should I provide a voice for Hamas's armed wing, the (young) men of the Izz al-Din al-Qassam Brigades, portrayed in that iconography standardized the world over of the mask and the green bandanna? Or, perhaps, I should enter an Israeli prison and interview those who organized the terrorist attacks, or the would-be suicide bombers who changed their minds and didn't blow themselves up?

No, there is no need for such volumes. The shelves of bookstores and those of many homes are replete with sensational titles, of front covers with hyperveiled Muslim women, of would-be suicide bombers cocooned in camouflage, of Arab children holding up guns, and so on. Few books, however, provide complex answers to the crucial question that emerged in the immediate aftermath of the Palestinian elections of January 25, 2006.

In those elections, Palestinians exercised their right and duty to vote with a deep and unanimously recognized sense of democracy. And they gave Hamas a decisive mandate. Why, at that particular point in time, did Hamas attract the support of the majority of Palestinians? Had the Palestinians, whose story we had all come to know over the past forty years, suddenly become supporters of terrorism?

This oversimplistic, Manichean explanation was offered by those who supported the chimera of a "guided democratization" in the Middle East, modeled on Western democracies. Such people, faced with the electoral result, would ask, how is it possible? How can it be that when we grace them with the opportunity to use the vote—that prince among instruments of Western representative democracies— that they, one man with one vote, end up choosing Hamas? These were the questions one heard in the immediate aftermath of the elections. The answers came. Perhaps—these voices asked—rather than protest at the scandal of Palestinians' choice, we should reconsider our strategy? The truth is that, given the electoral results, given that vote, the Hamas victory has to be erased. At all costs.

This is precisely what happened. In practice, Hamas's electoral success in 2006 was annulled by the international community, erased as though those very same heads of government had not earlier praised the presence of the Islamist party on the electoral roll. As though the polling booths had never been installed throughout the West Bank and Gaza. As though just under nine hundred international observers had never been installed and had never attested to the democratic character of the electoral process. "Free and fair," it was said at the time, an example of freedom and propriety, as all the reports compiled in the election's aftermath said. Yet, ever since the establishment of the Hamas government the following March, the international community bolted all exits and enclosed Palestinian politics in a pen.

Doors locked, windows barred, and still no answer to the fundamental question: Why did Hamas win on January 25, 2006? And this is itself a question that is only the latest in a long series of political questions, the tip of an iceberg of questions that are all the more urgent because they go to the heart of the Palestinian-Israeli conflict. Indeed, for precisely this reason, they require complex and exhaustive answers. The first answer—the hardest, the most controversial, but also the most clearly backed by both facts and experts—is that Hamas is not a terrorist organization, but rather a political movement that has used terrorism, particularly during a certain phase of its history spanning over two decades. The latest to attest to this is a man who cannot be accused of either collusion or sympathy toward the members of the Harakat al-Muqawwama al-Islamiyya: Tom Segev, a well-known editorialist for *Ha'aretz*—one of Israel's most popular broadsheets, particularly abroad—who, the day after the beginning of Operation Cast Lead, launched by the Israeli Defense Forces on December 27, 2008, wrote: "Hamas is not a terrorist organization holding Gaza residents hostage: It is a religious nationalist movement, and a majority of Gaza residents believe in its path."[1] This is a distinction that appears to take into account neither the fear of Sderot's inhabitants, nor of the suffering of the families of the over 500 victims of the suicide bombings that not only Hamas, but all Palestinian armed factions—including those linked to Fatah—carried out inside Israel between 2000 and 2005, the year of Hamas's declaration of a de facto truce. Men, women, and children. The civilians dead in the buses, in the cafés, on the roads of Tel Aviv, Jerusalem, Afula, Netanya, Haifa. Israelis, Jews, and Arabs, foreigners, soldiers on leave, mothers, students on the way to school early in the morning.[2]

Early, like that morning of January 29, 2004, when Ali Munit Youssef Jihara, a Palestinian policeman from Bethlehem, blew himself up in one of Jerusalem's downtown quarters, in a road with an evocative name, Rechov Azza—Gaza Road—fifty meters from the office of the then–Israeli Prime Minister Ariel Sharon, and fifty meters away from the Moment Café, which had been the target of another suicide attack two years before. At that time, I lived less than two hundred meters away from Rechov Azza. I didn't hear the explosion, as is often the case in these circumstances. I only heard about it later. What I *did* hear were the ambulances' strident horns, the crazed sirens and loudspeakers of police cars. They were telling me that there had been an attack. I made sure that my family was okay—my husband had left to take our son to the nursery—and then I rushed to Gaza Road, to see with my own eyes what a suicide attack meant: a bus, half of which had been blown away, so that the crumpled chassis was the only simulacrum yet visible, the symbol of all the broken lives, the tattered flesh, which, I was told, could be found blown onto the balconies of the buildings in the Rehavia quarter, a middle-class area that provides for the quiet retirement of professionals and intellectuals. Professionals and intellectuals like Zeruya Shalev—writer, author of familiar novels, whom I met four years after that January 29 at Moment Café, which had in the meantime changed its name to Resto-Bar. Life is made of human beings and of stories that touch us, and it wasn't until four years later that I discovered that she had been on Gaza Road just before I arrived, among the dozens injured in that attack, which had claimed eleven lives. She had been hit in the knee: she was on the sidewalk, with the bus having driven past her just before it exploded.

That attack was not claimed by Hamas, but not only did they not condemn it, they commended it. It was immediately claimed by Al-Aqsa Martyrs' Brigades, the armed faction close to Fatah, Yasser Arafat's party. It was my baptism for "that kind" of news in Jerusalem, where I had arrived just a month and a half before, in the still-bloody wake of the Second Intifada. Thinking about it again, composing the pieces of that personal, professional, and human mosaic that is one's life, perhaps it was precisely that attack which gave me a point of entry into the Palestinian-Israeli conflict. The lifeless shell of a bus, its rear portion blackened, yet intact around the driver's seat. And outside, along the perimeter designated by that symbol of suffering, a deep sense of unreality, of detachment between the image of the explosion and the silence of the aftermath: the "specialists" looking for anything that might be linked to the explosion, the sorry remains of human beings, the objects belonging to those who were on that Number 19 bus, the owners of the shops and the tenants sweeping broken glass off the pavement.

From then on, after that fateful January in 2004, my role in Jerusalem would become double: witness of the news by profession, and the city's resident and thus potential unwitting victim as a consequence of a choice we made as a family. It is precisely this dual role that made it impossible for me to shun questions, not to ask myself what it meant to live with that daily fear packed into a rucksack, into banal everyday gestures: getting onto a bus to go to work, entering a café, finding oneself in a car behind public transport and hoping it isn't a suicide bomber sitting on the seat on the other side of a glass windshield, or walking a little more briskly past the bus stop on Jaffa Road or the popular market of Mahane Yehuda because crowds are always dangerous.

But these were not the only questions I asked myself, precisely because it was my duty both as a professional and as a human being to dismiss neither questions nor possible answers. I have always wondered what might lead a twenty-year-old man, a teenager at eighteen, or a young woman of twenty-two to give up their own lives and cause the death of others. I have never thought that this might be a decision taken lightly: all one has to do is step into someone else's shoes, one's neighbor's shoes, to understand that a gesture so definitive, so totalizing, must be born of a feeling that is equally definitive and totalizing. Hate, pain, revenge: one can conjugate desperation however one wishes to, but what is sure is that a suicide bomber's heart is not light; he is not a sniper who fires from afar without putting his life on the line. A suicide bomber pays with his own life; he cannot go back, he cannot be "re-educated."

The common view in the West assumes that religion provides the crucial impulse to become a suicide bomber. Or rather, this account maintains that Islam promises so much in the afterlife that it makes death lighter. I have never fully believed in such a "religious" interpretation of this kind of suicide: in my opinion, this kind of act never loses its political significance, and this political significance falls entirely within the bounds of the Israeli-Palestinian conflict and of national claims. Indeed, confirmation of the political dimension of such an act can come from considering a simple fact: it is not only Islamist organizations like Hamas or Islamic Jihad that have used suicide attacks, but also Fatah and the thoroughly secular Popular Front for the Liberation of Palestine (PFLP). Of course, the fact that these organizations are rooted in more conventional post-1948 Palestinian nationalism in no way detracts from the urgency of the questions that the use of this kind of terrorism raises. It does, however, implicitly question whether it can be right to view Hamas solely in this "religious" light, and whether it might not be more intellectually serious to use more sophisticated interpretive instruments to understand this organization—those same instruments that have also been used for groups such as Fatah or the PFLP.

If these simplistic answers are unsatisfactory, then one must go beyond such simplistic interpretations. This in turn requires immersing oneself in the complexity of the Palestinian Islamist movement, an organization whose existence is based not only on an indefinite religious substratum, but that is, for all intents and purposes, a movement for political reform that cannot divorce itself from reality, from concreteness, from pragmatism. Reality, concreteness, and pragmatism paradoxically coexist with the military wing, with guerrilla, and with suicide attacks. Without an analysis of this complexity, it is not possible to gain an understanding of what has happened in Palestine not only over the past six years, but over the past two decades.

Faiqa's Pilgrimage

Faiqa, for example, was a member of the Palestinian People's Party, one of the two incarnations of Palestinian communism. She took part in the First Intifada, and for that she ended up in an Israeli prison. She was a strong woman, with a deep gaze, a full face, a dark complexion, and a head covered by a simple kerchief, a tiger-skin print *hijab*. I met her during the winter of 2008 in Kobar, a village just above Ramallah, a few kilometers from Birzeit University. Faiqa is not from Kobar; in fact, she has no links with what is little more than a village, known for being the birthplace of Palestine's best-known Barghouthis among the leadership. And yet, when I met her, she had recently arrived in Kobar on board a bus in order to convey her condolences to a widow she'd never met in her life, the wife of a man she had never met: a Hamas imam, one of the best known in the area around Ramallah. Faiqa had learned of the death of Sheikh Majid Barghouthi, who—an investigation would find a few weeks later—had died under torture. Sheikh Majid had been taken away by the men of the Mukhabarat, the Palestinian secret service, and had not left the interrogation room on his feet. The news of his death spread through Palestine. Al Jazeera had been to Kobar, headlining the ugly news, and Faiqa told me she had been unable to sleep at night because of it. She woke breathless, had trouble falling asleep again, and finally decided to go to Kobar even though she had nothing to do with that family or that political history.

If a woman with a communist past, with strong and intelligent eyes, travels through Palestine to pay her respects to a Hamas imam, what then is Hamas—not simply for its members, but for all of Palestinian society? Not just resistance, not just guerrilla. And not just a simple network of social services, prepared to supplement with their own "welfare-within-welfare" the Palestinian National Authority's provision, a provision that fourteen years after its inception has yet to reach all the inhabitants of the West Bank and Gaza. Hamas must represent something more, something that resonates with the expectations and prospects of the Palestinian people as a whole. It is in this dimension that one might begin to find an explanation for this movement's existence and its survival in a land that hopes one day to become a recognized state—viable, possible, real. Indeed, given that Palestinian "political Islam" has not disappeared like snow in the sun despite the military pressure that both Israel and the PNA have repeatedly exercised—including the assassination of Hamas's leadership—one must conclude that the Islamist movement must have provided an alternative to the secularists that was considered more than simply plausible.

These alternatives may appear unrealistic to a Western observer, including, as they do, the rejection of Israel, which Hamas inserted into its own infamous charter of 1988 that called for Israel's destruction, the suicide attacks on Israeli cities, and the launch of Qassam rockets in 2007–2008, all of which smack of total confrontation. But from a Palestinian standpoint, Hamas has provided only these kinds of answers: from its political stances during the First Intifada at least up until the electoral victory of 2006, it also highlighted the fragility of Fatah and of the PNA, and ultimately of the Palestine Liberation Organization (PLO) itself. This is particularly clear with respect to the question of peace with Israel, which was not achieved through the Oslo Accords. And indeed, far from contributing to peace, many now point at the Oslo process as having led down a dead end, legitimizing the Israeli policy of establishing "facts on the ground" regarding settlements[3] in the West Bank and in East Jerusalem, just as it legitimized Israeli control of water resources and of the economy.

A recognition of the weakest parts of the population and the conditions in which they live, political answers concerning the future for Palestine, and rigor in personal conduct—these factors, as much as national claims and protest against the corruption and cronyism of the PNA, are at the root of Hamas's electoral success between 2005 and 2006. I understood this when I saw Hebron—Al-Khalil to the Palestinians—for myself, a city that I have come to love during the last eight years of my life in Israel and Palestine. I cannot explain exactly why, not least because it is certainly not a fascinating city: it has many of the undesirable traits of the urban south of Italy and that sense of slowness and of tradition that I know well. Hebron is (correctly) considered Hamas's stronghold in the West Bank, as it proved during the elections of January 2006, or indeed as demonstrated by the delaying tactics the PNA employed in order to stall earlier local elections out of a fear of losing the most important city of the southern West Bank and thus control of one of the most important industrial and commercial nodes of Palestine.

I should not therefore have been surprised at the tens of thousands of people who descended from Hebron's populous hinterland, from the suburbs, the villages, the countryside, the hills, and of course the various quarters of the city on the eve of the 2006 general elections: minibuses bursting with whole families and green flags, all flocking to Hamas's final political rally. And yet, in the bitter cold of January, that part of Palestine that is made of normal people—made of many women and mothers, made of people who were not on the lists of clients or patrons of the *sulta*, the term by which Palestinians refer to the PNA—threw another question at me: Which Palestine did the West portray? Which pages and how many pages were dedicated to these families, the farmers, the poor, and the refugees, as well as the technicians and the professionals, who all wave the Hamas flag? Is it possible to paint all these people as willing backers of those suicide attacks with the same simple and brutal brushstroke? But if it is not possible—as it clearly is not—then who exactly are these people who have chosen Hamas, either as a party of government or as an expression of their own ideology?

The simple fact to start from is that media representations are inevitably simplistic compared to the complexity of reality, and that when it comes to the Middle East, it is precisely that representation that the West considers to be the only plausible version of reality. This may be the reality, but it does not mean we are justified—in my case, as a historian and a journalist—in setting that complexity aside, and in accepting unquestioningly simplifications that might serve this or that interest, but that never serve the truth. These are the reasons for my choosing to write on a subject that many consider not so much a difficult topic as much as an uncomfortable and provocative one: the first twenty-four years of Hamas, from its birth during the First Intifada of 1987 through the several phases that marked the Palestinian Islamist movement's history—that is, the organizational period, the long and painful season of the suicide attacks inside Israeli cities, the fight against the kind of peace process foreshadowed in Oslo, and the complicated relationship with Fatah, Yasser Arafat, and the PNA. And then, most recently, the political transitional period marked by the participation in the electoral process, Hamas's first government and the national unity government, until the coup that, in June 2007, led the Islamist group to take control of the Gaza Strip. The last chapter, added to the American edition, has been devoted to the aftermath of Operation Cast Lead and the Gaza blockade, as well as the Arab Revolutions and their influence on the internal structure of Hamas and on the national reconciliation process between 2009 and 2011.

Chapter 1

BETWEEN WELFARE AND RESISTANCE

Welcome to Hamastan

The wide slivers of plastic snap in the invisible wind that whistles through a long corridor closed off by slabs of cement eight meters high. Slivers of plastic and slabs of cement at Erez are the funerary monument of the Oslo Accords and of an ideal of economic development that had once seemed to be emerging over the horizon. This ideal had been realized in those Israeli industrial zones that had arisen in border areas, where Palestinians arrived from Gaza in the morning, provided cheap labor, then returned to the Strip in the evening. Then, when the conflict became even harsher at the outbreak of the Second Intifada, queues of Palestinians—in ever-dwindling numbers—began to appear throughout the long Erez corridor along the northern border between Gaza and Israel. In the unreal silence of the Erez dawn, one can nearly hear the footsteps of those workers, a black plastic bag in their hand with their food from home. All lined up, like legions, hundreds, thousands, waiting to pass through the Israeli military checkpoints at the border.

Now there is no one left in this corridor. Even the plastic and cement has disappeared: by 2010, in one of the seemingly never-ending "aesthetic" changes to the Erez crossing, the 200-meter-long corridor has transformed into a path edged by a metal net and a corrugated iron roof. Despite the changes, the silence remains the same.

At Erez, silence is amplified from the other side of the wall that separates Gaza from Israel by the improbably high ceilings of the enormous terminal that lies alone as though it is some kind of exhibition: a beautiful terminal, styled like an airport, and completely empty. As fate would have it, the terminal was completed after the dream of a transborder industrial zone had already been shattered by the failure of the Oslo process, by the Second Intifada, and by terrorism. All that remains of that pained humanity that crossed the border to earn its daily keep are the snapshots taken by photographers for the agencies. Not even the few remaining porters, often little more than boys, can break the stony silence of Erez. Without words, they help the few Palestinians who try to cross: the sick with their applications to be hospitalized beyond the border, the employees of international organizations on missions to Israel, and a few businessmen with special permits.

They are the ones who belong to the select few "special categories," the only Palestinians who have the good fortune of being able to leave Gaza. Ever since the summer of 2005, when the Israeli pullout from the area crystallized the frontier with Israel to the north and west, no one else has been allowed to leave the Strip. The roughly 9,000 settlers who used to live in Gaza—who, thanks to Tel Aviv's good offices, had established three settlement blocs in the Strip—are no longer there. Before falling into a coma, then Prime Minister Ariel Sharon had made the most momentous political decision since the Israeli pullout from southern Lebanon in 2000 by also withdrawing from Gaza, again unilaterally. Hamas's electoral victory of January 25, 2006, came a few short months after this unprecedented change, after Sharon had ordered the end of the Israeli presence in the Strip. And it was precisely in Gaza that Hamas had its stronghold.

Hamas's strength was one of the most important reasons given for the quarantine under which Israel increasingly placed Gaza until, in June 2007—in the move that would bring Hamas to power in the Strip—Gaza was completely sealed off from the rest of the world. But even in previous years, the number of Palestinians who could manage to get work permits in Israel had been steadily decreasing to the point of disappearing entirely, while an authorization to attend a university outside the Strip—whether in Egypt, in the United States, in Jordan, or in Europe—has always been considered a lottery prize, one to be claimed by only a few lucky ones among the thousands who graduate each year. A few others earn their keep working as porters at Erez. They work for years and years, and they wait for ever-fewer customers, most of them severely sick Palestinians who received a permit from the Israeli authorities after passing through a long procedure. The porters help elderly women and mothers with sick children, accepting a few shekels to physically transport them on wrecked luggage trolleys. The porters—who lived through the still-ongoing changes at Erez—greet the few rare guests who arrive from the other side of the wall: VIPs, journalists, nongovernmental organization (NGO) volunteers, diplomats, spies—all high-risk specialists, the only ones who care about the destiny of a place so distant from the daily life of the rest of the world. From the few experts who still pass through Erez, the young porters hope that apart from some loose change, they'll get a few cigarettes—one of the most expensive goods in the Strip, under the increasingly strict isolation imposed by the Israeli army and economy.

Welcome to Gaza. Welcome to one of the most desperate places on the planet even well before Hamas's rise to power. The records only half-describe Gaza's predicament: the highest population density in the world, the most consistent demographic increase in the region with over five children per woman, and since the second half of 2008, the unfortunate distinction of the highest unemployment level on the planet. A smack in the face, squarely delivered when the sun, sand, and dust break the desolation of Erez's long corridor. Off to the right, the empty shells of buildings destroyed by the Israelis for "security reasons" appear, destroyed so that the military's control might extend a few kilometers in from the wall at Erez, up to the buildings funded by Sheikh Zayed bin Sultan al-Nahyan, the old ruler of the Emirates who passed away in November 2004 at virtually the same time as Yasser Arafat.

A solitary red flag used to fly here—at least until the end of 2007— above the ghostly shell of rooms and pillars, atop the steel skeletons of the destroyed buildings of the broken industrial dream that was Erez: neither the green flag of Hamas nor the historical yellow flag of Fatah, but the adventurous banner of the PFLP, the "reds" of the Palestinian political arena, their banner flying and ready to take on the Israeli army's guns all by themselves.

That red flag, borne up by the wind, didn't last long. Just a few months and it disappeared. And along with it, the last building next to the wall that marked the border, completely flattened in order to allow the Israeli army a perfect view. All that remains now, immutable, is the rhythm of Erez clicking along.

Godot's silence, the silence of those who wait in fear for something to come along to break the monotony of desolation: tanks entering the olive groves of Beit Hanoun, a Qassam rocket launched toward the towns of the Negev, there, just beyond the border, and the Israeli air force's missiles ready for a targeted assassination. Or an entirely different situation, like the massive attack codenamed "Hot Winter," which took place over the space of barely six days between February and March 2008. The incursion resulted in 130 dead and 350 wounded among Palestinians, as well as two dead Israeli soldiers who had penetrated just over the horizon of Erez under tank and air cover into that self-same Beit Hanoun of Sheikh Zayed's buildings, and a little farther down into Jabalia, once a refugee camp and now a populous town.

It was said at the time that the operation was a response to the Qassam rockets, and to the more sophisticated Grad, which had been launched toward cities in southern Israel. And the rockets, in turn, were often launched as reprisals for a targeted assassination carried out not just in Gaza, but also in the West Bank, to demonstrate that at least as far as the armed factions were concerned, the two Palestinian entities were still united.

A few days' closure, with hell breaking loose next door. A few days during which that paradoxical silence and everyday routine are broken in the way that only low-intensity conflict can break them. It is in these moments that Erez changes, if only for a few days, before once again closing that doorway into hell, replacing Charon's sunken eyes with the tired face of a taxi driver, who drives you to Gaza's new reality: Hamas's political and administrative control of the tiny Palestinian strip along the Mediterranean coast.

As time passes, Hamas's power becomes more stable, as can be seen in the thorough, polite yet lengthy check of the visitors done by the newly appointed Islamist government's bureaucracy at the new gate a few hundred meters from Erez: a few border offices, policemen, and uniformed personnel carrying laptops with webcams to register the newcomer's name, passport, and face.

After the border check, it takes ten minutes by car to arrive at Gaza City. Ten minutes, the time required to spy on the lives of others from the window, light a cigarette, follow the profiles of crumbling buildings and then the open workshops along the road, the mule carts loaded with tires now drawn up beside Egyptian and Chinese-made motorcycles newly arrived through the commercial tunnels that link Gaza's southern edge with Egypt's Sinai. Ten minutes, and Gaza offers you its welcome, its Mediterranean air, its southern flavor. There are half-finished buildings ready to take on another floor, another apartment for sons and parents to be built quickly on the steel frames that are already there, poking through the roof, alongside drying laundry. Then there are the buildings of the *sulta*, that PNA that was born in Gaza in 1994, when the Israelis left the majority of the Strip overnight, and when the Palestinian exiles who arrived with Yasser Arafat took control of places—like the military governor's building, called Majlis al-Tashri'i by the Palestinians—that had until that moment born the mark of the occupier, first Egypt and later Israel.[1] Finally, there are tall buildings, especially those linked to the *sulta*, the public employees, the civil servants. A city grown upon itself at a dizzying rate. Concrete and little else, facing a sea both beautiful and wild. Beautiful, and polluted by waste dumped out at sea.

Unlike the unreal atmosphere surrounding Erez, Gaza is a city where everything is normal, but where normality is nothing but fiction, a screen upon which is projected a scene of ordinary life such as one might find in Rome, Cairo, or Tunis. Shops, traffic, shop windows, children coming out of school, markets with their stalls, mechanics, offices, and banks. A normal city, suspended in the clouds. Far away, beyond that strip barely forty kilometers long and ten wide that lies between Israel and the Mediterranean, is the outside world, the place that sometimes seems like a myth to Gaza's Palestinians, sometimes a distant memory, for which they are always nostalgic. Gaza is a place where time has been suspended. Here, a limbo of houses in sequence leaves the city indistinguishable from the countryside, the refugee camps blending into a seashore that becomes a window upon the Mediterranean: no longer the gateway to other places but simply a backdrop, sealed off from the outside world, just like everything else. Even during Operation Cast Lead, Israel's most violent military offensive against a Palestinian territory since the Six Day War of 1967, Gaza remained sealed off; even during those interminable days, it remained closed, imprisoned, with no one among the community of international journalists allowed to enter and to tell, independently and truthfully, the story of what was taking place.

Gaza is an anthill in which people live piled upon one another—one in which people generally can't, and often don't, want to leave. Entire generations of Gazans have never left the Strip, nor do they know what might be outside, save for the stories told by their grandfathers or the stories of some of their luckier neighbors who have been to Egypt to visit part of their family, thanks to an Egyptian passport or a special medical permit. Grandfathers dream of the villages they escaped from, certain that they would some day return—villages that are just over the border, just out of reach. And those who are well connected enough remember a day trip ten years ago to Jerusalem, just a few hours outside the borders of the Strip: dashing visits with the requirement to return before sunset when the permit issued by Israeli authorities expired.

From here, from the Strip, one can break out only through death—death brought by old age, or ever more frequently, death while still young. Perhaps this is why along the walls, on the large roadside billboards, and on the posters in shop windows the theme is ubiquitous: the martyrs, the *shaheed*, are the sole protagonists of an iconography that, like the history of Gaza over the last six decades, speaks only the language of conflict. Armed martyrs, killed in firefights with the Israelis or by missiles fired from an Israeli helicopter. There have been no suicide attacks in Israeli cities since 2005—attacks that in any case originated far more frequently from the West Bank rather than from Gaza. There are, however, unarmed *shaheed*: men, women, and children. All of them are listed under the same rubric—*shaheed*—which unites all the factions and the colors of all the flags that accompany posters, bills, and portraits in a now customary symbolism. There is no distinction.

The flag might be the green of Hamas; it might be the lemon yellow of Fatah, or the red of the PFLP. It might be black, like the bandannas wrapped around the foreheads of Islamic Jihad militants. The *shaheed* are *shaheed*; they belong to everyone, and the colors of the flags are mere embellishments, the distinguishing mark of a political "family." Their photographs, mounted with a symbolic backdrop that combines the Al-Aqsa Mosque with Kalashnikovs and the slogans of the resistance, flood the city's walls, its shop windows, the front entrances to its apartment blocs, and even its cars. Nothing to do with the iconography of Palestinian fedayeen: secular nationalist guerrillas from the 1970s, portrayed as cosmopolitan, urban, and educated.[2] Today, everything is different: religious symbols have become the line that joins Palestinian factions, alongside the figurative rhetoric of resistance. This is the only iconography that runs throughout the Strip, a constant reminder that Gaza is not a peaceful place, that it is not a fishing village, that it is not just poverty. There are poverty and war, pain and deprivation, destruction and the bleak horizon of a featureless future.

It is in this desolate land that Hamas has taken power, after the extreme violence between Fatah and Hamas militias in June 2007, when the attempt at cohabitation between the two main Palestinian political movements in a national unity government failed in a matter of a few, bloody days. Hamas came to power in the 2006 elections, but its power was halved by the duopoly that immediately followed: Mahmoud Abbas, president of the PNA, and prime minister and Hamas leader Ismail Haniyeh administering executive power. In June 2007, the PNA's duopoly became geographical as much as political: Abbas controlled the West Bank, Haniyeh Gaza. Hamas, therefore, came to administer sole power within the Strip, and it could have been no other way. Ironically, this watershed came a few months before the celebration of two important anniversaries: twenty years since the First Intifada, and the twenty-year anniversary of the foundation of the most important Palestinian Islamist movement. The June 2007 coup represented more

than just a symbolic watershed in Hamas's history: historiographi-
cally, it also marks the end of a long phase, the demarcation of a
"before" and an "after" in the evolution of HAMAS—the acronym
for Harakat al-Muqawwama al-Islamiyya—born from the Muslim
Brotherhood, an organization whose history in the region stretches
back to the early 1940s, a time during which the land was under the
protectorate of His Britannic Majesty, whose domains extended to
the land between the Mediterranean and the Jordan from the end
of the World War I until 1947.

The before and after in the history of Hamas itself tells an important story: from "Islamist resistance movement" to an organization
that directly administers power, whether by its own choice or otherwise. By the methodological standards of the history of Western-style
political parties, there would be nothing remarkable in such a watershed: from movement to institution, from opposition to government, from armed struggle to reentry into mainstream politics. But
in the Middle East, and particularly in Palestine, Western method-
ologies must always to some extent be revised, not so much because
the Israeli-Palestinian conflict has left its mark upon the birth and
life of Hamas, but rather because the movement's life has taken place
entirely within that conflict—including its history in power, which
is the fruit of reaching neither peace with the enemy (Israel) nor the
normalization of state life (under the PNA). Thus, even its time in
power has been lived entirely within the Palestinian-Israeli conflict,
and Hamas knew it could enter into the institutional machinery of
the PNA only by sharing the tragic fiction of an authority that is not
a state, and of a country that has neither recognized borders nor a
monopoly on the use of force. As a consequence of this unique Israeli-
Palestinian *sonderweg*, Hamas never rejected the idea of remaining a
resistance movement while also exerting power—whether as a government enthroned by the PNA that controlled the West Bank and
Gaza (2006–2007), or as a de facto government that wielded power
exclusively in the Gaza Strip from June 2007 forward.

From *Nakba* to Politics

Our story begins over sixty years ago, when the twentieth century had completely disrupted the life, rhythms, codes, and the very future of a small strip of land to the north of the Sinai, transforming what was an ancient commercial transit point between the Arabian peninsula and the Mediterranean into an antechamber of desperation. Over the span of a single night, the Gaza district—which included all of the southern part of Mandatory Palestine under British rule—lost most of its territory. After the first Arab-Israeli War of 1948–49 it became the "Gaza Strip," shrinking from a territory spanning nearly 1.4 million *dunums* to a diminutive space of 325,000 *dunums*, a sliver of land less than 400 square kilometers. On top of the loss of territory came the refugees—those Palestinians who fled what are today Ashkelon and Be'er Sheva, completely transforming the social, political, and economic life of this small territory as well as its demography. These were Palestinians who fled their villages thinking they would return in a few days, after the military operations were over. Or Palestinians chased from their houses not only to carry out a "border clearing"[3]—in the words of historian Benny Morris's exemplary description—but also to reduce de facto the Arab population in southern Israel in the years after 1948. This was a wound that Gazan Palestinians would remember through stories like the one of the expulsion from Majdal, a few kilometers away from today's Ashkelon. After the first Arab-Israeli War, many Palestinian inhabitants stayed in Majdal, but were concentrated in a single district, a district that the Israelis called "ghetto," from which around 3,000 were later deported to Gaza in 1950.[4] The 80,000 inhabitants of the area around Gaza City along the coastline from before 1948 were joined by a further 200,000 refugees. This exponential growth in population would prove difficult to absorb, modifying the basic social makeup of Gaza's ancient southern district and placing on the refugees the weight of a deep, rapid, and irreversible change. At the time of the First Intifada, toward the end of the 1980s, 65 percent of the half million people who then lived in Gaza were either refugees, their children, grandchildren, or great-grandchildren.[5]

These changes truly defined an era, while at the same time representing just one of the many somersaults that this millennia-old town has experienced throughout its history, traversed as it has been by different armies and civilizations, from the Pharaohs of ancient Egypt to the Persians, the Romans, and the British.[6] Throughout its history, Gaza was not always as it is today: poor, miserable, isolated, and cut off from the world. Gaza was the land of the Philistines, remembered in the Torah for the story of Samson and the temple of Dagon, and it lived through Alexander the Great's raids, as well as the Islamic conquest of 635 CE headed by Omar, one of the Prophet Mohammed's companions, during the first great expansion of the Caliphate that eventually made Damascus its capital. Then the British Mandate, agreed upon by Europe's Great Powers, brought His Majesty's troops to the shores of the Eastern Mediterranean after World War I. Pitched battles, horses' hooves, and warriors' raids all testify to ancient Gaza's political significance, portrayed in its borders and its palaces in a Byzantine mosaic conserved and arguably "produced" in Jordan—the famous *Map of Madaba*, crucial to understanding the area's geographical, human, and political importance. Here, where there were forums, theaters, stoa, and a church, Gaza is considered of such importance as to be ranked behind Jerusalem alone.

Gaza has had its golden age: central to Mediterranean trade and an important station for caravans in the commerce between the southeastern Mediterranean, the Arabian Peninsula, and the Horn of Africa, it was also a cultural hub of the late Hellenic period. Scholars remember it as the center of a literary and philosophical school that had the merit of bridging Eastern Christianity and Hellenism, and was in particular responsible for systematizing rhetoric thanks to names like Procopius, Coricius, and Aeneas, all active between the fifth and sixth century AD. During this same period, Gaza became the location for the development of an Eastern monasticism whose champions were the venerable old hermits Barsanufius and John, as well as their disciple Dorotheus, who preferred taking care of the sick to the life of a hermit. Gaza displayed the infrastructure of an important city: thermal baths, roads lined with columns, stadia, temples later made into churches, theaters, and places of entertainment. Comedy and satire were staged there, and mimes would act there. Around the third century AD, Olympic-style games were held there, while chariot races would take place in Gaza's hippodrome, famous across the contemporary Hellenic world.

While Gaza's ancient past was often glorious—and above all, *open*—its recent past and its present can be summed up with a single word: *closure.* In the six decades since 1948, Gaza has built its contemporary identity upon increasing geographical, political, and cultural separation. It is the simple chronology of events that testifies to the abruptness with which the territory was cut off from that selfsame hinterland it had always been linked with. After the first Arab-Israeli War of 1948, the Gaza region suffered a double trauma: the initial loss of the inland area and the north, as well as the drive toward the south under what amounted to an Egyptian protectorate, until the 1967 Six Day War, when—under Israeli occupation, paradoxically—Gaza rediscovered its links to the West Bank. After 1948, Gaza gradually changed from a port city and commercial hub to an island, a sliver of land physically separated from its past and suspended in its present, in which only refugees remain as storytellers—not least of all because Egypt itself was careful to avoid integrating the Strip into its own state structures. The nearly two decades of Egyptian dominion constituted the formative period of Gaza's current identity inasmuch as they consolidated a social code based on the traditional conservatism for which Gaza and its surroundings were already famous. Over the course of decades, the sociocultural edifice of Gaza's contemporary identity has been built both on refugees' unique relationship with their past—the time before 1948, which provides both a founding myth and a framework for contemporary social mores—and on their present *as refugees.* This edifice attempts to accommodate, to reinterpret everything in light of their practical necessities (work, maintaining the family, the house, the near future) and of their ambitions, such as returning to their home village, resisting the Israelis, seeking justice or revenge, or not accepting the miserable reality of refugee camps.

During those two decades, Gaza became a piece of Palestine, which no longer had any connections with either pre-1948 Palestine or the West Bank, itself under Jordanian control. Neither did it have close links to Egypt, aside from the kind of relations an "overseas territory" might have with its capital, located far away beyond the oceanic deserts of the Sinai: relations made of bureaucratic exchanges, requests for services, and the formation of elites. For Gaza's young, Cairo became the beacon for higher education: the campuses of this Arab megalopolis, from Cairo University to 'Ain Shams and—at least initially—its military academies became the places in which Gaza's technical cadres were formed: teachers, doctors, pharmacists, engineers, and other professionals. This attraction would continue even after 1967—the year in which Cairo's protectorate came to an end, replaced by the Israeli occupation—when, during the 1970s, Cairo hosted the generation of students from Gaza's refugee camps that would later constitute the core of Hamas.

Close connections with Egyptian politics, in truth, already existed, and it was precisely as a result of the relationship, dating back to 1935, with Hassan al-Banna's Ikhwan al-Muslimun (Muslim Brotherhood) that Hamas was formed. In that year, two members of the Egyptian branch of the Brotherhood—Sheikh al-Banna's brother, Abdel al-Rahman al-Sa'ati, and Mohammed al-Hakeem—had undertaken a tour during which they also met Hajj Amin al-Husseini, then Mufti of Jerusalem and considered one of the leaders of the Palestinian Muslim Brotherhood in the immediate aftermath of World War II. At the time, there were no organic or consolidated connections; it was more a matter of holding the first few meetings necessary to establish those associations that would later spread al-Banna's teachings. The turbulence of those years, including the anti-British and anti-Zionist revolt of 1936–39 as well as World War II, delayed the establishment of local branches of the Ikhwan proper. This took place in 1945 and 1946, and would not be located in Gaza by chance alone. There is no scholarly agreement concerning the precise timing of the birth of the first Muslim Brotherhood branch in Gaza City, although it seems likely, as Khaled Hroub argues,[7] that it was established after the end of World War II and was headed by Sheikh Zafer al-Shawwa, who came from one of the area's most prominent families. The city came to have four branches—among them the Rimal, Harat al-Zaytounah, and Harat al-Daraj areas—and later spread to outlying areas.

The participation of the Muslim Brotherhood in the first Arab-Israeli War of 1948 increased the consensus for the Ikhwan exponentially, particularly in Gaza. Hundreds volunteered, traveling from Egypt, Jordan, and Syria to join the conflict: this presence, while certainly not significant from a military point of view, is nonetheless important in terms of the Brotherhood's involvement in the "Palestinian cause," and a commitment that would later generate considerable support among the refugees in the Gaza Strip, who recognized the Ikhwan's courage in defending them and in being ready to take up arms during what became Israel's War of Independence.[8] Indeed, it is precisely the refugees from that and later wars who became the foundation for the success of the Brotherhood's particular brand of "political Islam" within the Gaza Strip. The Brotherhood provided a model for the identity of a land that war had transformed utterly, and that needed new ways to imagine itself. Two things happened in Gaza. First, the presence of 200,000 refugees fragmented a society that had relied on the balance of power determined by the local urban and commercial Palestinian nobility. Second, the Muslim Brothers provided immediate answers to the need for identity and for social cohesion—both needs particularly acute in the refugee camps among those who had been twice marginalized, first by the war and then by the camps, and who had lost all their bearings. The radical changes brought about both by the *nakba* ("the catastrophe," as Palestinians refer to the events of 1948) and by the presence of a new Islamist political group were crucial for Gaza's future. As Beverley Milton-Edwards writes in her detailed account of Palestinian Islamism: "The Muslim Brotherhood also played its part, advertently or inadvertently, in widening the gap between the politicized refugee community on the one hand, and the ruling families and their supporters" on the other.[9] Just as would later happen between Hamas and the PNA, the Muslim Brotherhood stepped into "the gap left by the Waqf authorities,"[10] the religious institution charged with overseeing not only the lands belonging to the "Islamic realm," but also with providing support for the poor. When the Waqf in Gaza proved "unable to support the refugee community and provide welfare," the Muslim Brotherhood's actions highlighted "the weakness of institutional Islam in the face of new changes."[11] And the Brotherhood provided its own answers, both ideological and practical—answers that the refugees found convincing.

And so, given the presence of the fertile terrain of the refugee camps coupled with the events in Egypt, and especially the history of the Brotherhood across Gaza's southern border, it is no coincidence that it is precisely in Gaza where the Muslim Brotherhood—and, after 1987, Hamas—found its stronghold. After a brief period during which the movement had been allowed to act freely, the Egyptian Muslim Brotherhood—and thus also the branches within the Gaza Strip—were banned by the Cairo authorities in 1949. The branch established by 'Aish Amira, however, did not close, and bypassed the ban by metamorphosing into a religious center, the Jamaat al-Tawheed (Society for Unification), which functioned as a cover in order to allow the Muslim Brotherhood to continue to work and retain its presence. In any case, the ban did not last long: the Egyptian monarchy was swept away on July 23, 1952, by the revolution of Colonel Gamal Abdel Nasser's Free Officers, who—along with other measures—reversed the state's hostility toward the Ikhwan, with which some of his Free Officers themselves had become affiliated.

During the first two years of the Free Officers' Revolution, good relations between the Egyptian Muslim Brotherhood and the new-born republican regime allowed Gaza's Islamists to carve out the necessary space to pursue their expansion and to consolidate, particularly within the refugee camps. Here, during the early 1950s, they were one of the largest organizations, with eleven branches and over 1,000 members. There are a few documents that remain from this period, providing information such as the oath of membership recited by members recruited in the Nuseirat refugee camp, one of the Strip's most important, carried out by placing a hand on the Qur'an and declaring, "I promise to be a good Muslim in defending Islam and the lost land of Palestine."[12] This unadorned formula sufficiently hints, in embryo, at the nationalist drive that is the hallmark of Hamas as much as—if not more than—other groups. Calling for the defense of that "lost land of Palestine" gave the Ikhwan's entry into Palestinian politics a political meaning so profound as to render adherence to the religious message only one part of militants' motivations for joining.

Thus, the Ikhwan was consolidating its position when relations between the Egyptian Muslim Brotherhood and the new regime in Cairo shifted radically in 1954, after a member of the Muslim Brotherhood made a failed attempt in October on Nasser's life. And thus the decision was made—on behalf of the person who would later become the icon of Pan-Arab Nationalism—to place Egypt's first president, General Mohammed Neguib, under house arrest. Relations between Nasser and Neguib had been deteriorating over the previous few months, not least over the Brotherhood, which was the last remaining mass movement in the country and which Nasser already wanted to ban. The failed assassination attempt allowed him not only to formally become the country's leader through a popular referendum in 1956, but also to undertake the wave of repression against the Brotherhood that would end in over 4,000 arrests and the death penalty for nearly all the upper echelon of the leadership. The harshness of the repression may not have forced Gaza's Islamists into hiding, but it certainly forced them to act under cover. The specific conditions of the Strip, under military protectorate, placed the local Ikhwan in a different position, creating the preconditions for a "Gazan way," a Palestinian nationalist interpretation of political Islam: Hamas. The difficulties in relations with the Muslim Brothers across the border forced local branches to define themselves increasingly in terms of the specifics of the Palestinian situation.

The Six Day War, an event that to this day represents a fundamental rupture both morally and culturally for the entire Arab world, left Gaza with no nostalgia for their Egyptian patron, especially among the ranks of the Muslim Brotherhood, which had paid dearly for the construction of the new Nasserite Republic. On the contrary, the war represented the moment at which Gaza's isolation was broken: the opening toward the West Bank and the progressive consolidation of the two parts of a new Palestine alongside Israel: Gaza and the West Bank united, along with East Jerusalem, under the United Nations' newly introduced phraseology of "Occupied Palestinian Territory"[13] as defined by the 1949 armistice lines. The Gaza Strip had constructed a new and complex identity during the two decades of Egypt's "protectorate." After 1967, it attempted to proceed in parallel with the West Bank, another scrap of Palestinian land that had been forced to rewrite its social codes as a result of its union with the Hashemite monarchy in Amman—a kingdom that, unlike Egypt, had attempted to assimilate the Palestinian territory to the west of the Jordan River into a "Transjordan," a large area dominated by tribal majorities. Thanks to history's quixotic trajectories, Gaza and the West Bank proceeded in parallel after 1967, but the geographic distance between Gaza City and Ramallah would never be entirely bridged, despite the Israeli occupation objectively having had the merit of bringing down the frontiers erected between the 1948 and the 1967 wars.

The parallels continued in relation to the history of Palestinian political Islam in both the West Bank and in Gaza. There had been little time to build a shared framework for the Brotherhood in the two territories before the Arab-Israeli War of 1948, but the seeds planted by Hassan al-Banna had nonetheless sprouted, taking root throughout the West Bank, including Jerusalem and particularly in the south. In Hebron, for example, a local branch of the Muslim Brotherhood was established largely due to the role played in the war by the battalion fielded by Egyptian Muslim Brothers.[14] Later, the division between the West Bank and Gaza interrupted this common development, and Palestinian political Islam developed in two different directions, influenced by their respective temporary patrons and by the socioeconomic differences between the two territories. While in Gaza the massive presence of refugees increasingly became the mainstay of the Brotherhood's—and later Hamas's—support, the situation in the West Bank was rather different. For one, this was because the landscape itself was different: despite having had its links to the coast and to important cities like Haifa severed, the West Bank still had important urban centers from Nablus all the way to Hebron. For another, the patronage was different: Jordan's young King Hussein had very strong links with the West Bank, toward which the Hashemite kingdom did not hide its expansionist aims.

Before 1967, the Palestinian territory located between the Jordan River and the armistice lines of 1949 followed the administrative norms set by Amman, from land registry to pensions, from commerce to textbooks, and including political relations between Palestinian notables and the Hashemite regime. Moreover, Jordan had become haven and home for many Palestinian refugees, to the extent that the country had become unique within the Arab world. Palestinian refugees were not treated as pariahs, confined to camps and the fragile status of statelessness, as they were in Lebanon and Syria. Jordan welcomed Palestinians and integrated them to the point of running the risk of profoundly modifying old political equilibria, as indeed happened. Palestinians were granted citizenship, evidence of which still exists today, particularly in East Jerusalem, where many Palestinian residents still retain their Jordanian passports, rendering them at least marginally less subject to the limbo to which Jerusalem's Palestinians have been confined since 1967, when the Jordanian Legion was defeated by the Israeli army, Amman's protectorate ended, and the Israeli occupation of Arab parts of Jerusalem began.

Thus, Jordan became not only the patron who controlled the West Bank, but also the power with which to negotiate and from which to receive suggestions and offers for the entire spectrum of Palestinian politics that took shape after the *naksa*. With regard to the sociopolitical groups, Amman was careful to construct a policy based on co-option, particularly with respect to elites. The case of the West Bank Ikhwan was no different, and it quickly established close relations with the Muslim Brothers in Amman. The Ikhwan in the West Bank was a conservative movement that initially concentrated on propagating Hassan al-Banna's school of religious and political thought throughout the population: its instruments were mosques and a network of social welfare services. After the 1948 war, the struggle against the Israelis was set aside. Rather, in line with the path followed by the Muslim Brothers across the Allenby Bridge, the West Bank Ikhwan's strategy included a reliance on what were overall good relations with the Hashemite regime, and with the monarch, King

Hussein, in particular. King Hussein, in turn, wished to preserve the delicate equilibrium upon which his family's power rested—a power rooted in the Franco-British decision to partition the Middle East, and thus an intrinsically fragile power, as was that of all the regimes born of Western colonialism in Arab lands.

The Muslim Brothers and King Hussein, therefore, wrote a history marked by fundamental compromise: the Ikhwan, in its Jordanian and West Bank branches, accepted Hashemite authority, avoiding questions as to its legitimacy, and in turn the dynasty founded by Abdallah did not place limitations upon the organization, which received the status and authorization necessary to run its charitable operations. The Muslim Brotherhood was one of the few legal organizations in the country. However, they had to ask for the regime's consent in order to open new branches—consent that they received, for example, in Jerusalem, Jericho, and Bethlehem. The Brotherhood regularly participated in elections and was represented by its deputies in Parliament. Of course, it had been a relationship with highs and lows, in which from time to time the Hashemite regime reined in the Brotherhood, only to later loosen its grip. Over the course of nearly two decades, therefore, the history of the Muslim Brotherhood—in Jordan as well as in the West Bank—had witnessed alternate stages of repression and of closer surveillance by Amman's intelligence services on the one hand, and of royal support on specific occasions on the other.

This understanding was not seriously questioned by either party, despite some hiccups along the way during the 1950s—for example, regarding the British presence in Jordan and Jordanian support for the Baghdad Pact, an anti-Soviet regional military alliance backed by Great Britain and the United States. What came between the monarchy and the Ikhwan was nearly always the former's pro-Western inclination. The monarchy was, however, careful in designing its foreign policy, blending apparently contradictory positions: pro-Western policies, support for Nasser's actions in the Suez in 1956, and attacks against the typically nationalist and socialist Pan-Arabism of the late 1950s. Save friction regarding concessions to "imperialism," the Muslim Brotherhood played the part of a largely "loyal opposition" for the Hashemite monarchy, with which—in the words of Yusuf al-'Azm, one of the movement's leaders and parliamentary deputies in Jordan—the Ikhwan effectively stipulated a "truce." "We were unable to open fronts with all sides at one time," al-'Azm explained to Ziad Abu Amr, a Palestinian historian of political Islam and the foreign minister of the national unity government of spring 2007.[15] "We stood with the King in order to protect ourselves, because if Nasser's followers had risen to power, or had a pro-Nasser government been established in Jordan, the Muslim Brotherhood would have been liquidated just as they were liquidated in Egypt."[16] Rather, the understanding between the Jordanian Brotherhood and the Hashemite regime suffered considerably as a consequence of events in the Palestinian political sphere, when the Jordanian regime and Palestinians clashed in the event that marked the lowest point of their relations: Black September.

The bloody repression of the fedayeen linked to the PLO—and of Yasser Arafat's Fatah in particular—decided upon by King Hussein in 1970 was linked to a period after the War of 1967 and the consequent detachment of the West Bank from Amman's direct control. It did, however, provide a good illustration of the West Bank Ikhwan's stance toward the monarchy, marked, as it was, both by a deep embarrassment and by a clear choice of sides—in favor of the Hashemite regime.

If not everything, then certainly much changed after the *naksa*—as Palestinians themselves refer to the human and political trauma of 1967—when the new borders and separations marked by Israel's blitzkrieg placed an even greater distance between what lay across the borders to the east and to the south of the Occupied Palestinian Territory. Paradoxically, it was precisely the distance established between Gaza, the West Bank, and their respective Arab patrons that made an entirely internal *sonderweg* possible, slowly detaching the destiny of the Palestinians—both to the north of Sinai and between the Green Line and the Jordan River—from that of their brethren who had become refugees abroad. In political terms, the claim to the common rights of the entire Palestinian people would never change, but it is beyond doubt that 1967 marked the divide between two phases of Palestine's social and political history: one in which the West Bank and Gaza existed within the patronage of Arab regimes, and the subsequent phase marked by a dialectic between the Palestinians inside territories controlled by Israel and the wider Islamist movement. What changed the balance of power between these different actors were the birth and the development of new political elites, as well as the deep changes to the social makeup of the West Bank and of Gaza, within which two new protagonists emerged: refugees and the young.

The Universities of the Revolt

"Hamas's founders? They became that by chance." These words uttered by Sayyed Abu Musameh, one of the Islamist movement's elder leaders, toward the end of October 2008 in his modest garden in Gaza City, hint at the political rationale behind the birth of the Islamic Resistance Movement.

Formally, Hamas was established on December 9, 1987, during a meeting of the Political Directorate of the Muslim Brotherhood held in the house of Ahmed Yassin. This took advantage of an unforeseen opportunity, namely, the outbreak of the First Intifada, which engulfed Gaza and the West Bank over the following two years. The project of an operational organization derived from the Ikhwan al-Muslimun, however, had already been in the air for years.

Abu Musameh, a thin man with a calm gaze, white hair, and a neatly trimmed beard, sporting an elegant gray shirt and dark trousers, explains: "The elections for the Muslim Brotherhood's leadership were frequent, as was its renewal."[17] He is among Hamas's longest-standing members, having entered the Muslim Brotherhood at the beginning of the 1970s while he was studying at the University of Damascus and experiencing—as all students did during those times—the ideological clash between the still-dominant Left and an increasingly influential political Islamism. Abu Musameh had been on precisely that journey—going from an initial fascination with socialism to his entry into the Muslim Brotherhood—at almost the same time as his wife, who now listens to her husband's story with that complicity typical of old spouses, her eyes sharp and deep, hardly veiled by the frame of her small spectacles.

Abu Musameh is considered one of the more pragmatic and moderate leaders in Gaza, in good standing with the entire political leadership. A man of the so-called second generation, after Yassin but before Rantisi and Haniyeh, he witnessed the early years of the Muslim Brotherhood. "You don't have to belong to the Ikhwan in order to be a member of Hamas, but all Palestinian Muslim Brothers are Hamas,"[18] is his way of explaining militancy in the Islamist movement, which casts light on the origins of the Harakat al-Muqaw-wama al-Islamiyya. "When Hamas was established during the First Intifada, its founders were there by chance: they were simply those who had been elected to the political office, the *maktab al-siyyasi* of the Muslim Brotherhood."[19]

Abu Musameh—himself the secret leader of Hamas for a year and a half around 1989—confirms the historical facts that have already been established, while affording a glimpse into the far more complex context within which the movement was born. The received historical truth about Hamas's birth is that it would not have taken place that December 9, 1987, had it not been for the Intifada, to which Hamas responded as a popular movement "from below" that accelerated the political tempo and left the Islamist leadership no choice but to enter into the political fray and attempt to ride the wave of the protest. The more complex picture, as it emerges from the different witnesses of the period, is that Hamas as a project was in the cards at least as early as 1983, and that it was the result of a continuous dialogue between the leadership of the Muslim Brotherhood abroad and the leadership in the West Bank and in Gaza.[20] This continuous dialogue was not simply the result of a discussion between these different geographical and geopolitical areas of the Islamist movement; it was above all a debate—one that bordered on outright confrontation and one whose outcome was far from certain—between two generations of members: the "old guard" who had reached Islamist militancy through the early Ikhwan (i.e., through co-optation by the companions of Hassan al-Banna) and the "young," those who had embraced political Islam during the 1970s. This latter wing included those who had been born between the 1950s and the beginning of the following decade, and who had come of age in the Palestinian high schools both within and outside the armistice borders of 1949 and, in particular, within universities throughout the Arab world and in the West Bank and Gaza.

The idea of establishing an operational branch of the Ikhwan—in other words, a branch that could also act on the ground against the Israelis—dates back to 1983, and was debated in the local circles of the Muslim Brotherhood outside the West Bank and Gaza. Osama Hamdan, born in 1964, was a young exponent of Palestinian Islamism who had entered the organization barely a year before the debates through a friendship with Khaled Meshaal, who he had known since he was fifteen. Hamdan explains: "At first, we tried to convince the leadership of the Jordanian Ikhwan of this project. It was not an easy task, but in the end, the leadership in Amman accepted our idea."[21] He tells of how "the younger generation was pushing for participation in the resistance, on the basis of a principle accepted by members of both generations, both in the West Bank and in Gaza, that the resistance should be undertaken only within the Occupied Palestinian Territory."[22] The difference between the Ikhwan on the one hand, and nationalist and left-wing factions on the other is obvious: there would no longer be guerrilla actions abroad, in the Middle East or in Europe, as had occurred up until that point. No more hijacking of airplanes or any of the other spectacular and bloody actions that had taken place across the Mediterranean. Instead, there would be clashes with the Israelis within the territory alone—without specifying whether this meant the territories occupied in 1967 or those of Mandate Palestine.

Until that moment, the Muslim Brotherhood had not participated in guerrilla actions against the Israelis in an obvious and integrated fashion. Indeed, for precisely this reason, they had earned accusations of not having been good patriots from nationalist quarters—the same nationalists who had given rise to the guerrilla war both inside and outside the Palestinian Territory: Fatah, the PFLP, the Democratic Front for the Liberation of Palestine (DFLP), and the many other factions into which Palestinian politics were divided.

There was some truth to this accusation. The choice of the generation of Islamists who had lived through the *nakba* had been to confine their religious and political activities to mosques and schools,
functioning as a cross between the Muslim version of "Sunday
school" and a small community center. This was not, given their
view of life and its relationship to religion, a voluntary restriction
in their horizons. On the contrary, the objective was more radical
and ambitious: to shape the "good Palestinian Muslim." This was the
goal, because returning to Islam was considered an absolute necessity for the very moral and political future of their generation. The
progressive distancing from Islam and from a conscious and rigorous
observance of faith in daily life had, from their point of view, been
the principal cause of the *nakba*. To redress this defeat, it was necessary to start from the pillars upon which a *normal* society is founded;
it was necessary to rebuild ethical foundations, the religious creed,
traditional and conservative values. And in order to do this, it was
necessary not only to address a perceived lack of religion, but also
to encourage a sense of basic social stability: family, health, freedom
from poverty, childcare, and the reconstruction of women's traditional role as an element of social cohesion, especially in conditions
as degraded as those found in the refugee camps. "After the wars,
from 1948 till 1973, the Palestinian nation was very sick. We had to
rebuild it on a psychological and social level in order to overcome our
wounds. The refugees were dependent on UNRWA aid, and therefore we had to rebuild the character, the self-confidence, the trust of
the Palestinian people." Thus recalls Jamila Abdallah al Taha Shanti,
a Muslim Brotherhood militant since 1980. Founder and chief of the
women's sector of Hamas, a deputy elected in 2006 elections, Jamila
Shanti links political and religious adherence with literacy and a society's identity with the search for a renewed dignity. "Young people
used to go from Gaza to Israel to work, instead of going to school,
driving Palestinians toward ignorance. We wanted to avoid illiteracy
and ignorance, and therefore we founded associations that promote
culture, sports, education, assistance."[23]

Upon closer inspection, then, there was a fully fledged political
program already contained within the social program of the Muslim

Brotherhood after 1967. Only by rebuilding a solid identity could there also be any hope of national redemption.

Ahmed Yassin had worked on precisely this program ever since he returned to live in the Gaza Strip after a period of studies in Egypt. A teacher by training, scarred ever since adolescence by a serious disability that would in time leave him wheelchair-bound and almost completely immobilized, Yassin concentrated on education through his militancy in the Ikhwan. As a member of the Muslim Brotherhood, he was arrested in 1965 when Nasser's regime tightened its grip upon the Islamist movement, but it was only toward the end of the 1960s that Yassin became a point of reference for the group of young men who would later become the Hamas leadership. Early on, the group gathered in al-Shati refugee camp. (Ismail Haniyeh, who would later become the first Hamas member to head a Palestinian government, came from this camp.) Later, activities moved to Gaza City and centered around the Mujamma al-Islami. The Islamic Center was born in 1973, the year of the Yom Kippur War. A range of connected activities came together around the mosque: a small clinic, a nursing school, a women's center, a committee to administer *zakat* (charity, one of Islam's Five Pillars), a sports center, a meeting room, and eventually schools, kindergartens, and a blood bank.[24]

This kind of community center was not a novelty in the history of the Muslim Brotherhood, nor—upon reflection, and with all the qualifications the difference in context requires—was it a novelty in the history of many Christian ecclesiastical communities in Europe. Starting from the church, the sacred place, activities such as the ecclesiastical communities' social initiatives enter the secular world. The goal is to help those social groups mostly exposed to weaknesses that are financial, and that often therefore involve also the moral, religious, political sphere. For this kind of ecclesiastical community, the religious dimension imbues its social activities with moral and spiritual values, helping to increase the cohesiveness of society as a whole. For the Palestinian Muslim Brotherhood, the objective was the same: to again infuse a society torn apart by the loss of land and by the scattering of local communities with a new resilience through a renewed faith in Islam. This Islam would be self-conscious and no longer traditional (as all those who have come into contact with the Ikhwan since the 1970s say, as though this very different, and one might say even secular, approach to religion had been the decisive factor in their entry into the movement).

The Ikhwan had already been establishing charitable organizations in the West Bank and Gaza since the 1960s. The difference was that traditional charities had not developed a political dimension—as the Mujamma al-Islami had done—a distinction that would become increasingly important as time went on, especially once the group of young militants who were to be decisive factors in the birth of Hamas gathered around Yassin. During this phase, Israel was not concerned about the presence of Islamist institutions. Indeed, in its own way, it favored them, both by not opposing them and by providing them with the necessary imprimatur of legality. This had already happened with the charitable organizations that had operated within the Palestinian Territory before 1967 and that immediately received the official consent necessary to continue their work in the West Bank and in Gaza, even after the Israeli occupation. It also happened in the case of Yassin's Mujamma al-Islami, which five years after its establishment in 1978 received a license to operate from Israeli authorities.[25]

This political stance—which Israel would maintain from 1967 until 1989, when Hamas was first included in the list of terrorist organizations—is at the root of the commonly held interpretation in the popular press that Israel itself created Hamas. During the first two decades of the occupation of the Palestinian Territory, Israel had in fact tolerated—and in some cases endorsed—the presence of the Islamists in the West Bank and particularly in Gaza. Such non-specialist interpretations of the rise of Palestinian Islamists are too simplistic for a movement that was never an instrument of external agents, but rather one that grew from within Palestinian society, where it gathered support not only for religious and social reasons, but also, ultimately, for political ones.

But there is also a grain of truth in the stereotypical reading of events. It is true that Israel, during a specific phase of the post-1967 occupation, allowed the Islamist movement room to maneuver by providing licenses to run social and socioreligious organizations such as the Mujamma al-Islami. It is also true that organizations linked to the Muslim Brotherhood were more easily able to obtain these necessary authorizations than similar organizations linked to nationalist and secular factions within the Palestinian political spectrum. In a 1981 interview with the *International Herald Tribune*, the military governor of the Gaza district, General Yitzhak Sager, said that the Israeli government had "given him a budget and that the military governorate had given it to the mosques. . . . The funds were used for both mosques and religious schools, with the purpose of strengthening a force that runs counter to the pro-PLO leftists."[26] As Beverley Milton-Edwards, one of political Islam's scholars, explains, these licenses were "all signs of classic *divide et impera* policy. Israel's benign encouragement of the Islamic movement was designed to strengthen Islam in the face of nationalists in the form of the Palestine Liberation Organization (PLO). By nurturing a conservative and traditional trend, the Israeli authorities hoped to diminish the progressive and radical appeal of the movement for national liberation."[27]

In truth, halfway through the 1980s an exception emerged with regard to the Islamist front's decision to concentrate its work on social services and on the formation of the good Muslim. This exception was the Islamic Jihad, a relatively new political organization born in 1982, yet following an already-long list of terrorist attacks against Israeli military personnel and against settlers. In itself, the arrival of Islamic Jihad on the political scene—itself established by two former members of the Muslim Brotherhood, Fathi al-Shiqaqi and Abdel Aziz 'Auda—had forced the Ikhwan to ask itself with increasing insistence the crucial question concerning its participation in the "resistance," namely, had the time come to add military activity, analogous to that undertaken by other Palestinian factions, to the socioreligious work the organization had been engaged in for decades?

It was the weakness of the PLO at the time that acted as a dampener in the discussion that took place between the younger generation of the Muslim Brotherhood both within and beyond the Occupied Palestinian Territory. The decision to establish an operational branch of the Palestinian Ikhwan was made in the immediate aftermath of

Operation Peace in Galilee in 1982 and of the ensuing occupation of southern Lebanon, which had struck the hardest blow of all against the PLO and forced Yasser Arafat and the organization's leadership to abandon the bases built in Beirut for an even more difficult exile. The images of the PLO's rout in Lebanon and of Arafat abandoning Beirut in August 1982 aboard the *Odysseus Elytis*—as well as the contemporaneous massacre the Lebanese Phalange carried out in the Sabra and Shatila Palestinian camps under the seemingly blind eyes of the Israeli soldiers—played an important role in convincing at least a part of the Palestinian Muslim Brotherhood to go beyond the religious and cultural dimension and to push for direct confrontation with the Israelis. The Israelis, for their part, had shifted their political center of gravity as a result of Likud coming to power after decades of Labor governments. The first right-wing government in Israel in 1977 and the strengthening of movements such as Gush Emunim (Bloc of the Faithful), the vanguard of the settlers who explicitly linked themselves to religious Zionism, had also made the context more favorable for the simultaneous growth of Palestinian political Islam.

The internal crisis of the Palestinian world, epitomized by the PLO's weakness, was, at any rate, only one of the forces driving a process—the emergence of political Islam—that went well beyond the confines of the West Bank and Gaza. Rather, it was part of a region-wide phenomenon that united Gaza City with Cairo, Ramallah with Damascus, Kuwait City with the other Arab capitals within which the student movement reached a level of politicization similar to that European universities had experienced a few years earlier. It was precisely within Arab universities—Palestinian institutions included—during the 1970s that the new elites that would have a radical impact on Middle Eastern history were forged, because it was here that the most important political clash of the time took place between the forces of the Left—particularly Marxists—and an emerging political Islam. These were the years immediately after the defeat of Arab forces in general and of Nasserite Pan-Arabism in particular in the Six Day War of 1967, as well as the years after the last Arab-Israeli War in 1973. The years, too, in which the policies pursued by Anwar al-Sadat sustained the growth of Islamism in universities and repressed left-wing movements. The revolution guided by Ayatollah Ruhollah Khomeini in Iran in 1979 took place halfway along a trajectory that had already been developing for nearly a decade in other venues, and was therefore neither a cause of Islamist growth in the Arab world nor a model that interested the majority of Islamists, as represented by the Muslim Brotherhood and by the range of movements that would later merge into the Ikhwan. If anything, the revolution in Tehran became a drive for Sunni Arab political Islamism to continue its struggle against local regimes, given what had happened to the Shah Reza Pahlavi.

Palestinian universities were no exception. Indeed, between the 1970s and 1980s a mass student movement took shape. Paradoxically, everything happened after 1967, when the Israeli occupation allowed the West Bank and Gaza to be reunited (so to speak) and, thanks to the decision by the administration in Tel Aviv to include among its principles the autonomy of education, severing it from the Arab countries that had up to that point been the destinations of choice for those Palestinian youth who wished to continue studying. Thus, the Muslim Brotherhood's so-called third generation took shape within universities, in those recently created in the West Bank, and—as far as Gaza is concerned—in Egyptian universities, which would continue to welcome quotas of Palestinian students until the mid-1970s. Even more than the activists of the secular and nationalist movements—of Fatah, the two Palestinian communist parties, and of the PFLP—young Islamists came from the lower social strata, not from those elites who had sent their children to study abroad before 1967. Many came from refugee camps and from rural areas and sought moral, political, and national redemption. But university campuses also offered political autonomy, which became a fertile terrain for the birth of an elite not completely dominated by the Palestinian leadership in exile—namely, that of the PLO, a new elite that would later give rise to the First Intifada. These students also benefited from a similar autonomy with respect to the mosques, where Islamist discourse was cultivated along traditionally conservative lines. The mosques were controlled by the Ministry of Waqf, the religious authority charged with administering Muslim property and therefore necessarily in direct communication with the Israeli administration of the Occupied Palestinian Territory. Universities, on the other hand, offered a neutral territory within which the seeds of political Islam could grow.[28]

The personal experience of Farhat As'ad—one of Hamas's leaders in the West Bank, who organized the campaign in the run-up to the Palestinian elections of January 2006—is exemplary in this sense and helps explain the extent to which the Ikhwan appealed to a generation of youngsters. In his words: "The son of refugees in the Ramle area, I grew up in a small village near Ramallah, A-Tira, in an environment within which being religious meant being tied to traditions more than it meant being conscious of being religious."[29] His personal watershed came after high school, when he met Bassam Jarrar, then one of the Muslim Brotherhood's best-known preachers. Farhat As'ad added that "Jarrar published texts that asked people to be conscious of their religiosity," explaining his own choice as a "passage from traditional religion to religion in politics"—a choice that many in the A-Tira College shared. "Between 1980 and 1982 the Student Council had been taken over by the Islamists. Over half of the students were from Gaza and were with the Muslim Brotherhood."[30] A-Tira College was only one of the cases that were repeated in Gaza City, in Nablus, in Hebron, and even in the secular and left-wing campus par excellence, Birzeit in Ramallah. The early 1980s saw the entry into Palestinian campuses of a new actor in student politics: political Islam. Despite repeated attempts by leftist nationalist factions to establish a common front to defeat the so-called amirs, the electoral lists linked to the Muslim Brotherhood gained a considerable degree of consensus well before Hamas appeared. Indeed, between 1979 and 1981 they gained control of the majority of technical institutes in the West Bank and in Gaza.[31] There would be victories and defeats of greater or lesser importance over the following years, but one element was certain: ever since the end of the 1970s, militant Palestinian politics within universities witnessed the birth of an additional protagonist, namely Islamism, which would later evolve into Hamas. The debate between different tendencies within universities would soon become outright political clashes reaching the highest levels—clashes in which, if anything, it was the campuses that became arenas for broader confrontations. The clashes that took place during the early 1980s—at the Al-Najah University in Nablus in 1981, at the Hebron Polytechnic in 1982, at the Islamic University in Gaza City in June 1983 (at the end of which there would be over 200 injured), and at Birzeit in Ramallah that same year—were the litmus tests of the growing conflict between the factions adhering to the PLO and the Islamist front, which did not belong to the PLO. In time, the conflict crystallized as a duel between Fatah and the Islamists, with the leftist factions taking on from time to time different attitudes toward their rivals.

As well as being a place of very real clashes between the PLO and Islamists, the Islamic University in Gaza City has always been of great symbolic significance for Palestinian Islamism: ever since its establishment in 1978, the Muslim Brotherhood explicitly considered it one of the pillars of their organization, both in terms of proselytism—as a tool for forming their elites—and as a stronghold of intellectual and political power within the Strip. The Islamic University, which still hosts thousands of students every year, has, for example, been the recipient of large amounts of funds from Gulf countries, such as the $150,000 donated in 1978 by the Islamic Development Fund, an outgrowth of the Organization of the Islamic Conference (OIC) and subject to the powerful influence of the Saudi royal family.[32] Ever since its establishment, and still today, a considerable slice of Hamas's cadres pass through the university's ranks. The university itself has been the terrain for political struggles, not centered so much on the internal equilibria of student politics (the Student Council has nearly always been controlled by a massive Islamist majority) as on the relations between the PLO, Fatah, and the Ikhwan in Gaza itself, where Yassin's political influence was increasing.[33] This also explains the "attention," so to speak, that Islamists reserved for Gaza University, the early history of which witnessed frequent intimidation—spilling over into threats and physical clashes—against secular groups. For the Muslim Brothers, the role of the university in Gaza as a power center could not be challenged.

For Palestine within the borders of the 1949 armistice, university politics became the place in which a new elite was forged, partially autonomous from the existing brands of traditional politics—autonomous at least from an intellectual point of view and in terms of local control, if not in financial terms. There were several different causes for the internal Palestinian elites' partial detachment from the PLO, from Fatah, and from the various factions into which the PFLP had divided over the years. To start, there was the PLO's defeat in Beirut, with the scattering of its leadership and of its activists in new refuges across the Arab world. Moreover, Israeli repression had itself contributed to the emergence of a younger generation of activists, as between September 1967 and the end of 1970 they deported hundreds of exponents of Palestinian cadres outside the Occupied Palestinian Territory, including at least 150 religious dignitaries, political leaders, mayors, teachers, professionals, and technicians, whose absence would not only impoverish the intellectual fabric of the West Bank in particular,[34] but would also open the door for the entry of a different elite.

In the Diaspora too, among the masses of Palestinian refugees, the generation shaped between the late 1970s and the early 1980s defined itself as an elite that had decided to count for something in future politics. This was especially true within the exile community across the Gulf countries, particularly in Kuwait. It was Khaled Meshaal himself, the man who had guided Hamas's politburo from abroad ever since the step back taken by Moussa Abu Marzouq halfway through the 1990s, who confirmed this version of events and gave a primary role to the so-called Kuwaitis. The Kuwaitis were those young Islamists who grew up in the Emirate's populous Palestinian Diaspora, where hundreds of thousands of refugees rebuilt a life for themselves, at least until 1991, the year Saddam Hussein's Iraq invaded Kuwait and the year the Gulf War started. For over four decades, after 1948 and even more so after the Six Day War, Kuwait had welcomed Palestinians with open arms. Palestinians, in turn, provided a more or less skilled labor force. The Palestinians had established a structured community, a sort of "Little Palestine," complete with associations, groups, and schools supported by the PLO. It was in one such school, for example, that a young

Khaled Meshaal—born in 1956, refugee from the village of Silwad near Ramallah during the *naksa*—had grown up. His presence, like that of many other men who would become Hamas leaders, was considered confirmation of the role and importance of the "Kuwaitis" in the birth of the Islamist movement in 1987. It is certain that in the history of the Palestinian Diaspora in the Middle East, the Emirate was the most fecund country for post-1948 politics. Yasser Arafat had been to Kuwait, Fatah's first strong nucleus took shape there, and the core of Islamist students, of which Meshaal was one of the best-known names, developed there.[35] The aftershocks the Islamist movements had to confront in the wake of the 1991 Gulf War confirm this version. Hamas fielded its good relations with the Emirate in order to tackle the consequences of Arafat's pro-Iraqi position.

Thus, after 1982, the parallel paths of Islamists within the Occupied Palestinian Territory and in the Diaspora merged into the operational branch of the Muslim Brotherhood in the West Bank and Gaza. The idea began to take shape a year later, when a secret conference of the Palestinian Ikhwan was held in Amman.[36] According to Khaled Meshaal, it was at this very conference that Hamas acquired the form in which it went public in December 1987: a structure formed by members from Gaza, the West Bank, and from exile. The Hamas project was thus built over the four years between that conference and the outbreak of the First Intifada. It was in 1983 in particular that the Muslim Brothers became more visibly present in demonstrations against the Israelis, particularly—and not coincidentally—in the demonstrations against the occupation of South Lebanon on the first anniversary of Operation Peace in Galilee, building up to actions defined as "civil resistance, including boycotts and clashes with Israeli soldiers, no longer extemporaneous, but decided from on high, by the institutions."[37] In 1986, the clashes between Palestinians and Israelis had become weekly events, while in parallel, still according to Khaled Meshaal's version of events, a decision was being made concerning the division of the organization itself into two sections, one that would remain internal in the Occupied Palestinian Territory, and another abroad.[38] That year also saw the definition of the organizational structure, of the political program, objectives, and leadership as confirmed by Hamas's representative in Lebanon, Osama Hamdan,[39] who would later be inserted by US President George W. Bush into the list of Specially Designated Global Terrorists alongside another five Hamas leaders.

In the meantime, in Gaza, Sheikh Ahmed Yassin was one of the few, aside from a group of loyal supporters, who knew about the intimate details of the project and who subscribed to it. In a post hoc reading, this is confirmed by his arrest. In April 1984, a military tribunal sentenced him to thirteen years in prison for possession of weapons, which were found at his house and at other locations. The security forces had quickly uncovered the group of people who, under Yassin's guidance, had begun to stash weapons: it was the first step toward armed struggle by at least a part of the Muslim Brotherhood, but at the time the Israeli investigators did not fully grasp the true significance of the project behind the hiding of a few rifles. The exit from the scene of the head of the Mujamma al-Islami, however, was only temporary, because Yassin was freed exactly one year later, in May 1985, as part of a prisoner exchange agreement between Israel and Ahmed Jibril's PFLP-General Command (PFLP-GC). The Hamas project thus resumed, avoiding the mistakes that had led to the Israeli discovery of the arms. Everything became more organized and, in particular, more clandestine. Alongside the Mujamma al-Islami, Yassin established at least two structures. One, the Munazzamat al-Jihad wa'l-Da'wa (better known by its acronym MAJD—Arabic for "glory"), guided by Yahya Sanwar and Ruwi Mushtaha, was a full-fledged security organization whose primary goal was to detect and strike the Palestinian informers whom the Israelis had managed to recruit over the years. The MAJD was tasked with gathering intelligence and punishing collaborators, such punishments including the death sentence. Attacks carried out in the Gaza Strip against the Israeli military and against settlers were undertaken by a separate organization, led by Salah al-Shehadeh, who would later also establish Hamas's armed wing, the Izz al-Din al-Qassam Brigades.

Yassin was acting without the knowledge of the traditional leadership of the Muslim Brotherhood. As Ismail Abu Shanab—who had until 1989 been the true (but secret) leader of Hamas, above even Yassin—explained to the International Crisis Group (ICG) a few days before being killed in a targeted assassination by the Israeli air force in August 2003: "The period 1983–87 marked the phase of direct preparation for resistance to the occupation, including armed struggle. Sheikh Ahmed Yassin took the lead in this, and did so independently of the Muslim Brotherhood."[40] In 1987, at the time of the First Intifada, two schools of thought still existed within the Muslim Brotherhood: the line of classical politics (al-siyyasa al-klasikiyya), which was endorsed by the older generation, while the so-called renewal tendency (tajdid), had in Sheikh Yassin its most notable exponent. It based its strategy essentially on two points: on the one hand, the use of tools of resistance such as strikes, demonstrations, and full-blown military struggle against the Israeli occupation; on the other hand, the expansion of those units that were already characteristic of the Muslim Brotherhood—namely the usra, families—through the appearance of more strictly speaking operational organs. It was clear that Yassin's strategy could not remain concealed for long. According to Osama Hamdan's reconstruction, the decision to publicly declare the birth of Hamas dates to October 1987.[41] The first document to use the organization's full name appeared in both the West Bank and Gaza on October 6—a document to which the press paid scant attention. The old generation then decided that it was better to shorten the name, just as Fatah had done many years before. Thus the acronym HAMAS was born.

The birthing process of the Harakat al-Muqawwama al-Islamiyya, however, was accelerated by an event whose historical importance no one had anticipated: the First Intifada burst onto the political scene in December, and everything in Palestinian politics changed.

It All Started in Gaza. A Coincidence?

The attacks against Israeli settlers and soldiers increased considerably over the years 1986–87, and not just in the West Bank, where the Gush Emunim, the ideological vanguard of the settler movement, had begun its expansionist adventure in the wake of the Six Day War by establishing Kiryat Arba not far from Hebron. Eventually, settlements had also appeared in Gaza, a sliver of land already crippled by poverty and by the presence of hundreds of thousands of refugees in the aftermath of the 1948 and 1967 wars. The first settlements, Netzarim and Morag, had been built in 1972, followed by a succession of small settlements throughout the following decade that were certainly important in terms of public opinion, but whose primary rationale was military and strategic. Settlements such as Nisanit and Elei Sinai had the primary objective of absorbing the inhabitants of Yamit, the Israeli settlement built in the heart of the Sinai and abandoned after the peace treaty with Egypt was signed. Other settlements had the strategic objective of splitting the unity and the communication lines within the Gaza Strip in order to obtain as complete a control of the territory as possible.[42] Settlements and military control also had other purposes, such as establishing a road network upon which Israelis and Palestinians would brush past each other on a daily basis. Such a situation could not, in a moment of tension, but give rise to a casus belli—like the one that sparked the First Intifada.

In 1987, Gaza was, in economic terms, a kind of dormitory. About 70,000 men would make the trip to Israel on a daily basis to work with legal contracts of employment, while it is estimated that another 35,000 would get there illegally. Thus, at least half a million people lived off those salaries earned in Israel—a predicament that left few opportunities for economic development within Gaza and that, on the contrary, forced the Strip into that unique condition of weakness that Sara Roy first dubbed "de-development": a process of "deliberate, systematic and progressive dismemberment of an indigenous economy by a dominant one, where economic—and, by extension, societal—potential is not only distorted, but denied."[43] This thesis blames the Israelis for having consciously prevented a gradual economic autonomy from developing inside the Occupied Palestinian Territory, Gaza included.

Off to work in Israel in the morning, back at home in the evening, returning to the Strip's refugee camps, to those towns hypertrophied after the mass arrival of refugees from across the border. On their way home were also the workers who, during the evening of December 8,

1987, were accidentally run over by an Israeli truck, two days after a settler was killed in Gaza by a member of the Islamic Jihad. Tension was therefore already high in the Strip. The opportunities for friction between Israelis and Palestinians as they brushed past each other on the roads of Gaza were frequent. Thus, when the two cars in which the Palestinian workers were traveling were run over, killing four passengers, it was as though a match had been struck next to dry hay. The hay took fire the following day in Jabalia, the refugee camp in the northern area of the Strip from which three of the dead came. The funerals in Jabalia became student protests, the protests became a revolt, and the Intifada spread first throughout Gaza and then all the way to the West Bank.[44]

Twenty-four hours after the accident in Jabalia, the political office of the Muslim Brotherhood was summoned in a small apartment in the poor quarter of Sabra in Gaza City. The location was the house of Sheikh Ahmed Yassin, who was already considered the Ikhwan's reference in the Strip. At the meeting were 'Abdel Fattah al-Dukhan, Mohammed Shama', Ibrahim al-Yazouri, Issa al-Nashshar, Salah Shehadeh, Abdel Aziz al-Rantisi, and the landlord, Ahmed Yassin. It was necessary to decide what to do after these disturbances, which— as would later become clear—had sparked something more significant than a simple confrontation between Palestinians and the Israeli army, but rather the most important revolt in contemporary Palestinian history. It was not the organized factions of the political landscape who planned the Intifada, which was truly—at its inception—a spontaneous movement, the most evident representation of the fact that in the Occupied Palestinian Territory a political consciousness was being born independently of the institutions of exile—the PLO being first and foremost among these. For Ahmed Yassin, the outbreak of the First Intifada provided an important opportunity to bring to fruition the project begun four years earlier. In Azzam Tamimi's words, the Intifada "provides Yassin the best moment"[45] to create Hamas, but it did not change its objectives.

The Intifada of the Stones—the Intifadat al-Oula, or the first uprising, as Palestinians call it—made a quick decision necessary, one made without further deliberations or delays. Overcoming the internal divisions and the doubts of the older generation of Muslim Brothers, who were also present at the founding meeting, the seven participants decided to accept Yassin's strategy: the Ikhwan must give itself an operational group capable of entering the fray and taking part in the Intifada. Hamas's founding document states: "When the idea matured, the seed grew, and the plant took root in reality detached from the temporary emotional outburst and unwelcome haste, the Islamic Resistance Movement came forth to perform its role of struggle for the sake of its Lord."[46] This document, which was made public nine months later, provided a glimpse of the trajectory that brought the project Yassin had pushed for to fruition, as well as a glimpse of the influence of the Revolt of the Stones in moving forward the timing of its founding. The decision to establish Hamas, however, was not simply the result of a historical accident, but rather born from the changes—not least the sociological changes—that had taken place within the Muslim Brotherhood, which during the second half of the 1980s no longer represented that mercantile and bourgeois class that had prompted its birth and growth in Palestine toward the end of the 1940s. Hamas, the Islamic Resistance Movement, is the result of historical changes in Palestinian society, devastated as it had been by the War of 1948 and by the establishment of the State of Israel. The decision to establish Hamas was made by those who sought refuge in the Strip after the *nakba*: of the seven participants at that meeting, six were refugees; only one was born in Gaza. They came from the small villages of rural Palestine, certainly, but they were also often professionals who held degrees of higher education. This was the profile of the new Islamist who gave life to Hamas.

The provenance of the refugees was not a simple sociological accident; on the contrary, it explains much of the program pursued by the Islamist movement, its strategies, and the very forms of resistance against the Israelis that Hamas decided upon during certain phases. Further, it speaks of the younger generation, who, after having pushed for Hamas's establishment, would become its leaders at the dawn of the new millennium.[47] Sheikh Ahmed Yassin, a teacher born in 1938, had arrived in Gaza from the village of al-Joura, near today's Ashkelon, which was also the hometown of the family of the future prime minister Ismail Haniyeh and of another leader of the 2005–2007 period, Said Siyyam. The latter, a strongman of the Executive Force, was killed during Operation Cast Lead on January 15, 2009, by an aerial bombardment that literally destroyed the Gaza City building he was in at the time along with one of his sons, his brother, and his brother's family. Nearly the same age as Sheikh Yassin was Mohammed Hassan Shama'a. Pharmacist Ibrahim al-Yazouri was only two years younger than Yassin and came from the village of Beit Daras. Then there were the younger representatives, in particular Salah Shehadeh and Abdel Aziz al-Rantisi. The former was a social worker, born to a family of refugees from Jaffa in al-Shati refugee camp in Gaza, while the latter was a pediatrician who had been born barely a year before the *nakba* in the village of Yibna, north of Ashkelon, and who had grown up in Khan Younis. Their names would become important among the Hamas *Nomenklatura* in Gaza—important enough that the Israelis planned between 2002 and 2004 to eliminate them. Shehadeh and al-Rantisi were fully part of that generation that marked a watershed in the history of the Palestinian Ikhwan.

What does this provenance mean in political and programmatic terms? First and foremost, it means that with Hamas, the question of refugees becomes central. Such a claim might appear paradoxical given the fact that in those very years, the nationalist and secular Palestinian leadership was epitomized by the Diaspora, the cadres in exile, and by groups of activists that moved from one Arab capital to another. And yet, over time, Hamas's roots in the world of refugee camps both inside and outside Palestine's pre-1967 borders became its distinctive trait with respect to other Palestinian political movements. The leaders have been and are still today nearly all refugees or sons of refugees, and in itself the two-pronged leadership—within the West Bank and Gaza, and outside the borders of PNA Palestine—confirms just how important this origin is for Hamas's very character. Moreover, it is this very origin that puts the question of refugees at center stage in the confrontation with Israel, explaining also why it has not been possible for the Islamist leadership to disavow the idea of a *return to Palestine*. Beyond any ideology, the very identity of a considerable portion of its cadres would have been at stake. Over the years, the right of return for refugees had always been formally asserted by the PNA, but in reality this right had been set aside when it came to crucial questions of Jerusalem, the Israeli settlements in the West Bank, and the final borders between Israel and a Palestinian state. But for Hamas, the idea of *refuge* remained a central, constitutive theme, not least because it has been in Gaza—whose population is largely composed of refugees—that Hamas has found its most fertile terrain.

Thus, it was not simply the "old guard" that was present at the meeting in Yassin's house. On the contrary, the presence of many from younger generations confirms that Hamas's birth took place as a kind of coup within the Muslim Brotherhood—a generational and social coup, an ascent to power by that growing wing of militants made of refugees, their descendants, and those new young professionals who had reached political maturity in Egyptian and Palestinian universities. Imad al-Faluji, a Hamas leader who was later expelled for taking what were thought to be overly pragmatic and flexible positions, for example, has stated that "the young people in the movement were violent and rebellious. They sometimes engaged in actions without consulting the traditional leadership, which was not fully convinced of the need for confrontation."[48] Sheikh Ahmed Yassin acted as a sort of link between these generations: much older than Hamas's recalcitrant young, yet very different from the mercantile class that had resisted the birth of Hamas, he shared with the younger generation their roots within the refugee camps that furnished the Islamist movement with both the bedrock of its support and the cadres of the organization within the Occupied Palestinian Territory over the first two and a half decades of its existence. It was particularly in the Gaza Strip's refugee camps that the new generation of the Muslim Brotherhood—and hence also of Hamas—was forged. The old guard, on the other hand, shared across the West Bank and Gaza a popularity within the ranks of that mercantile class that had been the hallmark of the early Ikhwan. For the period preceding 1967, it has been calculated that at least a quarter of the Brotherhood's membership was drawn from traders and landowners, and that about another 40 percent was divided among intelligentsia, workers, and peasants.[49]

Ahmed Yassin had to take on the opposition not just of the Ikhwan in Gaza, but also of the fractious West Bankers, where those who acted as a bridge between him and the Ikhwan took at least one week to overcome resistance within the organization, and it took forty days for them to get Hamas underway there, mostly thanks to the role played by Jamil Hamami in the Jerusalem area and beyond.

The first document signed with the organization's full name, Harakat al-Muqawwama al-Islamiyya, and distributed publicly a few days later on December 14,[50] bears all the hallmarks of a document written in a conflict situation, where the essential drive is toward the struggle. Within the folds of the call to arms ("Our sons and youths who love the eternal life in heaven more than our enemies love this life," "Our people know the way of sacrifice and martyrdom and are generous in this regard"), there are some political indications that would define Hamas in years to come, both in relation to the Israelis and to secular nationalist groups. In this sense, it is no coincidence that according to some, the document was penned by Abdel Aziz al-Rantisi,[51] one of the closest to Yassin and the most important leader of the Ikhwan's youth movement at that time. The document's central paragraph in itself says much about the slant that the new leadership wished to give Hamas in 1987: "The Intifada of our vigilant people in the Occupied Palestinian Territory comes as a resounding rejection of the occupation and its pressures, land confiscation and the planting of settlements, and the policy of subjugation by the Zionists."[52] Again: The Intifada has come "to awaken the consciences of those among us who are gasping after a sick peace, after empty international conferences, after treasonous partial settlements like Camp David." The document also justifies violence, which was considered necessary after over twenty years during which the Muslim Brotherhood had abstained from participating in guerrilla actions: Let the Israelis "understand that violence breeds nothing but violence, and that death bestows [nothing] but death. How true is the adage 'I am drowning: why would I fear being wet?'" The recipients of this message were addressed with the precision that is the hallmark of those who know their constituency well: "Our people, our cities, our refugee camps, and our villages." Hence the recipe, the same that the Muslim Brotherhood had prescribed, at least until a few years earlier: "The Intifada is here to convince [the Palestinians] that Islam is the solution and the alternative."[53]

Over the course of its history, Hamas has always described its origins, not without a good dose of ambiguity, as directly linked to the First Intifada. The leadership maintains that the first "martyr," the first *shaheed* of the Intifada, was in fact an activist of the Islamist movement who died in Jabalia—a way of clarifying that the link between the birth of the movement and popular revolt was unbreakable. However, as was the case for Fatah, the most credible explanation is that the Intifada was indeed a revolt born "from below" and from within the Occupied Palestinian Territory. If there is a measure of truth in Hamas's explanation of its own birth, this can be found in the relationship between the Islamist movement and popular uprisings, which was much more direct than the link between the revolt's leadership and the institutional structures of the organizations represented within the PLO.

In sum, even if Hamas developed along a trajectory prior to and independent of the Intifada, the choice of entering the political fray the day after the beginning of the Revolt of the Stones confirms that Hamas has always found its reason and its strength in its link to the population. This is the reason it is at root a mass movement, indeed perhaps more than Fatah ever was, particularly in that part of its history that linked it to its role within the PNA. This role transformed Fatah into a party-state, or at least into a party-government, which grafted the Authority, the *sulta*, over both the exiled leadership that installed itself in Ramallah after 1994 and the local Fatah potentates, who then over the years lost touch with their rank and file. Hamas, even more so than the Palestinian Muslim Brotherhood, had always been different, precisely because of its ability to keep its finger on the pulse of the population and of Islamist civil society more generically.

Thus, it does not seem to be a coincidence that Hamas's birth, albeit accelerated by events, took place after the Jabalia riots, which coalesced into a full-blown revolt—an intifada—only over the course of the following days and weeks. At least one part of the Muslim Brotherhood leadership in Gaza—namely, Yassin and the younger generation—appears to have intuited that the embryo of the revolt would not remain a flash in the pan, and that such a revolt was a wave that had to be ridden in order to bring to fruition the project that had been conceived four years before. The very idea of establishing an operational wing of the Muslim Brotherhood is in itself linked to the organization's relationship with its popular support. As Osama Hamdan recalls: "Among we Islamist students the question was: how can we build a resistance movement without financial support from Arab states and after the PLO's defeat in Lebanon? Other movements received support from individual countries—Fatah, for example, received support from Egypt. Our answer was: we must build our support among the people. And we knew the people."[54] Of course, this is a partial explanation, entirely internal to the organization of the relationship between the Muslim Brotherhood and the base from which it gathered consensus, yet the very importance given to this support as a determining factor in Hamas's establishment provides an indication of how important this connection was and continues to be.

The relationship with popular support and with the interpretation Hamas has offered of the Palestinian population's needs emerges not only from what the Islamist movement has done during its first two decades, but also from its internal documents. A political strategy document dated 1992, for example, claims that "our true power lies in our popularity while Fatah's instead is a combination of financial resources and control of the most important institutions."[55] Both the leadership of Hamas itself and Islamist scholars such as Azzam Tamimi speak of an undoubted sensitivity toward what the population thinks of the strategies the movement has adopted over time. Bassam Na'im, then health minister of the de facto government led by Ismail Haniyeh after the June 2007 coup, concludes that Hamas's choice to participate in electoral politics was rooted in the fact that people had grown "tired."[56] Palestinians were worn out by the wave of terrorist attacks and by the Second Intifada, and they would not have understood (or sustained) the continuation of widespread violence.

Chapter 2

SNAPSHOTS FROM HAMAS'S WORLD

The Orphans of Al-Salah

The sea just beyond the houses at Deir al-Balah is swelling. Yet, among the low-rising houses of the village—whose name means "monastery of dates" and which is famous for its palm trees and vegetation that make it look like a snapshot of an Egyptian suburb—the sound of the winter sea becomes hushed. It is not the sea's strong undertow that breaks the silence in Deir al-Balah in the middle of the Strip, barely ten kilometers from Gaza City, but the strident tones of the old loudspeaker that continuously croaks out slogans while the men of this quarter, accompanied by their sons, slowly move toward a space covered by a tarpaulin. Dozens of white plastic chairs await the funeral-goers on their way to express their condolences to the family and to fulfill the rites of mourning. The dead were members of Hamas's armed wing, the Izz al-Din al-Qassam Brigades, units that carry the name of the sheikh who led the revolt against the British Mandatory authorities and against Zionist settlements during the 1930s. Suleiman al-Houly was twenty. No one knows for certain how old Abdul Rahman Abu Ghaza and Salman Dakrani were. All three died when a missile launched by an Israeli jet hit the Kata'eb al-Qassam, the Brigades' branch in Deir al-Balah.

Deir al-Balah is still—at least in theory—divided between a refugee camp hosting 20,000 inhabitants and a town that is home to a further 50,000, but nothing remains of old Darum City's ancient past dating to the time of the Crusades and the Knights Templar, much less of its Bronze Age treasures, which can now be admired in Jerusalem's Israel Museum instead, having been taken away by the Israel Antiquities Authority. Indeed, many of the precious anthropomorphic sarcophagi ended up in the private collection of Moshe Dayan—a general well known for his archaeological "hobby"—only to be acquired by Israel's largest museum after his death. But Deir al-Balah is too enmeshed in this painful contemporary history—caught between the conflict and the deep blue sea, between dust and palms—to recall that it was once one of the cultural cradles of Hellenism. Before the withdrawal, before the closure of the Israeli settlements abandoned in August 2005, Deir al-Balah was crushed between the two settlements of Kfar Darom and Netzarim, disbanded when then-Israeli Prime Minister Ariel Sharon decided that defending some 9,000 settlers surrounded by a Palestinian population nearing 1.5 million was counterproductive. The conflict, however, was already part of the very fabric of society in Deir al-Balah well before the settlement enterprise got under way in Gaza. The two waves of refugees, which arrived in 1948 and in 1967, had utterly changed the area's very topography.

The Al-Salah branch is less than two hundred meters from the funeral tent. It is a branch that one cannot overlook: two schools, a sports field, a small hospital, offices, and large buildings, white and dignified, that everyone in Deir al-Balah knows because the buildings have come to signify support, education, health, medicines, gift packages, school bags, exercise books, and clothes. It was no coincidence that Al-Salah's now-exhausted coffers provided a monthly source of support for thousands of orphans. Al-Salah is one of the largest charitable organizations in the Gaza Strip. Established in 1978, it obtained a license to operate from the Israeli authorities. Among its leadership were 'Abdel Fattah al-Dukhan and Imad al-Faluji; the former was one of Hamas's founders, while the latter was a leader until his expulsion from the movement in 1995.

Al-Salah currently has eight branches across the entire Strip that undertake different support projects, from the poor to the sick, from orphans to students. One of the most important projects for this organization—a force to be reckoned with, within what in Western terms might be called the "third sector"—is its support for 15,000 children, of which about four-fifths are orphans. Orphans are, in fact, the principal clients of at least forty charitable organizations in the West Bank and Gaza.[1] Often these orphans have lost a father, as they are the children of the *shaheed*, the "martyrs." The word "martyr" can refer to anyone: the militant of either Hamas or one of the other armed factions who died fighting the Israelis, the militant who has undertaken a suicide attack, or someone who died in a workplace accident or as a result of a bombardment, whether as an intended victim or as "collateral damage." The other 3,000 students in Al-Salah schools, however, come from very poor families. Every child has his or her own personal file, with personal data that has been checked against existing records. The organization's now three-decade-long knowledge of the local context further protects against the possibility of fraud. The files are then sent on to one of the international organizations that send money from Europe or from Arab states, and through a tried-and-tested system of long-distance child sponsorship, every child receives a minimum monthly contribution of a hundred shekels, equivalent to about $30. Since 2005, however, receiving money through banks has become increasingly difficult, as foreign accounts have been frozen following the US decision to undertake precautionary measures against Al-Salah in 2003, with Arab banks following suit. Moreover, the checks placed on the charitable organizations in Europe that sent funds to Al-Salah have blocked at the roots the flow of funds that had previously been channeled toward Gaza. This has put the infrastructure of support—the network of assistance to the poor, to students, and to orphans—under considerable strain. Ever since the summer of 2007, all programs have been at risk, from donations to orphans to the distribution of gift packages, from food aid to school supplies.

During Ramadan, Al-Salah used to distribute food packages to poor families, and at Eid al-Fitr, the feast that concludes the month of fasting and that for Muslims is also the feast of important gifts, the association's roughly three hundred volunteers distributed clothes and the money collected through *zakat*. At the beginning of the school year, they provided school bags, exercise books, pencils, and so on: a small supply of educational equipment handed out to poor students irrespective of whether they attend a private school such as the ones run by Al-Salah itself, a state school, or one of the schools run by UNRWA (United Nations Relief and Works Agency for Palestine Refugee), the UN organization charged with assisting Palestinian refugees. In the 2007–2008 school year, Al-Salah provided school uniforms for 3,000 students. The organization's large school, inaugurated in 2000, has 1,000 students: half in the girls' section, and another 500 boys in the white building opposite. The buildings are large, simple, well-ventilated, and clean, and their walls are covered with the children's drawings. The mosque is next door. Nearby is a hospital, which opened in 2002 and is considered both the best in town and the best attended, since the cost of being cured is US$1.50—and not even that, if it is well known that a family is poor. Some 7,000 patients a month are cured by 120 doctors and nurses paid for by the organization, which also provides salaries for another 48 employees in branches scattered from north to south across the Strip, from Jabalia all the way down to Rafah, as well as around 100 teachers. The rest are all volunteers. Volunteering has an undeniable religious dimension. From a large and unadorned but clean office block, Salwa, one of Al-Salah's officials, explains: "Most of the doctors, of the nurses, and the staff are well-educated people, who could easily work with organizations, with the government, or with the UN. But they decided to work here precisely because of their religious commitment."[2] After Hamas's victory in the 2006 general elections, and even more so after the June 2007 coup, the situation for Al-Salah became truly borderline: "It's the hardest it's been in the organization's thirty-year history. We're suffering more now than under the Israeli occupation. The difference is that when the Israelis were here, Arab banks did not freeze our assets as they do now. But we are independent. We have no links with politics."[3]

This emphasis on the independence of charities from politics is a constant when one speaks to those in charge of charitable organizations, which are believed to be linked to Islamist organizations—both Hamas and others. Other charities, in Gaza as in the West Bank, offer the same refrain in the attempt to avoid closure, the freezing of their financial assets, and the drying up of their sources of funding. It happened in 2007 and again in 2008; it happened while the Second Intifada was at its height and before that during the early days of the PNA, when Yasser Arafat had ordered a few dozen organizations closed. All these measures—at least those undertaken during the 1990s—had not seriously challenged the existence of these charities. But, alongside the analogous measures implemented worldwide after September 11, 2001, and the particular strictures imposed upon Islamic charities, the closures of the last few years have had a greater impact on these organizations' ability to survive. After Hamas's June 2007 coup in Gaza, the PNA government in Ramallah, headed by Salam Fayyad, targeted NGOs and organizations that it considered to have links to the Islamist movement, charities included. The PNA either closed these organizations—citing various reasons, among them financial mismanagement—or required them to appoint PNA loyalists to their boards. According to Hamas sources, 150 NGOs have been affected by the Ramallah government's new policy.[4] From the middle of 2010 on, Islamist charities in Gaza began to implement investment projects aimed at maintaining the cash flow necessary to honor their commitments to the different social sectors they had historically assisted. According to the "Gaza street," some of the most important Islamist charities in the Strip own the Gaza Mall, opened during the summer of 2010, as well as some of the family amusement parks. Islamist NGOs have also used business enterprises, like the fish farm in Al Bustan Park along the coast between Gaza City and Jabalia, as a means of collecting and distributing the liquid assets that remain under siege.

The argument that Islamist charitable organizations have no links with Palestinian politics has never convinced any of these groups' counterparts—not the higher echelons of the PNA, not the Israelis, and not US authorities. Indeed, it was the web of controls established by the US Treasury that surveyed the financial records of the school in Deir al-Balah, and on August 7, 2007, Al-Salah was listed among the charitable organizations that, according to Washington, financially supported Hamas. To be precise, the United States included Al-Salah in the list of organizations under sanction kept by the Office of Foreign Assets Control, with the result that all bank accounts and any financial activity on US soil linked to the organization were frozen, and that US citizens have been prohib-

ited from financing or from having any connection with Al-Salah.
This was a decision made rather late, given that Al-Salah—which is
keen to be considered apolitical—was established thirty years earlier, with a license given by none other than the occupying power
itself, namely, Israel. The US Treasury Department argues that "the
Al-Salah Society supported Hamas-affiliated combatants during
the first Intifada and recruited and indoctrinated youth to support
Hamas's activities."[5] To support this statement, they point to Ahmed
al-Kurd's leadership of the organization when al-Kurd was mayor
of Deir al-Balah in February 2005, after Hamas trounced Fatah in
the municipal elections, gaining thirteen out of fifteen seats on the
town council. Ahmed al-Kurd was a Hamas leader in Deir al-Balah
in 2003, as well as a member of its *Shura* Council during the First
Intifada. For his part, Ahmed al-Kurd does not believe that Hamas
could have gained support through charitable organizations, which
he maintains distributed a negligible percentage of funds compared
to the amounts that international donors, for example, brought to
Palestinians. As al-Kurd puts it, "Islamic charity organizations didn't
pay out [even] one percent"[6] of the $6 billion that the international
community has donated over the past ten years. The US Treasury,
however, maintains that "the *Al-Salah* Society has employed a number of Hamas military wing members. In late 2002, an official of
the *Al-Salah* Society in Gaza was the principal leader of a Hamas
military wing structure in the Al-Maghazi refugee camp in Gaza,"
where at least a further five people, considered to be members of the
same organization, also had links with the charitable organization
at the same time.[7]

From this point of view, tracing a red line linking Al-Salah, Ahmed
al-Kurd, and Hamas appears straightforward enough. Just as it
seemed straightforward to Israeli authorities to trace a link between
Jamia'a al-Khairiyya al-Islamiyya (the Islamic Charitable Society) of
Hebron, Abdel Khaleq al-Natsheh, and Hamas. Ever since the time
of Amman's control over the West Bank, the Islamic Charitable Society of Hebron has been another colossus of the Islamic charitable
sector, so much so that its roots can be traced all the way back to
1962, when the Hashemite Kingdom first licensed it, opening an

orphanage for fifteen children. What followed was a history similar to so many other Muslim charities across the West Bank and Gaza: a history of licenses always renewed, first by Israeli authorities responsible for administering the Occupied Palestinian Territory, then by the PNA, while in the meantime the organization grew, as did the population it served. Thus, by 2008, the Islamic Charitable Society of Hebron ran eight schools attended by 4,500 students, two orphanages (one male, one female) totaling 240 children residing on the premises, two bakeries, a small textile factory, a central depot with three forty-foot-long industrial refrigerators, and several shops. One day in February 2008, the Israelis closed three schools and the girls' orphanage, confiscated the stocks in the depot, including the three refrigerators, closed the bakeries, and took away the sewing machines from the workshop located underneath the orphanage. The accusation was that the charity supported Hamas and that the head of the committee in 2002 was Abdel Khaleq al-Natsheh, who was well known and considered to be linked to Hamas's military wing in the West Bank. But he was also among those who subscribed to that famous Prisoners' Document that, in spring 2006, attempted to mend the rift between Fatah and Hamas, and to lead the Islamist movement toward the recognition—however qualified—of Israel. Another seven administrative staff and employees of the charity were imprisoned. The response from the Society's lawyer was that Abdel Khaleq al-Natsheh was not designated from within the organization itself, but appointed by the Ministry of Waqf (i.e., by the PNA itself): "So perhaps they should shut down the Ministry of Waqf,"[8] quipped legal consultant Abdel Karim Farrah. The Israeli authorities, however, did not accept this explanation.

Notwithstanding the closure order, the girls' school in one of Hebron's main streets is still open, and its classes run normally, with PNA textbooks on the desks just like the textbooks all other students use in the West Bank, East Jerusalem, and Gaza. The orphanage, where the girls receive meals of chicken and rice, is also still open. However, nothing could be done to save the textile factory. The workshop floors are empty, and young Maysoun Darwish is angry: "I'm an orphan; I've been here for fifteen years, since I was only nineteen. They paid me well, 1,300 shekels, just under $350. I can't find another job where they respect you like this, where they give you a good salary and where you work eight hours a day. There are ten of us in the family, and only two of my sisters work."⁹ Maysoun's story is similar to that of so many others across the towns, villages, and refugee camps of the West Bank. More than in the PNA's welfare net, the neediest families found solace in the NGOs, which receive support from abroad and particularly from the extensive network of Islamic charities. Al-Salah in Deir al-Balah and the Jamia'a al-Khariyya al-Islamiyya in Hebron are cases in point, two of dozens of possible examples, glimpses into a hidden but vast world of Muslim—and at times Islamist—organizations. The fact of the matter is that charities make no distinctions when they offer public services. Every Palestinian knows this. In Gaza City there used to be a small clinic in the town center, on a long but narrow road. It belonged to the Society for Public Support, and next to the main entrance, posted on the wall, were the plaques of US Agency for International Development (USAID) and the French, both of which had sent funds in years gone by. Word on the street was that the clinic was supposedly linked to Hamas, and yet it was the single most important center for childbirth, the one that most people trusted because it was the cleanest and because its doctors were good. All sorts of women went to the small clinic on Al-Mughrabi Road, both secular and Islamist: it had a catchment area 45,000 strong, 250 deliveries a month, and three operating theaters.

"Serving the people" is a recurring phrase when meeting members of Hamas, or those people who, although not militants, are close to political Islam. It is the heritage of an experience rooted in the Muslim Brotherhood that gradually evolved over time along increasingly national lines. A Muslim Brotherhood member "serves the people" in Egypt, where broadly Islamist voluntary organizations can be found throughout the country, although "they [are] not political in the narrow sense of the term" because they do not "advocate a particular political agenda or take part in the competition for political power."¹⁰ One "serves the people" in Palestinian society also, where mosques, schools, clinics, kindergartens, women's health centers, and sports centers have been hallmarks of social engagement—as well as of the promotion of Islamism, particularly since the birth of Ahmed Yassin's Mujamma al-Islami in 1973. As in Egypt, in the Palestinian Territory it has always been simplistic to think of a simple and linear direct connection between charities and politics, between the NGO sector and Hamas, despite the fact that very often one can find Hamas's leaders, militants, and activists within different organizations as teachers, doctors, technicians, or just as volunteers. This is because the social dimension is part and parcel of Hamas's identity: Article 21 of the Mithaq (Hamas's Charter) itself states that "part of social welfare consists in helping all those who are in need of material, spiritual or collective cooperation in order to complete various projects," and that Hamas members must "look after the needs of the people as they would their own needs" and "spare no effort in . . . realizing this and protecting them."[11]

Despite this, despite the fact that the NGO sector could be considered the base for Hamas's political mobilization,[12] charities cannot simultaneously be categorized according to such a limited framework as the history of the Islamist movement, nor can they be considered to be some kind of "piggy bank" that the Harakat al-Muqawwama al-Islamiyya simply draws on at will. This phenomenon is too widespread, going well beyond Hamas and the bedrock of its consensus and well beyond the history of the PNA—beyond even the competition between opposite factions. It is easy to find staff and employees with different political affiliations within charitable organizations. One only need browse independent studies, such as those published by the World Bank, the UN, or think tanks, to realize that the voluntary sector has over the decades become one of the pillars of Palestinian welfare, without which it would be impossible to provide assistance to the weaker strata of the population. A thin red line connects the Occupied Palestinan Territory before and after the establishment of the PNA, and this connection is precisely that of the voluntary sector, both secular and religious, which compensated for the shortcomings in public welfare, health, and education. According to a study carried out by the World Bank, the situation evolved from one in which, before the first Oslo Accords, NGOs covered the costs of 60 percent of primary health care and 50 percent of secondary health care, to one during the difficult years of the Second Intifada in which charities provided for extensive areas of the social fabric. When conditions for the population became much tougher with the outbreak of the Al-Aqsa Intifada in 2000, the support offered by charitable organizations became absolutely fundamental for many families' subsistence simply because the number of people in need grew exponentially. According to a study carried out by two UN agencies at the time, "NGOs and charitable organisations (as a whole) are the major service providers, reaching about 60 percent of the total beneficiaries from regular and emergency programs," thereby overtaking even UNRWA, the UN agency responsible for Palestinian refugees for the past sixty years, which accounts for 34 percent of provisions, and the PNA's Ministry for Social Affairs, which covers barely 6 percent.[13] One of the Islamist leaders at the time, Ismail Abu Shanab, was even more precise: in 2002, at the height of the Second Intifada, charitable organizations—whether linked to Hamas or otherwise Islamist—covered 15 percent of Palestinians' needs in Gaza.[14] The invocation of two such different time periods in recent Palestinian history as the pre-Oslo period and the Second Intifada is no coincidence. These are two phases during which "associational life in Gaza and in the West Bank arises in response to the absence of a legitimate national authority, and in conditions of occupation and deprivation."[15]

Islamist associations thus extend the range of their activities whenever the state sector pulls back on its own, whether this be the occupying power (Israel) or an entity such as the PNA. In this sense, the West Bank and Gaza are not much different from many other areas of the Arab world with respect to the existence of Islamic charities. One need only cross Gaza's southern border into Egypt and follow the trail of charitable organizations—particularly after the 1970s—to discover that the great increase in voluntary bodies was, among other things, the result of the economic and political conditions in which the most populous Arab state found itself. Particularly after Hosni Mubarak's ascent to power and Cairo's application for support in the form of the Structural Adjustment Programs (SAPs) guided by the World Bank and the International Monetary Fund, Egypt entered a phase during which charities compensated for a state welfare provision that was no longer able to satisfy the demands of the weaker parts of society—the poorest, the least protected—who made up a very considerable percentage of the population. The diminished presence of the public sector in areas such as health and welfare was therefore counterbalanced by an increase in the efforts made by charitable organizations linked to Muslim activism, which simultaneously created a fertile terrain for activism in Islamist opposition—particularly in the ranks of the Muslim Brotherhood. This dynamic characterized not just Egypt, but many other Arab countries in which the liberalization policies pursued by international economic institutions during the 1980s and 1990s had caused extremely serious social problems, many of which remain unresolved to this day. It is to these problems that Islamic charities have responded promptly. Of course, the Palestinian case has its own unique characteristics, beginning with its economy, which is based primarily on international assistance, and on the so-called aid industry. By the same token, however, Palestinian Islamist charities have reacted to crises while so-called public agents have displayed an inability to intervene to support the least protected in society.

Both in the Arab world and in the Palestinian context, health centers, clinics, and free medical centers, however, are only one of the aspects of the Islamist associational sector, albeit perhaps the most high profile. In reality, this sector has often been the one least closely linked to politics. The one exception, both in terms of the history of the Islamist volunteer sector and in terms of Palestinian civil society more generally, was the 1979 struggle for control of the Red Crescent, an important symbol of welfare provision in Gaza. The battle for control of the organization's board of directors took place before the birth of Hamas, but after Sheikh Ahmed Yassin's Mujamma al-Islami had already become an important actor in the landscape of the Gaza Strip's volunteer sector. Control remained with the Left, but Islamists reacted violently in the roads of Gaza City, ultimately culminating in an attack on the headquarters of the Red Crescent itself, which were destroyed and set ablaze, while its founder, Dr. Haidar

Abdel Shafi, one of the most important figures of Palestinian history, was threatened.[16]

In any case, the Harakat al-Muqawwama al-Islamiyya has built its ability to mobilize and disseminate its political message in other areas. Education is one example. As demonstrated by the history of the Islamic University, education—from kindergartens to advanced training—was considered one of the pillars of the Islamist presence in Palestine, although mosques remained the center for congregation, unification, and education. At a time when the First Intifada was at its height, Hamas's leader Mahmoud al-Zahhar and Eyad al-Sarraj, a well-known Gaza Strip psychiatrist and a secular-independent intellectual, had a long, intense discussion. The argument—as Sarraj recounts—was the first poll his center, the Gaza Community Mental Health Program, had conducted on political participation among Palestinians. The study found that only 11 percent of those questioned adhered to Hamas, and 21 percent to other factions. Sarraj recalls that "Abu Khaled [the name by which many of Gaza's inhabitants knew Mahmoud al-Zahhar] came to me and asked me how I had managed to obtain those results. He contested them in the following way: nearly all of Gaza is Muslim, half of it prays, a quarter prays in a mosque. Therefore that last quarter will meet someone from Hamas."[17] Mahmoud al-Zahhar's reasoning might appear simplistic, but it does confirm the importance that the Islamist movement has always given to education—secular as well as religious—as a way of proselytizing. The mosque had been the center from which the Mujamma al-Islami had developed, and it continued to play that role after the birth of the operational branch of the Muslim Brotherhood. Even given this, religion is one thing, while everything else, all that is political, is the result of efforts made by men, as Osama Hamdan himself points out: "The efforts of the political movement are not orders that come from God, they are a way of translating" the religious message into political practice.[18]

Nonetheless, the mosque remains central not only as a place within which other activities can take place, from Qur'an reading clubs to activities that in Christian terms one might call "Sunday school." The mosque is also the place to find preachers, imams, and a roll call of the more or less charismatic leaders with a distinct presence in Hamas's history, from Sheikh Ahmed Yassin himself to Ismail Haniyeh—who, even as a prime minister, never stopped attending Friday prayers at the mosque, or speaking from the pulpit—to West Bank imams such as Hassan Youssef and Bassam Jarrar in Ramallah, the conservative Hamed Bitawi both in Nablus and at the Al-Aqsa Mosque in Jerusalem, and Nayef Rajoub in Hebron. These are all religious personalities who also occupy leadership positions within Hamas—and who have all, incidentally, spent long periods in Israeli jails. Many other less well-known preachers, the so-called countryside imams, have also spent time in Israeli jails, but have remained anonymous in the media until some serious event such as their killing throws light on the role they played within the community.

The most recent case—which in some ways is typical—is that of Majid Barghouthi, who bore a famous family name and was the second cousin of Marwan Barghouthi, the Fatah leader who is serving multiple life sentences. Majid Barghouthi was the imam of Kobar, a small village, 4,000 strong, on the hills surrounding Ramallah: Hamas's imam. Because of his political affiliation, Majid had spent five years in Israeli prisons. As Kobar's inhabitants themselves say, he was well known among the population because for twenty-five years the West Bank's religious authorities—the Waqf—had sent him far and wide across the countryside to preach. After this—as is typical both in Islam and in other religions—Majid delved into more prosaic concerns, including joining a parents' association, as he himself was married with eight children (his first bearing the name Qassam). One day in February 2008, the Mukhabarat—Palestinian intelligence services—arrested him, believing they could extract from him the location of the weapons Hamas had hidden in Kobar. Majid died during the interrogation. The weapons were not found, but a commission to inquire into his death was established. The commission came to a harsh verdict on Palestinian intelligence, and after a few months, Mahmoud Abbas did not extend the mandate of the Mukhabarat's leader, Tawfik al-Tirawi. The whole village attended the funeral of Sheikh Majid, as he was known to his congregation, with local leaders at the forefront and Hamas and Fatah supporters

who both bore the Barghouthi name in attendance. These Barghouthis, both Fatah and Hamas, all went to give their condolences to
the family and the widow, a diminutive woman, pregnant with her
ninth child, in their small house on the outskirts of the village—a
house like any other, modest, constantly under construction, with
the steel rods of its cement pillars in full view, ready to welcome
another room, Hamas flags and the large banner bearing Sheikh
Ahmed Yassin's face hanging on its façade.

Majid Barghouthi's is a small, local story, one that explains far
better than many theories how much Islamist militants—preachers
included—are rooted in their communities, and not through some
kind of external intervention. It also shows how Palestinian society
displays far stronger bonds than those of mere political affiliation;
there are family ties, clans, local and religious affiliations. Eyad al-
Sarraj, who has worked in Gaza for decades and who has known
the Islamist movement's leadership and militants from the beginning, explains that from a certain point of view, it is indeed true
that Hamas acts according to the typical rules of tribalism: "They
have their own special identity, and they don't want to be part of the
wider group. In this case, identity is a barrier between you and the
other."[19] This behavior is congruent with a Hebron activist's explanation of the spirit of Hamas membership: "When you enter the movement, they tell you that you'll be a part of it until you die, but that
you won't be allowed to die until you have found someone who will
ensure continuity. It's a project."[20] The combination of these two elements—tribalism and proselytism—is part of the identity of those
who become members of Hamas, an identity that is still absolutely
similar to that of other movements that have their roots in Hassan
al-Banna's Muslim Brotherhood. This identity is one of the reasons
why it is impossible to talk about Hamas without reference to its
popular consensus.

Preachers and imams are part of this consensus, even though their
presence cannot explain the consensus entirely. Moreover—as with
all movements that are as pragmatic as the Harakat al-Muqawwama
al-Islamiyya—the instruments through which imams preach have
modernized, evolving over time in order to reach their audience

wherever it may be. Just like in other parts of the world, the audience in the Occupied Palestinian Territory often sits in front of the television. And just like in the rest of the Arab world, where religious satellite channels have markedly increased over recent years, with mirroring trends already witnessed in Italy (Tele PadrePio), in Europe (Radio Marija), and in the United States (Protestant televangelists), Hamas itself has also opened its doors to sermons over the airwaves. Younis Al-Astal, for example, is one of those who address the faithful. Born in Khan Younis, a graduate of a Saudi university, president of the Shariía faculty of the Islamic University in Gaza City, and elected to Parliament in 2006 with nearly 40,000 votes, he is one of the most radical figures within the Islamist movement in Gaza City. Al-Astal has always been known for his inflammatory tone, for his radical provocations, and for his hawkish line, one that he never conceals, even in front of the camera.

Of Music, Film, and Stereotypes

That Hamas militants do not have close links to the art world is a matter of fact that runs throughout the entire history of both the Islamic Resistance Movement and the Muslim Brotherhood. The movement's relationship with culture and entertainment, therefore, is similar to that which other Islamist groups generally display, with the partial exception of Hezbollah. In Hamas's case, just as in Hezbollah's, however, absolute statements cannot accurately capture a picture that has evolved over time, becoming increasingly complex, until it began to step back again after Gaza's isolation became complete. The message transmitted to young Islamists, for example, is not monolithic. They are not told that it is prohibited to watch television, that music is prohibited entirely, or that to adhere to a more orthodox vision of Islam one can listen to *nasheed* (Qur'anic chants) alone or, at best, music made up entirely of percussion. Reality is much more complex, and young Islamists range from those who watch films and television series without so much as a second thought, all the way to those who keep their televisions turned off, and feature a whole range of intermediate positions that may make little sense to a Westerner. In any case, the stereotype of the Islamist who rejects art, who rejects the technological dimension of an artistic message, or who simply rejects technology entirely does not capture the range of realities one finds in Hamas's world.

The clearest demonstration of this is the decision made by the movement during the Second Intifada to establish a radio station, the Voice of Al-Aqsa, which quickly became the Gaza Strip's most popular station. Then, in 2005, it established a television station that came on the air two weeks before the 2006 general elections in which Hamas had decided to take part.[21] Al-Aqsa began its programming on January 8 of that year, without the requisite license—as Rael Abu Deir, the station's director, comments: "We have been trying for a year (to receive a licence)."[22] It carried out limited technical tests in Gaza for three months and survived several attempts to take it off air by PNA institutions responsible for radio and television, and then, after Hamas's coup in June 2007, it became the voice of Gaza's de facto government. Hamas's decision to establish a television channel is directly linked to its need to provide its own version of the facts and to spread its own propaganda, as well as to consolidate a counterweight to Palestinian public television by providing its audience with a political and cultural image in line with Islamist thought, and to provide an interpretation of events different from that provided by Israeli and Western channels. After an initial period during which politics and religious education took center stage, the channel's programming was broadened to include sports and children's programs, both of these closely monitored by Israeli observers, who have often accused these programs of inciting hatred and of broadcasting violent, anti-Semitic messages. According to Hamas, the objective is not simply that of providing counterinformation; it is also—as the channel's administrators themselves say—to change Hamas's image: "To change the perspective about us among the world, believing that we are terrorists."[23] Fathi Hammad, the network's director—who was also elected to Parliament in 2006 and who, after Operation Cast Lead, succeeded Said Siyyam to become a powerful minister of the interior—explains: "We will prove to them that we are a people under occupation, resisting and struggling to get our rights, and not a selfish, terrorist people."[24]

Previous to the birth of Al-Aqsa, the relationship between Hamas and the media had not taken on a strategic significance comparable to that of the media's relationship with the Shi'ite Islamist movement in Lebanon (although Al-Aqsa would ultimately take as its inspiration the Hezbollah-run station Al-Manar) until the beginning of the current century, when Hamas decided to adopt a full-blown media strategy that went beyond the limited distribution available through the press. This strategy involved not only the radio and television stations in Gaza (starting with Al-Aqsa in 2005 and continuing with the Lebanon-based Quds), but involved also the development of several websites that gathered the information conveyed by the Palestinian Islamist movement.

If one cannot speak of a full-blown communications strategy during the early years of Hamas, at certain points of its existence the Islamist movement has certainly demonstrated an ability to take surprisingly effective advantage of the media landscape.

One example stands out above others, demonstrating just how much Hamas had already, by the early 1990s, come to understand the role of communications in its attempt to build a relationship with the outside world that went beyond the bipolar "Israelis vs. Palestinians" dimension. This is the Marj al-Zuhour case, in which on December 17, 1992, 415 Islamists—affiliated mostly with Hamas but also including members of the Islamic Jihad—were arrested in the West Bank and in Gaza by Israeli authorities and deported to Marj al-Zuhour in southern Lebanon. Very quickly, the deportees made the decision to remain in the open countryside, in harsh weather conditions (it was winter, and there was inadequate shelter). Designating Abdel Aziz al-Rantisi as a spokesperson, Hamas representatives adopted a media strategy that they had followed in the organization of the camp itself: they decided to manage Marj al-Zuhour as though it were a *non-temporary* camp. In a few short days, they adapted the existing camp to the landscape surrounding it, and assigned administrative roles on the basis of each individual's competence. In particular, the Hamas representatives established a full-fledged press center and selected spokespeople to act as liaisons with the international press—who flocked to Marj al-Zuhour within months—on the basis of the simple and effective criterion of linguistic competence. (It was not difficult to come by men who were familiar with several foreign languages, as many of those who would later become Hamas's cadres had pursued further education abroad. Four were in possession of doctorates, ten had master's degrees, sixty-nine had undergraduate degrees, five were journalists, eleven were doctors, and fourteen were engineers. For some, this level of linguistic competence was aided by their experience as journalists in Lebanon before being arrested and deported.) Thanks to this media strategy, the deportation to Marj al-Zuhour was constantly placed in the spotlight, both in the Arabic media and in the international press, so much so that it became a media boomerang for the Israelis and for Hamas. As Rantisi himself would later say, "It was a milestone. After that event, Hamas became an actor on the international stage."

However, it is the continuous presence of Hamas leaders on the television screen that changed the relationship between television and Palestinian Islamists. This presence became continuous with the birth of a twenty-four-hour Arabic news channel, which itself afforded new perspectives, new ways of understanding events, and—for its competitors—meant dealing with new criteria for newsworthiness. The entry onto the media scene of Al Jazeera toward the end of the 1990s, and in particular its coverage of Palestinian politics since the Second Intifada, changed Hamas's relationship to television, as well. Information channels were finally completely legitimized, not only in the eyes of the leadership who, thanks to press conferences and interviews, came into direct contact with the media, but also among that great majority of militants who could now easily turn on the television and zap from one satellite channel to another. Using television as a source of information became a normal, daily act, along the lines of what was already happening for other Islamist movements in other Arab countries.

But what happens when one moves from information to other programming; what happens in the shift from news to entertainment? It is precisely in the terrain of general television programming that the fissures between the more open sectors within Hamas and the orthodox ones become apparent. This distinction does not exclude any *place* Hamas is present in, from geographical areas such as the Occupied Palestinian Territory to the refugee camps in Lebanon, Syria, and Jordan, and even to the Israelis prisons where thousands of Islamists are detained. In jails, for example, because the rules of daily routines vary quite considerably between the secular members of the PFLP and Islamic Jihad's militants, prisoners tend to be grouped by political affiliation in order to satisfy a number of requirements, not only to avoid creating friction within individual cells between members of different factions, but also simply to make cohabitation easier. One of the rules is aimed at the presence and watching of television. There is general agreement that there should be no "variety" shows or other programming that might be considered "indecent" by more rigid Islamist groups, but the debate heats up when it comes to fiction. In the Arab world, fiction covers a great spectrum of possibilities, from the American action films that swamp Saudi satellite channels to the historical dramas produced predominantly in Syria, from Egyptian comedies of the last twenty years to dramas shot in Cairo or in the Delta countryside.

It is here, between cinema and television, that one can trace the line dividing the more radical factions of Hamas from those within the movement who are considered more pragmatic, or even moderate. Certainly, it is easier to discover such divisions this way than it is through those gestures—such as, for example, the willingness of an Egyptian or Tunisian Islamist either to shake a woman's hand in greeting or to avoid the handshake by putting his hand on his chest as an alternative sign of respect—through which one understands whether he is more or less open in his mores. The overwhelming majority of Hamas's leadership will not shake hands with a woman who is not wearing a glove, but nearly everyone watches television, even those considered the most conservative, and some among the Islamist leadership have very specific cinematic preferences. There are those who love films that deal with current events, such as Osama Hamdan, while others, like Ahmed Youssef, who once lived in the United States, prefer old American films. There are even those who are fanatical about Italian neorealist cinema, such as Mahmoud al-Ramahi, anesthesiologist, graduate of an Italian medical school, and one of the deputies elected in 2006 and then incarcerated by Israel until 2009, and then again in jail from November 2010. Many among the leadership do what most Arab Muslims do during Ramadan: they avidly follow the plot of *Bab al-Hara*, a *musalsal* (soap opera) set in a fictitious old quarter in Damascus during the golden age of anticolonialist nationalism, which has monopolized the television season since its inception in 2006. Many among the middle-aged cadres, then, share the same preferences as those in the wider Arab world who are neither militants nor Islamists. (Following *Bab al-Hara* is a bit like listening to the legends of Middle Eastern music, whether it is the old and always fascinating Lebanese legend Fayrouz for those who live further north between the West Bank and the Levant, or whether it is the music of singer Umm Kulthoum, the Star of the Orient, the legend of Pan-Arabism, the voice of Egypt for those in Gaza who gravitate further toward Cairo's cultural orbit.)

As television habits have spread within the Arab public, so too has the acceptance of television among Hamas's cadres and militants, limiting the actual prohibition on watching television to a very small minority. From sports to *musalsalat*, news, talk shows, and expressly religious programs, television has become a natural part of daily life, even among Islamists. Differences remain on music; the openness of the middle-aged generation (those who are now in their fifties) currently faces strong resistance in Gaza, where the "prison syndrome" radicalizes even minute details of social living. Singers like Umm Kulthoum—an icon of Palestinian nationalism for the generation that grew up in the seventies—are now considered *haram* (sinful) by Hamas militants in their thirties. Yet while these militants listen only to *nasheed*, they consider *halal* (permitted) the American action movies shown on MBC 2, the Saudi-owned, pan-Arab network that devotes its second channel entirely to Western movies.[25]

Hijab and Politics

"Hamas is now made up of more women than men."[26] One wonders whether this statement by Sheikh Hamed Bitawi is based on statistical evidence or on his experience as one of the Islamist movement's doyens, president of the Union of Palestinian Ulama and professor at Al-Najah University, although perhaps best known outside the West Bank and Gaza as one of Hamas's most conservative clerics. That there are many women within Hamas is an objective fact, one visible in the movement's mass demonstrations. Six were even elected to Parliament in the 2006 elections for the Palestinian Legislative Council (PLC), although there were quotas requiring a certain percentage of female representation (which Hamas in no way discouraged) to facilitate women's participation in the electoral process. Hamas is well aware that it can rely on an enormous slice of the female vote, which is perhaps the most conservative and the most tied to a traditional way of life, to women's role within it, and to the family.

However, even a cursory examination of the behavior of politically active women within Hamas shows how different and complex their behavior is today from the time of the movement's establishment. Throughout the 1980s, there was intense pressure placed on social mores and on the socioreligious code of conduct—pressure that came first from the Muslim Brotherhood and then later from the Harakat al-Muqawwama al-Islamiyya. Conservative pressures on women in particular date to this period, one example being the pressure placed on the women who attended universities to adopt a more sober and increasingly modest dress code. The justification for this, around the time of the First Intifada, was that Palestine was in mourning, that there was a struggle against the occupation, and therefore one could neither have fun nor betray vanity for one's body through clothes or makeup. It was as though every Palestinian should demonstrate personal mourning, which in the Arab-Islamic tradition—just like in many places in the Western world—means demonstrating with one's own body the pain of loss through overgrown beards, a lack of makeup, and modest dress in dark colors or black.

This is the moment, during 1988, when the first *hijab* campaign burst onto the political scene. Hamas began the campaign, but it met no opposition from the secular and nationalist factions that had merged into the Unified National Leadership of the Uprising (UNLU) that came to guide the Intifada. In Gaza particularly, women who did not don the veil were threatened and even targeted with stones, until the summer of 1989, when the UNLU itself intervened to try to take the question of *hijab* off the agenda of the Revolt of the Stones. This action came too late, as many of Gaza's women said at the time,[27] even though the UNLU's intervention helped to close the vicious circle by which the *hijab* was rapidly becoming a token of religious conformity under the guise of a nationalist symbol.

The end of the violent *hijab* campaign of 1988–89, however, was unable to stop the progressive drift toward a conservative code both of dress and of social behavior, particularly in areas such as Gaza and the southern West Bank that were already quite traditional. This is what the West calls the "Islamization" of Arab societies, a phenomenon that in many Western eyes has been uniquely linked to the exponential growth of Islam since the 1970s. In Palestine, however, the problem is that this so-called Islamization can be found throughout all political forces, even those that are defined simply—and simplistically—as secular, nationalist, or leftist. It would therefore be better to talk about the diffusion of socioreligious mores that turn toward tradition, or at least ones that move closer to the more orthodox understanding of faith shared by Hamas and Fatah, by town and country, by Hebron in the south and by the sophistication of Nablus.

Thus a considerable proportion of women in the West Bank and Gaza today don the veil, just as they do throughout the Arab world. Fatah's women wear it, Hamas's women wear it, and women who follow no particular political faction wear it. Having said that, it is also beyond doubt that this dress code is used to express one's ideas visibly, immediately, and publicly. This is also why Hamas women use it. It is a code that makes modesty its first rule, a rule to which all else comes second.. The symbol of this code is the *jilbab*, the long coatlike gown that covers women down to their feet in dull colors, a garment particularly popular among girls. Omar Barghouthi, a Palestinian choreographer and careful observer of popular culture, argues that this aesthetic code contradicts "that distinctive national element which pertains to Hamas." He maintains that the *jilbab* has nothing to do with Palestinian tradition. And yet it is worn especially by those women and girls who wish to demonstrate their allegiance to the Islamist message. "It's a uniform, it's monolithic, and it is definitely imported," Barghouthi says, recalling how different traditional Palestinian dress was, the exact opposite of a uniform: "Every woman was unique, because it was she who decided the design and style of the embroidery she sewed onto her dress."[28] And a number of individuals, particularly young women, clash with this monolithic image of Hamas's female side as women in uniform. Some of the daughters of Hamas leadership are far from both aesthetic and psychological stereotypes. It is possible, for example, to meet girls in jeans with flowery tops and matching foulards that cover their hair who have no compunction about voicing very different ideas from those of their fathers. This also goes for more conservative leaders, whose daughters might wear the *jilbab* and an even simpler veil around the face. In both cases, the girls appear neither submissive nor completely dominated by their fathers, but on the contrary, come across as young women with very sharp eyes, careful ears, and no sense of inferiority in relation to the guest, whether Palestinian or foreign.

Another feature of the Western stereotype of Islamist women is the recurring theme of Muslim polygamy, a subject often splashed across newspapers but never addressed by asking those involved for their thoughts. In the Palestinian context, polygamy is a highly restricted practice, both in terms of numbers and in terms of traditions. It is likewise restricted in Hamas's universe. When tackling the question with the movement's members, once the first blush of embarrassment has been overcome, one discovers that most men have only one wife and that the last case of polygamy in the family dates back a few generations. If anything, one detects in the unfolding stories of family relationships among the members of Hamas a certain complicity within couples, as though the couple were a tribe, a group apart, and clandestine in many moments of their lives, and as though political choices had to be made together if the couple were to continue together. One gets the sense when talking to these members that a political project often becomes a family project.

It is just one example among many, but Sayyed Abu Musameh and his wife confirm that they met when both were active members of the Muslim Brotherhood. Nor is it difficult to find women who have shared their husbands' political projects to the point of inheriting their political roles. In Palestinian politics, this happened within Fatah in the classic case of Umm Jihad, the widow of one of the movement's historical leaders, Khalil al-Wazir (also known as Abu Jihad), assassinated by what is thought to have been a Mossad commando unit in 1988. There are several similar instances within Hamas. One is the case of Mona Mansour—widow of Jamal, one of the West Bank's best-known leaders who was killed by the Israelis in a targeted assassination in 2001; she continued her husband's political work and was elected to Parliament in the 2006 elections. Another is the shocking case of Maryam Farhat, better known as Umm Nidal. Umm Nidal had also been elected as a member of Parliament, and in 2002 she appeared at her son's side in the video that surfaced after the event in which he claimed responsibility for the attack on the Atzoma settlement in the Gaza Strip, in which the young man died after having killed five people. Two of Umm Nidal's other sons had been killed in the Al-Aqsa Intifada, and Umm Nidal publicly declared that had she had one hundred sons, she would have wanted them all to be "martyrs," a statement that turned her into a symbol of Hamas's "martyrology" within the Strip.

Still, there are examples of polygamy within Hamas. One militant, who is himself monogamous, in love with his wife, and who would like her to complete her studies soon after years of looking after their six children, is surprised at curiosity on such matters, saying, "It is possible to have up to four wives, but it certainly isn't compulsory." However, the question that arises to a Western observer is how this choice is perceived by a woman, who finds herself having to share a man with someone else. A.—a Hamas militant who has been willing to tell me about her polygamous life—says, "If you don't have a problem talking about it frankly, I'll explain it to you." A. continues: "First of all, for us it is difficult to understand your lack of solidarity, the indifference of Western women toward other women who are lovers, or prostitutes, women with no protection, with no defense. You prefer that your husband have a lover, without that woman having any rights at all?" Then she changes her tone: "If you want to know whether I suffered when, after twenty years of marriage and of love, my husband told me that he wanted to take another wife, I will answer that yes, I did. I suffered a lot, and I immediately rejected the idea, telling him I did not agree." She is an intelligent woman, strong, not at all submissive, and initially she did not consent to her husband's desire. On the contrary, she had a say in a decision that involved the entire family, including her six children. She adds: "I thought about it again and again, and then—in the end—I understood one thing: had I not allowed him to take another wife, I would have lost him. So then I said yes. He took a wife who was much younger than I was, practically the same age as my eldest son. Now, when he is with me, I know he is mine alone, completely mine."[29] A. has no hesitation; she knows she means a lot to her husband. But her story is that of a woman who has had to come to terms with a choice she did not want, and it is also the story of a very strong person, who for that reason did not passively submit to polygamy, but met it head on, the way one does other events in the life of a couple—a lover, an illegitimate child, a divorce—events that are far from unknown in the West.

To Western eyes, this might appear paradoxical, but A.'s insistence on the matter of women's rights is central to Hamas's female militants who have decided to take an active part in politics. And it is precisely to Islam's scriptures that Hamas's most prominent exponents trace their struggle in defense of women's rights, in line with an Islamist feminism that has developed over recent years not only—indeed, not primarily—in the Arabic-speaking world, but also in Asian Islam and within Muslim communities living in the West. Samira Halaika, one of the six women elected to Parliament on January 25, 2006, on the Change-and-Reform list connected to Hamas, points out with ill-concealed irony that "in the Qur'an there is a *Sura al-Nisa*, a sura on women, but there is no *Sura al-Rijal*, a sura devoted to men." She adds: "The Qur'an already contains indications of all women's rights, first and foremost equality. Because no one is superior to anyone else in the relation between men and women. And there is not a single word in the Qur'an prohibiting women from working or from taking part in politics."[30] The part women take in politics also means supporting the men, who are "the first to be struck by the occupation," as Samira Halaika herself knows: her husband and eldest son were at certain times arrested, accused of belonging to Hamas. Women, she says, "cannot sit back and watch without doing anything. They must plug the leaks, since in society it is men who pay the price first. Women have many duties: taking care of the children, of the house, of the family, living up to their duties in politics, and fulfilling their duties toward society."[31]

"We had to reprogram our mentality according to the new situation, to confront the strikes. Compared with the male activists, chased by Israeli authorities, Hamas's women had more freedom of movement," explains Jamila al Shanti, one of the long-standing leaders of the women's division of Hamas, echoing Samira Halaika's words. "Women have to be strong. Behind a prisoner or a casualty, there is always a strong woman. Sheikh Yassin insisted on teaching women how to teach women, and opened the mosques to female activism."[32]

While Samira Halaika and Jamila al Shanti consider women's roles to be rooted in the contingencies of place and time and in the structure of the organization, Maryam Saleh, on the other hand, is the typical representative of Islamist feminism, starting with her curriculum vitae, which is entirely devoted to studying sacred texts and which boasts a doctorate earned in Saudi Arabia and a lectureship at Al-Quds University. Like many of her lawyer and Islamologist colleagues in other Arab countries, Maryam Saleh begins from an interpretation of the sacred scriptures in order to talk about women's rights from an Islamist perspective. Born in 1952 in a West Bank refugee camp, it is no coincidence that in March 2006 Ismail Haniyeh put Saleh in charge of the Ministry of Women's Affairs in the first Hamas government. According to Islah Jad, one of the most important Palestinian gender studies scholars, the paradoxical conclusion is that it is precisely "in the process of formulating a new reading for religious texts, a parallel process of "de-Islamisizing" the discourse on women's rights took place" within Hamas.[33] What does this mean? It means that the interpretation of sacred texts from a female perspective has given Hamas women a legitimacy that they otherwise would not have had, driving them to demand real equality in politics— something that has not yet occurred.

And yet, two events have shed a little light on the least well-known part of Hamas's history and give reason to believe that steps are being taken in this direction. The first was the female vote in the general elections of January 25, 2006, which was probably decisive for the Islamist movement's victory. And the second was the small platoon of women deputies who arrived in Parliament, allowing women to carve out for themselves a role that the more conservative sectors of Hamas would not have wanted. Jamila al Shanti's conclusion regarding women's roles in Hamas's Gazan wing is very clear: "I can affirm that we are not walking behind men. We are walking parallel." In political terms, this means influence, the ability to determine Hamas policy: "I am proud to say that women in Hamas play an influential role. We can delay the passage of a law, for example. We are represented at the highest levels of leadership; we have an important quota in the Shura council and in academic and educational circles as well."[34]

Chapter 3

CONSOLIDATION

"The Charter Is Not the Qur'an"

The story goes that in March of 1988, when the First Intifada was at its height, one of the Jordanian Muslim Brotherhood's leaders sent a message to Sheikh Yassin that was not at all reassuring for those who had established the Harakat al-Muqawwama al-Islamiyya barely three months earlier. It was the messenger himself, who wished to remain anonymous, who specified the content of the message: "Tell Yassin it's too much, we can't afford it." The Jordanian Ikhwan, in other words, was not able to maintain Hamas from a financial point of view, on top of which perhaps pressure in Amman was mounting to prevent the Ikhwan from openly supporting one of the leading actors in the Revolt of the Stones. Yassin's reply was perfectly in line with the spirit of any movement that sees itself as revolutionary: "We, however, will keep going. Tell the Ikhwan in Amman that if they are unable to maintain us from a financial point of view, to at least recite the *du'a*, the supplication to God. We will keep going regardless."[1]

Hamas's organizational and political machine was running and could not be stopped. In February, well before the Jordanian Ikhwan attempted to rein in the operational branch of the Palestinian Muslim Brotherhood, Hamas had for all intents and purposes become one of the protagonists of the Revolt of the Stones. The Hamas acronym appeared for the first time on February 11, 1988, at the foot of a flier, along with a claim of responsibility that could no longer be put off: Hamas, "the powerful arm of the Association of Muslim Brothers." Thus, it is with what scholars call the First Intifada's "fourth communiqué" that Hamas, with its own strategy, fully entered the fray of the Revolt of the Stones. The Islamic Resistance Movement established its own timetable for protests and its own collections for the victims of the uprising, and it began to hold alternative classes in mosques, allowing students to continue their studies during the period of strikes in universities and in secondary schools. Hamas was going through a phase in which it had to reinforce and advertise its identity while still maintaining a relationship of nonbelligerence, so to speak, with the UNLU, which included all the other secular and nationalist movements.[2] However, the honeymoon phase of the relations between secular groups and Hamas was over even before the end of spring, when the latter started to see itself as an alternative to the UNLU. Earlier, each group made attempts not to get in the other's way in calling for strikes or demonstrations, but now the swelling of Hamas's ranks led it to compete rather than cooperate—to the point of clashing.

The UNLU itself was explicitly linked to the PLO, after an initial period in which the leadership abroad was itself ignorant of what was going on in the West Bank and Gaza. And now, making relations between Hamas and the Unified Command worse, Yasser Arafat made his first choice for a diplomatic opening to the international community. Abu Ammar, Arafat's nom de guerre, was rapidly changing his strategy on the Palestinian question, riding the impetuous wave of the Intifada in order to achieve the status of sole Palestinian interlocutor to the international community. He achieved this to such a degree that in June 1988, during a meeting of Arab states convened specifically in order to deal with what was happening in the West Bank and Gaza—a meeting set up by Bassam Abu Sharif, then one of Arafat's most trusted advisors—the "two-state solution," one Israeli and the other Palestinian, was accepted for the first time in the guise of accepting UN Security Council Resolution 242 of November 22, 1967. The news of this turning point reached the streets in the Occupied Palestinian Territory just as it reached the eyes and ears of the rest of the world. It therefore appears to be no mere coincidence that during the very weeks in which Arafat was assembling his new strategy, Hamas decided to emphasize its role as an alternative not just to other factions in the West Bank and in Gaza, but to the PLO itself.

On August 18, 1988, Hamas published its charter, the Mithaq, its most debated, cited, and condemned document and one that was often used as a political bargaining tool. Article 13 expressly states that "the initiatives, what is called a 'peaceful solution' and 'international conferences' to resolve the Palestinian problem, are contrary to the ideology of the Islamic Resistance Movement, because giving up any part of Palestine is like giving up part of religion. The nationalism of the Islamic Resistance Movement is part of its religion; it educates its members on this, and they perform jihad to raise the banner of God over their nation."[3] Barely three months had passed from the distribution of this document when Arafat received the mandate required to negotiate for the birth of a Palestinian state in the West Bank and Gaza, with East Jerusalem as its capital. The Declaration of Independence was passed on November 15 by the Palestinian National Council (PNC) in session in Algiers. The road to Oslo had been opened, but Hamas had already decided not to travel it.

According to the most credible account, the text of Hamas's Charter was penned by Abdel Fattah al-Dukhan, one of the leaders of the Muslim Brotherhood's older generation in Gaza, who was among those present at the December 9, 1987, meeting at Sheikh Ahmed Yassin's house. Nearly the same age as Yassin and a refugee from the Ashkelon area, Dukhan also served as headmaster of the school in the Nuseirat refugee camp until he was elected to Parliament on the Hamas list in 2006 as the assembly's eldest member. It was therefore neither one of the new leadership's ideologues nor one of the future leaders of the Diaspora who wrote the Mithaq. The hand that wrote the foundational Charter, the militant text that over the years became a political manifesto that Hamas itself never debated, belonged to a teacher of fifty years, a preacher from one of Gaza's refugee camps. The Mithaq is an extremely long text in which several different levels coexist, from the typical language of Intifada propaganda leaflets to statements about current political events, from pedagogical messages to the most retrograde of stereotypes, including the citation of the infamously anti-Semitic *Protocols of the Elders of Zion*. Comprising thirty-six articles crammed with religious citations—particularly passages from the Qur'an, and also hadith, sayings of the Prophet

Mohammed—and quotations from poets and sages. The Mithaq is a text replete with slogans and long didactic explanations rooted in Islam's early history and the later victories of its great leaders, including Salahuddin al-Ayyubi, the Saladin who defeated the Crusaders.

The Charter's preamble speaks of the destruction of Israel, but through one of the three citations that appear at the beginning of the text rather than by means of a discussion. The citation is taken from Hassan al-Banna, who in 1948 said, "Israel will grow and will remain strong until Islam will eliminate it, just as it eliminated what came before it."[4] Paradoxically, however, it is not so much these words of the founder of the Muslim Brotherhood that created a nearly insurmountable obstacle to changing the Mithaq, but Article 11, which defines Palestine as an Islamic *waqf*, and therefore a land that cannot be subject to the disposal of men, but rather "an Islamic land entrusted to the Muslim generations until the Judgment Day."[5] Thus, adds the Charter's author, "no one may renounce all, or even part of it."[6] According to sources inside Hamas, it was on this article that internal debate had in recent years focused in order to try to allow what is, after all, a pragmatic organization to move beyond the formal impasse that had bogged it down. Hamas's Mithaq, after all, simply echoed what had already been said in a nationalist vein in the Palestinian National Charter, approved by the Palestinian National Congress on July 11, 1968, according to which "the liberation of Palestine, from an Arab viewpoint, is a national duty . . . and aims at the elimination of Zionism in Palestine." Eliminating that phrase, just like the other anti-Zionist elements in the Palestinian National Charter, was not the sine qua non condition for the negotiations between the PLO and Israel that led to the Oslo Accords. In practice, the question of its elimination was tackled only in 1996, after the PNA had already been established, and even then it was left formally unresolved.[7]

The history of the Palestinian National Charter has been taken as an example by many Hamas leaders to argue that their Mithaq has been used by Western governments as an alibi and by Israel to avoid contact with the Islamist Movement, especially after its decision to take part in electoral politics in 2005. Indeed, among the conditions imposed by the International Quartet (comprised by the United Nations, the European Union, the United States, and Russia) after the formation of the first Hamas government in the spring of 2006, there was also a requirement that Haniyeh's executive accept the agreements signed by the PLO and renounce those parts of its founding Charter that called for the elimination of Israel. For the Islamist leadership, however, recanting even parts of the Mithaq meant recognizing Israel without having obtained a reciprocal legitimization and, according to many among that same leadership, without having obtained an equally formal recognition not only of the Palestinian people, but of Palestinians as a nation. From a strictly political point of view, Hamas has always feared repeating the mistakes made by Fatah and the PLO, who gave away too much to Israel without receiving anything in exchange. On the contrary, during the life of the PNA and during the negotiations between the 1991 Madrid Conference and the 2000 talks at Camp David, Hamas had always opposed the stances of the PLO and of the PNA, which it considered lax. According to Islamist leaders, if they had a similarly flexible negotiating stance, it would lead to making significant concessions without substantial and tangible results in return.

The conclusion drawn by several Hamas leaders, however, is that the Charter's significance has in actual fact been overestimated by those who call for its disavowal, given that Hamas's founding charter has mostly been set aside, replaced over the decades by other documents that are far more important in defining the strategy and politics of the Islamist movement. There are even those who question the idea of the 1988 document as a founding charter. As Nasser al-Din al-Sha'er, a moderate Islamist from Nablus, puts it, "three people sat around a table and wrote it"—a trenchant definition that liquidated any further reflection on the Mithaq. There is one important exception—the single element that is truly controversial and that has prevented Hamas from modifying its Charter throughout its first two decades—namely, the definition of Palestine as a *waqf*, land belonging to the Muslim community as a whole. "I don't think that's true," Nasser al-Din al-Sha'er retorts. "Palestine cannot be considered a *waqf*, and I wrote about it in 1997."[8]

Nonetheless, Hamas's first document—the one on which the Islamist movement did not even open a discussion concerning either its wording or its substance and the only document rooted, at least through the conditions under which it was written, to the here and now of the Revolt of the Stones—has in practice become its most debated and most cited document outside the movement itself. Indeed, often it was the only document to have been translated from Arabic and used in high-level negotiations and meetings between governments, as well as the only object of negotiations. It is particularly the point relating to the existence of Israel that has monopolized the debate on Hamas. For its part, the organization has never repudiated this document, but over the years this point became the true obstacle to any opening toward the Palestinian Islamist movement, so much so that Azzam Tamimi, historian and author of one of the most in-depth studies of the movement, says that the Charter was "Hamas's worst enemy."[9] According to Tamimi, this assessment is shared by Khaled Meshaal, who has reportedly said that the Charter was written "by mistake"—a recognition made in private conversations by the leadership itself, albeit not in public. There are those who maintain that no one within Hamas can recall the Charter, nor cite from memory its main points, and that it is better known to the movement's opponents than to its own members. Others recall the way in which the Charter came to life, who wrote it, the historical moment, and the goals that moment entailed, giving such context a crucial weight when considering the contents of the document. Again, according to Tamimi, Hamas has said much in public since the mid-1990s that has contradicted the Mithaq.

Having said that, no one within Hamas's leadership is prepared to disavow the 1988 Charter. But the embarrassment it produces is obvious. In this as in other cases, the movement sacrifices its pragmatic side on the altar of its unity, because Hamas considers it essential that its unique democratic centralism not be undermined. Abandoning the Charter would not be possible even for those who opposed it from the very beginning unless an extensive discussion were to take place that included all of Hamas's different constituencies: its bureau abroad, Gaza, the West Bank, and the members detained in Israeli prisons. This is an example of what Mahmoud al-Zahhar defines as a "collective decision," or one made first within a single constituency and then adopted by the four groups as a whole, "but only [after] having listened to what each group has to say on the matter at hand." But once the collective decision has been made, "everyone is committed to abiding by it, irrespective of their own positions."[10] Only after such a decision was made by a majority could Hamas formally change its position on the Charter, which is currently being defended both by those who do not agree with it and those who do. Among the leadership who have been heard over recent years, the only one to have admitted his opposition to the Mithaq is Sayyed Abu Musameh, who in October 2008 revealed that both he and Moussa Abu Marzouq—one of the Islamist movement's most important figures abroad—had come out against the document.[11] Confirming Abu Musameh's declaration is a statement made by Abu Marzouq dating to the period after the June 2007 coup in Gaza, during which Hamas was trying to break an even greater international isolation than the one it experienced after its success in the January 2006 elections. In a comment in the *Los Angeles Times* of July 10, 2007, Abu Marzouq, in his position as second-in-command of Hamas's politburo and as a man considered to be the éminence grise of the expatriate center, wrote that the Charter made public in August 1988 has had its time, and indeed it must be understood in its historical context. The time in which it was written made the Charter "an essentially revolutionary document born of the intolerable conditions under occupation more than 20 years ago."[12] Abu Marzouq goes even further, making parallels between the Charter and other "founding revolutionary documents" such as the American Declaration of Independence, which "simply did not countenance (at least, not in the minds of most of its illustrious signatories) any such status [as independence] for the 700,000 African slaves at that time," or the Basic Laws on the basis of which Israel "declares itself explicitly to be a state for the Jews, conferring privileged status based on faith in a land where millions of occupants are Arabs, Muslims and Christians."[13] No *sonderweg*, therefore, for Hamas; on the contrary, according to Abu Marzouq, the experience of Hamas mirrors the experiences of other revolutionary movements. However, in Abu Marzouq's accusation, it is only to the Islamist Palestinian movement that the international community applies a double standard and demands that the movement reject the statements of the Charter immediately "as a necessary precondition for any discourse whatsoever."[14]

In truth, the first public statements that attempted to put the value of the Charter into its proper perspective had already been made during an earlier period, between 2003 and 2005, when Hamas was first discussing the possibility of entering electoral politics. The debate on the Mithaq, say Hamas sources, was one of the issues discussed in the Marj al-Zuhour deportee camp in South Lebanon in 1992,[15] but the first substantive public qualifications of the Charter began to appear toward the end of the Second Intifada, when the idea of Hamas's entering the PNA and a reformed PLO was beginning to win supporters. The list of such qualifying statements is long, and the most important of them are concentrated in the West Bank, particularly in the politically important center of Nablus. The most effective statement, from a media point of view, was made in September 2005 to the Reuters news agency by Mohammed Ghazal, head of the Civil Engineering Department at Al-Najah University. The Charter of 1988, he said, "is not the Qur'an," elaborating that "on the level of history we consider all Palestinian territories the property of the Palestinians, but now we are talking about the reality, about a political solution. Reality is something different."[16] Even Sheikh Hamed Bitawi—a religious authority in Nablus and president of the Union of Palestinian Ulama known for his radical positions—had no problem in confirming that "the Charter is not the Qur'an; we can change it. It is merely the summary of the Islamist movement's positions in its relation to other factions, and of its politics."[17] Aziz Dweik, founder of the Geography Department at Nablus University—who became speaker of the Parliament after the 2006 general elections but was later that summer imprisoned by Israel until 2009—went even further, clarifying the political and pragmatic necessity of moving away from the Mithaq. Speaking with Khaled Amayreh, a Palestinian journalist close to Islamist positions, Dweik said that

"Hamas wouldn't remain hostage to past rhetorical slogans such as 'the destruction of Israel.'"[18]

Ever since 2005, Hamas's leadership has produced documents and position statements as attempts to distance the movement from its founding document without entirely rejecting it. It has to be said that this attempt has not produced the desired effects, even though all the main figures in the Harakat al-Muqawwama al-Islamiyya have used multiple methods—including the mass media—in their attempt to open a channel not so much toward Israel but toward Western states, the United States above all. Ahmed Youssef, one of Ismail Haniyeh's closest advisors through June 2007, has often called attention to the fact that the Charter has been in practice superseded by other official documents.[19] Of these, a prime example is the electoral manifesto of the Change and Reform list, under the banner of which Hamas took part in the general elections of January 2006. Indeed, the manifesto takes the form of a document that goes well beyond the requirements of an electoral campaign in outlining the movement's policies. It is also completely different from the 1988 document; it was not written in a hurry, and it was less a vehicle of what was felt to be a revolutionary moment—the Intifada—and more an indicator of the discussions conducted (nearly always in secret) by Hamas both within and outside the Occupied Palestinian Territory. The electoral manifesto's complexity is such that it leads figures like Osama Hamdan[20] and Mahmoud al-Zahhar[21] to define it as the most important public document since the 1988 Charter. Given the difficulty of breaking the movement's international isolation without renouncing the Charter and given the impossibility of formally renouncing the Charter without an internal debate, Hamas's documents have become replete with atypical voices, particularly within articles signed by Hamas's most visible leaders and intended for American and British newspapers, but also in television interviews and other public interventions. Indeed, over the past few years these comments released to the press have been the primary window into the changes within Hamas that are taking place in terms of political strategy, even if the movement's basic ideology is unchanged. These political changes have not eliminated all ambiguities, but they have certainly attempted to soften certain positions, particularly at crucial moments, for example, during the delicate phase when Hamas explored the possibility of international legitimacy through participation in the institutions of the PNA. In the meantime, according to some exponents of Hamas, the secret discussion over the Mithaq kept going as it had for years, particularly centering on the article that defines Palestine as a *waqf.* Changing that point would allow the Islamist movement to cut the Gordian knot that prevents it from recognizing Israel and that still forces it to talk in terms of truce and not in terms of peace.

Outsiders . . .

The Hamas Charter had not yet been made public—and indeed had not even been written—when Mahmoud al-Zahhar met Shimon Peres for the first time. The Intifada had dramatically exploded less than four months earlier, and Hamas was still in the process of defining its role within the uprising when on March 28, 1988, then–Foreign Minister Shimon Peres asked to meet the person who was already clearly becoming one of Gaza's Islamist leaders. Sitting at his desk at the Foreign Ministry's offices in Gaza City, a tall building that in December 2007 bore evident signs of an Israeli bombardment, Mahmoud al-Zahhar emphasizes that he "did not go to meet him voluntarily. I was forced to."[22] In his office, unadorned with dark curtains drawn for security reasons, al-Zahhar recalls the circumstances under which, nearly twenty years ago, he found himself facing Peres and fifteen other people from the Israeli military and security establishment. Peres had one question: how to solve the Intifada? Al-Zahhar's response was the Islamists' first initiative with regard to the Israelis. "The offer I made him consisted of three points," he explains, namely, "Declare that you Israelis are ready to pull out of the West Bank and Gaza; [secondly,] place the Territory under the control of a neutral authority in order to minimize our suffering and end the occupation. Thirdly, the Palestinians would have to choose a representative by means of an election or even through an agreement in order to continue negotiations with the Israelis. We in Hamas, I told him, are not ready to negotiate independently, because what we are talking about concerns the national interest." Peres's answer was: We can pull out of Gaza immediately; we need six months to leave the West Bank; we'll postpone discussions with regard to Jerusalem. "And I told him that it would be very difficult to find anyone among the Palestinians who could accept Jerusalem being placed last on the order of discussions—Jerusalem should be first. I made a mistake at the time, because the Israelis did find someone who was not only ready to delay discussions about Jerusalem, but someone who was prepared to abandon it forever."[23]

As Mahmoud al-Zahhar recalls—and this is well known—there were other meetings in Tel Aviv (including with Yitzhak Rabin, then minister of defense) over a year after the meeting with Peres. The Intifada was not over, but the Israeli authorities had already arrested the men who established Hamas, with the arrest taking place just after the publication of the Charter in August 1988. Sheikh Ahmed Yassin had managed to escape arrest for a few months, time he spent building the movement's organizational structure, including the military wing that had begun to appear publicly, heralding the phase of the kidnapping and killing of soldiers. The Israeli government was still attempting to find a way to move beyond the impasse the Intifada had produced, and it was at exactly this time that the secret contacts that would lead to the Oslo Accords were being established with the PLO leadership in exile. In mid-May 1989, Rabin decided to make a final attempt, and met not only with a Hamas representative, but also with the other main Palestinian factions, including Fatah and the PFLP—all in all, about fifteen people. The meeting concluded without significant steps forward, with al-Zahhar suggesting to Rabin the same proposal he had made to Peres a year earlier. No precondition was set for that meeting, even though the Charter had already been published. In any case, Israel's attempts to talk to Hamas ended with that meeting, and over twenty years of uninterrupted clashes began between the many successive governments in Israel and the Palestinian Islamist movement.

Between the 1970s and 1980s, Israel had looked with a kind of benevolence upon the Muslim Brotherhood, which had made a bid in the West Bank and in Gaza to set itself apart from the nationalist, secular, and leftist factions. While the latter all engaged in the national liberation struggle, the Ikhwan concentrated on social and educational work through mosques and support centers. The birth of the Harakat al-Muqawwama al-Islamiyya brusquely changed the Israeli authorities' perception of the Islamist sectors of society. They quickly realized the difference between the Ikhwan establishment and its operations branch. Not two days after Rabin's last meeting with al-Zahhar, the Israeli army and the security services carried out a second massive wave of arrests against Hamas at the direction of the Israeli authorities. This time—according to al-Zahhar[24]—about 2,500 people ended up in prison, accused of belonging to the Islamist movement, which Tel Aviv authorities had included on the list of "terrorist organizations." In practice, Israel had decapitated Hamas, arresting not only Ahmed Yassin, but also Ismail Abu Shanab, probably without realizing that he was *the* leader of the movement at the time.[25] Two years later, Yassin was sentenced to life in prison.

Hamas was therefore suddenly forced to rebuild its network without the person who had most pushed to establish the organization after the First Intifada. It was at this point that the leadership in exile decisively came to the fore, a leadership born and bred in the Diaspora.[26] The Islamist movement was on its knees but was reborn thanks to the arrival in Gaza of one man with the specific goal of reestablishing the organization's structure, one man who would leave his mark on Hamas's history over the following two decades: Moussa Abu Marzouq.

Abu Marzouq was born in 1951 in the Rafah refugee camp in southern Gaza. With a degree in engineering from Egypt, an American green card, and a US doctorate, from the moment of his arrival Abu Marzouq took on the number one role in the politburo, the executive branch designated by the *majlis al-shura*, the consultative council that at different times comprised between twenty and fifty members both within and outside the Occupied Palestinian Territory. In Gaza, which he knew well not least of all because he had been one of those who established the Islamic University, Abu Marzouq managed to rebuild a network that could not be destroyed by a new wave of arrests. It is practically impossible to understand how Abu Marzouq managed not only to reestablish the group's structure, but also to put in place an organization that over the following two decades would manage to escape more or less intact despite waves of arrests, targeted assassinations of its leadership by the Israelis, and the closure of organizations considered to be connected to it. One of the explanations usually offered is that the network established within Gaza became increasingly dependent on the leadership abroad, which could manage Hamas even it its weakened state following the waves of arrests. Another hypothesis is that there was a continuous replenishment of militants[27]—implying a very close connection with the population and local communities—which provided Hamas with ongoing grassroots support. Confirming the latter hypothesis is the fact that Abu Marzouq remained a highly appreciated figure in the Gaza Strip, even many years after his reorganization work in 1989. In 2007, a prominent leader of Hamas in Gaza maintained that the organization was still based on the help provided by Abu Marzouq, and he is, in certain circles, even more highly regarded than Khaled Meshaal.

The reorganization of Hamas carried out by Abu Marzouq became a watershed in the Islamist movement's history, the point at which the equilibrium was established between the leadership inside the Territory—in the West Bank and in Gaza in particular—and their counterparts in the Diaspora. However, upon closer inspection, the period spanning the 1980s and 1990s was a difficult one, and not just for that part of the Islamist movement that remained within the borders of the Occupied Palestinian Territory, deprived as it was of its leadership incarcerated in Israeli jails. The Diaspora leadership was also going through a transitional phase, during which it reeled from the repercussions of the Gulf Crisis of the early 1990s, when Palestinians were expelled from Kuwait after Yasser Arafat had staked his position in support of Saddam Hussein. Despite the fact that the Harakat al-Muqawwama al-Islamiyya had been careful to keep its distance from Arafat's pro-Iraqi pronouncements, all Palestinians paid the price equally. From one day to the next, those in the West Bank and in Gaza lost a considerable slice of the remittances that had previously arrived from the Gulf, while those in the Diaspora, in the face of the Kuwaiti desire for vengeance, were suddenly forced to leave the Emirate and all they had managed to build over decades of emigration. Hamas was among the groups who bore the costs of this defeat. As Azzam Tamimi confirms, "[Hamas] carried out much of its work in Kuwait, from relations with the press to the organization itself."[28] Hamas had attempted to maintain a certain degree of ambiguity in its position on the 1991 Gulf War. This was for two reasons. On the one hand, from a general point of view, Iraq was achieving through the annexation of Kuwait what traditional political Islam considered to be one of its main objectives: to reunite the Arab Muslim world. On the other hand, from an ideological point of view, Saddam Hussein was still held to be one of the Muslim Brotherhood's most powerful enemies: the principal heir to Ba'athist secular nationalism who had invaded a Gulf country, one in which adherence to Islam was considered closest to the Ikhwan's desiderata.

The ambiguity of its position alone, however, was not enough to save Hamas from the consequences of the war. The Islamist movement was forced to choose another location from which to manage relations with the Occupied Palestinian Territory, eventually deciding on Amman, which from the outset had been designated as the location where the struggle with Israel would take place. The outside world—Arab states included—would not be dragged into that struggle, as had happened with the secular nationalist factions during the phase of hijackings and of terrorist attacks, which took place primarily in Europe. Even after the stinging experience of the PLO's expulsion from Beirut at the hands of the Israelis in 1982, Hamas chose not to embarrass the countries with which it had relations, and thus not to alienate the Arab world, to the point of not taking a position on the internal affairs of individual states. Ever since 1948, the Arab world's relationship with the Palestinians had always been built upon a very precarious equilibrium, which for some countries was made unstable both by the presence of refugees and by changes in the leadership of individual national regimes, and not least of all by the changes in strategy Arab governments adopted toward the Israeli-Palestinian conflict. The choice made by the Hamas leadership abroad was clear: it was better not to embarrass privileged inter-locutors, not least of all because they had to preserve themselves in order to be able to support the Islamist cadres within the West Bank and Gaza, who were far more exposed to Israel's reactions.

At the beginning of the 1990s, the Islamist leadership still main-tained good relations with Jordan despite the problems created by Arafat's position on Amman's larger neighbor, Iraq. This relation-ship was born of individual circumstances, such as the fact that some Hamas leaders had Jordanian passports and several of those inside the West Bank and Gaza had studied in Amman. There were also relations built with Jordanians through the Jordanian Muslim Broth-erhood in Amman, which had kept in touch with and supported the birth of Hamas, even at times against its own wishes. The credit that the Islamist movement gained, however, was based on the overall loy-alty that the Muslim Brotherhood had shown King Hussein in the years before the Six Day War. This credit, however, was slowly extin-guished during the first half of the 1990s. Over time, and through the consolidation of the Oslo process and of the PNA, the winds of peace swept up King Hussein as well, who signed a historic treaty with Israel on October 26, 1994. As a consequence, supporting the continued presence of Hamas's foreign bureau on Jordanian territory became increasingly difficult and embarrassing for the Hashemite monarch, particularly after a long season of suicide attacks began in April of that year in Afula, in the north of Israel, in response to the massacre carried out by Israeli settler Baruch Goldstein in the Ibra-himi Mosque in Hebron, where twenty-nine people were shot dead while at prayer. Hamas's leaders in Jordan not only failed to con-demn the suicide attacks, but in fact considered them a legitimate act of resistance to the occupation. Statements of this kind were released in Amman, increasingly embarrassing the Hashemite monarchy as well as the Jordanian Muslim Brotherhood.

The man who understood that the atmosphere had changed was Abu Marzouq, who still headed the politburo in 1995, and who was expelled from Jordan in the spring of that year. Looking for another host, he, in the end, resolved to return to the United States, the only country where he was able to live with his family, since some of his children were American nationals and he himself possessed a green card. However, Hamas's highest ranking leader was arrested on July 25, 1995, in the United States itself. This provoked yet another earthquake in Hamas's leadership, which had already been deprived of Ahmed Yassin, who had been held in an Israeli prison since 1989. Detained in an American jail, Abu Marzouq's case was resolved after a twenty-month struggle in the spring of 1997, when Israel, which had submitted a formal extradition request, let the procedure drop. The United States resolved to send Abu Marzouq back to Jordan, which had agreed to take him back, at least temporarily. In the meantime, however, Abu Marzouq's place had been taken by Khaled Meshaal, who until the moment of Abu Marzouq's arrest had been the politburo's second-in-command. Abu Marzouq's and Khaled Meshaal's roles had, in practice, been inverted. Abu Marzouq would remain in a rather unique position as a sidekick, leaving the stage to Meshaal, but without Marzouq's losing the status that would allow him to maintain independently a range of relationships across the Arab world, making him one of the few Hamas leaders capable—for example—of negotiating with Egypt.

. . . and Insiders

At the beginning of the 1990s, Hamas's structure within the West Bank and Gaza was still dealing with the consequences of Israel's frequent waves of arrests, which left Ahmed Yassin and many other Islamist leaders in prison. The attacks Hamas's military wing carried out against Israeli soldiers, however, did not stop. In fact, they reached a new peak in December 1992, with six soldiers killed in the course of a few days within the Occupied Palestinian Territory. The reaction by the Rabin government, however, came after the kidnapping of border guard Nissim Toledano on December 13, 1992, in Lod, within Israel. Hamas wanted to exchange Toledano for Ahmed Yassin, who was serving a life sentence, but Toledano was killed immediately, the very night of December 13, after Israel categorically refused to negotiate. Israel launched one of its most extensive arrest raids in the history of the conflict, detaining 1,300 people in the space of a few hours. Barely a few days after the tragic conclusion of the kidnapping, and despite a contrary ruling of the Israeli Supreme Court, the government in Tel Aviv decided to deport 415 Palestinians—mostly Hamas members, but also affiliates of Islamic Jihad—to southern Lebanon, which its forces still occupied at the time.[29] On December 17, hundreds of Palestinians, each with $50 in his pockets, were left in the security zone in southern Lebanon. After their attempts to return failed, the deportees of Marj al-Zuhour began the media and political struggle described in the preceding chapter, a struggle that would come to a conclusion only in the autumn of 1993, when the Islamists would return to the West Bank and to Gaza.

Thus, in the most difficult moments of its history, Hamas demonstrated a strategic skill rarely seen in other movements. Marj al-Zuhour is perhaps the most spectacular example of this because of the impact it had on different kinds of audiences. There can be no doubt of the influence this campaign had on Palestinians within the West Bank and Gaza, as well as on the refugee camps in neighboring countries. For the first time, however, the impact of Hamas's media strategy extended to an international audience as well, an audience who knew very little about Hamas, but who now began to familiarize themselves with the movement's faces, voices, claims, and political proclamations. Beyond that, Marj al-Zuhour became an event that increased Hamas's standing in Palestinian public opinion, which came to see the small refugee camp at the border with still-occupied Lebanon, within the security zone, as a way to achieve a kind of redemption. Hamas's militants defied Israel, and Israel was forced to give in.

What about Marj al-Zuhour transformed those ten months into a spectacular event that took on legendary proportions in everyone's memories, both among the 415 Islamist deportees and among those who were simply spectators? To start, Hamas managed to link Marj al-Zuhour directly with the *nakba*, the catastrophe of 1948, so that their victory would overturn—if only symbolically—those decade-old events. On the very night of their deportation, the Islamists immediately decided that they would remain inside the buffer zone inside which the Israelis had left them, rather than moving on to Lebanon, where they would have swelled the ranks of the hundreds of thousands of refugees who already lived between Sidon and Tripoli. The challenge was: "We either manage to get back to our land, or we stay here." Having failed in their first objective, the deportees decided to remain in the open countryside during an extremely harsh, cold winter. They received help from the International Red Cross and established what Mohammed Nimer calls a full-fledged "Islamist society."[30]

The 415 deportees built a camp that relied on the skills of several of those present: engineers and technicians organized logistics; university professors conducted classes for the students; doctors took care not only of those at the camp, but also the population of nearby villages. A tent mosque was erected to hold religious services and classes, and a medical tent provided shelter for the sick and maintained reports and statistics on the population's health. Those among the Hamas leadership who were there recall that the camp was organized according to geographical criteria—with a tent for Nablus, one for Hebron, another for Gaza, and so on—as a way of maintaining local ties and of respecting the traditions and affiliation of each militant.[31] At the same time, the Hamas deportees took advantage of the unique opportunity Marj al-Zuhour offered them to get to know each other and to debate among themselves. Many of the movement's members had never met, so Marj al-Zuhour is remembered as one of those extremely rare occasions in Hamas's history in which the cadres managed to overcome the sputtering lines of communication they had been used to, strengthen their bonds, and debate the group's overall political strategy. Beyond that, Marj al-Zuhour also became a place where Hamas members could meet with other Islamist movements. Abdel Moneim Abul Futuh—one of the Egyptian Muslim Brotherhood's leaders until he was expelled by the Ikhwan after the January 25 Revolution and his candidacy for the Egyptian presidency—for example, recalls how he was able to meet Abdel Aziz al-Rantisi only rarely during his days as a medical student in Egypt, but how they were able to meet again in Marj al-Zuhour when Abul Futuh brought aid from the Egyptian Doctors' Association to the deportees.[32] Both in the analysis of the different cadres and in the memory of the Hamas deportees, Marj al-Zuhour has been always considered vital for the new strategy of the movement. During the long months of deportation, leaders and militants were in constant discussion, transforming the camp into an ongoing political congress, one that elaborated the movement's new overall strategy, reorganized its structure, and opened contacts with the other Islamist organizations in the region and with an international audience. The Marj al-Zuhour conference even discussed the project of establishing a political party separate from the movement's structure, as was realized three years later in the Hizb al Khalas experiment.[33]

For Israel, the deportation quickly turned into a political boomerang, one resolved only with the Islamists' repatriation, achieved after long negotiations. For the Rabin government this was a defeat, one that mirrored Israel's unilateral withdrawal from Gaza several years later, in the summer of 2005. In that case as well, Hamas used the withdrawal of Israeli soldiers and settlers to declare victory on the field. In 1992, as much as in 2005, a solely military and security-driven response brought neither immediate success nor lasting victory for Tel Aviv. On the contrary, in Marj al-Zuhour, Hamas managed to emerge as a much stronger player in the Middle East conflict, having not only achieved media prominence, but also arriving on the scene of the Israeli-Palestinian conflict as a new protagonist, one that had previously been little known outside the confines of the crisis.

After its setback with the Marj al-Zuhour deportees, Israel avoided deporting Palestinian activists en masse for some time. By 2009, however, it had again begun to resort to similar measures, ones that affect not only political rights, but especially civil rights and international laws. After Operation Cast Lead and the subsequent political consultations in Israel, the newly elected rightist coalition government headed by Binyamin Netanyahu adopted a tougher policy, one with the general goal of dissolving traditional ethnic and religious identities and applying stricter regulations on Palestinian residency in Jerusalem. The first outstanding example of these tougher citizenship and residency policies was the "Hamas Four" incident, which began on July 1, 2010, when three men entered the International Red Cross building in East Jerusalem. Among them were two members of the Palestinian Legislative Council, Ahmed Attoun and Mohammed Totah—both of whom had been elected under the Hamas-backed Change and Reform bloc—as well as Ismail Haniyeh's former minister for Jerusalem affairs, Khaled Abu Arafeh. The men asked for asylum under the International Red Cross and for protection from forcible transfer by an occupying power under Article 49 of the Fourth Geneva Convention. The three political figures remained inside the Red Cross compound to avoid arrest and deportation, while Israeli authorities stripped their residency and erased their files in the registry office. Although the men were Jerusalemites, and although none of the three had been charged with any crime in this case by the Israeli police, their residency rights were erased due to their political orientation and their supposed Hamas affiliation. For months—months when Jerusalem became an extremely sensitive issue in the Israeli-Palestinian conflict—the three men's case, together with the case of Hamas MP Mohammed Abu Teir, then in detention, remained unresolved. The incident prompted comparisons to Marj al-Zuhour. In both episodes, Hamas militants decided not to bow to the wishes of the Israeli authorities, with the Hamas Four choosing to remain in Jerusalem rather than moving with their families to the West Bank. As at Marj al-Zuhour, the Four confronted the Israeli attempts at deportation and "showed steadfastness" in an attempt to attract international attention.[34] However, according to Hamas sources, "four men are not 415," meaning that the Hamas Four incident cannot be compared with Marj al-Zuhour and the iconic role it played in the movement's historical memory.

Even outside that memory, the 1992 deportation represented a watershed moment in determining the balance of power among the Palestinian factions. For Yasser Arafat, the events at Marj al-Zuhour confirmed that Hamas could not simply be eliminated from the Palestinian political scene; at best, it could be contained. Without Hamas, managing Palestinian politics would become impossible.

This held true even after the beginning of the Oslo peace process, which Hamas, considering "that peace" unjust, opposed from the outset. This "no" to Oslo was never in doubt within the Islamist movement. For one, Hamas saw Oslo as a betrayal of Palestinian aspirations, one that did not lead to the objectives Hamas had set for itself both in its foundational Charter and elsewhere. Moreover, the peace process declared the PLO the "legitimate representative of the Palestinian people," which in practice definitively ended Islamist attempts to join the PLO with a status similar, if not equivalent, to that of Fatah. These attempts had taken place throughout the entire phase that preceded the 1991 Madrid conference, the first public step in the peace process.[35]

For the Islamist movement, however, opposing the Oslo process did not mean opposing the idea of the PNA that emerged from the Oslo negotiations. Although Hamas had never wished to be part of the PNA structure, it was careful to maintain an open relationship with the authorities in charge of that structure—although this relationship worked through channels that were not always publicly visible. The relationship was born from the necessity of administering the West Bank and Gaza and of attending to the population's basic necessities. In Osama Hamdan's words: "We boycotted the *political* dimension of the Authority, in the sense that we wanted no part in the PNA. But the administration of daily matters could not be undertaken separately. This is why we took part when it was a matter of supporting Palestinians in their daily lives."[36] There are many cases of such participation in the daily life of the community, perhaps most prominently the preparatory work certain Hamas-affiliated intellectuals carried out through the center responsible for developing the national curriculum for PNA schools. This participation also explains why the debate over this curriculum was not reopened after Hamas's rise to power in March 2006, nor did it become the object of a political-cultural clash. On the contrary, the curriculum had been agreed to by groups spanning the entire political spectrum in the West Bank and in Gaza. Aziz Dweik, a teacher at Al-Najah University in Nablus, who became the Parliament's speaker after the 2006 elections, had taken part, for instance, in developing an eleventh-grade geography curriculum.[37]

This does not mean that relations between the PNA and Hamas

were always idyllic. On the contrary: after an initial honeymoon period that lasted a few months after the establishment of the PNA in Gaza in 1994, Hamas tried to exert pressure on Yasser Arafat's Authority. This first clash was a demonstration that the Islamist movement called for in November of that year at the Palestine Mosque in Gaza City. PNA security forces, which had been deployed around the sacred building clashed with the demonstrators, killing thirteen of them. This early clash looms large in the narrative that Hamas on one side and Fatah on the other have constructed regarding the history of their relations, epitomizing its highs and lows. Over the years, and particularly since 2003, relations between Hamas and the PNA have been influenced both by events on the ground—such as the suicide attacks undertaken by the Islamist movement's military wing—and by developments in the peace process between the PNA and Israel.

One thing, however, seems certain: the door between Hamas and the PNA was never slammed completely shut, even when Yasser Arafat chose the path of repression by undertaking waves of arrests that would periodically drag hundreds of Hamas militants to prison, or even when it was revealed that Mohammed Dahlan's Preventive Security Forces had tortured prisoners. It is from this point, in the mid-1990s, that Gaza's strongman Dahlan became Hamas's adversary par excellence by dragging Islamist leaders and militants to jail. Mahmoud al-Zahhar, among those arrested, tells in an autobiographical volume both of the torture he underwent and of the offensive acts carried out against prisoners, such as having his beard forcefully shaved off.[38] Dahlan's role in the repression of militants during the 1990s is one that none of the militants can forget, particularly during the period when he served as a close advisor to President Mahmoud Abbas.

Yasser Arafat, however, did not use only the "stick" of arrests to maintain power. He also tried to involve Hamas, especially when he understood its strong roots within Palestinian society and in Gaza. And the Islamist movement, for its part, reacted to the advent of the PNA by asking itself how it should adapt its role. Should it evolve into a political party and take part in elections regardless, or should it remain distant from a new all-Palestinian institution that might arrive in the West Bank and Gaza?

This was a slow debate, one that went on for years, and one that played itself out in documents. All of these documents have been internal and secret; only rarely have a few reached the outside, and those that have reached the outside have been read only by highly specialized audiences such as historians and political scientists. Those who have read these internal documents, however, find a Hamas that expresses itself in terms very different from the rhetoric of the founding Charter of 1988, from the Intifada leaflets, and from the fiery public proclamations. Instead, the documents outline full-fledged scenarios for the leadership, enabling it to decide whether to change the basic nature of Hamas. Epitomizing these kinds of documents is a discussion paper dated 1992—that is, before the signing of the Declaration of Principles and the handshake between Yasser Arafat and Yitzhak Rabin on the White House lawn in Washington on September 13, 1993. The central question in this document is: How should we behave in the event of elections? And the answer is: We must choose between four clearly distinct alternatives. We can take part in the elections, boycott them, boycott them by means including force, or participate in them under a different name.[39]

Thus, in these internal documents, the possibility of establishing a full-fledged political party became real. Across the Arab world, there are several examples of this. Above all, there is the experience of the Jordanian Muslim Brotherhood, which divided the Ikhwan proper from the Islamic Action Front and presented itself to voters as the Front.[40] One of the possible scenarios envisaged by the 1992 document presages what would happen in 2005, when Hamas undertook the most important change in its history by deciding to participate in parliamentary elections. The 1992 document states: "Our goal might not be to win a majority, but, rather, to achieve a significant [political] presence, which would secure the movement's power and political weight."[41] The Palestinian case, however, was different, and Hamas did not yet want to give up the term "resistance," which had marked its birth in 1987.

According to Ghazi Hamad: "It is true; we discussed whether we should establish a political party or not, because we had before us a new system. And a party would have been a good instrument to establish contact with the PNA. In this way, Hamas would have remained the resistance movement, without becoming entangled in politics."[42] Hamad thinks back to a time now long gone, while he talks about the debate over the establishment in Gaza of what would later become the National Islamic Salvation Party (Hizb al-Khalas al-Watani al-Islami) in 1996. Hamad spoke in October 2008, exactly two months before Israel began Operation Cast Lead, and at the time, the Gaza Strip had already been isolated for months. Ghazi Hamad, born in 1964 in the Rafah refugee camp in the southern Gaza Strip, continues to be among the more pragmatic, moderate Hamas leaders. He has been part of the movement from the very beginning and is a classic example of those young men who adhered to the Muslim Brotherhood at the start of the 1980s. During the hardest moments of 2008, Ghazi Hamad managed to carve out a political space for himself in a context in which it was mostly others, the hawks, who were doing the talking. His account of Al Khalas experience is in some ways a journey backward, in which the past merges with events that occurred many years later. As he says: "Within Hamas, we began talking about the party in 1994, then it was debated with the PNA, and the final decision was taken a year later, once Yasser Arafat had also given his consent." But 1995 was a tense, difficult period. In 1994 Hamas had already begun to undertake suicide attacks. (Hamad calls these attacks "military operations," thereby setting himself apart in the language he uses not only from the hawks, but also from the majority of the rest of the Islamist movement, which calls these suicide attacks "martyrdom operations.") In the end, the party was established in 1996 after the first general elections, which Hamas boycotted. Al Khalas would be short lived, with the entire experiment lasting less than four years and entirely confined to Gaza after a failed attempt to create a West Bank branch.[43] Ghazi Hamad, however, calls it "a fantastic experience," the end of which meant "Hamas lost much." Al Khalas had established good relations with the PLO, and Arafat had even given his blessing, despite knowing all too well that the party was established and financially sustained by Hamas.

Among the party's principal figures were Hamas's more pragmatic leaders. Ghazi Hamad, who was its spokesperson, reels off names like Yahya Moussa, Salah al-Bardawil, Ismail al-Ashkar, and Ahmed Bahar—all figures who in 2006 would become deputies in the Palestinian parliament's second legislature. Salah al-Bardawil goes further, affirming that "without the four-years-long experience of Al Khalas, Hamas would have not participated in the 2006 political elections. Al Khalas political thinking became political practice." Analyzing the brief history of Al Khalas, Salah al-Bardawil describes it as the embryo of a political party that ran the civil life of Hamas; it trained the activists on issues that would become crucial some years later, among them electoral campaigning, parliamentary life and rules, and relations with the PNA.[44] As Hamad recalls: "Most of the party members were open-minded; they had a new vision of politics. Hamas, however, was still too sensitive on certain topics, so much so that the relationship between Hamas and Al Khalas did not go beyond a typical father-son relationship. The message was: you are under my supervision, under my eyes, and you can do nothing without coordinating with me. So, well, we did not succeed in establishing a greater distance between us—Al Khalas—and Hamas. We did not succeed in cutting the umbilical cord. In that particular political situation, it was not easy for us to take decisions far from Hamas's gaze, as they were ultimately our point of reference, as well as our funders."[45]

Tensions rose in 1999, when Al Khalas started to take part to the PLO's central council as a participant, in spite of Hamas's opposition to such involvement. Hamas's leadership thought that any Al Khalas involvement in the PLO's structure would undermine Hamas's strength in the negotiations it was undertaking with Abu Ammar to join that body and gain more significant representation than the limited access offered by Arafat. At the end of the arm wrestling between Hamas and its party, and under heavy pressure caused by the outbreak of the Second Intifada, Sheikh Ahmed Yassin decided to close the experience and to integrate Al Khalas with Hamas. "And all became Hamas again," Salah al-Bardawil summed up. And yet the experiment was not without consequence: in the ongoing discussion on participation, Hamas—says Bardawil—"took some steps back and agreed on elections, paving the way for Al Khalas to run the new era of Hamas."[46]

In short, in 1996, resistance and politics could not part ways. "At the time," Hamad concludes, "Hamas was not politically mature enough to give the party freedom to maneuver. Hamas dominated the party, and its control was too strong . . . even to allow it to take part in the 1996 elections. At the time, I argued . . . that we should have taken part. But that decision would take Hamas another ten years."[47]

It is true that for months Hamas debated whether or not it should take part in the first general elections in the West Bank, Gaza, and East Jerusalem. However, these would be the first elections for the PNA, and at the time the Islamist movement was not collaborating with that body due to its opposition to the Oslo process and the kind of peace that the Accords envisaged. Yasser Arafat tried up until the last moment to reach an agreement with Hamas, and the negotiations, which involved both the leadership in the West Bank and Gaza and the leadership abroad, were conducted outside the Occupied Palestinian Territory, a choice that allowed the Islamist leadership to meet and avoided the delays inherent in a long-distance discussion. In December 1995, the PNA convinced the Israelis to allow Hamas members to leave the West Bank and Gaza, and a rare meeting attended by the entire Hamas leadership convened in Khartoum, Sudan. The lively discussions went on for four days and concluded that taking part in the 1996 elections would be impossible.

According to Osama Hamdan, "It made us laugh when we heard the voices [that claimed] a *fatwa* had been issued prohibiting taking part in the 1996 general elections. During the previous months no such *fatwa* was issued: it was a purely political decision. Boycotting the elections must be considered a democratic decision, just like participation is a democratic decision."[48] Eyes on the present, Hamdan recalls the other elections, the first of the PNA era, that Hamas decided not to take part in. It was not a *fatwa*, that is, a religious edict, which prevented Hamas from taking part. Hamdan's interpretation is confirmed by Sheikh Hamed Bitawi, a religious authority in Nablus, who newspapers at the time indicated as the source of the *fatwa* against the elections. "It's not true," Sheikh Bitawi says, sharply bringing this discussion to an end on the veranda of his Nablus apartment on the city's hillside. "I never issued any edict. The decision was made by the movement. I issued dozens of *fatwas*, but on entirely different topics: against the opening of the casino in Jericho, or against the festival which was being organized in Sebastya, just outside the city of Nablus."[49] Osama Hamdan explains that "Fatah was asking us not only to take part in the elections, but also to put an end to the resistance. We, on the other hand, argued that it was necessary for another Palestinian group to say no, that Oslo would not have worked. The Israelis had not recognized the Palestinians as a nation, but only as a people present on the land. As though we were renting an apartment."[50]

Thus, the choice to take part in electoral politics was in fact possible in 1996, when the PNA's first general elections were called. Despite the "no" from the Hamas summit in Khartoum, part of the movement's members from the West Bank and from Gaza wanted to participate badly enough to choose a provocation: it presented a list of candidates, among them well-known figures, including the three leaders Ismail Haniyeh—who would in future become the first Hamas member to fill the post of Palestinian prime minister—Sa'id Namruti, and Khalid Hindi. They registered their names as independents at the electoral office, only to later withdraw them on January 2. The Hamas leaders themselves explained the reasons behind their gesture, as the *Jerusalem Post* reported on January 19, 1996: "We mandated ourselves to be a safety valve when Hamas's relations with the PNA were in crisis," adding that "in nominating ourselves for the forthcoming elections, we believed in serving Islam and the homeland. But due to the eruption of a state of confusion within the Islamic circle, and despite our conviction in the value of our beliefs, we decided to withdraw our candidacies."[51] The pressure to withdraw those candidacies came from the result of the debate between two different political positions. The first, which emerged within the internal leadership, viewed electoral participation favorably and received support from those members who were closely linked to society, to chambers of commerce, to the student movement, and to trade unions.[52] Although this was a minority within the movement, it was a significant one, within which several members who participated in Al Khalas experiment—such as Ahmed Baher—were active. The second school of thought, with which the leadership in exile in Amman was associated, was against doing anything to mitigate the clash with the PLO and Fatah, which began when negotiations with the Israelis were undertaken, first at the Madrid conference and then during the Oslo process.

One of the Palestinian journalists who has followed this question more closely, Khaled Amayreh, from Hebron, argues that an "acrimonious internal debate" took place between the hardliners and the minority who believed that participation was the lesser of two evils. One of the hardliners was one of the best-known Islamist preachers of the time, Bassam Jarrar, who in early December stated that "the decision to boycott . . . is definitive and irrevocable because these elections will be an enormous farce aimed at legitimizing the Oslo Accords and to perpetuating the occupation and usurpation of our land by Israel."[53] The clash reached its apex on December 10, when the movement's spokesperson in Amman, Ibrahim Ghosheh, announced the election boycott the same day demonstrations were held in Nablus, at Al-Najah University, to mark the eighth anniversary of the beginning of the First Intifada and of the establishment of Hamas.[54] Osama Hamdan recalls that "Haniyeh was attacked in Gaza for his decision to present himself as a candidate, so we decided to discuss it with him ourselves, and he decided to withdraw his name from the list."[55]

It is said that after a specific request from the PNA, Hamas had decided to suspend attacks in a sort of electoral truce, as four Hamas leaders told Islamist journalist Khaled Amayreh. This period of time would have been determined by "Palestinian national interests," although any Israeli attack against Hamas would have meant the end of the truce. Hamas's internal debate on a truce, however, was interrupted by the killing on January 5, 1996, of Yahya Ayyash, nicknamed "the Engineer" (*al-muhandis*), who was one of the commanders of the Izz al-Din al-Qassam Brigades, Hamas's armed wing, which had decided to come into the open in 1992. For the members of the Kata'eb al-Qassam, as for the Israelis, Ayyash, a thirty-year-old engineering graduate from Birzeit, was the instigator and planner behind many suicide attacks and, more importantly, specialized in the preparation of explosives. At the time Israel did not admit to the "targeted assassination," but Ayyash topped its blacklist, and the killing of the Engineer was so sophisticated that it pointed to Israeli involvement: Ayyash died when the mobile phone that an acquaintance had loaned him exploded while he was making a phone call in Beit Lahya, in the northern part of the Gaza Strip.

After Ayyash's assassination—one of the most spectacular undertaken by the Israeli security forces—two distinct opinions clashed with each other, at least according to the scant news available on the secret internal debate. The first option—to which members like Mahmoud al-Zahhar in Gaza and Jamil Hamami in the West Bank subscribed —supported the view that retaliation using suicide attacks would have provoked a disproportionate Israeli reaction, and would have reignited the clashes between the PNA and Hamas. For the military wing, the Izz al-Din al-Qassam Brigades, not to react at all would have been perceived as a sign of weakness and would have jeopardized Hamas's credibility.[56] As the facts themselves demonstrate, the hardliners won the day, and in February and March four of the bloodiest ever suicide attacks were carried out. Two of these took place on the same day: one near Jerusalem's central bus station, with a final tally of twenty-six dead, and the other in Ashkelon, where a suicide bomber blew himself up near a crossroad popular with hitchhikers. On March 3, nineteen people died on the Number 18 bus on Jaffa Road, Jerusalem's busiest road. The following day, another thirteen people were killed by a suicide attacker in Tel Aviv in the equally central Dizengoff Center. Sheikh Jamil Hamami, one of Hamas's founders, left the movement immediately after the bloody sequence of these four attacks. Israel launched a wave of arrests that brought around 1,000 Hamas members into Israeli prisons, and Arafat's PNA did the same, even though it later slowly released them. This was one of the harshest moments to date in the entire Israeli-Palestinian conflict. Yitzhak Rabin had been killed a few months earlier, on November 5, 1995, at the hands of a right-wing Israeli extremist, and then Hamas restarted its attack. This end of the Oslo dream and the climate of fear it produced profoundly affected Israeli elections, facilitating a sharp turn to the right. Labor's hold on government came to a sudden end, and Likud's new man, Binyamin Netanyahu, rose to power.

With his actions, Netanyahu immediately showed that the Israeli government's politics would be different from that of Shimon Peres, roundly defeated in the elections. Specifically, Netanyahu showed that he would not follow in the footsteps of Yitzhak Rabin in the first few months of his mandate, when he gave the go-ahead to contin-ued settlement expansion, particularly in the Jerusalem area, toward Bethlehem, with the birth of the large Har Homa settlement on the hill known to Palestinians as Jabal Abu Ghneim. Later, the opening of the Hasmonean tunnel in Jerusalem's Old City toward the end of September 1996 triggered a mini-Intifada that left 54 Palestinians dead and 800 wounded, as well as 14 Israeli soldiers killed. This act was called a provocation not only by the Palestinians, but also by the Jordanians who supervised the Muslim sacred places in Jerusalem.

And yet Hamas did not react with attacks, despite the fact that this was the peak of the suicide attack phase. In contemporary accounts, this moderation was seen as one of the reasons for Hamas's increasing popularity, alongside the PNA's decision to free hundreds of Islamist militants. This tacit truce with Israel, however, did not last long. On July 30, 1997, two consecutive suicide attacks were carried out in the large popular market of Mahane Yehuda, in the heart of Jerusalem's commercial district, resulting in a tragic balance sheet of 16 dead and 178 wounded. Two months later, on September 4, just before a visit by US Secretary of State Madeleine Albright to Israel, a second bloody suicide attack took place a few hundred meters from the site of the July 30 attack on the Ben Yehuda pedestrian road.

Yet while the phase of suicide attacks was in its fullest flower, some-thing that on its face appeared paradoxical was at work behind the scenes, the details of which would emerge only years later. It was still September 1997 and barely two weeks had passed since the last attack in Jerusalem when King Hussein of Jordan communicated personally with Israeli high officials, asking them to relate to the prime minister that Hamas was prepared to offer Israel a thirty-year truce.[57] According to revelations made by former Mossad Chief Ephraim Halevy in 2004, the offer of a thirty-year truce came from Sheikh Ahmed Yassin, who was then being held in an Israeli prison.

Exactly three days later, Prime Minister Netanyahu called the Hashemite monarch—but not to discuss Hamas's offer. Instead, his purpose was to resolve an embarrassing incident that had just taken place: two Mossad agents had been captured in Amman as they attempted to poison Khaled Meshaal. The story of the attempted assassination of September 25, 1997, is well known, beginning with the aggression against the head of Hamas's politburo by Israeli secret service agents who injected Meshaal with a synthetic opiate, fentanyl. The Hamas leader's bodyguards captured the two agents, and Meshaal was taken to a hospital and saved, as Israel was forced to pass on the details of the antidote. Meanwhile, diplomatic services worked overtime, and it was King Hussein who personally took charge of the negotiations, which led to the release of Sheikh Ahmed Yassin and twenty-two other Palestinian prisoners.

This was the price Netanyahu had to pay not only for the failed assassination attempt on Meshaal, but also for a diplomatic incident that involved one of the few Arab states friendly to Israel: Hussein's Jordan. For Netanyahu there was a superficial victory in the fact that Hamas's leadership had to leave Amman and that in the near future it would find a home in Damascus. In practice, however, the Meshaal affair was a double defeat for Netanyahu: it definitively soured relations with the Hashemite monarch, relations that had already been tested by Likud's choice to freeze the Oslo process, and it resulted in a political boomerang vis-à-vis Hamas, who saw their most charismatic leader, Ahmed Yassin—who everyone thought had been definitively sidelined from the political scene thanks to a life sentence—return to the fray as an active force.

Yasser Arafat visited Ahmed Yassin in the hospital in Amman, where he had immediately been taken to assess his precarious health, as a quadriplegic, after eight years in prison. Arafat made the best of a bad situation. According to leaks to the press at the time, in a parliamentary meeting the following October 8, he accused Jordan of "trying to create a base for itself in the West Bank via the Hamas movement."[58] Meanwhile, Sheikh Ahmed Yassin returned to Gaza, where he was met by massive crowds. After just two months, he started a diplomatic tour that would bring him to Egypt, Saudi Arabia, Qatar, Iran, Kuwait, the United Arab Emirates, Yemen, Sudan, and Syria. Hamas has yet to stage another event on such a large scale. In a television interview after the killing of Yassin in a "targeted assassination" in the spring of 2004, Halevy confirmed that once out of prison, Yassin had reiterated the offer of a *hudna* (truce), albeit one that had been reduced to ten years. But Israel was not interested in truces.

Chapter 4

FROM THE "UNDERGROUND" SHEIKH TO HUMAN BOMBS

The Preacher at the Workers' Mosque

"This is the first time the Arabs have their own Tel Hai."[1] Tel Hai, Upper Galilee, March 1, 1920: a place and a date of historic importance in Israel's collective memory. It is associated with the figure of Joseph Trumpeldor, a Russian Jew who died to defend settlements from the attack of a group of armed Lebanese men, and a symbol of the early Zionists' self-defense. The Palestinian Tel Hai would take place a little further south, in the Jenin area, where the forest of Ya'bad stood. This, at least, was the interpretation offered by David Ben-Gurion, Israel's founding father, upon recalling Sheikh Izz al-Din al-Qassam, killed on November 19, 1935, by British soldiers who were hunting down al-Qassam and his companions for the crime of setting up clandestine armed groups against His Majesty's Mandate and against Zionism. "This is the first time that the Arabs have seen that a man can be prepared to give his life for an idea," said Ben-Gurion, who immediately realized how important the figure of Sheikh Izz al-Din al-Qassam would become for Palestinian nationalism. But the origins of Sheikh al-Qassam's importance predated even this event, reaching back all the way to the 1920s, when news began to circulate of a Syrian imam who took care of the poor, the disinherited, and the workers in Mandate Palestine's largest port, Haifa. Nearly ninety years later, the architectural profile of Haifa—the only large mixed city in Israel—is unrecognizable. The Sail Tower, its tallest skyscraper, carves out the sky in the distance, with its imposing vertical curve resembling a full sail in the wind. But the intense green of the Al-Istiqlal Mosque can still be clearly seen. The mosque has recently been restored. Dating to the modernist period, it was established in 1923, only to be raided by the British, bombed by the Italian air force as it left its Aegean bases in the summer of 1940, and stripped of its lands by Israeli authorities after 1948. Yet today it remains the most important and the most active mosque in the city, the seat of the Shariía court and of the *waqf* administration. Al-Istiqlal Mosque, however, owes its fame to its history, a history that reaches beyond Palestinian borders. At the beginning of the 1920s, this place of worship had only recently been opened when a man was called to be its preacher, a man who despite his old age quickly became well known among the workers who had arrived in Haifa from the surrounding villages, drawn there by the prospect of earning a little money. This Syrian preacher went to look for the faithful in the most degraded areas of the port city, in the streets where prostitution and dives were rife. He had absorbed various schools of Islamic thought: among them, Sufi mysticism, which his family practiced, as well as the reformist impulse that dominated Cairo's Al-Azhar University at the time. Al-Azhar was the most prestigious seat of Sunni Islamic learning. The newly appointed preacher at Haifa's Al-Istiqlal had studied there during the very same years as Mohammed Abdu and Rashid Rida were teaching—intellectuals whose profound influence would be felt across the various schools of Islamism throughout the Arab world.

His name would become so famous over the space of a few years that his killing by British soldiers at the end of 1935 was seen by some historians as the trigger that set alight the Great Arab Revolt just a few months later, a revolt that would devastate Mandate Palestine between 1936 and 1939. And yet, no one would have guessed that the name of this Sheikh would become the label for a particular way of seeing political violence among Palestinians and across the Middle East, both as the name of Hamas's military wing and as the name chosen for the rockets that the Islamist movement—as well as other factions—launched against southern Israeli cities.

Sheikh Izz al-Din al-Qassam was probably born in 1882 in the Syrian village of Jebla, near the coastal city of Latakia. He left Al-Azhar University not only with a background as a preacher, but also imbued with the nationalist Arab culture of the early twentieth century. Al-

Qassam's role as a preacher in his small home village soon became a tight fit, and after his first involvement in the struggle against French colonialism, he was forced to escape Syria, finding refuge in the port city of Haifa in 1921.

Izz al-Din al-Qassam's preaching in the Istiqlal Mosque quickly made him famous, although it was his role as cofounder of one of the city's most important trade unions—the Young Men's Muslim Association (YMMA)—that opened the door to political activism. Along with Rashid al Hajj Ibrahim, the local director of the Arab Bank, Izz al-Din al-Qassam took an active role heading one of the associations that best embodied the radical Palestinian nationalism of the period and its disaffection with elites, with landowners, and with the ineffective politics of Arab parties. His leadership role within the YMMA also allowed Sheikh al-Qassam to work alongside nationalist activists, such as the members of the Independence Party, Al-Istiqlal, and to become acquainted with the other leading figures in Jerusalem and to put pressure on them. He attempted to involve the Mufti of Jerusalem, Hajj al-Amin al-Husseini, in a more radical vision of the clash against the British, but without success.[2] Nonetheless, his daily work with the poorest and most marginalized sectors of society characterized Izz al-Din al-Qassam's social and political engagement. It was to Haifa's urban proletariat, the workers in the suburbs of a port city that was undergoing rapid expansion, that al-Qassam offered a "reformed"—according to his own interpretation, a "purified"—vision of Islam, and provided social services such as literacy courses. In the last phase of Sheikh al-Qassam's life, peasants from Galilee—who the preacher encountered during his frequent journeys in the countryside in his capacity as a wedding official—joined the ranks of the weakest in this industrialized city, and al-Qassam looked among them for followers, as well as for recruits into the mujahideen that he was in the process of establishing. It was this dimension of his activities that allowed al-Qassam to become one of the few political figures capable of "appealing to the frustration and the anger of the popular classes" in Palestine.[3] The Great Arab Revolt of 1936–39 soon after his death would later make clear to everyone not only the rising tensions among the Palestinians, the British, and the Zionists, but also the class divisions that had become more acute after the world economic crisis of 1929.

His political activism was directed not only against British colonization, but also against Zionism at a time when the Yishuv, the Jewish communities, were experiencing their greatest influx of immigrants. Between the 1920s and 1930s, authoritarian winds blew across Europe: anti-Semitism grew in Poland to the point of sparking the "fourth *aliyah*," which by 1928 had brought 70,000 Jews to Palestine. By 1935, Nazism consolidated its grip on power in Germany and passed a raft of increasingly repressive legislation against Jews, while Italian fascism also became increasingly repressive. As conditions for Europe's Jews became increasingly harsher throughout the 1930s, Jewish immigration to Mandate Palestine increased exponentially. The Yishuv doubled in size in the space of four years, with the Jewish population growing from 175,000 in 1931 to 400,000 in the spring of 1936, while the purchase of Arab land went from 20,000 *dunum* in 1932 to over 60,000 *dunum* in 1934.[4] This was the most delicate phase in the life of Mandate Palestine: harsh times, and times of change not just for Zionism, but also, in parallel, for Palestinian society overall.

After a first phase during which he concentrated on preaching and on the dissemination of ideas, al-Qassam moved from straightforward political activity during the early 1930s to the establishment of full-fledged armed groups who carried out attacks against the kibbutzim, which had become the symbols of Zionism. It was this path that would ultimately lead al-Qassam to the Ya'bad Forest. In November 1935, the Sheikh had gone on the run with a handful of men, barely a dozen of his most trusted companions. According to the most reliable reconstruction of events, it appears that the decision to go into hiding was taken after a consignment of weapons hidden in a cement cargo was discovered by pure chance in the port of Jaffa. According to later historical reconstructions, the weapons, sent by an unknown exporter, originated from Belgium and were destined for the Haganah.[5] For al-Qassam, that chance discovery proved that there was no more space for a political solution to relations between the Palestinians, the Jews, and the British. According to the Sheikh, it was necessary to choose an armed jihad. The period of armed struggle, however, did not last more than a few days. After going into hiding, Sheikh Izz al-Din al-Qassam was immediately sought by the British, who killed him in an ambush.

His funeral became an event—proof of the strength of disaffection among the population, and a demonstration of just how popular al-Qassam's ideas had become, beyond and despite the politics of Palestinian elites. In Haifa, people attended the funeral in the thousands, signaling what would happen just a few short months later with the outbreak of the Great Arab Revolt proper. Five days after Sheikh Izz al-Din al-Qassam's death, some Arab parties demanded from the High Commissioner a memorandum to stop Jewish immigration, which in 1935 had reached its peak with over 60,000 arrivals in a single year. After the forty days of mourning, Haifa witnessed another demonstration in al-Qassam's memory, which became a trial of strength for those nationalists who were less closely linked to the traditional centers of Palestinian power. The tension showed no signs of abating: the seeds of revolt had already been sown, and the spring of 1936 witnessed the explosion of the most important Arab insurrection, the thawra. This revolt did not stop at clashes with the British and with the Yishuv, but displayed an important dimension that is entirely internal to Palestinian society, a social conflict which borders on civil war. The conflict had gone down in history as the symbolic clash between the kaffiyeh and the tarboosh, between the campaign's all-white head cover—not the checkered version known today—and the fez that the Ottoman administration had introduced and that had come to symbolize urban modernity. Back then, the kaffiyeh was not just the national symbol, but also the "symptom of antagonism against privileged urban notables."[6] Sheikh Izz al-Din al-Qassam had encouraged this antagonism through his proselytism in the Galilee countryside.

A constant pilgrimage began just after the burial of the Sheikh's remains beneath a large marble tombstone in Balad al-Sheikh on the city's outskirts. The pilgrimage to the stone continued uninterrupted until 1948, when the 5,000 inhabitants of Balad al-Sheikh were forced to flee during the *nakba*, and in time the village became part of the new Israeli municipality of Nesher.

Sheikh al-Qassam is a legendary figure whose stature and significance goes beyond his ideological and religious stances. The Sheikh of the Masjid Al-Istiqlal, the Independence Mosque, was the hero of the nationalist revolt against British colonialism and against the Zionist project. He was the man who took up arms without waiting for the decisions of politicians, and who, if necessary, took them up against their machinations and against the establishment—in a word, against Palestinian notables. Thus, before being "recruited" by Islamist mythology, Qassam was part of the national heritage for all Palestinians, the archetype of a nationalist hero. It is no coincidence that Communiqué No. 2 during the First Intifada, published on January 13, 1988, began by addressing the "masses of our great people. A people of martyrs, nephews of al-Qassam. Brothers and companions of Abu Sharar, Khaled Nazal and Kanafani. People of the Revolt, which is taking strength from the roots of our homeland since 1936."[7] Qassam was also the symbol of the revolt against the politics of compromise followed by the notables—he was therefore also the symbol of a revolt that bypassed the elites' own strategies. As Elias Sanbar—Palestinian historian and intellectual, and for years the life force behind the *Revue des Etudes Palestiniennes*—recalls: "Before adopting the name 'Fatah', the idea of calling the military wing of the movement 'Al-Qassamiyyun' was also considered," because the militants saw their movement as a rupture with respect to the historical process.[8] *Qassamiyyun*, or *Ikhwan al-Qassam*, the Brothers of Qassam, was also the name of those brothers in arms who had followed the Sheikh in his decision to wage an armed struggle and later to go underground, becoming—for at least some of them—protagonists of what would later be called the thawra, the Great Arab Revolt of 1936.

Although it did not immediately appropriate the figure of Sheikh Izz al-Din al-Qassam, Hamas embraced the myth wholeheartedly during the First Intifada, emphasizing that the Great Arab Revolt was an *armed* revolt, just as the Kata'eb al-Qassam Hamas established at the beginning of the 1990s to oppose the Israelis were armed. Hamas's founding Charter, for example, says in Article 7 that "the Islamic Resistance Movement is a link in the chain of jihad against the Zionist occupation. It is tied to the initiation of the jihad by the martyr Izz al-Din al-Qassam and his *mujahid* brothers in 1936."⁹ In this context, it becomes clear why Izz al-Din al-Qassam became a model for Hamas. His religious background, his commitment as a preacher, his nationalism, and his transition toward armed struggle all went to the heart of the Islamist movement's two ideological and cultural pillars: loyalty to the religious message and national struggle, along with attention given to the poorer social groups, attention that Izz al-Din al-Qassam had always shown, and that was not the basis of the notables' consent. There is, in other words, a connection between al-Qassam's followers from the poorer parts of the Palestinian countryside and Hamas's close relationship with those places where the weaker sectors of Palestinian society—villages to refugee camps—are found.¹⁰ This emphasis on the mythology linked to the Sheikh also meant that the historical role of the Egyptian Muslim Brotherhood came to be de-emphasized, despite the fact that it had itself taken up arms both against its own British Protectorate and to aid the Palestinians. Both Egyptian and Syrian Muslim Brothers, albeit with only a few hundred men, took part in the 1948 war; this participation was so widely publicized that, at the time, it became one of the principal reasons for the consensus the Brotherhood was able to gather, particularly among the refugees in Gaza. Indeed, the choice of armed resistance originated in Cairo through the influence of the Egyptian Muslim Brotherhood. Hassan al-Banna began to take an interest in the Ikhwan's infiltration of the army ranks already in 1936. Al-Banna set himself two specific objectives: first, the liberation of Egypt from British occupation, and second, the prevention of the birth of a Jewish state in Palestine. According to scholars, the first cell of Muslim Brotherhood officers dates to 1943–44, when World War II was in full swing.¹¹ It was from this "special section" of the Egyptian Ikhwan, which had trained on the Muqattam plains near Cairo, that the battalion that left for Palestine was selected to take part in the first Arab-Israeli War in 1948.¹²

The history of the Palestinian Muslim Brotherhood, however, sharply diverges from its counterparts between 1948 and 1983, during which time the Brotherhood effectively distanced itself from armed struggle. This choice, to which exceptions were made only in a few episodes during the 1967 War, was probably also at the origin of the break between the Muslim Brotherhood and the two leaders who would later become among the most prominent within Fatah: Abu Jihad and Abu Iyad. The difference in approach became clear in 1956–57, when Israel occupied Gaza for a brief period during the Egyptian protectorate. Some within the Ikhwan—Abu Jihad included—formed an armed cell, but the Muslim Brotherhood rejected the idea of directly confronting the Israelis, causing the group of militants to form "a separate organisation—a movement that would have no visible Islamic coloration and that would have its goal of liberating all Palestine through armed struggle."[13] This was the embryo of what would become Fatah.

It is for this reason that Hamas cannot trace its own models for armed struggle in the Muslim Brotherhood, and is therefore forced to go back in time to the myth of Izz al-Din al-Qassam in order to present its own archetypes of resistance to the general public. However, the myth goes beyond the historical genealogy that Hamas attempted to establish between the "Qassamite" armed groups that emerged at the time of the Sheikh and the armed groups that emerged in the period after Israel's birth in 1948. The citations that recall al-Qassam became evident when Hamas decided to make the jump from an armed struggle against military objectives to what might be called its own "strategy of tension"[14] during the mid-1990s, namely suicide attacks inside Israel. The use of references to Sheikh al-Qassam was clear from the very first suicide attacks Hamas carried out: the bombings that the Islamist movement decided to undertake in 1994 as a response to the massacre carried out inside the Ibrahimi Mosque in Hebron on February 25 of that year by right-wing Israeli settler Baruch Goldstein. Paradoxically, traces of Sheikh al-Qassam can be found within the mosque massacre itself, when Goldstein opened fire on the faithful at prayer during Ramadan, killing twenty-nine people: the extremist Israeli movement Kach, to which Goldstein belonged, had profaned al-Qassam's tomb in Balad al-Sheikh in December 1993, just a few months before the Hebron Massacre.[15] Amer Salah Amarnah, the twenty-two-year-old suicide bomber who carried out one of the attacks following the Hebron

Massacre for which Hamas claimed responsibility—the attack in Hadera on April 13, 1994—was originally from the village of Ya'bad in the Jenin area. This seemed to be no coincidence, as it was precisely in the Ya'bad Forest, on November 19, 1935, where Izz al-Din al-Qassam was killed by British forces. Violence had returned to the heart of the conflict between Israelis and Palestinians, albeit this time no longer under the guise of war, of hijackings over European skies, or even of the stones of the First Intifada, but with a devastating weapon: suicide attacks.

Tracing Baruch's Footsteps

In the Middle East, and in Israel and Palestine in particular, dates are important. Dates are tombstones that mark an infinite history of loss. They are also milestones that carve out different narratives: in the two parallel yet intertwined historical trajectories, dates describe the situation, responsibilities, and guilt of each party and its adversary. If, on the Israeli side, the chronology of suicide attacks is an integral part of the attitude the Israelis take toward armed Palestinian factions, on the other side there is one day that will never be forgotten—and not just by Hamas militants. It is February 25, 1994, during Ramadan: the final Friday of what for Muslims is the most sacred month. In Hebron, as in Jerusalem, the number of faithful who gather in mosques increases during this period; some say there were 800 present on the morning when Baruch Goldstein, a radical settler, extremist Kach movement militant, and Brooklyn-born doctor, opened fire with his Galil automatic rifle inside the Ibrahimi Mosque, the most sacred after the ones on the Haram al-Sharif in Jerusalem. It is said that he fired at least one hundred bullets. On the ground, after it was all over, there were twenty-nine dead among the faithful and a far higher number of injured. Goldstein himself was beaten to death by the outraged crowd.

That day, which went down in history as the Hebron Massacre, is also considered in Palestinian accounts to be a watershed for Hamas. The Islamist movement claimed responsibility for its first suicide attack—in Afula, in northern Israel—exactly forty days after the massacre. In the Arab and Muslim world, the mourning period lasts precisely until the fortieth day, when the deceased are remembered at a family gathering that closes the period of grief. In the reconstruction later offered by Hamas militants, it was the Hebron Massacre that led the Harakat al-Muqawwama al-Islamiyya to conclude that terrorism should become the principal instrument of the struggle against Israel. Further, it should be a struggle in which civilians would not be spared, just as Goldstein had targeted civilians—and what is more, targeted them in a holy place, during Islam's holiest month—to carry out the folly of his political act.

The Israeli government's condemnation of the terrorist attack was not enough to stop Hamas, which considered the massacre at the mosque—within which the remains of Abraham himself are preserved—a point of no return. The government's condemnation was perceived by Palestinians as only one side of the coin, the other side being the funeral procession that accompanied Goldstein from Jerusalem to the radical settlement of Kiryat Arba, near Hebron. Palestinians witnessed hundreds of settlers gathering around Goldstein's tomb hailing him as a hero, and they knew that on the tombstone—in Kiryat Arba's park, which is dedicated to Meir Kahane, the rabbi who founded the Kach movement—Baruch Goldstein is called a "saint," a man "killed to sanctify God's name."[16] Palestinians also knew that the more extremist among the settlers trace an analogy between Goldstein's act and Samson's biblical gesture—dying in the act of destroying the temple of the Philistines. The precedent of political suicide was also hinted at by Moussa Abu Marzouq, currently second-in-command of Hamas's politburo abroad, who said in an interview with *Time Magazine* in 2002—while the Second Intifada's bloodiest wave of suicide attacks was taking place—that "Hamas was actually not the first group to resort to these operations. Israel began these operations when the Israeli terrorist [Baruch] Goldstein dashed to al-Khalil Mosque and killed twenty-seven [*sic*] people there while they were praying inside the mosque."[17]

Many years later, Sheikh Ahmed Haj Ali argued that "had there not been the 1994 Ibrahimi Mosque massacre, there would have been no suicide bombings."[18] Haj Ali, the leader of the Muslim Brotherhood in the West Bank, born in 1941, was elected by a landslide in Nablus in the January 2006 elections on the Change and Reform ticket while held in an Israeli prison under administrative detention. He is not alone in making this point. In an interview dating back to 1998, and therefore preceding the emergence of a political line that later aimed to soothe the West, Abdel Aziz al-Rantisi, one of Hamas's most radical leaders, said that suicide attacks "began after the massacre committed by the terrorist Baruch Goldstein [in the Hebron mosque in 1994] and intensified after the assassination of Yahya Ayyash."[19] All the leaders who were asked what the massacre at the Ibrahimi Mosque represented gave the same answer: it was a turning point in determining whether to choose an armed strategy. Osama Hamdan, Hamas's representative in Lebanon, states that "before the Hebron massacre armed operations had soldiers and settlers as targets" and goes so far as to claim that "the Israeli authorities had at the very least been informed of what was about to happen" by radicals among the Israeli settlers.[20] Ahmed Youssef, one of the most moderate leaders within Gaza, echoes this position, arguing that "history would have been different had Hebron not happened— a real crime against humanity. Without Hebron, Hamas would not have been able to justify suicide attacks."[21] According to this interpretation, the use of suicide attacks was a sort of retaliation in kind, an equal and opposite measure, to the actions carried out by one man, Baruch Goldstein, who knew full well when he entered the Ibrahimi Mosque that he would not leave it alive and that he was going to sacrifice himself in a suicide that was as insane as it was political. A similar interpretation was also offered by Ismail Abu Shanab, one of the main figures in the negotiations that led to the truce of June 2003, later killed by the Israelis after a suicide attack—one of the bloodiest—in Jerusalem the following August. Abu Shanab told the experts of the International Crisis Group that the Hebron Massacre "did not leave us any choice. They attacked us at our weakest point, so we had to do the same in return. We did not want this kind of struggle, but were left with no choice."[22]

The reading Hamas offers of the massacre in the Hebron mosque is, therefore, unambiguous. And it was indeed after the massa-

cre that the Islamist movement began to recruit groups of youngsters unknown to Israeli authorities, youngsters who had not been
arrested or stopped by the police, who were untraceable in the dossiers on Palestinians, and who would carry out what—according
to the dominant philosophy within certain sectors of Hamas—had
become a martyrdom, thereby becoming *shaheed*. According to Beverley Milton-Edwards, it was through this philosophy of martyrdom
that Hamas "elevated the act of *jihad* in the aftermath of Goldstein's
Jewish equivalent."[23] In this sense, the decision to blow oneself up,
causing death and destruction all around the explosion, was not
simply offensive: "*jihad* is, in this context, an act of defence, the suicide bombings are a retaliation against an aggression."[24] According
to Milton-Edwards, this is because the legitimization of the attacks
is found in a verse of the Qur'an that exhorts the faithful to "fight
in the way of God those who fight with you . . . And slay them
wherever you come upon them, and expel them from where they
expelled you."[25] In the same interview to *Time Magazine* cited earlier, Abu Marzouq offers a kind of periodization of Hamas's armed
struggle: the first two years, until 1989, without resorting to military
operations; then, until 1993, clashes with "light arms against Israeli
soldiers," operations defined by the then head of the politburo as a
"popular demand" in order to react to the killing of the boys who
threw the stones in the 1987 revolt. Then, when the Israelis began
to "face Palestinian civilians with weapons . . . we could have done
nothing but to answer with the same weapon."[26] An eye for an eye,
a tooth for a tooth.

However, reprisals and revenge did not stop at the first suicide
attack. Nor at the second. Within a brief space of time, the reprisal
mutated into a "strategy of tension" that aimed to inflict as much
damage as possible upon the emerging peace process and the Declaration of Principles by Rabin's Israel and Arafat's Palestine. The Hebron
Massacre became secondary in the legitimization of the use of suicide
attacks, to the point that Hamas no longer spoke of revenge and of
civilians killed just as Baruch Goldstein killed civilians. There was
no longer talk of a symmetrical reaction to the crimes committed
by Israel against Palestinian civilians, or of a classic "eye-for-an-eye"

logic. The justifications Hamas used changed. In order to legitimize indiscriminate attacks inside Israeli cities—in cafés, in buses, and at crowded crossroads—it began to argue that Israeli society was militarized, that it was a society in which everyone undertakes military service and remains reservists until they are at least forty. Hamas thus attempted to legitimize its continued use of terrorism by stretching the concept of a "soldier," and therefore of a combatant, such that the victims of suicide attacks were no longer civilians. This trajectory by some within Hamas appears to confirm what some of the most pragmatic leaders have said, namely, that it is not at all clear that all of the leadership agreed with suicide attacks, at least from an ethical and political point of view. One of the longest-standing leaders in Gaza, Sayyed Abu Musameh, has stated that he "did not support the suicide attacks" and that already "in 1990 there was an internal document in which he stated his opposition to violence perpetrated against civilians and against Arab soldiers." This is also confirmed by Ahmed Youssef, who wrote to the leadership of the Islamist movement in 1998 advising that suicide operations be stopped, and that given the reactions these had triggered around the world, another method of opposing the Israelis should be found.[27]

Negotiations to suspend the suicide attacks would achieve some temporary successes, particularly within the Palestinian world, but these periods of calm—which were neither written about nor publicized until they had been broken by a new attack—were, however, always temporary. One such period of calm, for example, had been obtained by the PNA in September 1995 and lasted through the months prior to the first Palestinian elections. These were months during which Hamas was discussing whether it should be taking part in the elections inside the territory under the PNA's as yet embryonic control, and the very same months in which the Islamist movement was establishing a full-fledged party, Al Khalas.

This unwritten calm was broken on January 5, 1996, by the targeted assassination of Yahya Ayyash, "The Engineer." Israel always wanted to maintain its freedom to act, and would strike against the instigators of the suicide attacks even if it meant that on some occasions diplomatic possibilities would be sacrificed on the altar of a military solution to the terrorist threat. Ayyash's case was exemplary in this sense. He was the organizer of numerous suicide attacks, and despite the fact that Shimon Peres's government foresaw that the Engineer's assassination would trigger a response from Hamas's military wing, particularly at a very delicate time when the Islamist movement was engaged in animated discussions over its participation in elections, the Israeli government preferred to eliminate him.

The main question, which has not yet been met with a definitive answer at a historical and a political level, concerns what kinds of relations there might have been between the political and military wings within Hamas. After all, the Islamist movement was born on December 9, 1987, under a specific banner that explained its objectives and modus operandi: "Islamic Resistance Movement." Resistance is the core around which Hamas has always revolved, even before its formal birth. Both times Sheikh Ahmed Yassin was arrested, before and after 1987, he was imprisoned because he was implicated in organizing armed groups. However, things appeared to change after the reorganization carried out by Abu Marzouq in 1989, the year after which political leaders tended to increasingly emphasize—at least in their official declarations—the separation between political and military wings, and between Hamas as an Islamist movement and the Izz al-Din al-Qassam Brigades. Fatah would later do the same, during the Second Intifada, with Al-Aqsa Martyrs' Brigades, an armed but independent group. However, the key question remains unresolved—just as the relationship between Ireland's Sinn Féin and the IRA at the apex of the Troubles remained unresolved, or indeed the relationship between Herri Batasuna and ETA in the Basque Country, or between certain African liberation movements and their respective armed wings—at least as far as the details of organizational structures and internal communications were concerned.

How much did Hamas's political wing know about the military wing's plans? In brief: All the political leaders insist that they did not know anything concerning the Izz al-Din al-Qassam Brigades's plans. This would suggest a degree of autonomy rooted in the very clandestine organizational structure around which Hamas is constructed. If known leaders, who have a public profile, knew of the military wing's plans, it would obviously be easier to obtain from these public leaders the information necessary to prevent the attacks. It is not a coincidence that over the years little more has been known of military commanders other than their names—second- if not thirdhand information mixed in with other urban myths surrounding the figure of the guerrilla fighter. There are revelations concerning the more recent leaders, such as Mohammed al-Deif or Ahmed al-Ja'bari, journalistic scoops that arise from time to time when reporters manage to get a tour of the sites from which Qassam rockets are fired from Gaza against southern Israeli cities, or when they manage to meet a militant or even a commander. Nonetheless, the veneer of secrecy remains intact, to the detriment of the image of the Islamist movement, which remains confused.

The umbilical cord to that central word in Hamas's definition—"resistance"—has never been severed. According to Islamist leaders, this is because the Israeli occupation is not over. In this sense, the Islamist movement cannot achieve a fully postconflict posture while the conflict itself endures. At the same time, the question concerning the real relationship between Hamas's two wings remains unresolved. One thing is certain, however, and that is that the political wing has never disowned the military wing, even during the harshest phase of the suicide attack strategy, even when the embarrassment of certain political leaders in taking responsibility for some of those attacks at particular historical junctures was evident.[28] The unspoken agreement, therefore, appears to be that the political wing should never and can never disown the military wing. Eyad al-Sarraj made the psychoanalytic point with regard to Hamas's structure that the organization acts according to the classical rules of tribalism, closing ranks at moments it considers vital.

A question follows from this: what freedom of action has the military wing had over the two decades of Hamas's existence? The latitude it has had has certainly been significant, especially at certain specific moments. This independence has strongly influenced the course of events, such as during the terrible months of the spring of 1996, for example, which were punctuated by a series of bloody suicide attacks. The later phase, after Hamas had undertaken the path of electoral participation, was similarly marked by the kidnapping of Gilad Shalit in June 2006, just as negotiations between Mahmoud Abbas and the Hamas-led government were in full swing, not to mention Hamas's armed takeover of the Gaza Strip exactly a year later. Aside from the attack against the commercial district of Dimona in February 2008, which was believed by the Israelis themselves to have been carried out by splinter groups, the commitment that had been made by the Islamist movement at the beginning of 2005 to end the series of terrorist attacks has been adhered to by the Izz al-Din al-Qassam Brigades.

Was there a formal consultation process inside Hamas to decide whether or not to stop the suicide attacks inside Israeli cities, limiting the resistance to within the Palestinian territory occupied in 1967? Both in the West Bank and in the Gaza Strip, Hamas leaders are cautious to answer this kind of question. Some declined to comment. Others confirmed that the four constituencies have been consulted on the "increase or decrease of the resistance,"[29] that is, on suicide attacks in Israel.

Once that particular "strategy of tension" was over, Hamas's armed wing appears to have restricted itself to a classic military posture, so to speak, or at least to one rooted in conventional guerrilla tactics. Specifically, it resorted to two elements: the launch of Qassam rockets, and the establishment of the Executive Force as a full-fledged military body. The *tanfisiyya*, which had been established in Gaza in April 2006 by the then–Interior Minister Said Siyyam in the Hamas government, did not limit itself to being a counterpart to the forces set up by Fatah and the PNA presidency, but has increasingly become a military organization, with its three-thousand-strong force doubling its numbers within the following two years. This kind of military posture crystallized after Hamas's June 2007 coup in Gaza, which enhanced the role of the armed wing in the movement's structure. Indeed, Hamas's seizure of power in the Strip paved the way to a less clandestine, more visible presence of the military wing, which from 2007 to 2010 became less the image of a resistance guerrilla and more that of a tool in the hands of the administrative and governmental structure. "Before, resistance has been fought by the PA.

But now there is a Hamas government, and the fighters can move more freely. Because Hamas is still a resistance movement," explained Mushir al Masri, one of the leaders of the young generation and the youngest member of parliament elected in 2006.[30]

The Lost Generation

The years of violent conflict during which Hamas struck at the heart of Israeli cities also created another target, an entirely Palestinian one, namely, the gradualist policies Yasser Arafat pursued with respect to the peace process. Abu Ammar knew Hamas's opposition to these policies well and reacted with an iron fist. In Gaza, Mohammed Dahlan was charged with making the arrests, carrying out about 2,000 of them against Hamas members, an act that made him into the figure most hated by the Islamist movement's militants.[31] The choice of repression was implemented in particular after the last wave of suicide attacks were carried out during the summer and autumn of 1997 under a Netanyahu government, which by then was well established. The roundups carried out against Islamist militants during 1997–98 are remembered by Hamas's political leaders as one of the reasons they put a stop to suicide attacks until the new—and extremely sad—phase of the devastating attacks of 2001–2004, while the Second Intifada was in full swing. In truth, there are also those who speak of an undeclared agreement between the Islamist leadership and the PNA to restrict Hamas's operations to the Occupied Palestinian Territory until 2001, suspending attacks inside Israel.[32] After his return to the Strip, it was Yassin himself who, on October 19, 1997, proposed a period of calm. In exchange, Israel would have had to suspend military repression and economic sanctions—conditions that Israel never adhered to.

Hamas, however, decided to continue its undeclared unilateral truce, not so much with Israel as with Arafat. The truce was broken only once Hamas threw itself fully behind the Second Intifada many months after the revolt triggered by Ariel Sharon's September 29, 2000, visit to the al-Haram al-Sharif under the protection of 1,000 police officers. Indeed, Hamas's entry into the Second Intifada dates to the spring of 2001, after Ariel Sharon's victory at the polls—which marked Ehud Barak's political as well as electoral defeat—and after a ratcheting up of the Israeli army's repression against demonstrations in the West Bank and in Gaza, which brought the count of Palestinian victims to over 300 in the space of five months. On March 4, 2001, a man blew himself up on Herzl Road in the heart of the coastal city of Netanya, killing with him three people and injuring dozens more. At the same time, that Sunday, Ariel Sharon was in the process of securing a majority for his government in the Knesset. Hamas did not claim the attack immediately, but the previous day the military wing had let it be known in a declaration that it would resume attacks, and that ten suicide bombers were ready to blow themselves up.

According to experts, Hamas's entry into the Second Intifada was therefore late. Graham Usher, among the journalists who know Palestinian matters best, wrote that "for four months, the temper, tactics and imagery of the revolt were dictated largely by Fatah, especially by its vanguard tanzim 'organization' led by the now imprisoned Marwan Barghouthi. Hamas only fully entered the fray with the February 2001 election of Ariel Sharon as Israel's prime minister and in response to his vow to bring security to his people 'within 100 days.'"[33] It was only after Sharon's victory, therefore, that Hamas, "with a nod from the tanzim, took the qualitative turn to suicide bombings in Israel as the uprising's signature and most lethal weapon."[34] The Islamist movement, however, rejects this interpretation. Farhat As'ad, who acted as coordinator for the activities connected to the Second Intifada on Hamas's behalf, tells a different story: "Three days after the beginning of the Intifada, we held a meeting among the representatives of the different factions. Marwan Barghouthi for Fatah and Ahmed Saadat representing the Popular Front for the Liberation of Palestine were also present. It was an extremely intense meeting, lasting several days."[35] This means, still according to As'ad, that Hamas was present from the very beginning, although it took some time to piece together an effective operational structure, "at least two or three months in order to re-organize,"[36] since Yasser Arafat's security forces had incarcerated a considerable portion of the movement's leadership. In order to strengthen Hamas's interpretation of these events, Farhat As'ad also explains that "most of the demonstrations were organized by us, and our people were present, although the other factions had asked us not to display Hamas's green banners."[37] On the contrary, the Islamist movement, according to its leaders, was the only one to call on Palestinians to resist Ariel Sharon's visit to al-Haram al-Sharif before it took place.[38] In truth, Sharon's famous stroll near the Al-Aqsa Mosque on September 29, 2000, took place at the end of a lengthy period in which tempers had overheated on the question of possible Israeli sovereignty over the Holy Mosques, as well as the activism of radical Israeli fringe groups such as those encompassed under the umbrella of the Temple Mount Faithful movement.

If the question of Hamas's immediate participation in the Second Intifada remains controversial, this cannot be said about the doubts that the Islamist movement had concerning Yasser Arafat's true objectives on at least the early incidents that would later give rise to the Al-Aqsa Revolt. As Osama Hamdan recalls, "Abu Ammar thought that in this way he could exert pressure on Ehud Barak. The question we asked ourselves was the following: if Arafat wants to use the Intifada for the same objective, namely the implementation of the Oslo Accords, what should Hamas do? Participate or abstain?"[39] Mahmoud al-Zahhar shares Hamdan's interpretation regarding the role of Yasser Arafat in galvanizing Palestinian rage at the beginning of the Al-Aqsa Revolt. In an interview with a Gaza-based Hamas television station in October 2010, al-Zahhar, one of the movement's longest-standing members, confirmed that Arafat "realized that negotiations without claws will produce nothing" and "sensed the importance of resistance on the negotiation table, and that it's one of the tools [with which] to face occupation. Therefore, he worked to use it to his advantage." Al-Zahhar went even further, allegedly saying in a closed session with students in Gaza that Abu Ammar "recommended that Hamas carry out a number of military operations in the heart of the Hebrew [*sic*] state."[40]

For months, Hamas debated how best to take part in the Intifada. Specifically, it debated whether it should resume terrorist attacks.

The Palestinian "street" and political observers both kept their attention fixed on the military wing, the Izz al-Din al-Qassam Brigades, asking why they had not yet taken part in the uprising. The scales would eventually tip in the hardliners' favor, mirroring what other factions were already doing. This triggered a vicious cycle of suicide attacks and targeted assassinations from the spring of 2001 all the way through to 2002. A new generation of very young militants was forged in this fire, a generation that took part in the Second Intifada under different flags: Fatah's yellow banner, Hamas's green, the PFLP's red, and the Islamic Jihad's black. But while the flag colors differed, the streets across the West Bank and Gaza were the same, and the bond formed between young men of different political affiliations was the one upon which the post-Arafat political transition would later be built. Youth belonging to Fatah, to Hamas, to the PFLP, and to Islamic Jihad fought together and died together. Going back to separate barricades was no longer possible, at least for part of the Palestinian youth, which in this sense distanced itself from the isolated citadel of politics, a process the great Palestinian writer Sahar Khalifeh recounts in her novel dedicated to the Second Intifada and to Nablus, *The End of Spring*.[41]

And yet, paradoxically, it was precisely while the Second Intifada—one of the most tragic and violent pages of the Israeli-Palestinian conflict, on both sides—was still raging that an entirely political debate began within Hamas on the question of its participation within the PNA, a debate that ran in parallel with hypothetical discussions of a truce with Israel.

Hudna, Tahdi'ah, Truces

Over the course of the first twenty years of its formal existence, Hamas has at various stages suggested to Israel not only temporary truces, but has also accepted on a de facto basis the possibility of reaching agreements on the West Bank and on Gaza—that is to say, on the territory occupied in 1967. Such a move would mean reconciling the never-renounced objective of retaking the entirety of pre-1948 Palestine with the more pragmatic objective of accepting a Palestinian state within the lands conquered by Israel during the Six Day War. Despite the ambiguities, all the movement's political leaders—from Ahmed Yassin to Moussa Abu Marzouq, from Mahmoud al-Zahhar to Khaled Meshaal—have accepted the 1967 borders, albeit without resolving the ambiguity not just on the de facto recognition of Israel, but also on the difference between a temporary solution and a definitive one, between a *hudna* and peace.

Ever since the early years of its existence, Hamas referred to the concept of *hudna* in order to exit the impasse of a possible agreement with the Israelis, a clear and decisive appeal to an Islamic concept. With respect to the idea of *hudna*, Hamas's historical and theological point of reference is the 628 CE Treaty of Hudaybiyya, made in the sixth year after the *Hijra*. Along with his followers, which tradition numbers around 1,400, the Prophet Mohammed decided to undertake the so-called Lesser Pilgrimage to Mecca, following the convention of being unarmed on the journey. Makkans, however, prevented the Prophet from completing the pilgrimage, forcing him to undertake lengthy negotiations that were eventually completed under a tree in Hudaybiyya on the caravan trail between Medina and Mecca, where the respective ambassadors signed a ten-year truce. According to the text of the treaty, "There will be no fighting for ten years in which people will be safe and stop from attacking one another. And amongst us what is vice should be prevented, and there shall be no theft or treachery."[42] The exhausting political debate between Hamas and the international community concentrates on breaking the *hudna* and on the significance of the truce for Muslims at the time of Hudaybiyya. The crux of the question is whether the *hudna* is a way for Hamas to strengthen itself during a period of weakness in order to later return to attacking its enemy. Some say that the Prophet Mohammed himself broke the Hudaybiyya truce, but in this case also interpretations differ. Islamologists say that neither the Prophet Mohammed, nor the Muslims, nor their allies broke the truce, but that after one year the truce was broken by the Banu Bakr tribe, which was connected to the Makkan aristocracy, the Quraysh tribe. Both the Banu Bakr and the Quraysh attacked the Banu Khuza'ah tribe, itself in turn linked to the Muslim side. Moreover, again according to scholars, the violation of the truce did not occur immediately, but after an exchange of letters and of envoys between the Prophet Mohammed and the Quraysh tribe.

This is the *hudna* to which Sheikh Ahmed Yassin referred in his numerous offers to Israel of a *hudna* for varying lengths of time, dating all the way back to 1993.[43] It is to that armistice, for example, that Moussa Abu Marzouq referred in 1995, outlining a possibility that would be reiterated to the international community particularly from the Second Intifada onward, including the offers that Hamas leaders would make after their ascent to power in 2006. The then head of the politburo had told Khaled Hroub that there was "a way of accepting an interim solution that is consistent with the Shariía, namely an armistice (*hudna*). This differs from a peace agreement in that the armistice has a set duration, and it does not require acceptance of the usurpation of [our] rights by the enemy."[44] As Professor Shaul Mishal, an Israeli expert on Hamas, has written: "By interpreting any political agreement involving the West Bank and Gaza Strip as merely a pause on the historic road of *jihad*, Hamas achieved political flexibility without forsaking its ideological credibility."[45] Moreover, "having adopted the strategy of a temporary settlement, Hamas was ready to acquiesce in the Oslo process without recognizing Israel; to support the establishment of a Palestinian state in the West Bank and Gaza Strip without ending the state of war or renouncing its ultimate goals; and to consider restraint, but not to give up the armed struggle."[46] According to Mishal, "a political settlement in the short run was interpreted as being complementary, not contradictory, to long-term desires."[47] At the apex of the Second Intifada, the "spring of fire" of 2002, Israeli cities were, in the space of two months, scarred by dozens of suicide attacks undertaken by all Palestinian armed factions, while some of the most important Palestinian cities such as Jenin and Nablus were devastated by Operation Defensive Shield. At this point the third-ranking member of the Hamas *Nomenklatura*, Ismail Abu Shanab, made Israel an offer and chose a very specific platform from which to do it: an interview with an American newspaper, the *San Francisco Chronicle*. After generations who had fought wars upon wars, Abu Shanab told Robert Plotkin, "now there is a generation who needs to live in peace, and not worry about their safety."[48] Abu Shanab, born in 1950, was talking about the generations of leaders born in Gaza's refugee camps; their idea was to delay talk of "historical issues," to "speak [instead] of historical Palestine, and practical reality," bearing in mind that "when Palestinians and Israelis live among each other in peace, they may cooperate with each other in a way that everyone will be satisfied."[49] This offer was in line with other proposals made in previous years by Sheikh Yassin, but Abu Shanab's in 2002 took on far greater significance because it was made immediately after the Arab League summit in Beirut. During the meeting, the then–Saudi Prince Regent Abdullah presented a plan, later approved, in which he offered Ariel Sharon peace and security in exchange for land. There could be peace between the Arabs and Israel if Tel Aviv pulled back to the armistice lines of 1949, the so-called Green Line. Something shifted, despite the violence. Between 2001 and 2002, it appears that Hamas decided to adhere unilaterally to a de-escalation on at least three occasions. But it was in the summer of 2002 that Palestinian factions came closest to reaching a ceasefire—Hamas included, as it was then the group with the greatest "firepower"—and this at the very same time that Yasser Arafat had decided to place Ahmed Yassin under house arrest after yet another wave of suicide attacks.

At the center of negotiations was a man considered to be the best when it comes to establishing fruitful contacts with Islamist groups, both Palestinian and Lebanese. He is probably the European who knows Hamas and Hezbollah best, thanks to a thirty-year career in the British foreign intelligence service. Alastair Crooke was the MI6 man in Israel and in the Occupied Palestinian Territory until he moved into conflict resolution early this century on the strength of an unquestionable competence in Middle Eastern matters. He contributed to the April 2002 report on the Second Intifada drawn up by US Senator George Mitchell. He acted as security consultant for Miguel Moratinos, then–EU special envoy in the Middle East and later Spanish foreign minister, and he was one of the closest advisors to the EU's Javier Solana, "Mr. Foreign Policy," on the Middle Eastern file. In that role, he helped facilitate the truce of 2003.

The previous year, Alastair Crooke headed the European security team and contacted Palestinian factions in order to arrive at a unilateral ceasefire, or *tahdi'ah*: a period of calm that would, above all, put an end to suicide attacks within Israeli cities. The EU consultant met with key figures, including Sheikh Yassin in Gaza,[50] and negotiations with Fatah and Hamas proceeded at such a pace that a public announcement by all the factions of a ceasefire having been reached was imminent. Just a few more hours and the agreement would have been made public: Hamas had agreed to stop suicide attacks, as Fatah requested. On July 22, 2002, however, a one-ton bomb was dropped on the agreement—the full weight of the ordnance dropped by an Israeli F-16 fighter on a four-story building in Al-Darj, an area in Gaza City, which contemporary reports describe as densely populated—just like the rest of the city. Fifteen people died, among them nine children and three women, while another 159 were injured. The objective of this "targeted assassination" carried out by the Israeli air force was the head of Hamas's military wing, Salah Shehadeh, who was among the fifteen victims, along with his two bodyguards. According to the government in Tel Aviv, Shehadeh had to be killed because he "was among the founders of the Hamas and directly responsible for initiating and directing dozens of attacks carried out over the last two years, in which dozens of Israeli citizens have been killed and hundreds injured."[51] The communiqué added that he was also "behind the financing of laboratories for the production of Kassam missiles and was personally involved in the purchase and manufacture of arms."[52] Regarding what the press had for years called "collateral victims," the armed forces declared that "if their information had indicated with certainty the presence of innocent civilians in Shehadeh's vicinity, the timing or the method of the action would have been changed."[53] But even within Israel the military's explanations did not stop the outcry, so much so that a state commission was set up to investigate the targeted assassination, while abroad the requests to investigate Avi Dichter, then head of the Israel Security Agency, mounted.

After the spectacular assassination of Salah Shehadeh, the agreement was called off, negotiations were suspended, and even champions of moderation toward the West and toward Israel such as Hosni Mubarak published statements the harshness of which can be understood only in the light of what would later come to be known publicly about the negotiations over the *tahdi'ah*. Shehadeh's assassination, Mubarak said at the time, "shows the Israeli Prime Minister [Ariel Sharon] was probably not happy with these initiatives and said, 'I will go ahead with this strike to sabotage these efforts.'"[54] At the same time, Mubarak was echoed by a good friend of the West in the Palestinian camp, Yasser Abed Rabbo, who repeated the same accusations on the pages of the Arab newspaper *Al-Hayat*: the massacre in Gaza City's Al-Darj quarter was an act of sabotage against the agreement that was about to be signed thanks to the joint efforts of the PNA, the Jordanians, and the Saudis.

In August, according to a poll conducted by the Palestinian Center for Policy and Research, Hamas overtook Fatah in potential voters' preference for the first time, gaining 27 percent of the potential vote, while Yasser Arafat's party collapsed from 32 to 26 percent.[55] Crooke's own direct recollection was that once the *hudna* began to be debated for the first time with the Egyptian leadership in Cairo in 2002, "Hamas responded affirmatively to a query on whether they would agree to remove civilians from the conflict. This response was passed to both American officials and to Israel. After shuttling between [an] American and a senior Israeli official in different locations in Cairo, the definition of who would be removed from the conflict was specified and a larger agreement to end violence targeting civilians seemed likely. However, Israeli Prime Minister Sharon rejected the proposal. In all, Hamas proposed to remove civilians from the conflict on three separate occasions. All three proposals were rejected by Israel."[56] The attempts Hamas and then–US President George W. Bush's administration made to suspend suicide attacks in September 2002 met with no greater success.

Nearly a year would have to go by before talk of *hudna* could restart, albeit this time solely within Palestine. The turning point came in 2003, with the first *hudna* reached by Palestinian armed groups entering into force on June 29. The architect of the June 2003 truce was without doubt Mahmoud Abbas, who Yasser Arafat had designated prime minister a few months previously. It was Abbas who attempted to include Hamas in negotiations because—according to sources within the Islamist movement itself—given that the bloodiest attacks had been carried out by the Harakat al-Muqaw-wama al-Islamiyya, its signature on the agreement would reduce Israeli civilian victims of the Intifada by 70 percent. An initial agreement with Hamas would then make it easier to reach an agreement with the armed group linked to Fatah, Al-Aqsa Martyrs' Brigades. The negotiations were difficult and bloodstained for both sides. So much so that before the *hudna* could be reached on June 9, Israel tried to assassinate Abdel Aziz al-Rantisi by firing seven missiles from two helicopters at his jeep. The Hamas leader was wounded, as were another twenty-four people, including one of his sons, while one of his bodyguards and a woman who was passing by were killed. Barely forty-eight hours passed before Hamas responded: a suicide attacker, disguised as an Orthodox Jew, got on a Number 14 bus and blew himself up halfway down Jaffa Road, in the commercial center of Jerusalem. Sixteen people were killed and about one hundred injured. But on June 29, Palestinian factions nonetheless agreed on a ceasefire—a ceasefire, however, that did not last long and that was broken beyond repair when Israel killed a Hamas leader on August 21. The target of the five missiles Israel launched was Ismail Abu Shanab, the most moderate among the Hamas leadership, the very person considered to have been the architect of the *hudna*, and even more importantly, the one who, from the height of his position as third-ranking member of the Hamas *Nomenklatura*, was the first to speak of the possibility of a Palestinian state alongside an Israeli state. Although no "dove," Abu Shanab was pragmatic, and he believed that the establishment of a Palestinian state was what his generation sought above all else at that historical juncture. He had also stated that he could not foresee what future generations might seek, thus recalling the temporary nature of the decisions Hamas could take concerning Palestine—a *waqf* land, the land of Islam, and thus not merely a homeland. His death, according to the accounts of pragmatic leaders within Hamas, had a considerable effect on them. Years later, in 2008—in a very different Gaza City from 2003, and one that a few months later would be targeted by Operation Cast Lead—Ahmed Youssef recalled that "the day before, [Shanab] had made a good public statement. I had called him on the telephone. I was still in the United States at the time."[57]

Israel's killing of Abu Shanab came in reaction to the bloody attack a few days earlier in the heart of Jerusalem, between Road No. 1 and the Orthodox quarter of Mea Shearim. The attack claimed twenty-three lives, including eighteen Israelis and five Americans, and injured about one hundred. The suicide attack was claimed by Islamic Jihad, but the attacker would later be identified as a Hamas member. This circumstance forced Abdel Aziz al-Rantisi to admit responsibility for the attack, although he defined it as an isolated incident, a reaction against the Israelis' assassination of an Islamic Jihad leader. Three weeks later, the Israelis themselves obtained confirmation that the attacker had acted alone, without having received an order from Hamas leadership. He came from Hebron, just like the Islamic Jihad leader who had been assassinated just five days before the suicide attack in Jerusalem.

But it was this August 2003 attack that provided a push from within the European Union to include Hamas on its list of terrorist organizations. Up until that moment, the political wing of the Islamist movement had been saved—so to speak—from the blacklist on which the Izz al-Din al-Qassam Brigades had already been included in 2002, alongside Al-Aqsa Martyrs' Brigades, the Islamic Jihad, and the PFLP. With a decision taken on September 12, 2003, the European Union's Council, under the Italian presidency (Foreign Minister Franco Frattini signed the act), added the whole of Hamas to the list of terrorist organizations. This inclusion, at this particular point, blocked any negotiated attempt by Javier Solana's men—Alastair Crooke foremost among them—to arrive at a lasting ceasefire with the Islamist movement.

Ismail Abu Shanab's assassination halted everything. The chain reaction of suicide attacks and Israeli retaliations began again: Hamas claimed responsibility for two attacks carried out on the same day, September 9, one against Israeli soldiers who were hitchhiking just outside the Tzifin military base (resulting in nine dead and thirty wounded), the other in the heart of Jerusalem, in the well-off German Colony quarter, just opposite one of the best-known cafés in the area, the Café Hillel (resulting in seven people dead and another fifty wounded.) The following day, the Israeli air force destroyed the two-story home of Hamas leader Mahmoud al-Zahhar in the heart of one of Gaza City's poorest quarters, Al-Sabra, where Ahmed Yassin also lived at the time. Al-Zahhar, his wife, and his daughter were injured, as were eighteen other people, while al-Zahhar's son Khaled and one of his bodyguards were killed.

Behind the scenes, however, the doors had not been bolted shut, and there remained an open channel for dialogue aimed at overcoming the internal divisions within Palestinian politics. Indeed, this possibility for dialogue remained open despite the PNA institutions being racked by yet another crisis. Having failed in its attempt to obtain stronger powers to reorganize and rationalize the maze of labels into which the security sector in the West Bank and in Gaza was divided, on September 6 Mahmoud Abbas resigned and was replaced by Ahmed Qureia, also known by his nom de guerre Abu Ala, who was now tasked with reconciling Palestinian politics. Or at least with trying to.

When, under Egyptian pressure, the twelve factions met in Cairo in early December 2003, the main theme was still that of the *hudna*, as well as the question of the relationship between Fatah and Hamas. It should have been simply a question of internal Palestinian politics, but it quickly became clear that this was not the case. There was an unacknowledged presence: Israel. Invisible and unspoken as its presence may have been, it was still one whose influence was clearly felt—especially at a particular point during the proceedings in some of the words spoken by members of the Egyptian intelligence services. Osama Hamdan recalls that "the Egyptians asked some very specific questions: What is the definition of civilians and of militants in the resistance? At that point, we understood that the questions had been set by the Israelis themselves, because these were precisely the crucial points in Tel Aviv's requests. We probed some individuals who were well informed, and we discovered that Ariel Sharon, who was then prime minister, had sent Ephraim Halevy to Cairo.

We asked for confirmation, and got it: Halevy was in the Egyptian capital."[58]

Until a few months earlier, Halevy had been one of Sharon's closest advisors, but had resigned in June after Dov Weisglass had taken on a more prominent role. The former chief of Mossad—an organization within which he had worked for twenty-eight years—Halevy had been the "prince's advisor" during the Oslo years and during the years of bitter disappointment that followed, as well as the man called upon to resolve problems in difficult moments. For example, Halevy had been the one involved in the return of the two agents responsible for the failed poison attempt on Khaled Meshaal in Jordan in 1997. Did Halevy's presence in Cairo therefore mean that the situation in December 2003 was a delicate situation? Osama Hamdan recalls that they "had put forth a proposal: stop all attacks against all civilians, Israelis, and Palestinians."[59]

The Egyptian response arrived after barely three days, and was negative. The then second-in-command within Egyptian intelligence cited the position of his boss, one of the most powerful men in Egypt, saying, "Omar Suleiman says it cannot work."[60] Hamdan continues, "We understood that Israel had rejected the offer. We later learned that Halevy had advised accepting the offer, but that it was Sharon himself who had rejected it."[61] But it was also the disagreement between different actors on the Palestinian political scene that ensured the negotiations would fail—in particular, Abu Ala's attempt to obtain everything he wanted at once. His request was not only that the parties should agree to another *hudna*, but that he personally be given the authority by the factions to negotiate on their behalf with the Israelis. A "no" was inevitable, and the agreement fell through.

Chapter 5

THE MARCH WATERSHED

During a slow and dreary November 2004, Palestine was suddenly plunged into mourning. Far away from Ramallah, and after days of agony, Yasser Arafat died in a military hospital on the outskirts of Paris. His funeral was held in Cairo, away from the Haram al-Sharif in Jerusalem, the city in which he wanted to be buried. Later the same day, his body was transported to the Muqata'a in Ramallah, where he had spent the last two years of his life under Israeli siege and where he was laid to rest in a corner of the large courtyard. Three years later, his successor Mahmoud Abbas would dedicate a mausoleum to Abu Ammar. But with the disappearance of Arafat, Palestinian politics was abruptly faced with having to start a new chapter in its history without its founding father, the man who was the symbol incarnate of the possibility of its independence and of its redemption, the man—as many on the streets of the West Bank and Gaza still say—who had managed to put Palestine back on the map.

Abu Ammar's death changed everything for Fatah, for the PNA, and also for Hamas. Like Fatah, the Palestinian Islamist movement had been without its leader and its symbol for some months now. On March 22, 2004, the targeted assassination of Sheikh Ahmed Yassin—ordered personally by then–Israeli Prime Minister Ariel Sharon—was carried out at dawn by the Israeli air force. Yassin was returning from the Mujamma al-Islami Mosque, which practically faces the house where he had lived most of his life, a modest house in the equally modest al-Sabra neighborhood of Gaza City: low houses that look out onto narrow, unadorned streets that boast a few shops, a mosque, and lots of children during the daytime. As dawn was breaking, Sheikh Ahmed Yassin was leaving the mosque after reciting the first prayer of the day, his quadriplegic's wheelchair being pushed down the street, when a missile launched from an Apache helicopter killed him at the age of sixty-six, along with seven other men, including three bodyguards and others among the faithful. Sixteen people, including two of his eleven children, were left injured.

The news spread quickly across the Palestinian Territory and across the entire Arab world. That morning in Jerusalem, everyone sensed that something momentous had happened. It was not that the streets were very different, apart from the heightened state of alert that had increased the number of soldiers and border patrols, especially in East Jerusalem. The difference was elsewhere, an intangible and anguished feeling carried on the air. From the early hours of the morning until nightfall, the loudspeakers of Jerusalem's mosques bore Qur'anic chants across the city, giving the day a unique feeling, one that would be repeated only one other time, on November 11 of that same year, upon the death of Yasser Arafat in that hospital on the outskirts of Paris. Sacred chants were repeated, bringing people together across the Palestinian Territory, just as Palestinian politicians were brought together, overcoming—if only for a brief moment—the divisions between Palestinians and between Arabs, between the faithful and the lay, between governments allied with the West and those allied with the "Axis of Evil." For days, squares across the Arab world, the region's television networks, and the online forums increasingly popular with the young were replete with photographs of Sheikh Yassin and particularly of the wheelchair to which he had been consigned for half a century. A wheelchair was brandished at his funeral and in the street protests that shook the entire region, as was its blackened skeleton, adopted in cartoons and caricatures as a kind of logo of resistance: resistance against Israelis, against the United States who sided with the Israelis, and against Arab regimes who were accused of acquiescing.

All of a sudden, Hamas was orphaned—not simply of the man who had established the Islamic Resistance Movement at a meeting in his home in December 1987, but of the figure portrayed in public as its spiritual guide. This loss was not unexpected, not least because Sheikh Yassin had escaped a previous targeted assassination attempt carried out by the Israeli air force while he was in a meeting in September 2003. The former teacher, who had been a quadriplegic since his teens, escaped with a wounded hand, but Tel Aviv's warning was clear: the list of Hamas members it was targeting included the highest echelons of the political leadership, such as the then third in command in Gaza, Ismail Abu Shanab—who had just been assassinated the previous year—or Mahmoud al-Zahhar.

Israel's strategy did not stop even after Yassin's death, a decision that surprised no one, least of all Palestinian Islamists. Yassin's rapidly chosen successor was the fifty-five-year-old pediatrician Abdel Aziz al-Rantisi, one of the *Nomenklatura* considered by the Israelis to be among the movement's most inflexible. This appointment indicated Hamas's choice to counterattack, explicitly avoiding any softening in its positions after such a severe blow as the assassination of its founder, who was widely thought to be Hamas's most representative public figure, at least in terms of his media profile. Rantisi, already considered by many a "dead man walking," had already been targeted by Israel's air force in June 2003 in an attack that left the pediatrician and heir apparent seriously wounded. Indeed, Yassin's successor would not last long: barely a month had gone by before Rantisi died in another targeted assassination on April 17. The most accredited interpretation of these events that circulated among Hamas leaders at the time was that Ariel Sharon intended to put the leadership under as much pressure as possible. Sharon was believed to be concerned above all with the question of who would become Arafat's successor, and by targeting Yassin and Rantisi he was supposedly aiming to eliminate those who were considered to be most charismatic by the Palestinian population: Abu Shanab, Yassin, Rantisi, Ismail Haniyeh (who was wounded in 2003), and Mahmoud al-Zahhar. Indeed, before that, a targeted assassination in Nablus in July 2001 had killed two of Hamas's best-known leaders in the West Bank, Jamal Mansour and Jamal Salim. Whether the interpretation offered by Hamas's leaders is true or not, it is certain that ever since the start of the Second Infitada, Israel had intensified its use of extrajudicial killings, which reached their peak with Yassin, but did not stop there. After Rantisi's assassination, another attack was carried out beyond the Occupied Palestinian Territory, in Damascus, host to Hamas's leadership-in-exile. Toward the end of September 2004, Izz al-Din al-Sheikh al-Khalili, who the Israelis considered to be a bridge between Hamas's military wings in the West Bank and in Gaza, was killed when a bomb under the driver's seat of his car was set off in the suburbs of the Syrian capital. Within the perverse logic of attack and counterattack, and in a spiral of revenge, the assassination of al-Sheikh al-Khalili was the Israeli response to the simultaneous attacks carried out against two buses that had racked the commercial districts of the main southern Israeli city of Be'er Sheva toward the end of August. The Izz al-Din al-Qassam Brigades had claimed the attacks in a leaflet found in Hebron, the city the two suicide bombers were from. The bombers themselves had intended to seek revenge for the deaths of Ahmed Yassin and of Abdel Aziz al-Rantisi.

Its founding leadership decimated over the previous few months, Hamas did not melt away like snow under the sun, but instead managed to organize and carry out bloody attacks such as the simultaneous bombings in Be'er Sheva, a city until then thought to be outside the reach of terrorist attacks. Hamas's military wing wanted the attacks to be spectacular. However, there were also obvious political implications in the Be'er Sheva suicide attacks, since they proved wrong the expectations of those who had ordered the decapitation of Hamas. The Israeli government publicly declared that its strategy's objective was to erode the consensus that favored the Islamist movement, and to stop the attacks inside the country. Indeed, the years following Yassin's assassination went in entirely the opposite direction: deprived of its best-known leaders in Gaza, Hamas went beyond the consensus it had gathered through its activists and through its provision of social services, transforming that support into political allegiance and electoral success. In an ex post facto reading offered by some among the Islamist movement's leaders, the physical elimination of some of its leaders in the spring of 2004—particularly Yassin and Rantisi—had no effect on the debate already going on within the organization concerning whether or not to participate in the PNA's institutions. Osama Hamdan points out that "the debate had already begun, even though it was only a theoretical question at the time. Halfway through 2004, the PNA had not yet decided whether it would hold a general election."[1]

Yet something did change within Palestinian politics. From a symbolic point of view, Yassin's death, followed by Arafat's only eight months later, brought to the surface a process that had already been taking place among the cadres of all political groups, namely the emergence of individuals who had until that time been living in the charismatic leaders' shadows. Yassin's and Arafat's traumatic departure from the Palestinian scene forced both nationalist and Islamist political elites to deal with the absence of the two leaders from their respective camps. There were no more symbols, no more father figures, no more fathers of a nation. There were no more totemic figures in whose shadow one could work. Thus, ever since 2004, leadership change took on a convulsed, even confused rhythm, one that became increasingly violent as time went by. At the root of all this was the question of power sharing, one that Fatah hadn't experienced since the PNA had transformed the leading party of the PLO into a party-state. For its part, after Abu Ammar's death, Hamas changed its strategy, moving from dealing with the PNA behind the scenes to a more public relationship. This relationship, now out in the open, brought to the fore a debate that, although it dated all the way back to the height of the Second Intifada in 2002, had previously remained within the confines of the Islamist movement's leadership: namely, whether or not to participate in the PNA institutions. As Ghazi Hamad, one of Hamas's moderates, explains: "We started talking about political participation when the situation in Palestinian civil society during the Second Intifada had deteriorated to the point that the PNA had been considerably weakened."[2] Hamad, who had himself been arguing since the mid-1990s for the need for a political leadership detached from the resistance, recalls: "The question was: how can we form a national leadership in order to shore up the PNA? We began discussions about this already in 2002, a debate which centered primarily around Gaza, and in which all leaders took part, from Ismail Abu Shanab to Mahmoud al-Zahhar, including Abdel Aziz al-Rantisi. The next step, however, happened because of Arafat's death."[3]

Thus, Arafat's death accelerated this debate. Hamas's internal discussions concerning participation in the PNA were given a public face immediately after Abu Ammar's funeral, in the form of the question of succession to Arafat and of presidential elections, which were hastily organized. The chosen date was January 9, 2005, about two months after the death of the PNA's first president. A candidate was chosen with equal speed in order to avoid leaving the PNA in the midst of a leadership vacuum that would have been very delicate to manage. The name that emerged was Mahmoud Abbas, the old Abu Mazen, the man who had shared Arafat's decisions concerning Oslo only to later come close to a head-on clash with him when, after having been appointed prime minister in spring 2003, the president denied him the powers required to reform the PNA, and particularly to simplify the plethora of its security organizations. In the January 2005 presidential elections, Abbas ran, for all intents and purposes, unopposed. Only Mustapha Barghouthi—the most notable exponent of Palestinian civil society, and the best known abroad—decided to present his candidacy. Barghouthi obtained an unexpected and very respectable share of almost 20 percent. This result in itself testified to the political maturity reached by the Palestinian electorate, despite the few opportunities it has had to exercise its right and duty to vote.

Hamas decided not to field candidates for the presidential elections, but also not to adopt a confrontational stance with respect to the elections themselves. Rather, the Islamist movement did not expose itself much, leaving its adherents free to vote as they chose. Indeed, something profound had already happened within the wider Palestinian electorate, signaled just before Christmas, on December 23, 2004, when the first local elections since 1976 were held in the West Bank, since the Israeli occupying forces decided to renew local administrations. It was Yasser Arafat himself who had buckled under pressure from advisors and politicians and allowed ballot boxes to make the decision on renewing those local authorities that he himself had selected in 1994, mostly from within Fatah, at the birth of the PNA. Ten years on, municipal councils were in trouble: if, during the first phase of the Oslo plans, they had been through a transition away from Israeli military occupation toward local autonomy for some towns, they had since experienced the blood and the ruins of the Second Intifada and finally witnessed the de facto cantonization of the West Bank with the return of the Israeli army to the Palestinian Territory and the proliferation of hundreds of checkpoints that fragmented the West Bank.

The elections held on that December 23, 2004, were limited, just a first taste of the ones that would take place in four separate stages throughout 2005. Barely 140,000 voters were called to renew twenty-six town councils. The councils to be renewed had been carefully chosen from among those where Hamas was weakest. Among these, there was only one city of any size: Jericho, one of Fatah's fortresses. But the result was explosive: a massive 84 percent of voters participated, and while Abu Mazen's party won a majority in seventeen councils, Hamas gained control of nine, with a total of 75 seats to Fatah's 135. In Jericho, victory went to a mixed list, with Fatah unable to win a single seat. The conclusion was not just that Hamas was on the rise, but that it would be a key player in the post-Arafat transition process. Forecasts that predicted Fatah as the clear winner clashed with reality on the ground. Even as a partial test, these first municipal elections suggested that Hamas was strong not just in Gaza, but that it had built and consolidated its consensus even in the West Bank, which was traditionally linked to Fatah and which had in recent years been divided into urban islets surrounded by the Israeli army.

The result of the local elections, so clearly favorable to Hamas, was also a message to Abu Mazen, the only possible candidate in presidential elections, given that Marwan Barghouthi, Fatah's secretary general for the West Bank, was in an Israeli jail serving five life sentences. Fatah's unexpected electoral weakness confirmed that the real game would begin after the presidential elections planned for January 9, when a different range of seats and constituencies—representation in the Palestinian Assembly—would be up for grabs. Only then would the real balance of power in the post-Arafat period become clear.

The pressure Hamas exerted on the January 9 elections, however, went beyond the matter of the electoral outcome. The Islamist movement had in practice complicated the electoral process as a result of the intensification of its battle with the Israelis in Gaza, which involved the launching of mortar shells and rockets against settlers and soldiers in the weeks prior to the elections. The clash was not simply military; it was also political. Israel, particularly on its political right, with the Likud party split in half, was debating the question of a pull out from Gaza: a withdrawal that the Israeli parliament was discussing just a few days before Ariel Sharon's enemy, Yasser Arafat, would die. The then-leader of the Tel Aviv government had put forward the idea of withdrawing soldiers and settlers from the Gaza Strip in a February 2004 interview with the Israeli daily *Ha'aretz*. To push this proposal through, Sharon was facing the deepest split ever seen in Likud just as the post-Arafat transition was being prepared.

The idea of an Israeli withdrawal from Gaza, however, had not influenced the behavior of Palestinian armed groups. On the contrary, these groups had continued to affect internal Palestinian politics in their own way both before and, as would become clear by mid-January, after the elections. It was at this point that a suicide attack at the Karni crossing, which joins Gaza to Israel, froze the tentative preliminary talks between Sharon's advisors and Abu Mazen's. The attack, which left six Israeli civilians and three suicide bombers dead, was claimed by Al-Aqsa Martyrs' Brigades, the group close to Fatah; by Hamas's own military wing; and by the Popular Resistance Committees. The armed strategy continued to parallel the political.

Tensions remained high within the Palestinian Territory. Notwithstanding the continuous clashes between the Israelis and all the armed factions in Gaza, however, the Palestinian electoral machine did not stop, and the presidential vote took place with a high turnout. The elections themselves, carried out under the supervision of about 800 observers who had arrived in the Occupied Palestinian Territory from all over the world, were democratic. Mahmoud Abbas not only won the election against his only real opponent, Mustapha Barghouthi, he also achieved an overall majority of preferences expressed. Over 70 percent of those eligible to vote participated, and of these 62 percent chose Abbas, who—despite not exactly running away with victory—could therefore be said to have achieved a consensus beyond party lines. It was of course true that Hamas did not express a preference in the electoral competition and that it did not put forward its own candidate. But it was also the case that Hamas's abstention was "soft"; it was a way of signaling that with the beginning of a new chapter in the PNA's history, the Islamist movement had crossed a Rubicon in deciding to participate in Palestinian institutional life.

Abu Mazen could not win Hamas's consensus directly. His history as the protagonist of the Oslo process and the history of the Islamist movement's leaders who had since the First Intifada consistently opposed such a peace were too different for that. Things could have been different had other candidates for the presidency been nominated. Marwan Barghouthi, for example, had refused to be listed, even as a purely symbolic presence, as some had suggested during November 2004. Had Barghouthi been the presidential candidate, Hamas might well have considered voting for the leader of the *tanzim*, who after all was the leader of the Second Intifada lionized by the media and with whom Hamas had agreed regarding strategy during Al-Aqsa Revolt. This much was hinted at by Mohammed Jamal al-Natsheh, one of the best-known leaders of Hamas in the Hebron area, interviewed in a Be'er Sheva prison just days after Abu Mazen was elected president of the PNA.[4] Putting forth Marwan Barghouthi as a candidate would have brought together the so-called street, the battleground of the Second Intifada, with "the cell" within which about 8,000 Palestinians—many of them activists of Al-Aqsa uprising—were detained. That said, Abu Mazen was far from unpopular with Hamas, which, on the contrary, saw him as necessary precisely in order for the Islamist movement to enter the PNA structures and thus to share power. On the other hand, a "Hamas president" would never have been able to meet with either the Israelis or those states that are crucial to the solution of the Middle Eastern conflict. In this sense, it was much better to have as head of state a well-accepted and esteemed figure such as Abu Mazen, who would be in a position to meet with

Ariel Sharon and be welcomed in Europe and in the United States as a representative of Palestinian moderates.

Mahmoud Abbas became PNA president in the context of a political landscape that was very different from the one that preceded it: Yasser Arafat, the founding father, was no longer there, and Abu Mazen had a very different character than his predecessor, who had been famed for his histrionics, for his extroverted nature, and for his passion. In some ways—certainly in terms of his public image—Abbas was Arafat's exact opposite. He also represented a different way of conducting internal politics, as well as a different assessment of international patrons and of adversaries. Abu Mazen had also been the main Fatah leader to favor the co-option of Hamas into the PNA ever since 2003, hoping this would provide a way of reining in its military power and of controlling its political influence. However, in the aftermath of Arafat's death, Abu Mazen quickly realized that controlling Hamas as a political force had become a difficult task indeed. The Islamist movement showed every intention of not remaining in the shadows but of fully entering the Palestinian political arena with a specific agenda. This agenda was not limited to participation in PNA institutions, but aimed more broadly at reforming the organization that had traditionally been given the mandate to represent the will of the Palestinian people: the PLO. This quickly became clear after Abu Mazen's inauguration as president, when on January 23 Hamas and Islamic Jihad declared a unilateral suspension of attacks on Israel in order to allow President Abbas to negotiate a ceasefire with Israel. This was also a starting point for negotiations between Palestinian factions, once again with Egypt's mediation, in order to reach a de facto unilateral ceasefire with Israel. The Cairo Declaration of March 17, which stipulated the continuation for the entirety of 2005 the "atmosphere of calm" with respect to Israel, explicitly stated that the factions had collectively "agreed to develop the Palestine Liberation Organization on bases that will be settled upon in order to include all the Palestinian powers and factions," and to "form a committee to define [the] bases" on which to do so.[5]

It was not the first time that Hamas had called for the reform of the PLO. Between 1992 and 1993, it had suggested to Yasser Arafat an agreement whereby the Islamist group would have held 40 percent of the representatives within the PNC at the same time as it entered into a profoundly reformed PLO. Hamas leaders had traveled to Tunis, when Arafat was exiled there, to discuss a possible thawing of relations, and they later participated in a meeting held in Khartoum mediated by the Sudanese Islamist leader Hassan al-Tourabi.[6] Abu Ammar, however, had rejected these overtures, wanting to avoid placing Fatah and Hamas on the same footing within Palestinian representative institutions.

In the meantime, however, times had clearly changed, not just because Arafat was no longer there, but because Fatah was weak from the point of view of its base support, and Hamas was demonstrating with each passing day its intention to take full part in the representative institutions available to Palestinians. Within the Islamist leadership in the West Bank, Gaza, and abroad, the winning strategy between 2004 and 2007 was participation. Hamas decided to stop its boycott of the PNA and instead to enter its halls of power. It chose to do so first and foremost through the instrument of electoral consensus, thereby remaining strictly within the representative branch of government.

The first step was participation in local elections. In truth, entering the public sphere at a local level had never posed either an ideological problem or a problem in terms of political practice for Hamas, as this was a primarily administrative form of participation and therefore perfectly coherent with its focus on the provision of welfare and of services that were in the interest of the community and that the Islamist movement had already been pursuing for years, following in the tradition established by the Muslim Brotherhood. Running local administrations was never considered incompatible with a political stance opposed to the PNA. The 2004–2005 elections, however, took on a very different meaning: they represented a "soft" entry into the institutions of the PNA, as well as providing a necessary test of the real consensus they met with at the grassroots level. The municipal elections in the West Bank produced a result the Hamas leadership itself had not expected. The subsequent test, the elections held in Gaza on January 25, 2005, just a few days after the presidential election, confirmed that the Strip was (nearly) under the control of the Harakat al-Muqawwama al-Islamiyya. For the newly sworn in Abu Mazen, the message from Hamas was clear: its goal was sharing power. However, as would become clear in the following two years, this was a contingency for which Fatah was not prepared.

The Turning Point

Gaza was practically a full house for Hamas: 7 municipal councils out of 10, with 75 council members out of 118, and a widespread consensus in that first round of local elections, with over 80 percent of registered electors turning out to vote. As was the case for the West Bank, the elections were no more than a test, since barely 90,000 Palestinians were called upon to designate administrators for the small municipal councils scattered across the Strip. There were two exceptions to this: Deir al-Balah and Beit Hanoun, towns that also have large refugee camps known for their daily confrontations with the Israelis. The completeness of its success was one of the main factors that made Hamas decide to take part in the general elections. As Ghazi Hamad recalls: "The people were voting for us, and this was a sign that the Palestinians wanted a change of leadership, as demonstrated also by the fact that we had just won in areas where we had not been strong until that point."[7] The victory in local elections was useful to Hamas, which decided to cash in on the political credit it earned in the following days, when the question of dialogue between the various Palestinian factions returned to the fore.

At the heart of yet another meeting between the various Palestinian factions, again mediated by the Egyptian authorities, was the question of a *hudna* with Israel, a truce that would silence the armed groups and that again became prominent after the election of Mahmoud Abbas, himself one of the authors of the truce of June 2003. There was a much bigger item on the menu, however: Hamas's entry into the PNA structures that took place on March 17, the date that marked a turning point for Hamas, the date of its formal decision to participate in the political process. This was the day of the Cairo Declaration, which committed thirteen Palestinian factions to a year-long "calm." This document contains the crucial passage that indicates a watershed moment for Hamas, stating that the factions "agreed on the necessity of completing total reform in all areas, of supporting the democratic process in its various aspects and of holding local and legislative elections at their determined time according to an election law to be agreed upon," which should be based "on an equal division (of seats) in a mixed system."[8] The Islamist movement had therefore chosen to take part in elections with a majority decision taken by its leadership. This shifted the movement's center of gravity, giving greater power to the pragmatic wing, which in 1996 had been forced to buckle under the pressure of the majority, giving up the prospect of running in the first general elections for the PNA.

The reasons for this change were rooted in contemporary circumstances, which differed from those in 1996 in several important points. Azzam Tamimi's words succinctly sum up both the atmosphere in 2004 and what would later take place in 2005 with the Israeli withdrawal from the Gaza Strip, an event that was nothing short of a watershed in Palestinian politics: "Oslo was dead. Arafat and Yassin had gone. The Israelis were leaving Gaza."[9] The debasement of the Oslo process, eventually dealt a mortal blow by the Second Intifada,[10] was therefore crucial for Hamas's own transition. It became one of the key features of the Cairo Accords of March 2005, which included the participation of groups like Hamas, despite the explicit prohibition on armed groups taking part in elections contained in the 1995 interim agreements between Israelis and Palestinians.[11] Thus, for Hamas it would have been easier to accept a formal entry into the PNA by way of a parliamentary presence if some of the bonds of the Oslo Accords—which had rendered the Authority dependent on Israel—had been loosened.

In 1996, the push to take part in elections had been backed by very few individuals, among them Ismail Haniyeh. Ten years later, however, all the groups that made up the Hamas leadership gave the involvement in PNA institutions the green light. The decision did not come without difficulty or without strenuous resistance from certain quarters. Hamas had long debated—and had long been divided—on this question, so that finding a majority to coalesce around the idea of taking part in a public arena so particular and so incomplete as the PNA was not an easy task. In the end, as has always been the case throughout Hamas's history, the Islamist movement accepted the will of the majority, according to a process very similar to the "democratic centralism" that was the hallmark of mass structures such as those of Communist parties, ultimately defending the final decision and overcoming earlier splits. The communiqué with which Hamas announced its decision to take part in elections in itself provides insight into Hamas's internal structure: the announcement was made—not coincidentally—in Nablus, where the opposition to participating in the PNA had been strongest. The local leader was Mohammed Ghazal, and the date was March 12, just days before the Cairo Declaration.[12]

These kinds of processes are in any case never linear, particularly when the transition from an armed resistance movement to a political party does not take place during a period of peace and stability. Rather, Hamas's shift toward participation occurred in a context of mutual hostility: the struggle between Israelis and Palestinians, which has never once stopped over the course of six decades. In other words, the transformation Hamas underwent after 2004 did not follow the expectations of standard conflict resolution theories. As Alastair Crooke points out, "Hamas and other Islamist groups continue to see themselves as resistance movements, but increasingly they see the prospect that their organizations may evolve into political currents that are focused on non-violent resistance."[13] The problem was that Hamas's ability to maintain the strength of an armed group was in itself part of the reason the movement was able to maintain its legitimacy and support among its base. These were not veterans of a conflict who had to be helped to rejoin society in peacetime, nor was this a transition toward solely moderate Islamist positions. Hamas was still Hamas, even after it chose to take part in the PNA's representative institutions, even after it became obvious that between 2004 and 2007 the pragmatic wing of the so-called doves managed to gain a majority consensus among activists.

At the same time, Hamas also sensed weariness in the Palestinian population after four years of Intifada, and decided to suspend suicide attacks against civilians inside Israel—a point on which the people's passive consent was eroding. Bassam Na'im, one of the leaders in Hamas's middle-age generation, retrospectively analyzed the choice of fully taking part in the sphere of representative politics, explaining that "the occupation and the resistance were fragmenting Palestinian society. It was for this reason that we chose to try to take part in the institutions."[14] The Hamas leadership understood that ordinary people were worn out, showing just how sensitive the Islamist leadership had been to the mood of Palestinian public opinion from its inception to more recent stages of its history. What people thought in the villages, in the refugee camps, and in the large urban centers in the West Bank and in Gaza all weighed on the decisions of the Islamist movement. Vice versa, the capillary reach of Hamas's social and political programs in the Occupied Palestinian Territory provided the Islamist movement with an accurate map of the current political situation. What Ghazi Hamad wrote barely three weeks before the elections, when there was still a possibility of delaying them, is telling in this respect: "Hamas, however, is unlikely to resort to violence. The lack of law and order, which in the public mind is blamed on the PA and the absence of the security forces, is a major reason for the growing popularity of the movement. Hamas would not want to come to be seen as a contributing factor."[15] Hamas was therefore clearly very sensitive to consensus, just like other organizations based on mass mobilization.

As with other decisions in the movement's history of more than two decades, Hamas decided to take part in general elections only after having held consultations in all four of its constituencies—Gaza, the West Bank, the prisons, and abroad. Scrolling down the still-unfinished list of decisions on which Hamas's constituencies have been summoned up to vote reveals a strong pragmatism that deals with political contingencies outside of mere ideological rigidity. Hamas asked the constituencies to vote, for example, on the movement's admission to the PLO in 1991, when the constituencies were only three due to the limited numbers of prisoners detained in Israeli jails. In 1997, the four constituencies approved Sheikh Ahmed Yassin's proposal on a *hudna* with Israel, based on a Palestinian state on

1949 armistice borders, Jerusalem as capital, and the refugees' right of return. Then, after 2004, the consultations were on the electoral program, on the exchange of prisoners between Israeli soldier Gilad Shalit and one thousand Palestinian detainees in the Israeli jails, on the reconciliation process between Fatah and Hamas, and even on the opening of a dialogue with the European Union.[16]

The 2005 decision process pertaining to the question of the PNA elections is an interesting case study in fully understanding the way in which Hamas's internal structure reacts to political requests that entail an important shift in the movement's strategy. In each of the constituencies, members voted, expressing their opinion on the question of participation in elections and thus on whether or not to enter the PNA. Witnesses testified that it was a long process, due to the difficulties of carrying out the internal consultations. There is obviously no hard data concerning the results in each of the four constituencies, though the Hamas leadership outside the Occupied Palestinian Territory argues that two-thirds of the leadership abroad declared its support for participation, overturning the position reached in the debate over the 1996 elections. In the West Bank and in Gaza, the majority had come out in favor of participation. Ahmed Youssef, who was Haniyeh's closest aide during the first Hamas-led government, even claims that it was precisely the leadership inside the Territory that overcame the resistance of the leadership abroad.[17] The most important factor, however, appears to be the prisons, which are interesting not only because of the result, but because of the way in which the consultation took place.

For Palestinians, the cycle of arrest and release from Israeli prisons is not considered to be a mark of shame. It is estimated that from 1967 on, at least 700,000 Palestinians have passed through Israeli jails; in every family, in other words, there is or was someone who is defined simply as a *prisoner*, whatever the reason for their arrest. It could be black market labor, or political militancy, or membership in an armed group, but in all cases one is and remains a *prisoner*. The experience of jail, therefore, is so widespread, so common, and so constant in the history of Palestinian society that particularly as far as political party militants are concerned, it is never considered a hiatus from active political life. One is a militant outside, and one contin-ues to be a militant behind bars also. Militancy can also start inside a cell, as in the case of Ayman Taha, Hamas's spokesperson in the Gaza Strip. The son of one of the leading figures in the Muslim Brother-hood and then in Hamas, Ayman Taha recalls that his affiliation with Hamas didn't start because of his father's role and influence inside the Islamist movement, but rather because of the traditional means of recruitment: at the age of nineteen, in 1989, he was imprisoned by the Israeli authorities and tortured in front of his father's eyes.[18]

Therefore, Hamas considers its prisoners in jail as a full-fledged constituency, on par with geographically defined groupings. Detain-ees have the same right to take part in the decision-making process and a full voice in discussions. Indeed, at times, they paradoxically have an even greater freedom to work on the movement's strategy and to enter into dialogue with other factions.

Between 2004 and 2005, the imprisoned constituency of Hamas approved participation in general elections. It did so notwithstand-ing the myriad of obvious difficulties involved in communicating between prisons, not least by taking advantage of the Israeli prac-tice of frequently subjecting inmates to transfers from one prison to another to pass messages between groups. A quarter of Palestinian prisoners (up to 2,400 detainees, Hamas militants included) were concentrated within Ketziot, a prison that journalists and inter-national observers managed to gain access to only with great dif-ficulty. The stories of those who have been there describe Ketziot as a camp within which detainees live in large tents, a prison that is completely different from the model detention centers in Be'er Sheva in the south or Hadarim in the north. The Hamas council in prisons consisted of twenty-three members. A wide majority, between sixteen and seventeen, spoke out in favor of participating in elections. Those who opposed participation were not opposed to taking part in the PNA institutions per se, but feared what in fact later occurred: namely, that the international community would not accept the Islamist presence within the PLC, and least of all would they accept Hamas's presence in government. Those who supported participation, on the other hand, believed that being able to influence PNA decisions was in itself worthwhile. One of those who took part in the discussion recalls that weighing heavily on the final decision was a document written by Sheikh Hassan Youssef—one of the most respected Islamist religious and political authorities in the West Bank and an imam at the central market mosque in Ramallah—in which he declared that he did not expect Hamas to obtain a majority of seats. Thus, the question of actually winning the elections—a victory that would have been very arduous to manage—was not even on the radar screen.

In any case, deciding to take part in elections was no simple matter for Hamas activists and had to be analyzed in all its possible aspects. The debate over participation in the 2006 elections shows just how independent Hamas's decision making was from patron-client relations of power and how it was instead a response to specific political problems. In prison, as in the other constituencies, Hamas militants imagined the possible scenarios of an electoral participation. One possibility was that the movement would run lower-ranking members of the organization for leadership posts, rather than its most high-profile personalities. A second possibility was to take part, but with only a limited number of candidates, mirroring a decision made by the Egyptian Muslim Brotherhood in the 2005 general elections. A third possibility considered was entering into an electoral coalition. The first scenario was quickly discarded; the absence of recognizable names would diminish the possibility of a strong showing and would leave the movement open to criticisms of being weak and of not representing a significant part of the population. It was the same fear of showing weakness through an unsatisfactory result that also undermined the option of forming a coalition. The a posteriori example suggested by an Islamist leader from the West Bank was the following: Mustapha Barghouthi had obtained an excellent result in the presidential elections of 2005, but his support dropped considerably a year later during political and legislative elections. According to this Hamas leader, "Had we, for example, decided to enter into a coalition with [Barghouthi], and had we then obtained the result which the ballot box later delivered, the interpretation would have been different from the reality: it would have been said that it was Barghouthi and his National Initiative that had received the people's support."[19]

The second scenario—the one based on a strategy similar to that adopted by the Egyptian Muslim Brotherhood during elections for the renewal of the People's Assembly, Egypt's lower house—was the most intensely debated. Egypt was going through a lively phase at the time: the opposition to President Mubarak had raised its head, and the reformist wing of the Muslim Brotherhood had established contacts with its secular counterparts. The Ikhwan's traditional caution, however, led the largest Islamist movement in the Arab world to avoid challenging Mubarak and scaring off the international community. The Ikhwan, which as a political organization was illegal until the fall of Hosni Mubarak, had bypassed the prohibition on participating in the elections by running as independents, but it feared that its participation might be read as an omen of a possible electoral victory and a sudden change of regime in Cairo. In order to avoid such fears, the Ikhwan decided to field a number of candidates equaling less than a third of the seats in the Assembly. Even if they had all been elected, Egypt's political balance would not be upset. The Egyptian Brotherhood was thus not aiming to obtain a majority in parliament, but merely to consolidate its options in the legislative branch of the political system in hopes of a de facto legitimization of its presence. Hamas, on the other hand, had not adopted the Egyptian Brotherhood's cautious strategy, even though some among the Gaza leadership—like Sayyed Abu Musameh— had unsuccessfully attempted to push for a strategy similar to the Ikhwan's in Cairo.[20]

Another factor that contributed to tipping the balance against limited participation was Mahmoud Abbas's decision to push the elections from July 2005 to January 2006. The fear that delays would increase the possibility of fraud had become increasingly pressing, and Hamas's leadership decided that it would be better to field as many and as high-caliber candidates as possible in order to compensate for the fraud that they believed was not simply a possibility but a certainty. The movement had commissioned independent polls—although sources do not indicate which groups carried them out—in order to find out how many votes Hamas would obtain were it to take part in the elections scheduled for the summer of 2005. The results indicated around 30 percent. When the date was moved to the following January, these polls were repeated, but the results never went above 40 percent. According to well-informed sources, which asked to be kept anonymous, it was precisely the decision by Mahmoud Abbas to postpone the elections that shifted the mood of the electorate: "Paradoxically, what earned us more votes was the postponement to January. It was the people first and foremost who feared fraud and wished to punish Fatah as the leading faction in the PNA."[21]

For Hamas, the point was not even the specific electoral system under which to hold the elections. The important thing was deciding whether to enter the competition or whether to repeat the choice made in 1996. Having crossed the Rubicon of participation, other considerations were seen as merely secondary. Thus, in the Cairo Accords of 2005, in which Hamas signed up to participate in general elections, the Islamist movement concentrated on a single point: namely, that candidates would not be asked to make any commitments in relation to the Oslo Accords. The agreement itself, at any rate, lay outside the scope outlined by the peace process established by the agreement between Arafat and Rabin, because Israel had no say in either the electoral law or in the organization of the elections themselves. Hamas—not least of all because it considered itself sufficiently strong in terms of its popular consensus, regardless of the precise architecture of the elections—therefore decided to ignore in large part the technicalities of the electoral law, leaving other factions free to choose them. Indeed, it was Egypt that pressed for a mixed system, and an agreement between Mahmoud Abbas and the PFLP in that direction was ultimately reached.[22] Hamas would also not oppose the "pink quotas" that mandated the seating of a certain number of female representatives and that had been established especially for this second election to the Palestinian legislature. Surprisingly, these would make a crucial contribution to the Islamist movement's victory.

A Silent Presence

The Cairo Declaration of March 17, 2005, with which the Palestinian factions approved a year-long *hudna*, was Abu Mazen's calling card during the opening stages of his presidency. It was with this immediate and striking success that Abbas presented his credentials to the international community as the right man for negotiations, perhaps even able to bring back on track the "Road Map for Peace," which had been derailed before it had even started. Even Israel should have been content with such an important result as a unilateral truce declared by all Palestinian armed factions, providing Israel's cities— which were at the time still under the threat of suicide bombings— with a breath of fresh air.

For Ariel Sharon, however, the agreement reached in Cairo also meant that Hamas was back in the game, thereby also indirectly declaring the failure of the strategy of targeted assassinations against the Islamist movement's leadership that had been initiated by old General Arik himself, Ariel Sharon. Killing Shehadeh, Abu Shanab, Yassin, Rantisi, and the dozens of other more or less prominent Islamist leaders was not enough to break the consensus that the heirs to the Muslim Brotherhood's "operational branch" had received. On the contrary: popular support was consolidating and transforming the movement into an electoral force to be reckoned with. Moreover, Hamas was drawn into the political limelight precisely at the moment Sharon was finalizing the most important decision of the last few years of his political life: the withdrawal from Gaza.

Ariel Sharon's new unilateralist strategy had an explosive impact on the Palestinian political transition. Already in February 2004, thanks also to a level of consensus that Israeli prime ministers had not received either domestically or internationally for years, the former general proposed Israel's "disengagement" from Gaza, and quickly brought this to fruition in 2005. Withdrawing from Gaza meant dismantling that complex machinery of occupation that had controlled the Strip ever since 1967, despite the installment of the PNA in 1994. The Israeli settlements, which had appeared in strategically important locations to split the Strip into three sections, had allowed the government in Tel Aviv to justify its military presence in order to defend the inhabitants of the settlements. But government support for the colonial enterprise in Gaza had not paid off the way it had in the West Bank. In Gaza, the settlements' populations had never reached significant numbers, but were limited to barely a few thousand people around whom a costly security machinery had been erected, one that included military outposts, soldiers, and no-man's lands. Within that machinery rested pleasant compounds with villas, flowerbeds, and swimming pools, all of these surrounded by a Palestinian population that was growing exponentially, reaching by 2008 an estimated 1.5 million, with all of them confined to refugee camps and overcrowded cities.

Over thirty years after the construction of the first Israeli settlement in Gaza, the settlers movement's greatest supporter, Ariel Sharon, decided that the price for Tel Aviv was too high both in financial terms and in moral and political ones. Gaza could not be controlled short of a systematic occupation, the price of which would be too high, not least of all in terms of human lives among the military. It would therefore be better to abandon it and to manage the problem of the Strip from the outside by means of a cordon sanitaire around its borders. Five years after the withdrawal from south Lebanon ordered by Ehud Barak, Sharon chose for Hamas in Gaza a strategy analogous to the one adopted against Hezbollah in the southern areas of the Land of Cedars: an attempt to control from a distance, rather than to become bogged down in an increasingly hostile territory, not least of all because this territory was increasingly dominated by Hamas. Despite strong opposition, particularly by the settlers' lobby, Sharon managed to convince both Israelis and the international community that the withdrawal was necessary. First and foremost among the international supporters was US President George W. Bush's administration, who viewed the Gaza withdrawal as the breaking of an impasse in a Palestinian-Israeli conflict that had lasted for far too long.

Neither Israeli public opinion nor the international community understood that Sharon's unilateralism would bring with it the bitter fruit of a crisis in Palestinian politics that was becoming increasingly difficult to control with the tools that had been used up until that point. Indeed, the Israeli withdrawal from the Strip had the effect of increasing support for Hamas. Hamas never gave up the possibility of armed resistance against Israel, and the withdrawal of Israeli soldiers was viewed by everyone as a victory of the Islamist movement's strategy of never giving up ground, as Fatah had, on the contrary, repeatedly been seen to do. Among Palestinians, many said and continue to say that resistance has paid off, while Fatah's and the PNA leadership's acquiescence toward Israel has only brought losses for the Palestinians: the Israelis had never stopped building settlements in the West Bank, and the separation wall is proceeding apace, swallowing up vast tracts of land.

The withdrawal from Gaza was over by early August 2005 without encountering too many problems, aside from the resistance of a few thousand die-hard settlers who did not want to leave the Strip. Neither the PNA nor Hamas placed obstacles in the path of the Israeli withdrawal. Hamas, however, immediately cashed in on its winnings, describing the withdrawal as the result of the successful strategy it had always adhered to: armed confrontation against occupying forces, and no concessions on the peace process. Resistance, the Islamist movement said, brought true results on the ground, and the withdrawal was a clear demonstration of this fact: Israel was abandoning Gaza, just as it had abandoned Southern Lebanon. Hamas was like Hezbollah, and it was celebrating this victory at precisely the time it was preparing to meet voters. Israel immediately understood that unilateral withdrawal from Gaza ran the risk of its most explosive effects being felt through the ballot box, and Sharon attempted in all sorts of ways to prevent Hamas from taking part in the elections. Indeed, bowing to pressure from abroad, particularly from Egypt, Abbas had already delayed opening the ballot boxes to voters by six months from July 2005—the eve of Israel's withdrawal—to January 2006.

Israel's pressure would last until the day before the elections themselves, echoing the same doubts expressed by Mahmoud Abbas's own entourage, particularly former Interior Minister Mohammed Dahlan, an ambitious leader himself about whom the media had run wild over recent years. On the one hand, Dahlan had been described as a Fatah leader accused of corruption and of running various monopolies in Gaza, including the crucial monopolies of cement and fuel. On the other hand, he was portrayed as a figure well received by the United States, by the UK, and by Tel Aviv. Indeed, according to the Israeli press itself, the Israeli government had even hoped that Dahlan might control Gaza after Sharon's withdrawal in August 2005. As Dahlan himself revealed to David Rose, the investigative journalist who published US plans to prompt a Palestinian civil war just after Hamas's electoral victory: "Everyone was against the elections"— everyone, that is, "except Bush," who "needed an election" in the Middle East.[23] No one within the administration would ever have expected Hamas's victory. Recalling the post-electoral atmosphere, a Department of Defense official told Rose: "Everyone blamed everyone else. . . . We sat there in the Pentagon and said, 'Who the fuck recommended this?'"[24]

Meanwhile, a few months earlier in Gaza, in September 2005, the Izz al-Din al-Qassam Brigades were celebrating the withdrawal as their own victory, distributing fliers with the typical iconography of the resistance—the pictures of its seven commanders—while Mohammed al-Deif, the leader of the Brigades, even gave a rare television interview, coming out of hiding in order to break his silence.[25] Israel realized, after its withdrawal, that its pullout was managed by Hamas as a full-fledged political victory, and that the cordon sanitaire set up around Gaza had not resolved Israel's security problems, first and foremost for those towns in the Negev that were being targeted by homemade rockets fired from the Strip (and in particular after September 23, when in an apparent accident during the celebrations for the withdrawal being held in the Jabalia refugee camp in Gaza the camp was devastated by the explosion of some of the rockets).

The Sharon government's response to this doubly negative result was once again entirely and solely military. After the withdrawal, Israel carried out an offensive that included a massive if limited intervention in Gaza using artillery and the air force, as well as a campaign of arrests that struck not Hamas's military wing, but its political wing in the West Bank—the one that had most pushed for the Islamist movement to participate in the general elections. About 250 Hamas supporters were arrested in September 2005, mostly activists, candidates in the forthcoming elections, professionals, and municipal council members throughout the West Bank from Bethlehem to Hebron, from Nablus to the heart of Ramallah. All those arrested were supporters of Palestinian Islamist movements, both Hamas and Islamic Jihad. This wave of arrests was part of a wider operation known by the code name "First Rain," which began after Hamas launched a clutch of Qassam rockets on Sderot and on the Negev. First Rain concentrated on Gaza, but also expanded into the West Bank. The tactic adopted appeared to focus on arresting many among the cadres of Islamist organizations, particularly targeting certain leaders considered to be crucial both to Hamas's political strategy and to the popularization of its ideas among the more disadvantaged sections of the population. Two names exemplify this pattern: Sheikh Hassan Youssef and Sheikh Ahmed Haj Ali. Freed barely a few months earlier after his latest sentence served in an Israeli jail, Hassan Youssef was considered one of the Hamas leaders best disposed toward its transformation into a political structure. Another such leader was Mohammed Ghazal, Hamas's leader in Nablus, and the very same leader who, in an historic press conference, stated that "the Charter is not the Qur'an," implying that the infamous reference to a call for the destruction of Israel could indeed be taken out of the Charter. Sheikh Ahmed Haj Ali, for his part, was a figure already very popular in Nablus and had himself spoken in favor of a Palestinian state within the 1967 borders.[26]

The postponement of the general elections to January 2006, the Israeli withdrawal from Gaza, and the Israeli army's iron fist in the West Bank—none of these events helped Fatah. Abu Mazen's party did not come out strengthened from these incidents because Fatah did not tackle the central issue: namely, the question of how well its cadres represented its support base. Tackling this question would have been possible only through Fatah's famous sixth congress, often announced since 1989 but not actually convened until August 2009. Instead, Fatah betrayed the depth of the split running through it by releasing two separate lists of candidates prior to the general elections. In competition with each other, these two lists reflected the fracture between the young guards gathered under the banner of *Al Mustaqbal*, or The Future, and the old militants who had experienced the Tunisian exile, known as the *Nomenklatura*. It was Marwan Barghouthi from his Israeli prison cell who in the end mediated between these two factions and managed to knit the fracture between his own followers. Qaddura Fares—one of the best-known leaders of the intermediate generation, who had the ear of Fatah's base and a long history of imprisonment in Israeli jails—would later call the unification of the two lists "the biggest mistake of my life."[27]

Hamas, for its part, used the delay in order to better prepare its electoral machinery, oiling the cogs of the new instrument it had taken up and preparing what would become its political manifesto: the electoral program of the Change and Reform list, the banner under which the Islamist movement ran. The preamble, the eighteen points, and the brief conclusions this program came to all revealed an important change. With the decision to take part in elections, Hamas had chosen to restrict its geographical ambitions and to become in a sense even more exclusively Palestinian than it already was.[28] The manifesto, however, remained Hamas's most important public document since the 1988 Charter, as the Islamist movement's leaders readily admit, especially those who agreed to participate in the first Hamas government explicitly based on that manifesto. For example, Nasser al-Din al-Sha'er—an independent and one of the best-known intellectuals in Nablus, later appointed to the post of executive deputy prime minister by Ismail Haniyeh—considered it to be the document "from which Hamas's political transformation begins."[29] The manifesto is light years away from the foundational Mithaq, written at the outset of the movement's life to mobilize the masses of the Intifada and motivate new activists. The electoral manifesto was in its every fiber a manifesto for a government; it was detailed, in depth, and not at all vague in defining social, educational, health, and youth policies. It was specific in calling for Shariía to be the "principal source"—and one should note well that it did not speak of Shariía as being the "absolute" source—of legislation in

Palestine, just as it was specific in stating that "Islam and its cultural results constitute our framework of reference and our way of life in all its political, economic, social, and legal aspects."[30] The military front remained in the background, as a simple reference to the need not to abandon the resistance. For the remainder of the text, the question of armed resistance was given no space at all, rendering the document therefore exclusively civilian, and implicitly delegating resistance to the military wing and to armed factions in general.

By the same token, however, the manifesto of the Change and Reform list included a range of terms from a political dictionary light years away from the one used in 1988, a semantic arsenal very close, in fact, to that of Western-style democracies. For example, the list attempted to "build an advanced Palestinian civil society that is based on political pluralism and the alternation of power," and called for a separation of judiciary, executive, and legislative powers in the Western European mold. Most importantly, in the section entitled "Public Liberties and Citizens' Rights," the manifesto talked of citizens "equal before the law" and of "citizens equal in rights and duties" for whom "security and protection for his or her life and properties" had to be provided. Toward the general public, therefore, a policy of "equal opportunities" had to be adopted, "reinforcing the culture of dialogue and respect for all opinions that do not contradict the people's faith or their civilisation heritage."[31] Within the general body of the citizenry, it was necessary to "guarantee women's rights and accomplish the legislative frameworks for supporting them and endeavor to enable women to contribute in social, economic and political development," as well as to "[highlight] the role of women in building the society," albeit within an Islamic framework.[32] In line with the choice of terms through which the list presented itself to voters—"change" and "reform"—Hamas indicated point by point what reforms were necessary and what change it envisaged both in terms of the Islamist movement itself and in terms of wider Palestinian society. From a certain point of view, it was from this document that, according to some experts, the new Hamas could be dated: a less revolutionary and more bureaucratic organization, a Hamas that would over the course of the following two years try—without success—to seek acceptance from the international community.

Hamas itself had already undergone the experience of administering those towns it had won control of at the ballot box during the 2005 municipal elections, an experience that it could cash in on in its relations with international actors. In the months during which Hamas led these municipalities, the common trait shared by all Islamist administrators was pragmatism. There were no ideological overtones, and aside from a few exceptions, no attempt to ride the wave of Islamization in the main cities. Indeed, according to International Crisis Group experts, through its "pragmatism, and even willingness to deal with Israel on day-to-day operational affairs, Hamas rule at the local level has been almost boringly similar to its predecessor. Local politicians emphasise themes of good governance, economic development, and personal and social security, leaving specifically religious issues and the conflict with Israel to the background."[33] Examples of such secret contacts between Israelis and representatives of the Islamist movement are many. One of the most indicative is the meeting between a Hamas administrator and an Israeli official that took place in the Jenin area in the first months of 2006: in a car, far from prying eyes, the officials discussed how to deal with a problem that went beyond ideological and physical barriers: namely, the threat of a bird-flu epidemic.

More than imposing, Hamas's mobilization around the Change and Reform list was capillary. It reached the cities, the refugee camps, and the villages, and it involved not only Gaza's entire social fabric, but—and this was where the real surprise came—also all of the West Bank, from Nablus to East Jerusalem, from Hebron to Bethlehem. The campaign machinery was set in motion from the very moment the candidates were selected. Candidates did not put themselves forward for inclusion on the electoral ticket, but rather were selected by each group and cell individually. Each selected member was then free to accept or reject the candidacy, although—as Hamas activists themselves say—refusal was not a positive gesture, as it "means that one does not wish to serve the people." The procedure of local candidate selection was one of the all-but-marginal reasons for Hamas's victory, because it was only those who were believed to be the best, the most dependable, and the most representative who were put forward for selection. Confirmation came not only from the decisions made by Hamas activists, but from the results obtained by the majority tickets, which were the most faithful reflections of local consensus. It was the electorate—which was certainly not made up purely of Islamist activists, but rather by a silent majority who were neither Hamas militants nor believers in its ideological infrastructure—that rewarded the choice of candidates based on their personal respectability, their credibility, and their honesty, as well as on what they had accomplished on the ground.

Political choices were then supported by a full-fledged campaign machine, coordinated and administered by those who had already gained some experience in such matters. One of the most important names in the campaign's preparation was Farhat As'ad, whose experience came from his university days. Between 1995 and 1996, for example, he had, as Hamas coordinator for all Palestinian universities, planned and managed elections to student councils. On the surface, such a choice might appear at best limiting, even amateurish. But as Farhat As'ad himself says with the benefit of knowing other factions from the inside—particularly the Fatah youth leadership—and with the benefit of having coordinated Second Intifada activities as well: "University elections had always been political."[34] He knew both the opposition and the rationales they would follow well, just as he knew young Palestinians, who—unlike their counterparts in the West—constituted the largest portion of the electorate.[35] The results were plain for all to see in the last rounds of municipal elections between September and December of 2005: Hamas won the West Bank urban centers, which were traditionally considered Fatah bastions, including the Christian-majority town of Bethlehem and the northern towns of Nablus and Jenin. Hamas also carried the important Ramallah suburb of Al-Bireh, as well as Rafah, Beit Lahiya, and Al-Burej inside the Gaza Strip. Moreover, Hamas benefited from an organizational structure that had long been put to the test in its role as a clandestine organization, and that spanned the entire Palestinian Territory, reaching into villages, refugee camps, and even individual homes.

This preparatory work quickly became apparent inside Hamas's strongholds, such as Hebron, a traditional constituency of the Muslim Brotherhood ever since the establishment of its earliest Palestinian branches. The final rallies held two days before the legislative elections of January 25 gave a sense of what Hamas had been able to achieve in its first electoral experience over the space of a few short months. Two brothers, Jibril and Nayef Rajoub, were the main contenders for support in the city. Jibril—a Fatah strongman linked to the PNA's security apparatus in the West Bank—addressed a crowd of at least 5,000 Fatah supporters in the large open area outside Hebron Polytechnic. Most of the listeners were young, many very young, with a few older figures among them. All of them, however, shared signs identifying them as Fatah supporters: the Palestinian flag, a scarf echoing the kaffiyeh, or perhaps one of the baseball caps that Fatah's electoral machine had distributed throughout town. There were very few women, however. All the others, numbering in the tens of thousands, were on the outskirts of town, attending Hamas's final electoral rally and listening to Sheikh Nayef Rajoub, Jibril's younger brother and one of the most prominent candidates on the Change and Reform list. Women—wives, mothers, and daughters, many with their children in tow or crammed into cars in which · entire families had taken refuge—were here en masse. Women from the villages of Hebron's vast hinterland, women from cities, women like Samira Halaika, who would later become one of Hamas's deputies. The vast majority were wearing a simple *hijab*; a few donned the *niqab*, which also covers the face. Many brandished Hamas's green flag and perhaps wore a Hamas cap. Women, in Hebron as elsewhere, have often been the key to Hamas's electoral success.

Chapter 6

ABUL ABED'S DOUBLE-BREASTED SUIT[1]

The Day that Shook the PNA

The momentous day of the elections came without the silent guest who had, over the past five years, affected Palestinian politics so deeply. Ariel Sharon had exited the Israeli political scene in mid-December, felled by a stroke, and vanished completely at the beginning of January 2006 when he entered the oblivion of an irreversible coma and thus a clinic for long-term patients in the Be'er Sheva area. Palestinians went to the polls while in Israel the post-Sharon transition was in full swing, guided by Ehud Olmert, one of his closest advisors, who not only had to take on the mantle of prime minister, but also guide the party Sharon had established—Kadima—through its troubled birth pangs. The Israeli weakness at the very time of the Palestinian elections made the shadow Israel cast over the elections appear less overbearing. But it was just an illusion, one that lasted barely the length of that sunny winter morning during which, across the West Bank, Gaza, and East Jerusalem, Palestinians celebrated democracy.

The head-to-head race continued throughout day, up to the last voter who crossed the threshold of one of the more than 1,000 polling stations that had been set up. Participation was extremely high, with a constant flow of voters from the early hours of the morning. Just short of a million Palestinians took part in the January 25 elections, 77 percent of those were eligible to vote. Eleven electoral tickets contested 66 seats elected under proportional representation, and a long list of 414 candidates vied for the other 66 seats appointed under a majority system. There were long, orderly lines outside the polling stations in the West Bank, in Gaza, and even in East Jerusalem, where in some areas Palestinians could cast their vote only in front of an Israeli employee at the local post office. There was a sense of duty bursting from every pore of the returning electoral workers, punctilious in the fulfillment of their offices. There was an understated joy in those who had voted and could demonstrate, with barely concealed pride, a finger marked with indelible ink, a sign that the ballot box contained their vote. There was the patience of those tens of thousands of people who got through the Israeli checkpoints dotted across the West Bank in order to reach their constituency, sometimes helped by international observers who arrived in the hundreds to witness the proper progress of the election. For Palestinians, January 25, 2006, was a long sequence of these snapshots, a day that for everyone emphasized an incredible sense of collective responsibility. In the memory of those who voted, the second general elections during the PNA's short history were considered an important event, one of the few moments in which everyone, without exception, felt like a citizen, an arbiter of their own destiny, above and beyond the conflict. Despite the presence of the Hamas-chosen Change and Reform ticket, no one had prevented the elections from taking place, neither the EU nor the United States. Israel had attempted to prevent or at least delay the vote in the West Bank, which it had completely occupied during the Second Intifada, but ultimately allowed the elections to take place.

Hamas had been accepted by the international community, both by the West and by Arab countries closest to the United States. The Quartet had itself given its go-ahead at a meeting on the sidelines to the General Assembly's session in the UN's glass building in New York a few months before the elections. The UN Special Envoy to the Middle East Alvaro de Soto later recalled how he agreed with then–UN General Secretary Kofi Annan, as well as his colleagues, among which were US Assistant Secretary of State David Welch, the EU's Marc Otte, and Alexander Kalugin of Russia. De Soto also recalled that "Abu Mazen's cooptation strategy was being endorsed" by inserting into the final part of the Quartet document a sentence that was not read in public. This sentence indicated that all parties should cooperate with what the Palestinians would decide, despite the fact that there was a fundamental contradiction between taking part in elections and controlling armed militias.[2] Alvaro de Soto recently explained that the Quartet didn't put any obstacles or constraints on Hamas's electoral participation. "The Quartet, which the Security Council turned to as the authoritative spearhead of ME diplomacy, in fact did the contrary: In its 20 September 2005 statement after meeting on the sidelines of the UN General Assembly, the Quartet in effect endorsed Abu Mazen's strategy of co-opting Hamas into the democratic field. Abu Mazen moved in that direction unhesitatingly less than two months after his election [as PNA president] by persuading Hamas, at an Egyptian-sponsored meeting in Cairo with the factions, a) to announce a *hudna* and b) to agree to participate in the elections (originally set for July, then unilaterally postponed by Abu Mazen until January 2006). Hamas' agreement to implicitly accept the Oslo framework (by competing for the PA elections which wouldn't have existed without Oslo) was seen as a positive development by the Quartet."[3]

Cold statistics then tell the story of the participation of the 832 international observers present at the January 25 elections in the Occupied Palestinian Territory, 184 of them from the European Union and 150 from the United States, as well as former US President Jimmy Carter, who had facilitated peace between Israel and Egypt; a former prime minister who was involved in international political interventions in Bosnia (Carl Bildt); former ambassadors; members of Western parliaments; and so on. All 832 observers said that the Palestinian elections of January 25, 2006, were so democratic as to be exemplary. No one had told the Palestinians that their right and duty to vote, their freedom to choose their own leadership would be conditional on its outcome. On the contrary, Hamas's presence was considered—particularly by the Europeans—to be a fundamental step toward the co-option of the Islamist movement within democratic institutions, with the publicly declared objective of facilitating a gradual moderation of Hamas's more radical positions. It was on these basic premises that on that fateful day Palestinians thought they were entirely free to choose as they saw fit, to vote according to conscience, to put a cross next to their favorite candidate freely and independently, as one does in a democracy. In short, they felt entirely in charge of their own destiny, without dictates imposed by the international community, in what were considered by international monitors the freest, most democratic, and fairest elections ever held in the history of the Middle East and of the Arab world. And on that day, defying all expectations, a majority of Palestinians voted for Hamas—defying all the experts, the pollsters, the journalists, and the observers, who up to the last moment refused to believe the result that came from the ballot boxes.

The following day, the counts began to tell a different story, very different from the one that had been imagined up to that point. The official result, published by the Central Election Commission and approved by hundreds of international observers from all over the world, said Hamas won seventy-four seats, while only forty-five deputies would sit in parliament to represent Fatah. Minor tickets shared the remaining thirteen seats. At its first showing in an election, Hamas obtained an astonishing result, winning 56 percent of the PLC seats. For Fatah, a phase of harsh recriminations began. Hamas faced an equally difficult phase: a movement that had always defined itself in terms of resistance and opposition now had to become a party of government.

As a matter of fact, Hamas's electoral earthquake took even its own leaders and activists by surprise. Just days before the elections, militants and cadres had shown great self-confidence. They were confident they could achieve a good result. Indeed, the projections that were being provided to journalists would have approached the actual outcome: a clear, decisive victory for the Islamist movement. But a more careful look reveals just how unexpected the result was for Hamas itself. None of its leaders have ever admitted this publicly, but privately they have confessed that they were the first to be surprised to find it was they who emerged victorious from the ballot. Ghazi Hamad, one of the most pragmatic leaders of Hamas, implicitly confirmed this in a letter he wrote outlining the reasons for his resignation from the post of spokesperson for the national unity government just after the June 2007 coup in Gaza. According to Hamad, during its period in government and in its political actions,

"Hamas got extremely confused and experienced a lot of surprises because of an absence of planning and an absence of readiness for the rapid changes that were taking place."[4] Rapid changes, Hamad adds, to which the movement responded with "traditionalism and lethargy," because "Hamas did not change its ideas, its mode of work, or its beliefs."[5] In a later reflection on these events, Hamad went further, explaining not only the emotional impact of the victory, but also the reasons that Hamas, at a certain point, felt paralyzed by its success: "With the 2005 watershed, we had decided to enter parliament; we hadn't decided to enter the PNA."[6] In other words, Hamas was neither interested in nor committed to entering government; they were purely interested in acting as "a strong opposition," to use Salah al-Bardawil's definition. "We envisaged two stages. During the first transitional step we should be a strong opposition and protect our national interests in parliament through the legislative work. At the same time, we planned to create a new environment, a new network with Arab and international interlocutors. Only in the second stage we contemplated the idea to move to government."[7] Hamad concluded: "This is why Hamas was confused. The time we had was too little for us to suddenly change our ideology, to balance ideology and politics, to be both resistance and authority."[8]

It is certainly true that the vote defied the pollsters, that reality overtook the wildest expectations, but this reality begs the question: why did the Palestinian electorate decide to vote en masse for Hamas, punishing Fatah so utterly?

The 2006 general election was neither simply nor even primarily a protest vote. Yet this was the way it was interpreted by Western governments and even by a considerable part of the media circus. Some, in good faith, thought that only a protest vote could lead a movement like Hamas to victory, a movement that would have led Palestinians to have to start all over again on a new and much more difficult path toward negotiation with the Israelis, going back to the drawing board with regard to the PNA and indeed the entire post-Oslo era. Others, with somewhat less good faith, used this explanation to feed Western politicians and public opinion-makers the most simplistic possible interpretation of the way in which Palestinians exercised their rights as voters. Following—or at least using—this logic, the political actors that would later administer the boycott and progressive ostracizing of the Hamas government that had emerged as a result of those elections on January 25 reached the harsh conclusion that it was the very objective of "exporting democracy" to the Arab world that needed to be reconsidered—not because one should not export democracy as a matter of principle, but because exported democracy had nearly always allowed Islamist movements to win.

What happened on January 25, 2006, was different, very different indeed, from this explanation. Palestinians in the West Bank and in Gaza came to the ballot box after having experimented with the use of their vote over the previous year. They were not, therefore, living a moment of collectively heightened emotions about seats, ballots, and indelible ink, because the vote was something they prized or because it was only a distant memory. They had elected Mahmoud Abbas exactly one year before; the decision that Abu Mazen should succeed Yasser Arafat was not made only by Fatah's or the PNA's clients. Within that clear majority that had designated Abbas as PNA president, there were also sectors of society linked to Hamas. There was, in other words, a very specific political reason Palestinians voted for Hamas. It was a reason that pertains to the decisions formally taken by the Islamist movement on January 23, 2005: the unilateral truce agreed to with the Islamic Jihad, despite the fact that the latter had broken it several times. Still, this truce put a de facto end to the period of terrorist attacks carried out by Hamas inside Israel's 1949 armistice borders.

The end of suicide bombings within Israeli cities, the substantive end of the Second Intifada, and Hamas's decision to participate in Palestinian electoral politics were all interpreted by the Palestinian population as a specific *political proposal*: an alternative to those who had ruled thus far. In and of itself, this proposal in practice placed new limits upon Hamas's strategy for resistance. The Islamist movement was not, therefore, chosen simply as a protest against the corruption, cronyism, and inefficiency of Fatah, a party that often blurred its boundaries with those of the PNA itself. This corruption coincided—from a chronological point of view, if nothing else—

with the failure of the peace plan traced in Oslo. It also coincided with the "facts on the ground" the Israelis had established to the detriment of the geographical and political continuity of any future Palestinian state, namely the continuous expansion of settlements and the colonial project underpinning them. Hamas's choice to take part in Palestinian electoral politics—a unilateral choice to which it strictly adhered—was made by the Palestinian population as a signal that a new phase was truly emerging from the ashes of the Second Intifada and from Arafat's death. In this phase, Hamas gained in political terms from its actions on the ground: armed confrontation with the Israelis and also care for the weakest in society.

Hamas leaders were regarded as honest people who had not enriched themselves at the expense of others, but who, on the contrary, kept living in normal parts of town and in the refugee camps. Ismail Haniyeh's case is exemplary in this sense: he lived in Gaza's al-Shati refugee camp, home to many among Hamas's middle generation, as well as, for a long time, to Sheikh Ahmed Yassin. Indeed, despite the fact that many Hamas leaders speak of the Mithaq with embarrassment, the Charter itself contains indications of some of the moral practices that have been followed by at least three generations of activists and leaders. Article 21 says, "It is a duty of all members of the Islamic Resistance Movement to share the people's happiness and grief, and they must consider it their duty to meet the demands of the people and to do what benefits them."[9] It was precisely this presence within society, bringing together administration of public life and participation in that life, that paradoxically mended that fracture between state and civil society that scholars have often pointed to in Palestinian politics. It was a fracture between institutions and social networks, between a power structure that, under Arafat, was managed in a paternalistic and authoritarian manner and a network of organizations that constituted an entirely parallel reality. It was Moussa Abu Marzouq who offered just such an interpretation in a surprising interview with the *Washington Post* barely a week after the electoral victory. Abu Marzouq defined the electoral result as "a grassroots alternative [that] grew out of the urgency of this situation."[10] The second-in-command of Hamas's politburo abroad therefore confirmed the theory of the "twin track" approach the organization took to the question of political participation in the West Bank and Gaza after the Oslo Accords took force. From the birth of the PNA until the January 2006 elections, there have been two ways of taking part in public life: one could take part within the PNA structure, and therefore from inside the power system established by Yasser Arafat, or one could take part within civil society. In Palestine, this meant a complex structure of NGOs, charities, trade unions, professional orders, women's rights associations, and local committees dotted across the land, any of which might be secular or religiously inspired organizations, progressive or conservative. Often these organizations emerged during the First Intifada, grew over the following two decades, and had flexible relations with the PNA itself. At certain stages, this dichotomy between civil society and PNA institutions coincided with the division between the Palestinian society left inside the West Bank and Gaza after the 1948 and 1967 wars and the elites who had returned from exile in Arafat's tow to take up the most important positions of power within the PNA.

Although Abu Marzouq himself belonged to those exiled elites, just like the majority of PLO members—particularly from Fatah— who arrived in the Occupied Palestinian Territory in 1994, he nonetheless understood one of the most important factors in explaining what happened on January 25, 2006. It was precisely that civil society—the tip of the iceberg of the silent Palestinian majority that had lived all the stages of Palestinian history after 1948 from the inside, from the West Bank and Gaza—that gave Hamas the chance to govern. Why? In his *Washington Post* article, Abu Marzouq argues that Hamas was seen as "a positive social force striving for the welfare of all Palestinians" because of "its legacy of social work and involvement in the needs of the Palestinian people." He also provides a sense of the deep ideological change afoot in Hamas when he describes the "heart of the mandate" for the deputies elected on the Change and Reform list as "alleviat[ing] the debilitating conditions of occupation, and not [the establishment of] an Islamic state."[11]

It was as though, through the January 2006 elections, Hamas had come full circle and returned to being the Muslim Brotherhood, shedding the fatigues of a revolutionary movement and once again replacing them with a double-breasted suit. Harkening back to social conditions on the ground, as Abu Marzouq did, was crucial because it recalled the Palestinian Ikhwan's politics, particularly that of the post-1967 period, when the Muslim Brotherhood under Sheikh Ahmed Yassin decided to focus on the shaping of "good Muslims," on the educational sector, and on networks of social organizations in order to consolidate the movement's roots. The heritage that Abu Marzouq recalls comes back to the fore while again emphasizing the dichotomy between the party-cum-state Fatah and its opposition. This opposition had chosen to grow and to seek representation within civil society organizations alone, to the point that in referring to secular groups and NGOs, some people even say that "civil society is the opposition."[12] In this definition, which at first sight might appear too simplistic, one finds the key to understanding the 2006 elections: this was not a protest vote, unless one thinks of it as a way of "grading" the PNA leadership and those parts of Fatah that did not find their raison d'être in their relationship with their base and with popular consensus.

Hamas vs. Fatah

An old family car proceeds slowly along the narrow road that winds around the perimeter wall of the Muqata'a, the presidential palace where Yasser Arafat rests and in which Abu Mazen resides. The car attempts to make its way through the jungle of cameras, microphones, and reporters from all over the world. The driver is not used to Ramallah, nor—in this case—is he used to the power centers of the PNA, the epitome of which is the Muqata'a itself, which still bears the scars of the Israeli siege of 2002 on its walls and in its large courtyard. The Muqata'a is the place where the Palestinian parliament was sworn in on February 18, inaugurating its second legislature. This is the parliament of Hamas's electoral revolution. The car's windows cannot conceal the disoriented looks on the passengers' faces—men only, in this case—crammed into the seats, with their beards neatly trimmed and dressed in their best suits for the occasion. The women follow soon after in other cars. These were the Islamist deputies who arrived, supremely punctual, at the presidential palace to take part in the PLC's inaugural first sitting. On their faces—a little lost, but not at all cowed—was the look of those who are about to enter a political game they are not used to, which is made of a particular code of conduct, of a certain care in one's presentation, and of the rules of protocol. Not to mention power. Hamas's new deputies were not used to the circus that is politics, just as they were not used to the assault of journalists who were waiting for them en masse outside the gates of the Muqata'a's back entrance. The journalists were there for them, because Hamas's representatives were the only novelty in an assembly that—on the basis of the composition and performance of its predecessor—would not have otherwise attracted much interest outside Ramallah. Newcomers to the parliamentary game, the new deputies betrayed the embarrassment that grips all those who are about to take such a step into the unknown; they betrayed as well what they call their spirit of service towards the Palestinian community. It might be difficult to comprehend for a Westerner, but in the eyes of the new deputies there was a deep respect for the responsibilities that come with the role of a parliamentarian.

Hamas deputies were new to this kind of life, but they were certainly not naïve. Parsing the list of those elected to the second Palestinian legislature in the West Bank reveals a kind of catalog of Islamist activism: technicians, businesspeople, university professors, teachers, preachers, ordinary citizens, and a small contingent of women. While most of these women had been elected primarily because of the "pink quotas," some were also symbols of that Islamist feminism that had taken root over the last few years across the Arab world, Palestine included. Many of these members of parliament had been Hamas militants ever since the establishment of the operational arm of the Palestinian Muslim Brotherhood. The elder statesman of the group is Abdel Fattah al-Dukhan, who had taken part in the founding meeting at Ahmed Yassin's house on December 9, 1987, and who is considered the author of the Charter. A dozen deputies had lived through the Marj al-Zuhour deportation episode, while others represent the younger generation who had entered politics during the first twelve years of the PNA's life. Many of them shared the short but vivid political experience of Al Khalas. In a Ramallah blessed with a brilliant sun and swept by the sharp wind of a Palestinian winter, the detachment of men and women elected on the Change and Reform ticket were the first to arrive. They had chosen to undergo the twists and turns of the dozens upon dozens of kilometers of hills around the West Bank in order to avoid the checkpoints, and they had reached the city the previous night. From Nablus, from Hebron, from Jenin, from Bethlehem, from all their constituencies, the distance is barely half an hour's car ride, an hour at the most. But the West Bank is dotted with hundreds of Israeli roadblocks that split the land, and the deputies had chosen to avoid unpleasant surprises. The rumor that would not go away was that the Israeli army had decided to block Hamas's parliamentarians, preventing them from arriving on time for the PLC's inaugural session and President Abbas's speech.

Those fears of a boycott by Ehud Olmert's government were all but unfounded: there were several absences that day in Ramallah. Of course, those held in Israeli prisons who had been elected to parliament were missing, a group that included such prominent names such as Fatah's Marwan Barghouthi and PFLP leader Ahmed Saadat (who was held in a Palestinian jail in Jericho, from which location an Israeli military raid captured him a month later). But not just the incarcerated were missing. Most visible among the absences were the Hamas deputies from Gaza, who the Israeli authorities had prevented from traveling to Ramallah. Gaza's Fatah deputies, on the other hand, had been allowed to travel. The Strip grew ever more distant from the West Bank, its only connection now a videoconferencing link between Ramallah and Gaza City, conditions that confined the Gazan part of the assembly to a pen isolated from the rest of the world. After the Israeli withdrawal in August 2005, the Strip was farther away, surrounded by a cordon sanitaire that closed it off not just along the two land borders it shares with Israel, but also on the southern border at Rafah. This last Gazan town before the Sinai is the gateway to Egypt, where the European Union's monitoring group led by Italian Carabinieri (EUBAM) was deployed following the international agreement sponsored in November 2005 by US

Secretary of State Condoleezza Rice. Those absences from Ramallah's Muqata'a, just like the videoconference that introduced the new members of the Palestinian legislature to each other, provided a clear signal of what was happening. They immediately made clear the geographical and political difficulties that an Assembly cleft apart would face during Mahmoud Abbas's presidency. President Abbas himself decided to skip formalities and go straight to the heart of the matter: Hamas's entry into the PNA. The president confirmed that the Islamist movement, which had won the elections, would be given the task of forming a government, with all that this entailed at the level of economic reform, of managing security organizations, and a range of other matters, including relations with Israel and with the international community. Despite the fact that negotiations over the formation of the new government were still going nowhere, Abu Mazen clearly stated his intention to safeguard these international links by living up to the commitments undertaken in the Road Map in order to protect the PNA from the increasing isolation of the Palestinians that Israel was attempting to bring about.

Israel's was a preemptive pressure, and one that from the outset relied on the economic and financial blockade of the Territory. This was considered the most effective weapon, and the one whose consequences were most immediate. The blockade had, for all intents and purposes, already begun in January with the failure to pass over to the PNA the tax revenues that, according to the Paris Protocol attached to the Oslo Accords, Israel was to collect on the Authority's behalf. Israel also prevented about 4,000 workers from entering the country from Gaza. Tel Aviv decided to freeze the roughly $50 million in monthly taxation payments, only to unfreeze them a few days later, in February, because Hamas was not yet in power. In doing this, the Israelis were following the practice of turning the tap of resources off and on at will, a practice already established during the Second Intifada. The message was clear: Israel was not willing to tolerate a government in which Hamas played a role, least of all the role of an executive.

But this was not all. Already in February rumors circulated about the new strategy taking shape in government circles both in Israel and the United States. The idea was simple and perfectly in line with the Bush administration's Middle East policy after the objective failure of its first phase, during which it attempted to export democracy to the Arab world. If the Arabs—in this case, the Palestinians—were unable to use the instruments of Western-style democracy to choose secular governments that were friendly to the West, if they would rather choose their representatives from the ranks of political Islam, then democratic practices must be channeled into directions more congenial to the wishes of Washington and its allies. This meant using methods such as regime change, despite the fact that this had consistently proven a failure during the second half of the twentieth century in the Middle East. As they had done with the overthrow of Saddam Hussein in Iraq, and as in the classic case of the CIA intervention against Mossadeq's liberal revolution in Iran in the 1950s, the United States decided that Hamas also had to be overthrown, regardless of the fact that it had obtained a mandate from a majority of Palestinians in elections that the very same George W. Bush above all others had demanded, and regardless of the fact that Hamas had received consensus without coercion, as international observers had witnessed. This consensus should have told Americans and Israelis a long story about the flawed politics of the first twelve years of PNA government, about the way in which humanitarian aid had been handled, and not least of all about the mistakes made at the very outset of the peace process outlined at Oslo.

The strategy of strangling Hamas, of boycotting the PNA while it attempted to find a way to share power between secularists and Islamists, however, did not meet with the slightest hesitation. Already in February, before any government had time to emerge from the new balance of Palestinian political power, the *New York Times* revealed decisions being made in Washington's back rooms. According to the most prestigious American newspaper, the United States and Israel were considering "destabilizing" the future Hamas government by strangling the PNA economically. The strategy was simple: no money to the Palestinians, in order to force President Mahmoud Abbas to call new elections and bring about a Fatah victory. Were it just a throwaway suggestion, it would not have been a scoop. But according to Steven Erlanger, author of the article, the highest echelons of the US State Department and of the Israeli government were debating the strategy. Confirmation was indirect. A few hours after the article's publication, Israeli Defense Minister Shaul Mofaz, speaking after a meeting with Hosni Mubarak, placed Hamas-led Palestine squarely within the Axis of Evil, alongside Iran, Syria, and Hezbollah, in that order. In the meantime, Israeli Supreme Court Vice-President Michael Cheshin stated that the PNA was by now a "de facto enemy state."[13] Tel Aviv, in short, proceeded with the strategy Ehud Olmert had indicated the day after the Palestinian elections, the strategy explained to the international community by Foreign Minister Tzipi Livni on her international tour, which began in Cairo and concluded in Washington on the eve of the first sitting of the Palestinian parliament.

The *New York Times* scoop would be only the first in a long list of leaks throughout 2006. Soon, full-blown scenarios elaborated by the various actors in this play emerged. It was primarily US diplomacy and its military who on several occasions indicated that they feared the failure of Washington's involvement in Palestinian internal affairs. According to these plans, from the outset the key to Hamas's fall was Fatah. Fatah, in its role as party-cum-state, should be the political group that replaces Hamas. To do this, the idea that Hamas had won the elections had to be undermined. Ever since the day after the January 25 elections, one can find two interpretations of the election's results. The first, and the most direct, is that Hamas won the elections by a clear margin. The competing explanation was that Hamas received a greater number of votes only because its secular counterpart Fatah had reached the ballot divided, and that it had been damaged by the mixed electoral system—a system that, incidentally, Hamas had played no part in choosing. This second interpretation was based on one indisputable fact: namely, that Fatah had been fragmented up until the last days before the election, just as it had been over the course of the past few years under Arafat. Fatah was split between the cadres that had come to the fore during the First Intifada on the one hand and the old "Tunisians" on the other, between the youths of the Second Intifada and the corrupt bureau-

crats in Ramallah, between the base exposed to the winds of change
sweeping through Palestine and the stultified establishment. This
split could not be resolved save through the technicalities of electoral
law or the composition of individual lists of candidates; it was so
deep that it could be dealt with only through the cleansing of a general congress. Fatah, however, had been unable to organize its sixth
congress in seventeen years, not least of all because of an inextricable
mire of reciprocal vetos.

Thus Fatah had lost. It had clearly lost both the electoral test and
the test of internal reform. Yet none of its leaders really admitted
defeat. On the one hand, this was because such an admission would
have meant driving the crisis even deeper. On the other, this was also
because the international community had always accepted the more
benevolent and technical explanation of the January 25 result, even
pushing Fatah itself to support such an interpretation. In political
practice, the implication of such a revisionist position was that from
the very beginning Fatah never seriously sought a compromise with
Hamas in order to overcome the aftershocks of the Islamists' success,
and instead the party allowed itself to be seduced by the (international) sirens who predicted the fall of Hamas as soon as it had been
"tainted" by power. At the same time, the Islamist movement was
faced with the task of reconstructing its strategy within the PNA
entirely from scratch, no longer from a position of parliamentary
opposition, but as a party of government. In its report on the Palestinian situation in mid-2006, the International Crisis Group stated
that "Fatah, unable to fully accept its electoral loss, has continued to
act as if it remains in power, treating the new government as usurp-
ers, temporarily in possession of positions and institutions that are
rightfully its own," while Hamas, "unprepared for its parliamentary
triumph and even less to govern alone, has behaved as if it were still
in opposition, relying on political posturing and denunciations of
subversive plots as substitutes for hard decision-making."[14]

The struggle between Hamas and the West, as much as between
Hamas and Fatah, began immediately, and was played out on several
different fronts. Two of these were decisive for the way in which one
of the most difficult—and most controversial—chapters in recent

Palestinian history would play out between 2006 and 2007. The first site of conflict was the international funding the PNA received and the economic blockade that would soon be in place. The second site, and one that was only superficially internal to Palestinian politics, was the administration of security and the use of force within the West Bank and Gaza. In parallel, confrontation with Hamas took place in the media, centering on the question of the Islamist movement's recognition of Israel, since the 1988 Mithaq had never been formally modified.

However, it was on the question of funding that immediate pressure concentrated. The Quartet was a multilateral consultation group on the Middle East established in 2002 during one of the most violent phases of the Palestinian-Israeli conflict in order to breathe new life into the "two-state solution" through the US-devised Road Map, a peace process to which the PNA and Israel had to adhere in order to reach their objectives. Within the Quartet, the United States had the dominant role, leaving Russia, the EU, and the UN with much ambiguity over their roles and very little room to maneuver. This was especially true of the UN, which over the course of the following two years would see the more or less controversial resignations of its various Middle East envoys. It was the United States in particular that pushed for the Quartet to use the instrument of international funding in order to demand that the PNA adhere to its existing agreements, even if Hamas were to lead the new government, while knowing full well that the Authority's very existence depended on the considerable help forthcoming from abroad. After the disaster of the Second Intifada and the ensuing military reoccupation of the West Bank, the unilateral withdrawal from Gaza, and the increasing isolation of the Strip, and not least of all the twelve years that spanned the PNA's existence and that were marked by a corrupt and cronyistic administration of public life, it was not surprising that the Palestinian economy was in a miserable state. A deficit of at least $700 million was growing at a seemingly unstoppable rate, a result in large part of Israel's failure to pass on the tax revenues it had collected. It was precisely on this point that Israel applied pressure, initiated by the interim Prime Minister Ehud Olmert, who delayed the payment of the funds due to the PNA. This measure provoked harsh reactions from both the PNA and from UN Middle East Envoy Alvaro de Soto; these reactions, however, never resulted in consequences.

At the same time, the Quartet began to move. Already on January 30, after having "congratulated the Palestinian people on an electoral process that was free, fair and secure,"[15] the Quartet approved a document that established three conditions that any future government was expected to meet. With a formulation that was neither an ultimatum nor a threat of sanction—at least not formally—the Quartet was firm in the demands it made of its interlocutor. The document said that the Palestinian people had the "right to expect that a new Government will address their aspirations for peace and Statehood" and welcomed "President Abbas' affirmation that the PNA is committed to the Road Map, previous agreements and obligations between the parties, and a negotiated two-state solution." However, the Quartet changed its language when it imposed the condition that "all members of a future Palestinian Government must be committed to nonviolence, recognition of Israel, and acceptance of previous agreements and obligations, including the *road map.*" Then, the corollary: "It was inevitable that future assistance to any new government would be reviewed by donors against that Government's commitment" to the three conditions. For the PNA, that word, "assistance," meant everything. It meant the enormous amount of funding that the United States—but more especially the EU—provided to the PNA, a body that often ended up acting merely as a kind of accountant, handing out aid, as the Palestinian economy was unable to stand on its own two feet and was forced to rely on international assistance. In this way, the international community demonstrated how completely unprepared it was to elaborate a more sophisticated and less superficial strategy after the developments that in the space of barely five months had radically changed the political landscape of the Middle East, with Israel's withdrawal from Gaza, the sudden departure of Ariel Sharon from the political scene, and finally Hamas's unexpected victory. Alvaro de Soto, who participated in the meetings, confirmed that the Quartet's line had been decided by the United States, whose representatives, Elliot Abrams and David Welch, went so far as to imply that had the UN not acquiesced, US funding to the UN itself might have be threatened.[16]

The $50 million in monthly revenue that Israel had decided to freeze toward the end of February represented a considerable portion of the Palestinian budget, which passed on to the new prime minister a continuously rising deficit of around $700 million. The tax revenues amounted to about a third of total income and were used mainly to pay the salaries of the 140,000 PNA employees—including the 58,000 on the payroll of various security bodies—which accounted for the income of around one-fifth of the population. Israeli, and later international, pressure had a specific target, even before a Hamas government had been formed: the petit bourgeoisie linked to the PNA, who were thought to be the true weak link and the pivotal element of popular discontent. By linking aid to compliance with the three conditions indicated in the January 30 declaration, the Quartet immediately traced a line Palestinians could not cross. In the following two years, the Quartet as a group never distanced itself from this stand and avoided any possibility of opening a channel with Hamas.[17]

The Quartet and Israel's actions confined acceptable politics in Ramallah and Gaza City to clearly defined and nonnegotiable borders, a confinement that immediately influenced the negotiations between parties concerning the establishment of a new government. These restrictions would also affect the actions of Abu Mazen's presidency, which from that moment forward moved along two different paths. On the one hand, there was the problematic relationship with Hamas, which would receive several ultimatums from Abbas until the June 2007 takeover by the Islamist movement in Gaza. On the other hand, Abbas continued a distinct policy aimed at strengthening the presidency so as to make it a center of power. The presidency might provide an alternative to those parts of the PA that would be run by Hamas after the result of the elections, particularly as far as relations with the West were concerned. This twin-track policy had at its core the management of security bodies, and began precisely on January 28, the moment the official results were declared. Immediately, Mahmoud Abbas ordered the main armed groups—the preventive security, police, and intelligence services—to report to him and not to the prime minister or the minister of the interior. This deprived Hamas of one of the pillars of executive power. But this was only the first change in the running of Palestinian security organizations, changes that paradoxically moved Abu Mazen toward the positions held by Arafat, particularly in 2003. At that time, Arafat had not wanted to relinquish control of security organizations to the government, then chaired by Abbas. Abbas had handed in his resignation precisely after losing the battle for control of these armed groups. The problem was real: the Second Intifada had caused the proliferation of the Palestinian security forces, and the fragmentation of the West Bank carried out by the Israeli army had accelerated the decentralization of these apparatuses, which young local warlords were beginning to take control of and which were concentrated primarily in the northern areas, in Nablus and Jenin above all.

The message conveyed by the international community was clear: there was only one person with whom it wished to speak—Abu Mazen. It was not prepared to entertain relations with Hamas, whose power had to be diminished to the point that it would become insignificant. But it was precisely this agreement to exclude Hamas that diminished Mahmoud Abbas's role in Palestine and, more importantly, created increasingly serious problems within Palestinian society as time went by. The fact that Mahmoud Abbas was so clearly and extensively supported by the West weakened him among the Palestinians who had democratically invested Hamas with executive power within the PNA. With the obvious exclusion of Abbas's clients, those security bodies linked to Fatah, and the presidential office, Palestinians increasingly perceived Abbas as being supine to the will of an international community that refused to recognize the legitimately elected government—unless that government was willing to accept the conditions imposed by the Quartet.

Yet Abbas accepted this role, and in this spirit he kept the security organizations linked to the presidency on a short leash, a tactic encouraged not least of all by the advisors close to him. First and foremost among these advisors was Mohammed Dahlan, viewed with increasing ill favor by Hamas just as he was held in increasingly high regard in certain Western circles. Before conferring Hamas with an exploratory mandate to form the new executive office, Abbas attempted on February 20 to further concentrate the exclusive control of the use of force in the presidency by reshuffling the upper echelons of the security establishment, a move with serious implications for relations between Hamas and Fatah. A few hours before meeting Ismail Haniyeh, the man Hamas had indicated as a possible prime minister, Abbas increased the powers of the new person in charge of preventive security, a man whose field of action had ever since mid-2005 included not just Gaza but also the West Bank: Rashid Abu Shbak. Abu Shbak was Fatah's strongman in the Strip, but more importantly, he was the right-hand man of one of those closest to Abbas, namely Dahlan, who in this way could control internal security from a distance. Thus, consultations for the birth of the Hamas government were undertaken in an atmosphere of mutual suspicion, with trenches already dug, thereby sinking the idea Hamas had been cultivating before it even had a chance: building a coalition that might be as wide as possible, and that would have included Fatah.[18]

Swords into Government

Every now and then, there are episodes in a person's life that look a lot like history turning the tables. Ismail Haniyeh was thirty-four years old and was known to few in Gaza outside Hamas circles when he put himself forward as an independent in the 1996 elections for the PLC. That candidacy was withdrawn after only a few days, but perhaps it was this provocation that won him the often-sought role of bridge between the Islamist movement and the PNA. This role was not as important as the one that Ismail Abu Shanab had taken on over the course of those same years, but Haniyeh's relations with Fatah members were certainly good, and his job of maintaining contacts between the PNA and the office of Sheikh Ahmed Yassin had helped that particular facet of Hamas's overall strategy. This strategy was not to seek out confrontation with the *sulta*. Rather, Hamas kept channels open through which much took place, including, at times, full-fledged collaboration on issues that concerned the immediate needs of the Palestinian people. Exactly ten years after his provocative candidacy, Ismail Haniyeh became the symbol—albeit perhaps more for the Western media than for Islamist militants—of what Hamas might become. Hamas in a suit: a movement that might even overcome international ostracism and, with a little effort, come to be accepted.

Abul Abed, as everyone calls Haniyeh in Gaza, has built a good name for himself. His reputation starts with his home in al-Shati refugee camp, where his family arrived in 1948 after fleeing from the village of al-Joura, near Ashkelon. The camp was also home to Sheikh Yassin, and Haniyeh served as his assistant from 1997 to Yassin's assassination in 2004. Ismail Haniyeh had lived in al-Shati—the "beach camp," as its name indicates—ever since 1962. "I was born here, I was raised here, I walked the streets here. I must stay with my people," he told a journalist with the Associated Press[19] to explain why he continued to live in a two-story building in the seaside camp with his family, his wife, his thirteen children, his brother, his cousins, his uncle, and other relatives all around him. Ashkelon, barely fifteen kilometers away, is just visible in the distance from al-Shati. The family lived on a meager UNRWA monthly contribution. And even after Mahmoud Abbas declared him a potential prime minister and charged him with the effort of forming a new government nearly a month after the elections, Haniyeh remained in al-Shati: the work desk of Abul Abed could be found in the bedroom of this large but unadorned house with a side table, Haniyeh's computer, and a television nearby. While he worked, the prime minister-to-be personally supplied the adjacent houses with electricity from his generator.

By betting on Haniyeh, therefore, Hamas chose a leader who was an appropriate choice both politically and symbolically. Haniyeh's was a rather new face, and one unknown to Western audiences, despite Haniyeh's work in Yassin's office. But most of all he was a figure who had yet to draw upon himself the extremely harsh attacks that the Israelis had launched upon Khaled Meshaal or Mahmoud al-Zahhar in Gaza. Ismail Haniyeh was the most expendable name in Hamas's Gazan leadership, which, after the killing of Yassin and

Rantisi, was said to consist of a triad that comprised al-Zahhar, Said Siyyam, and Haniyeh. Despite being considered Hamas's moderate face, Abul Abed still sported a curriculum typical of a Hamas activist of his generation. He entered the Muslim Brotherhood during the course of his studies in the Department of Arabic at the Islamic University in Gaza, headed the Islamist student bloc during the mid-1980s, and later took part in the First Intifada, spending six months in an Israeli jail in 1988, only to be arrested again the following year and sentenced to three years in jail. Haniyeh was also part of the Marj al-Zuhour community in 1992, and worked after his return closely with Yassin. He even was with Hamas's spiritual leader during the first attempt on the sheikh's life on September 6, 2003.

The original idea—at least according to the version of events provided by Hamas's leadership in exile—was not to establish a government composed solely of Hamas members. On the contrary, the first effort went toward building a coalition government, in the hope of allowing the Islamist movement a gradual entry into the halls of power. The first to be surprised by the margin of the January victory, in fact, was Hamas itself. The Islamist movement had been prepared to enter parliament and to take on the mantle of a constructive opposition to the established power of Fatah within the PNA. Hamas was ready to set out on the road toward reforming the PNA and the PLO—starting with the PLC—from the inside by passing new laws and by taking increasingly effective control over the *sulta*'s administrative actions. It had studied this role as a constructive opposition so carefully, in fact, that it had described it in great detail on the Change and Reform ticket's electoral manifesto. Yet while reform and change were to be implemented from within parliament, Hamas certainly had no intention of implementing them from within the PNA's executive branch. And yet Hamas's preelection plans became meaningless the day after the voting, when the Islamist movement found itself in power, with the enthusiasm of a solid majority of Palestinians in the streets behind them, yet with no experience at all in the administration of the *sulta*. As Ghazi Hamad explains, using an apt comparison: "After the victory in 2006, we had no other choice but to form a government. It was a bit like changing tires on a racing car mid-race."[20]

Within the leadership, the first reaction was to push for a coalition government. Two or three days after the January electoral victory, Hamas strongly put forward the idea of such a national unity government, trying to find some way to compromise with Fatah's political program in order to obtain its administrative support. Khaled Meshaal himself spoke personally of this possibility with Mahmoud Abbas, offering him a "president's government." Abu Mazen did not discard the offer and even called it "a good idea, one which we should work on."[21] The Hamas leadership interpreted this response as Abbas simply wishing to procrastinate to the point of making the Hamas attempt fail, at which point Abu Mazen himself could appear to be the only person capable of rescuing both Palestinians and Hamas. Confirmation of this interpretation comes from Alvaro de Soto, whose confidential end of mission report was handed in a year later, in May 2007, along with his resignation. The report was an impassioned, extremely harsh indictment that brushed nothing under the carpet and that painted a frustrating picture of what the international community had consciously done in order to prevent any reconciliation between Fatah and Hamas, and through this avoid any possibility of Hamas being able to soften its political stance. Coincidentally, de Soto's entire memo would be sent to the *Guardian* in mid-June, just as the last battle for control of the Strip was raging. De Soto, a UN official with much experience—"twenty-five years plus a few days in the United Nations," as he writes "in his End of Mission Report" with more than a little irritation—lived through the entire behind-the-scenes history of the post-Arafat period, from June 2005 until the eve of the Hamas takeover in Gaza two years later. According to de Soto, "a National Unity Government with a compromise platform along the lines of [the] Mecca [Agreement of February 2007] might have been achieved soon after the election, in February or March of 2006, had the US not led the Quartet to set impossible demands, and opposed a NUG [national unity government] in principle."[22] More than that, the UN official recalls that "at the time, and indeed until the Mecca Agreement a year later, the US clearly pushed for a confrontation between Fatah and Hamas."[23]

Hamas, however, did not give up. Consultations continued, both before and after the official mandate had been given to Ismail Haniyeh. Several names had been put forward for the prime minister post over the course of the weeks before Haniyeh himself would be formally named for the position. Among the other candidates were businessmen from Gaza and from the West Bank—Jamal al-Khoudari and Mazen Sinokrot, for example—who were well known for their good relations with the international community. Hamas, however, concentrated on the most political name it could find, and although Haniyeh was a moderate choice, Hamas failed to convince other Palestinian political parties to support him.

Many explanations were put forward for this failure. Khaled Hroub, for example, one of the most respected experts on Hamas, ascribed the lack of agreement on a political program for the Hamas-backed government to two factors: "Hamas's failure to acknowledge the PLO as the sole legitimate representative of the Palestinian people and its refusal to subscribe to the UN resolutions on Palestine and Israeli-PLO agreements."[24] Others, such as Ziad Abu Amr, later foreign minister of the 2007 national unity government and one of the most important scholars on Palestinian political Islam, attributed the failure to Hamas's inability to be flexible in giving away certain posts. In Abu Amr's words, "when [Hamas] talks about powersharing, it means something that won't take away its decision-making power. . . . [Hamas] could have compromised far more easily now with its big majority [in parliament]."[25] One fact remains interesting regardless: the program for the national unity government that Hamas presented to the other parties in the new parliament (as well as to Islamic Jihad) contained none of the anti-Zionist and anti-Israeli rhetoric of the 1988 Charter, in an obvious attempt to open a channel with the international community, especially through Articles 9 and 10 (out of the full thirty-nine), both of which dealt with the question of respect for UN resolutions and agreements with Israel. Furthermore, other parts of the document referred to Palestine exclusively as the territory within the Green Line, although the document retained enough ambiguity to maintain the support of the militants and to avoid caving in completely before the Quartet's demands.[26]

As for the rest, the government's objectives were the same as those in the electoral manifesto: fighting corruption, defending weaker parts of society, great importance given to welfare, and an obvious attempt to reassure its secular counterparts in Palestinian society. Specifically in Article 6, the government undertakes to "build a society and institutions on democratic foundations that guarantee justice, equal participation, and political pluralism; stress the rule of law with complete separation between powers where the independence of the judiciary should be guaranteed and human rights and basic liberties protected."[27] However, all this was not enough to convince the other parties, not even the Left represented by the PFLP, which had earlier been more willing than other groups to enter into a government with Hamas, a move unthinkable a few years before.

The idea of a coalition having failed, the Islamist movement had to resign itself to forming a government of its own. As the Hamas leadership recalls, even the circles closest to Abu Mazen believed that Ismail Haniyeh would meet with Abbas merely to inform him of Hamas's failure to form a coalition executive branch. But Abbas himself was surprised when Haniyeh instead delivered a forty-minute speech, one that ended not with his letter of resignation, but with a list of the twenty-four ministers in his single-party government. The list included leaders of the Islamist movement, deputies elected on the Change and Reform list, and independents considered close to Hamas.

It was what some called a government of experts. The team included university professors, professionals with doctorates from Western—often American—universities, as well as specialists, technical experts, intellectuals, and lawyers. The minister of finance post was given to Omar Abdel Razeq, holder of a doctorate in international economics and mathematical economics from the University of Iowa and a professor of economics at Al-Najah University in Nablus. The well-credentialed Abdel Razeq was the archetypal Hamas government minister. At nearly fifty, he is from the same generation as Haniyeh, the new Interior Minister Said Siyyam, and many other colleagues, and shared the respectable academic track record common among many of the new cabinet members. Health Minister Bassam Na'im, a doctor at the large Shifa Hospital in Gaza City, had a degree from a German university as well as a doctorate. Samir Abu Eisheh, minister for planning, was a professor of engineering at Al-Najah University. Another seven ministers were also engineers: Jamal al-Khodari, charged with communications and new technologies; Ala al-Din al-Araj, the businessman appointed to the treasury; Joudeh George Murkos—the only Christian in the team—who became minister for tourism; as well as Minister for Public Works Abdel Rahman Zeidan; Transport Minister Ziad al-Thatah; Chief of Staff Mohammed Awad, deputy director of the Islamic University; and Khaled Abu Arafeh, a businessman. The list continued with Minister for Information Youssef Rizka, who had a doctorate in Arabic and was a literary critic; Maryam Saleh, minister for women's affairs, with a PhD in Shariía jurisprudence; Justice Minister Ahmed Khaldi, considered one of the top experts in legal disciplines, as confirmed by his position as head of the committee charged with drawing up a Palestinian constitution and his position as dean of Al-Najah University School of Law; Minister for Agriculture Mohammed al-Agha, who earned a doctorate in environmental studies and hydrology from Manchester University and who was a visiting professor at the University of Virginia in the United States, as well as in Manchester and in Bremen, Germany. There were also those who referred to themselves as independent, such as Nasser al-Din al-Sha'er. Two and a half years later, in the autumn of 2008, al-Sha'er would call his presence in the government "a service rendered to our people." The very same phrase is used by another West Bank minister, Labor Minister Mohammed Barghouthi, who adds that he would have felt "more at ease in the national unity government" formed in March 2007, given his position as an independent.[28] Al-Sha'er, one of the best-known intellectuals in Nablus, has a doctorate in comparative religion from the University of Manchester and was for years the dean of the School of Law and Islamic Studies at Al-Najah University. He has always described himself as a moderate Islamist along the same lines as Turkey's Recep Tayyip Erdogan, and he has challenged the fact that many experts, scholars, and journalists identified him as Hamas's point man in the West Bank—part of a *Nomenklatura* that remains secret—based on the fact that he became deputy prime minister in Haniyeh's first government. He maintains that he had been forced to take on that role because Israel had restricted the freedom of movement of the Palestinian leadership in Gaza, effectively halving the real control the prime minister had over his government. In his words: "Something had to be done."[29]

The government Hamas had to form single-handedly thus located itself squarely in the tradition of Hassan al-Banna's Muslim Brotherhood, which had always drawn its activists and future leaders from the liberal professions. The striking number of scholars, professors, and those who held more than one degree in Haniyeh's government, however, did not succeed in appealing to the international community, much less to the Israelis. Degrees, doctorates, and academic titles did not help Hamas much in the arduous task of gaining acceptance for a government without allies, particularly without Fatah. The professors—Haniyeh first and foremost among them—had donned double-breasted suits, but they made no concessions to Israel; indeed, they still refused to recognize it formally, and they continued to reject the conditions that the Quartet had set. A readiness to dialogue combined with inflexibility on fundamental questions—this is how the story of Hamas's leadership of the PNA unfolded. Ultimately, Hamas did not want preconditions because it was those preconditions—at least according to the interpretation the Islamist movement had always given of the Oslo process and of Arafat's conduct—that had from the very beginning precluded any possibility of real negotiations: there were too many concessions on the Palestinian side, with nothing but delays to show for them. At the same time, Hamas did not want to spook the West, and above all the Islamist movement wished to avoid a situation in which Western governments would rally around Israel in its refusal to negotiate with Hamas.

In order to break the negative image and increasing isolation that had come to characterize Hamas over the course of the last twelve years, ever since the suicide bombings began inside Israeli cities, the Islamist movement undertook a media offensive aimed at showing the world a different face of the movement. No longer would the name "Hamas" signify attacks on Tel Aviv buses or Jerusalem cafés; instead it would signify a movement that had committed itself to the parliamentary route to trace a possible path to peace, albeit one that followed a different path than Oslo's. The task of painting a new political picture of the Palestinian Islamist movement was left to those leaders who had greater access to Western media. This is what Khaled Meshaal and Moussa Abu Marzouq, the two highest-ranking members of the movement's leadership abroad, did through two interviews published simultaneously on January 31 in the *Guardian* and in the *Washington Post*. There were significant differences between the interviews: Meshaal was more concerned with reassuring the millions of refugees who had fled in 1948, while Abu Marzouq sought an opening among American liberals when he asked the United States to "abandon its position of isolation and join the rest of the world in calling for an end to the occupation, assuring the Palestinians their right to self-determination."[30]

Having said this, it was not so much the Damascus leadership but rather the Hamas leaders inside the Occupied Palestinian Territory, and the pragmatists in particular, who formulated the clearest description of the "New Hamas" as it related to Israel, to the West Bank and Gaza, and to Palestine as a whole. It was Ismail Haniyeh, the moderate leader within the Strip, who delivered the message (before he even became prime minister), this time not from the generalist platform of a large broadsheet, but to the experts of the International Crisis Group—the European think tank that between 2004 and 2011 published the most in-depth and reliable analysis on the Palestinian situation. According to Haniyeh, "The real problem is that we are not a state but the government of an authority existing in territory that does not meet the criteria of a state. I say clearly that if Israel wants to end this situation it must agree to a fully sovereign Palestinian state. If this does not happen the conflict will continue." Abul Abed went further, reaching the crux of the matter:

> The solution is a sovereign Palestinian state encompassing the West Bank and Gaza Strip, with its capital in East Jerusalem. This does not obligate me to recognize Israel. The real-

ity is that Israel exists and is a state recognized by many, and I have to deal with this. There is no law compelling me to recognize it; the subject of recognition is not on the agenda. The solution is in the hands of the Israelis. We demand that it announce its commitment to a Palestinian state with its capital in Jerusalem, and clearly announce and fully respect a schedule for implementing this. We are under no obligation to offer initiatives and we do not provide political positions free of charge.[31]

"We expected some difficulties, but we didn't expect a boycott of that magnitude against the Hamas government. We foresaw that the international community would impose some conditions on us, but we didn't think that it would impose a yes-no alternative," Salah al-Bardawil recalls.[32]

Consequently, Hamas was playing a game on a razor's edge, a game in which the Islamist movement pulled on a rope without thinking that it might break at any moment, a game in which flexibility could all too easily be mistaken for a breach in Hamas's defenses, one that the opposition might exploit. This was a game that also clashed with Tel Aviv's absolute inflexibility in the run-up to the Israeli elections scheduled for March 28. If Hamas continued to call for the liberation of the Occupied Palestinian Territory—albeit signaling several times that it meant the land within the 1949 borders—then most Israeli politicians continued to regard an agreement with the PNA as impossible.

During one of the most delicate periods of the Israeli-Palestinian conflict, Hamas's single-party government, guided by one of Sheikh Ahmed Yassin's advisors, was formally installed on March 29, the day after the Israeli elections that confirmed the victory of Kadima, the centrist party established by Sharon. Additionally, the racist right made major inroads in the Israeli elections, as epitomized by Avigdor Lieberman's Yisrael Beitenu, a movement supported primarily by immigrants from the former USSR. After Kadima's (partial) success, would-be Prime Minister Ehud Olmert restated his promise: if it was not possible to reach an agreement with the Palestinians on peace,

Israel would continue its unilateral policy of "disengagement" from certain areas of the West Bank. The United States under George W. Bush followed Israel's script, and from 6:00 p.m. on March 29—at the very moment Ismail Haniyeh's ministers were sworn in—the Bush administration forbade US representatives from having any contact with the Hamas government. An uncompromising confrontation became inevitable, one that took the form of a progressive and near-complete economic blockade of the PNA—a blockade whose consequences Gaza would suffer above all others.

Indeed, even before the Hamas government had been approved by the parliament, the Strip's economic isolation was already a reality. On March 11, 2006, Israel closed the Erez crossing completely to Gazan laborers. In March, the "flour crisis" began, a food crisis caused by Israel's closure of the Karni commercial crossing into the Strip, which prevented food from entering Gaza for forty-eight days out of the previous two months. UNRWA sounded the alarm, as a week of continuous closure at the crossing not only forced Gaza's bakeries to close, but also reduced to a bare minimum the UN food reserves that provided aid to Palestinian refugees. It fell to the Fatah government led by Ahmed Qureia, Fatah's eldest leader (who held power in the days leading up the swearing in of the Hamas government), to stigmatize the closure of Karni and the crisis it caused. Mazen Sinokrot—the minister of economy in the Qureia government and a West Bank businessman well known both for his wafer biscuits and his moderate Islamist stance—laid the blame for the humanitarian disaster squarely on Israel's decision to close the border crossing for "security reasons," with only occasional and unpredictable periods at which the crossing was open. The decision to keep Karni closed left Palestinian agricultural produce that was ready for export rotting in trucks. This included produce from the former settlers' greenhouses, which James Wolfensohn, the former head of the World Bank and the Quartet's special envoy for Israel's disengagement from Gaza, had vigorously struggled to allow Palestinians to keep after the withdrawal. Palestinian leaders all reached the conclusion that Israel was using the Karni closures for political reasons: the closures put pressure on the PNA, not just on Hamas. In the case of this particular crisis, the situation was resolved—albeit only partially—thanks to negotiations involving Israelis, Egyptians, and Palestinians that were carried out at the residence of the American ambassador in Israel. As a result, a dozen trucks loaded with flour were allowed to pass through Karni in order to resupply Gaza's bakeries, which had shut down due to the lack of ingredients. The episode had lasting significance, however: it epitomized the way that border crossings with Gaza would work over the coming years, a situation that culminated in the border being completely sealed off after Hamas's "coup" in June 2007. The border would be opened or closed depending on several variables, foremost among them the Qassam and other rockets fired toward Sderot and other towns in the Negev by different armed groups within the Strip. In addition to this, there were security procedures requiring borders to be closed on Jewish holidays, for example.

Thus, the humanitarian emergency in Gaza, Hamas's stronghold, developed in parallel with the transition from the old PNA, which had been in power for the past twelve years, to the new PNA, through which the Islamic resistance movement made inroads into the nerve centers of Palestinian public life. Yet even given these inroads, little seemed to have changed for Hamas: the diplomatic isolation, the political pressure, and the political discourse that either failed or was unwilling to move beyond the adversarial dimension of Palestinian history all remained from the days when Hamas had adopted terrorism as a tool of political struggle. The little change was for the worse: to these problems was now added the economic blockade, which struck not just the Islamist movement but Palestinian society as a whole.

Given that it would be too simplistic to lay full responsibility for this lack of change solely at Israel's door or at that of the international community, the most important question is this: what was the root of Hamas's inability to display any flexibility when faced with the demands made by the international community? One possible answer is internal. All of a sudden, without any sort of transitional phase, Hamas went from being an opposition movement to being the group responsible for governing the territory administered by the

PNA—an institution it had never wanted to be a part of. It would be impossible for such a sudden change not to have a major impact both on Hamas's ideology and on its politics. And yet, in reacting to this change, Hamas was unable to move beyond its preexisting political and organizational structure, which represented the main "obstacle" to responding swiftly to external demands. Hamas's "democratic centralism"—the very decision-making process it had always followed, involving internal debate and full consultation of its four constituencies—was responsible for the sluggish pace of Hamas's reaction to changing events, the pace at which it still reacts today. Its responses—made purely by means of statements from the leaders who have the highest media profile—resulted in statements that often remained ambiguous. Having said that, Hamas's ambiguity often looked, from the outside, like steadfastness—the very steadfastness that voters had rewarded by punishing Fatah for its flexibility.

The first few months of the Haniyeh government were extremely difficult. Funds were scarce, especially after Israel ceased handing over tax revenues, and the PNA's deficit increased from month to month as a result. The European Union was at a loss for how to react: it did not wish to interrupt aid to the general population, but at the same time it did not want to have to work through a Hamas government to deliver that aid. In June, it would find a way of resolving the dilemma by means of a "Temporary International Mechanism" (TIM) that would allow at least a part of the PNA salaries to reach employees, for a total of around $140 million. The UN encountered greater procedural difficulties: they maintained relations with the cabinet ministries while avoiding as much as possible any contact with individual Hamas-affiliated ministers. Their interaction thus became entirely bureaucratic. The government attempted to parry this blow, but had to enter into the organizational machinery without any help from its predecessors in those same ministries. At the same time, Hamas had to resolve immediate problems such as the payment of public employees' salaries in arrears, a real Sword of Damocles hanging over the government's head. Teachers, for example, represented a third of the salary bill to be paid, and as Nasser al-Din al-Sha'er, himself a teacher, said at the time, "some of them haven't been paid for nine months; it's an accumulated problem. There's not a single dollar left in the ministry. The private sector is suffering too. We can do nothing without aid. People are already suffering. We don't know how long they'll be patient."[33] Hamas's leaders attempted to convince its counterparts that the lack of monies would strike all Palestinians, without regard for political parties. Salah al-Bardawil, Hamas's parliamentary spokesperson, used his own case as an example: toward the end of November 2006, nearly one year after turning in his resignation at his previous job in order to run in the general election, he had only once received half of his deputy's salary, along with two down payments that amounted to $300 and $400 respectively.[34] The government tried to provide some respite for its employees by handing out down payments on salaries when it could, but this was ultimately useless: strikes, particularly among the public sector employees where Fatah's presence was very strong, were a constant thorn in the Hamas government's side throughout the year it remained in office. Among Islamists, it was argued that the strikes were politically motivated, but this didn't change the result: because of the lack of funds, the population was on its knees.

The Hamas leadership attempted to take on these insurmountable problems in various ways. At the same time as it attempted to open a breach in the barrier that the West had put up, it sought support elsewhere. Support from Iran was a foregone conclusion, but this was not enough, especially from a political point of view. The goal was to win the support of Hamas's Arab brethren, but the Arab League was increasingly divided. There was the moderate front, which included the pillars of US Middle East policy led by Egypt and Jordan. Then there were the Gulf countries, which felt increasingly uneasy because of the growing tension all around Iraq and Iran; and finally countries like Syria, which during this phase was increasingly associated with the Axis of Evil drawn up in Washington. To obtain the support of an organization like the Arab League, increasingly fragmented and unable either to formulate a vision for a Palestinian future or mediate effectively between Abu Mazen and Hamas, was practically impossible, and at any rate the Arab League's support did not go beyond promises of massive financial help. Of the tens of millions of dollars that had been promised, however, not much would actually make it into the Palestinian Territory.

Moreover, Hamas was unable to distinguish between its role as a movement and its role as a government, between political leaders and members of the executive branch. Khaled Meshaal, for example, immediately attempted to position himself as one of Hamas's most authoritative leaders by setting out on a tour of those capitals that were willing to extend their welcome. Meshaal's role helped Hamas overcome its isolation on the one hand, but on the other it diminished the role of the Hamas-led government itself. Keeping in mind that the movement itself—which never shed its veil of secrecy, even after entering the PNA institutions—has never been easy to decipher, the few statements made in this regard by the Hamas leadership play down the evident distinction between Hamas as government and Hamas as movement. There should have been no ambiguity, however, at least in theory. Yet Khalil al-Hayyah, one of the best-known public figures in Gaza, explains that taking on an important position in the government automatically meant losing one's role in the movement's decision-making bodies. Hayyah points out that "they remain members of Hamas and contribute to its internal discussions, but you can't, for example, be a PNA minister and at the same time remain a member of the Consultative Council [*majlis shura*] or Politburo [*maktab siyasi*]."[35] If this is true from the standpoint of internal organization, the image that the public and other governments perceived was that Meshaal was taking on multiple roles at the same time: he was at once the leader of the movement and the ambassador of a government whose members could hardly leave Gaza and the West Bank, the public face that governments registered and to whom they reacted.

Meshaal's Palestinian critics argue that his main objective was to become a kind of new, Islamist Arafat. Be it as it may, it was Meshaal who succeeded in breaking the Palestinian government's isolation by going to Ankara for his first meeting with a foreign state of note. Turkey is a NATO member and has at that time mitigated tensions with its neighbor, Syria, which plays host to the Hamas leadership abroad. As such, it would be in an ideal position to take on the mantle of facilitator for negotiations. Moreover, Turkey also remained the only state in the region that could claim to be a traditional friend of Israel, as a state that was readying—albeit with some difficulties—to join the European Union. Finally, Turkey's government is also the first in the Near East to have chosen the path of moderate Islamism, as represented by the AK Party led by Prime Minister Recep Tayyip Erdogan. It was not a coincidence, then, that Meshaal asked Ankara's leaders for a meeting, nor that the Turkish government was very careful in its handling of that visit in mid-February 2006: yes to a meeting with then–Foreign Minister Abdullah Gul, no to a one-on-one meeting with Prime Minister Erdogan. For Khaled Meshaal, the Turkish leg of his tour was in any case already a media success. Even more important would be his meeting in Russia, one of the Quartet states that was vying to raise its profile in the Middle East once more. Vladimir Putin wanted a greater role in the Quartet and decided to meet with Hamas. This happened not least of all because, from a formal point of view, Putin was the only Quartet leader who could meet with Hamas. The United States included Hamas on its blacklist of terrorist organizations, with the EU eventually following suit, not least of all thanks to the encouragement of the Italian government led by Silvio Berlusconi during Italy's six-month presidency of the EU in 2003. Moscow, on the other hand, was bound by no such commitments, and Meshaal could in this way break international ostracism to launch his offer to Israel from the Neretva stage. Hamas's political bureau abroad said: "If Israel declares that it is ready and shows commitment to withdraw from the lands occupied in 1967, if it guarantees the return of refugees, dismantles the colonies, and demolishes the separation wall and releases prisoners, our movement will take steps towards peace."[36]

This offer, however, was not followed by any thaw in relations whatsoever, neither by Israel nor by the Quartet. For the international community, Hamas could not make any half-hearted commitments to recognize Israel; recognition was either full or nothing. (This position, however, made no concessions to the first law of diplomacy: negotiation.) Yet Hamas was unable to move beyond a position of principle, a position consolidated by too many failures in various peace processes over the years—not least among them Hamas's own terrorist phase, which had ensured the failure of any steps forward, and which provided Israel with an argument for its having established its "facts on the ground." Hamas, however, was not a monolith. If Haniyeh was its moderate face, if Meshaal was the leader who in time was making concessions to pragmatism, there still remained a more radical wing that was not limited to the Izz al-Din al-Qassam Brigades and that considered themselves independent of the rest of Hamas in certain respects. There were hawks within the strictly-speaking political movement as well, notably Said Siyyam and—to a lesser extent—Mahmoud al-Zahhar. Moreover, the more conservative wing of Hamas, the one most closely linked to the "resistance" phase and less closely associated with the "political" phase, did not make the job of ferrying Hamas toward moderation any easier. On the contrary, the conservative wing undertook actions that only deepened the divide between Hamas and Fatah. These actions mostly centered on questions of security and of the balance of power between the different armed groups in Palestine's security forces, reflecting a mindset in approaching relations with Fatah that had been heavily influenced by the Second Intifada. The actions of the conservative wing spent political capital and diminished the capacity for action by Hamas's moderate wing. They also entrenched the international community's position, which was never much in doubt. Other nations would not support Hamas's "doves" by allowing for diplomatic openings. To do so would only have consolidated the Islamist movement's negotiating power.

Chapter 7

HAMAS VERSUS FATAH

Prison Diplomacy

The clash over the question of recognizing Israel transcended borders and in particular went beyond the streets of Palestine, which faced its own immediate and more pressing problems: salaries, of course, but especially violence among armed factions. As the factions committed to one side or the other of the duopoly that had come to dominate the PNA leadership, it was above all the Gaza Strip that paid the price for the tension that had by now become a staple of everyday life. Weapons appeared on the streets; shots were fired in broad daylight; people were hit in the legs; the opponent's militants were kidnapped for a few hours here and there; warnings were issued. In Gaza the safety of the population—even that of children going to school—was no longer put at risk by Israeli soldiers, but by the Palestinian militants.

It was Hamas versus Fatah, and the clashes got worse by the day. The armed groups linked to the two main Palestinian factions became the real protagonists of the confrontation, both as instruments of political conflict and as groups who exerted pressure on their own leaderships. The friction reached all the way into the security institutions, which in spring 2006 were still in the process of being reformed. In April, Abbas reinforced the Presidential Guard and made it answerable directly to him, and also established an organization tasked with monitoring the borders, which in practice meant the crossing between Gaza and Egypt at Rafah. Hamas responded by establishing the Security Forces Unit, a body that took its orders from the Haniyeh government's interior ministry, thereby challenging Abu Mazen's authority. Heading what would later be called the Executive Force[1] (or *tanfisiyya* in Arabic) was Said Siyyam, well known as one of the movement's hawks and one of the men who had contacts not just with Hamas's military wing, but with other armed factions within the Strip. Indeed, many say it was Siyyam himself who pressed for the Force's establishment.

The Executive Force brought together the groups that had been established and consolidated during the Second Intifada. Thus, it was not just Hamas's militants who joined the Executive Force, but more importantly the members of the Popular Resistance Committees (PRC), as well. The PRC was itself heterogeneous and not integrated into the Islamist movement. In a move that appeared to be aimed at strengthening links with the PRC, Siyyam appointed as director general of his ministry the founder of the PRC, Jamal Abu Samhadana, who was also second on Israel's most-wanted list. Abu Samhadana's appointment, therefore, was yet another spark over a very dry pyre, and one that could not but seriously embarrass Abbas, who sure enough immediately—yet unsuccessfully—attempted to block it. The Executive Force initially comprised 3,000 men but practically doubled within a few months. The perception was that the Force had been established for two reasons: to reinforce and "regularize" the military tools at Hamas's disposal in the Gaza Strip and to establish an organization strong enough to confront the Preventive Security Force—which had traditionally been close to Dahlan—head-on. The sheer numbers were still relatively small, compared to the 60,000-strong forces controlled by the presidency. The 3,000 men initially incorporated under Siyyam's *tanfisiyya*, however, gave Fatah more than a little to ponder, not merely because of their training and their cohesion as a force and their religious zeal, but because they heralded a confrontation that could be expected to be bloody, given what had already happened in the Strip.

In a surprise move, however, this cycle of violence was broken on May 11 by the prisoners held in Israeli jails, the only group within Palestinian society whose moral standing was high enough to bring both Hamas and Fatah together at the negotiating table. If in mid-2006 national dialogue was restarted, it was because a document drawn up by the prisoners and signed by the most important leaders of each movement emerged from the Hadarim penitentiary in cen-

tral Israel. The so-called Prisoners' Document contained few novel-
ties compared to what had been said a few weeks earlier by Hamas
leaders in the West Bank and in Gaza, who had attempted to reconcile ambiguity and flexibility with statements that differed merely in
their tone. The document is blunt: Palestine is the land within the
1967 borders, including the West Bank, Gaza, and East Jerusalem.
Refugees have the "right of return." Hamas and Islamic Jihad must
become PLO members. Internal Palestinian divisions and armed
confrontation between factions must cease. And there must be a relationship of reciprocal respect and trust between the PNA presidency
(Abbas) and the prime minister's office (Haniyeh). Thus, the document attempted to bring together essentially internal matters, such as
the clash between factions, with the need to break the PNA's increasing isolation. This international isolation forced Palestinian prisoners
to dedicate the first of the eighteen points of this document, entitled
the "Document for National Reconciliation," to the question of the
geographical boundaries of Palestine. The first point stated: "The Palestinian people in the homeland and in the Diaspora seek to liberate
their land and to achieve their right to freedom, return, and independence and to exercise their right to self-determination, including
the right to establish their independent state with al-Quds al-Sharif
[Jerusalem] as its capital on all territories occupied in 1967 and to
secure the right of return for the refugees and to liberate all prisoners
and detainees based on the historical right of our people on the land
of the fathers and grandfathers and based on the UN Charter and the
international law and international legitimacy." In this sense, the text
was a perfect example of a balancing act. The recognition of Israel
was as implicit as it was in the statements the Hamas leadership had
previously made. The tool was the recognition of the PLO as "the
legitimate and sole representative of the Palestinian people wherever
they are located": the PLO itself recognized Israel in its own charter,
and as the document stated, Hamas and Islamic Jihad must become
members of the PLO. Equally, the document made implicit statements when it referred to its support for "the right of the Palestinian
people in resistance . . . focusing the resistance in the occupied territories of 1967."[2]

The way the document is phrased speaks volumes about the extent to which every word had been carefully weighed in the internal debate among prisoners so that there might be a de facto recognition of Israel, while not discarding either references to historical Palestine ("land of their fathers and grandfathers") or refugees' right of return. The terms used were drip fed into the document after a slow debate involving all the prisons and all the factions represented there. In fact, the idea of a national platform that might overcome the divisions between factions had been floated at least since Arafat's death in late 2004. In this sense, the Prisoners' Document was not a bolt out of the blue, nor an agreement imposed from above. Firsthand accounts[3] state that a draft document, handwritten on large yellow sheets of paper, had been circulating in the Be'er Sheva jail as early as January 2005. The person who showed me the draft was one of those whose signature later appeared on the published "Document for National Reconciliation": Mohammed Jamal al-Natsheh, another member of Hebron's Natsheh clan. Elected in 2006 along with the deputies on the Change and Reform list, he was one of the Hamas leaders who were taking part in the national dialogue between Palestinian factions. Those sheets of paper, pored over in a cell in the Be'er Sheva prison a year and a half before the publication of the Prisoners' Document, provide an indication of just how much this political self-analysis was a direct result not of the January 2006 elections, but rather of the generational change brought about by the Second Intifada.

This analysis, moreover, was supported from outside the prisons by those among the Hamas leadership who had themselves formerly been detained and who at that point found themselves at the center of the political action in Ramallah or in Gaza City. From this point of view, it was no coincidence that the first signatory of the Prisoners' Document was Marwan Barghouthi, who was not only Fatah's most famous and most popular leader in Palestine, but also the only one in the Fatah leadership who all factions would listen to, Hamas included. Well before the Islamist movement's electoral victory, Barghouthi had given a memorable interview to Al Jazeera in which he argued that there would be only one possibility for the future PNA government: national unity. In the interview aired on

Al Jazeera Arabic the day before the elections, Marwan Barghouthi referred to the need of a national unity government. The unity he spoke for was the unity between "blood brothers," those who had been brought together by their "resistance to the Israeli occupation." In making this claim, Barghouthi placed the prisoners at the heart of Palestinian politics. Although at the time this might have appeared merely as an attempt to stop the prisoners from being forgotten by those who were then in charge of public life, it would later become clear that it was a prelude of things to come. If a dialogue between Hamas and Fatah was possible at such a delicate stage in Palestinian politics, it would be achieved only through the prisoners.

Reaching an understanding behind bars was not a problem for the two factions. The other high-profile signatory of the Prisoners' Document was Sheikh Abdel Khaleq al-Natsheh, Hamas's highest ranking prisoner.[4] Such an agreement should not have come as a surprise precisely because national dialogue between factions was a practice that had been going on for a long time, at least among prisoners. The jails themselves were often organized according to the political affiliation of the prisoners: all those belonging to Islamic Jihad were held together, just as Fatah, PFLP, and Hamas members were. However, prisons were also places in which the forced proximity of detention and the shared nature of their punishment provided a common ground from which a conversation might begin, not least of all thanks to the neutral "terrain" of the often long detention sentences handed down to many of the detained activists. If anything, the problem lay with those outside the prison walls and at the highest levels of the very same factions whose imprisoned members, from their cells, had reached an agreement while their counterparts continued to confront each other on the streets of the Strip. For the leaders in Ramallah and in Gaza City, the problem was how to diminish the importance of that document written by the prisoners who were the living definition of suffering and of heroism in the eyes of Palestinian society. In the ongoing debate, such a document could not simply be ignored. And so, barely two weeks after the Prisoners' Document's public distribution on May 25, Mahmoud Abbas put the document to a referendum. The PNA president did this at the very beginning of the conference on national dialogue to break the impasse that Hamas above all had contributed to bringing about: Hamas had delayed giving its public approval to the document in order to allow its internal debate to take its course. Although Abu Mazen emphasized that his proposal was not an ultimatum, it certainly looked like one, particularly because of the time limits he placed on the discussion: only ten days' time to agree on a program of national unity, without which a referendum should be called within forty days. A referendum with a single question: would the PNA approve of the Prisoners' Document?

Mahmoud Abbas was counting on two elements. First, that the document might be decisive in attempting to overcome international isolation, as it contained a de facto recognition of Israel. Second, that from the point of view of internal Palestinian politics, the document pushed Hamas into a corner, since it could neither reject nor accept it entirely without first consulting all of its constituencies.[5] This was also the intention of some of Abu Mazen's closest advisors, as one of them, Yasser Abed Rabbo, candidly explained behind the scenes during those days to the officers of the American consulate in Jerusalem: "Abed Rabbo saw the referendum offer as a useful political ploy to corner Hamas and give Abu Mazen an excuse to dissolve the government if Hamas refused a referendum."[6]

Ismail Haniyeh's answer to Abu Mazen's proposal, delivered the day after, during the sermon for Friday prayers, was directed at the second element mentioned above, implied in his request that the document be submitted to a popular vote. Before the gathered faithful, in the tone of a tribune, the Palestinian prime minister issued a warning: "Even if they besiege us from every side, they should not even dream that we will make political concessions." He did not, however, name the assailants or the concessions that would hypothetically be demanded. The imprecision was not a coincidence, because that very same ambiguity gave Haniyeh some maneuvering room in the negotiations that had already begun on a de facto basis. Haniyeh made a move of his own through his interior minister, Said Siyyam, whose street reputation was as one of Hamas's toughest leaders in Gaza. While Haniyeh was directing his words of warning toward Abu

Mazen, he was also launching his own proposal, a proposal that was perhaps less eye-catching, but certainly more concrete. Said Siyyam ordered his men in the Support Force—a force formally established on May 17 against the will of the presidency—to leave the streets of the Gaza Strip and to confine themselves to the group's headquarters. The intention was obvious: namely, to reduce the friction with the security forces linked to the PNA presidency, and to send Fatah a message of peace after a hard, bloody week that had left at least a dozen dead between the two factions. Besides, the referendum could help Hamas overcome the difficulties in its position relative to its recognition of Israel, as it would be able to appeal to the will of the people. Moreover, a referendum could provide an opening for Hamas to be able to accept the Saudi plan proposed by then–Regent Abdullah during the Arab League summit held in Beirut in the spring of 2002: an Israeli withdrawal to the 1967 borders, in exchange for security and peace with the whole of the Muslim and Arab world. In reality, however, Haniyeh's message did not have the desired effect. Although negotiations continued, as happens often in the Arab world, by the beginning of June the struggle between the presidency and the Hamas government had nearly reached the boiling point.

Without any doubt, the Prisoners' Document broke the vicious cycle that had begun just after the elections with the Quartet's ultimatum. Abdel Khaleq al-Natsheh's signature at the foot of those eighteen points, however, shattered the static image Hamas had given itself until that point. There has been no confirmation to date by the protagonists themselves, but one may hypothesize that the Hamas leaders within the Israeli jails attempted to put pressure on the movement's leadership both within the Occupied Palestinian Territory and abroad, pushing them to adopt a less ambiguous position—not on the question of recognizing Israel so much as on the delimitation of Palestine to the 1949 armistice borders. An indirect confirmation of this hypothesis can be drawn from the silence with which the document was met by the Hamas leadership in the West Bank, in Gaza, and in Damascus. Had Sheikh al-Natsheh's position been the result of Hamas's normal decision-making process, with the four constituencies voting on the decision to be made, the response from the leadership abroad to the document's publication would have been immediate, without uncertainty or embarrassment. But the decision-making process in this case was not normal, and nearly two months passed before Hamas was finally ready to accept the document, even to the point of making it the basis of the agreement between Abu Mazen and Haniyeh (whose signature came only after certain changes were made, reflecting some sense of the tough internal debate that had taken place over those two months). Ultimately—as Mustapha Barghouthi, among others, argue—the moderate wing won out over resistance from the leadership abroad.[7]

As expected, it was the very first article of the document that underwent changes. The changes, however, were not regarding the defininition of Palestine along the 1949 armistice lines as the West Bank, Gaza, and East Jerusalem, but on two even more controversial points: the presence of Israeli settlements in the West Bank, and the fate of the refugees from between 1948 and 1967. In the context of the peace process as defined by the Road Map and George W. Bush's position from spring 2005, the Palestinian assertion of any right to "remove the settlements and evacuate the settlers and remove the apartheid and annexation and separation wall," as well as the question of "annexation and separation" itself, meant an implicit halt to any negotiations that involved territorial exchanges or concessions concerning the Green Line. During a meeting with Ariel Sharon the previous year, Bush had clearly modified the US position, declaring that the 1967 line was no longer realistic due to the "facts on the ground" that Israel had created with its large West Bank settlements. The Prisoners' Document, as it was modified and then approved on June 28, 2006, put the brakes on the prospects for a compromise on borders—just as it hardened its position on the question of refugees—by adding a proviso that would make any negotiation far more difficult. According to the modified version of Article 1, the refugees had the right to return to "their homes and properties from which they were evicted and to [be compensated for] them."[8]

That fistful of words added to the document had considerable consequences for the Palestinians' flexibility in any possible negotiation with the Israelis. The changes brought the focus squarely back to the

Green Line, and demonstrated just how much the Islamist leadership both in Gaza and in Damascus—both leaderships extremely and personally sensitive to the question of refugees—wished to leave their mark on the document.

Hamas had regained its unity after its internal consultation process, and the relationship between the PNA presidency and Haniyeh's government seemed to be growing more and more positive. To take one example, it previously would not have seemed possible for Foreign Minister Mahmoud al-Zahhar to pass through the Rafah crossing under the watchful eye of the Presidential Guard with suitcases containing $20 million, just as Abbas and Haniyeh were engaged in negotiations over the Prisoners' Document. Abu Mazen responded to critics by saying that the money would go straight into the treasury's coffers and would therefore not be available for Hamas's private use. This monied crossing was repeated shortly thereafter with Information Minister Youssef Rizka, who carried $2 million in cash across that same border crossing into Gaza, thereby circumventing the increasing isolation that by this point had made it impossible to receive funding from Arab countries through foreign banks.

Hamas and Fatah reached an agreement over the Prisoners' Document, but it came too late. At dawn on Sunday, June 25, a number of militia men carried out an ambush on Israeli soldiers just beyond the Kerem Shalom crossing. The attack took a heavy toll for Israel: two soldiers were killed and a young Israeli corporal, Gilad Shalit, was kidnapped. After twelve years without such a kidnapping, Shalit's kidnapping dropped like a bomb, not just on internal Palestinian politics, but also on the attempt to build a new relationship between a new and pluralistic PNA and the community of Western states. Three groups claimed responsibility for the kidnapping: part of the Hamas military wing, the PRC, and a new group that called itself the "Army of Islam." In their claim, the authors put forward two reasons for their actions: first, the Israeli incursion on Rafah carried out on June 24—the first since Sharon's unilateral disengagement—which had left two Hamas fighters dead, and second, the targeted assassination that had been carried out on June 8 against Jamal Abu Samhadana, the leader of the Executive Force. Some said that the tunnel that the Palestinian militias had dug to reach the other side of the Kerem Shalom crossing had been completed for months, meaning that the operation had been planned far in advance. And yet, the attack also seemed to have been designed by some faction within Hamas's military wing to undermine any possibility of an agreement between Haniyeh and Abbas. It is, however, virtually impossible to establish whether that act, which part of the military wing carried out, had in fact been ordered from within the political establishment. Ever since the Hamas reorganization that Moussa Abu Marzouq had carried out in Gaza, the military wing was independent from its political counterpart from an operational point of view. This decision had been taken after the arrests at the end of the 1980s that had decimated the movement—not least of all due to the information about military activities furnished by collaborators. The independence of the movement's two wings had therefore been considered vital in order to avoid the possibility that Israel might attempt to track down and destroy the entire organization.

And indeed, Israel's military reaction to Gilad Shalit's kidnapping was not far off from such an attempt. Early on, military operations were "limited" to raids that targeted infrastructure and to the entry of tanks into the old airport at Dahanya near the Israeli border. Three bridges were destroyed, as was the power station on which half of Gaza's population depended, leaving 700,000 people without electricity or water. Having done this much, Israel decided to raise the stakes by targeting the Hamas leadership. On July 2, it bombed and destroyed Ismail Haniyeh's offices, although he himself was not present at the time. Three days earlier, in a move intended to put pressure on those who had kidnapped Gilad Shalit, the Israeli authorities had arrested and imprisoned sixty-four of the most prominent Hamas leaders in the West Bank and in East Jerusalem. This was only the first in a number of raids that would in the end result in the arrest of eight ministers, twenty-six PLC members, and various other leaders of the Islamist movement's base. The first wave of arrests, carried out at dawn on June 29, apprehended Minister of Economy Omar Abdel Razeq, Minister of Planning Samir Abu Eisheh, the

Minister for Decentralization Issa al-Jabari, the Minister for Prisoners Wasfi Kabaha, the Minister for Social Affairs Fakhri Turkman, the Minister for Jerusalem Affairs Khaled Abu Arafeh, the Labor Minister Mohammed Barghouthi, and the Minister for Religious Affairs Nayef Rajoub. On August 5, Israel came for PLC Speaker Aziz Dweik, whose health was fragile, and on August 19, they came for Deputy Prime Minister Nasser al-Din al-Sha'er. These were the two best-known figures among Hamas moderates in the West Bank, and both were very well known in Nablus. The list continued with the Minister for Public Works Abdel Rahman Zeidan, who was arrested on November 3.⁹ Despite all of this, Israel had thus far been unable to get Gilad Shalit back. And so the military stranglehold tightened: 178 Palestinians were killed in the space of a month and a half, property was destroyed, and a humanitarian emergency was created. One would assume that media attention would result, but in the meantime, the thirty-three-day war between Israel and Lebanon had erupted, diverting cameras. On July 12, just after the initial Israeli attack on the Gaza power station and Haniyeh's offices, Hezbollah opened a second front by performing two raids, with eight Israeli soldiers killed and two more kidnapped. Tel Aviv responded with unprecedented harshness, which the Party of God had not expected: Over 1,200 Lebanese were killed in little more than a month through intense bombardments carried out against Beirut and in the southern portions of the Land of Cedars. Hezbollah responded with Katyusha rockets that struck not just in the Galilee area, but reached as far south as Haifa. The conflict was finally halted when an agreement was reached, not least of all thanks to the efforts made by the Italian diplomats who succeeded in drawing in the United States, Israel's greatest ally. The spotlight had moved temporarily from Gaza to Lebanon, until it would again turn south in September to the developing humanitarian emergency.

In the meantime, something had changed not only within the Haniyeh government, but more generally throughout Palestinian institutions. Dozens of ministers and PLC members were now in Israeli jails, but the Executive had not resigned, as some American strategists had expected. Moreover, the Prisoners' Document, which had been drawn up over the course of a year and a half of debates, remained the agreed-upon basis for a national unity government. Once again, president Abbas and Prime Minister Haniyeh met to try to reach consensus on such a unity government. The meeting caused the United States considerable concern, not least of all because by this point it was putting pressure on Abu Mazen to dissolve the Hamas government. According to information gathered by David Rose in his now-famous investigation published in *Vanity Fair*, it was the Bush administration's Secretary of State Condoleezza Rice who in early October presented Abbas with an ultimatum. During face-to-face talks with Rice in Ramallah, the PNA president attempted to buy time over an *iftar* meal for the breaking of the Ramadan daily fast, trying to delay the fall of the government until after the Muslim festivities of Ramadan, and then of Eid al-Fitr, the great feast that concludes the holy month of penitence. Abbas's behavior was indicative of the degree to which he could not be considered an impartial figure inside the Palestinian political and institutional equilibria.

According to Rose, Rice quipped after meeting with Abbas that "that damned *iftar* cost us another two weeks of Hamas government,"[10] a comment that demonstrates the hurried nature and recklessness of American foreign policy in the Middle East at the time, a characterization confirmed by Alvaro de Soto's own impressions. According to the UN representative, at least during this period, Abu Mazen never abandoned his attempts to co-opt Hamas. "The United States, which appear[s] to listen to a small clique of Palestinian interlocutors who tell them what they want to hear, seemed to believe on any number of occasions that Abu Mazen was just around the corner from taking Hamas on," notwithstanding the fact that this misjudged "both the man, and the balance of forces he faced."[11]

It was from this point, from early fall 2006 forward, that a race against time began, one in which all participants were attempting to reach goals that were, if not wholly contradictory, certainly very different. On the one hand, Washington was pressing for a resolution to the Palestinian impasse that would involve a "straightforward" fall of the Haniyeh government and the ejection of Hamas from the corridors of power. The "talking points" note the State Department drafted for the American consul in Jerusalem, Jake Walles, leaves no room for doubt: "Hamas should be given a clear choice, with a clear deadline: . . . they either accept a new government that meets the Quartet principles, or they reject it. The consequences of Hamas' decision should also be clear: If Hamas does not agree within the prescribed time, you [Abbas] should make clear your intention to declare a state of emergency and form an emergency government explicitly committed to that platform."[12]

In yet another struggle, several governments of European Union member states—particularly those where right-wing leaders had recently been replaced by left-wing ones—supported the attempts at mediation provided by Mustapha Barghouthi. Barghouthi was and is a well-known name in European intellectual circles and had good connections within governments. In addition to these qualifications, he was known as a secularist, had taken part in the First Intifada, and headed one of the Palestinian NGOs that received the most support from abroad, the Union of Palestinian Medical Relief Committees (UPMRC), which had been established in the 1970s. Additionally, he had run against Abbas in the presidential election, receiving a considerable level of support, and was the leader of his own small independent political party. Thus, for many reasons, Barghouthi was the ideal candidate to don the mantle of a mediator. From his office in Ramallah, the headquarters of his NGO, Barghouthi told his story: "My mediation began in early October, a very intense 'shuttle diplomacy' which took place particularly with Khaled Meshaal and Mahmoud Abbas. During that period I also met Condoleezza Rice and a considerable number of EU Foreign Ministers."[13] As he explains, "There were objective elements which were pushing in the direction of an agreement: Hamas was suffering as a consequence of the embargo because of the impossibility of governing and because of the strikes. Fatah, on the other hand, had not succeeded in reaching its objective of bringing the government down either through strikes or through the referendum."[14] Barghouthi's mediation reached its peak in November 2006, when Meshaal and Abbas signed an agreement of which Barghouthi possesses the only original copy. This agreement, however, fell through on November 30, when Abbas announced that negotiations had reached a dead end, fading away any hope for an agreement.

What had happened? During his interview, Mustapha Barghouthi asked for a sheet of paper and was given a notebook with lined pages. With a series of lines, he drew the wings inside both Fatah and Hamas, tracing fractures and factions within each political group. At the close of 2006, Hamas was divided into three groups: the doves, the pragmatists in the middle, and the hawks—a tripartite division that demolished the interpretation then widely circulating in the international media of a movement simply split into hawks and doves. The problem was that at a certain point, both hawks and doves found themselves agreeing that Haniyeh should stay on as prime minister in the new government of national unity, a position that would make such a government increasingly difficult to form. On the other hand, pragmatists—by and large, the Hamas leadership abroad—would have had no problem in accepting another name for the post. According to Barghouthi, among these pragmatists was Khaled Meshaal himself. Barghouthi's attempt at negotiation was directed primarily at Hamas and aimed at getting the pragmatists to come around to the positions that the other leaders in Gaza and the West Bank had already adopted. As Barghouthi himself said: "The unfair portrayal of Meshaal was pointless. For me, it was important to speak with him."[15] Barghouthi believed that Hamas was determined to retain certain posts, such as the post of prime minister, but was flexible on other ministerial posts, including the foreign ministry and the treasury. "They wanted to become part of the system, of the Authority," he argues, "and they were especially determined to see the democratization of the PLO. Indeed, in the early stages of negotiations, they wanted the reform of the PNA to proceed in parallel with the reform of the Palestine Liberation Organization. As the negotiations went on, Hamas accepted that these reforms should take place gradually."[16]

During the negotiations, Ismail Haniyeh had set off on the hajj, the pilgrimage to Mecca, on the occasion of the Islamic holiday Feast of Sacrifice. For Haniyeh the practicing Muslim, this was an essential pillar of faith. For Haniyeh the politician, it was the begin-

ning of a tour of Arab countries that would allow him to overcome
the local and reductive dimension of the Gaza Strip in order to raise
his political profile. He returned from Mecca with his head shaved,
as is the custom, and wearing the kaffiyeh. In the contemporary
Arab world, the kaffiyeh has two symbolic meanings: it emphasizes
Hamas's nationalist image by bringing Haniyeh's image closer to
Arafat's, and it allows Haniyeh and Hamas to present themselves as
true Arabs who follow the sunna, thus distancing themselves from
charges of being Tehran's agent in the Sunni world. The prime minister of the Hamas government had decided to cut short his diplomatic tour in order to return to Gaza after a new wave of violence
had been sparked by a failed attempt to assassinate a high-ranking
member of Fatah's intelligence service that resulted in the death of
his three children and a bystander. The following day, a judge linked
to Hamas was executed. Adding to the extremely high tension on
the streets, a struggle for power developed among Haniyeh, Egypt,
and Israel: the Tel Aviv authorities were blocking Haniyeh's return
due to a suitcase with $35 million that he was carrying in a bid
to bypass the embargo. After lengthy negotiations that resulted in
the money being deposited in an Egyptian bank, Haniyeh returned
on December 14 through the Rafah crossing, still policed by Abu
Mazen's Presidential Guard.

At this point violence broke out. One of Haniyeh's bodyguards
died and twenty-seven other people were injured in an exchange of
fire in what became one of the high points of the armed confrontation between Hamas and Fatah. The accusations made by the Islamist
movement were clear: it was Mohammed Dahlan who had orches-
trated the assassination attempt on Haniyeh, and Abbas was morally
responsible because control of the Rafah crossing was in the hands of
the Presidential Guard. Fatah rejected the accusations, Abbas threatened to call an early election, and violence spread through the streets
and towns of the Gaza Strip, with the risk of spreading to the West
Bank, as well.

The United States continued to view the *fawda*, the chaos into
which Palestinian politics had descended, as an instrument through
which to topple the Hamas government. The US administration rep-

resentatives said this plainly in diplomatic meetings. Alvaro de Soto notes in his "End of Mission Report" that during a meeting with diplomatic representatives in Washington that took place toward the end of January 2007—by which time Gaza's streets had become a battleground for Fatah and Hamas, a near civil war in which civilians were regularly killed and injured—one of the US envoys twice remarked upon how much he "liked this violence" because it showed that "other Palestinians are resisting Hamas."[17]

There were, in other words, far too many external pressures for an entirely internal mediation to have any chance of success. Barghouthi continued to carry out his duties as facilitator, but the situation was at an impasse, one broken only by an Arab patron who decided to leave the sidelines and intervene, throwing all his considerable weight into the discussion. This patron was not Egypt, which at this stage appeared to lag behind events, not least of all due to its own internal political problems, to which Hosni Mubarak was paying greater attention. The regional landscape had changed, and domestic politics had a considerable impact on Cairo's ability to mediate internationally—so much so that Egypt had taken for itself only a small stake in the pressure being applied by Arab countries upon Palestinians—namely security matters— and Egypt was limited to negotiating truces that were reached and then breached on a practically daily basis, lasting no more than a few hours before it was necessary to negotiate another all-too- temporary truce. Saudi Arabia, on the other hand, took on the lion's share, namely the Gordian knot of the conflict between Fatah and Hamas. The Saudi intervention—which was based on a decision by the recently enthroned monarch King Abdullah, and which brought the king's full influence to bear on the Islamic resistance movement—was based on two factors: first, the religious role of the Ibn Saud dynasty in the Sunni world, and second, Riyadh's ability to mediate directly with Washington. Moreover, Saudi Arabia had the benefit of occupying a special place in Palestinian politics, not only because of the financial assistance it had supplied for decades, but also because it was one of the few countries that had long-standing good relations with the Islamist front, despite being one of the United States' closest allies in the region. And of course the Saudi royal family was the "custodian of the two holy places" (the mosques at Mecca and Medina) in more than just name—a function that was used, along with the perception of Riyadh's neutrality, as leverage in order to place pressure upon the two Palestinian groups. Abdullah's decision should not have come as a surprise: in 2002, the then–Crown Prince Abdullah had already been the protagonist of a comprehensive peace plan based on the "land for peace and security" principle. This was the only peace plan the Arab world had offered Israel in nearly a quarter of a century.

It was the last wave of violence at the beginning of January 2007—with a bloody outcome of eighty deaths in the streets of Gaza City—that finally prompted King Abdullah to act. In addition, Riyadh was concerned about the growing influence Iran might have gained on the Islamist front and believed the time had come to exert its own pressure in order to rein in Tehran's ambitions. Thus, Saudi Arabia decided that the time had come to force Khaled Meshaal and Mahmoud Abbas to sign an agreement. Further, Riyadh decided that this discussion and signing should take place in a highly symbolic location—namely, Mecca. There, the agreement could be debated and signed far from the tense atmosphere of Gaza, and Meshaal and Abbas even had their picture taken together at prayer, both presenting themselves in the plain white garb of pilgrimage. According to Osama Hamdan, however, it was Hamas's military pressure in the Gaza Strip that drove Fatah—Mohammed Dahlan, to be precise, the most strenuous opponent of the national unity government—to accept the Mecca negotiations. Dahlan himself even took part in the negotiations, at which cameras and photographers captured his darkened and irritated expression. Hamdan argued that "in a few hours we had taken the outposts occupied by the Preventive Security in the north of Gaza. This was the reason why Dahlan took part in the Mecca negotiations. He believed he had the support of Israel and of the United States to become the future Palestinian president."[18] Providing a glimpse into the balance of power within Palestinian politics, Hamdan continues: "I had told him well before Abu Ammar's death, during a meeting in Cairo, after Dahlan had attacked us, falsely accusing us of the death of a Fatah member that one cannot become Palestinian president without Hamas's consent."[19]

On February 8, Mahmoud Abbas and Khaled Meshaal reached an agreement on a national unity government. It was a detailed agreement, and one that betrayed the difficulties both sides had in trusting one another. Abu Mazen designated Ismail Haniyeh as the new administration's prime minister with a letter of charge that indicated the distribution of roles among the twenty-four ministerial positions available. Hamas retained the post of prime minister along with another eight ministerial posts compared to Fatah's six, while five went to independents and four to other political groups. Among the most interesting appointments were those of Salam Fayyad, a much-loved figure within the international community, to the treasury, and Ziad Abu Amr from Gaza, a scholar of "political Islam" and thus well acquainted with Hamas, as foreign minister. The Islamist movement, on the other hand, lost the key post of minister of the interior, but it reserved the right to put forward an independent figure, Hani al-Qawasmeh, approved by Abbas. As expected, the president's letter mentioned relations with Israel and with the international community, asking the prime minister to "commit to the higher interests of the Palestinian people" and to "work in order to achieve its national goals as was approved by the PNC, the clauses of the Basic Law and the National Reconciliation Document [i.e., the Prisoners' Document]," and to "respect international resolutions and the agreements signed by the Palestine Liberation Organization."[20] Haniyeh signed this letter a week later, on February 15, after resigning from his previous premiership. From Damascus, Moussa Abu Marzouq explains the difference between the Hamas leadership and Abbas thus: "The main difference between us, perhaps the only difference, regards [the] agreements" previously signed by the PLO. Abu Marzouq adds: "It is now a matter of one word. We said we would honor past agreements; Abbas wants us to comply with them. But some of these agreements go against Palestinian interests. We can talk with Israel and others on how best to correct some of these agreements."[21] Mustapha Barghouthi echoes this sentiment, emphasizing that "the last Quartet document before Mecca asked that the national unity government reflect the conditions it requested in its program, not that it adhere to these. Then, after the government had been formed, they changed their minds."²²

In practice, the agreement reached in Mecca was in substance the agreement Barghouthi had negotiated toward the end of November, with the Saudi seal of approval. The only difference was that the February 8 agreement, unlike the November agreement, contained Ismail Haniyeh's name as prime minister. The agreement reached in the shadow of the Kaaba—which the protagonists could see from the windows of the Saudi Royal Palace in the very heart of the Sunni Muslim world—was received on the Palestinian street as though it were little short of a miracle, a triumph of common sense during a delicate and dangerous phase of the PNA's brief existence. Palestinian politics had certainly been through periods of extreme litigiousness and even insoluble conflicts between strong personalities within the PLO leadership—particularly between the late 1970s and early 1980s—as well as divisions and splits involving the established parties. But the physical level of these clashes had never reached such an intensity or produced such a high level of casualties. The specter of a civil war—a civil war fought by armed groups, and one which certainly did not extend into or involve the civilian population—was transforming daily life in Gaza. The civil war was limited to security organizations. In the latter years of Abbas's career, the reduction of these organizations had become his major priority and the strategy by which he hoped to reopen the peace process with the Israelis. Despite this, the security organizations had not melted like snow in the sun upon Abu Mazen's rise to the presidency.

And yet, in a way, it is precisely the degree to which such clashes involved only armed groups rather than a broad civilian resistance that provided an indication of just how much the street fighting had become a piece of a political game that to different degrees and in different ways involved several international actors, as well as Ramallah and Gaza City. The Bush administration's support for the security organizations linked to the PNA presidency was proclaimed in broad daylight. It was justified in terms of the need to strengthen the only partner that both the Americans and the European Union considered reliable: Abu Mazen. Between the end of 2006 and early 2007, however, the flow of funds, the increasing presence of American officers in Jerusalem, Jericho, and Ramallah, and the preparation of protocols and of training camps in Jordan and in Egypt gradually shifted the emphasis of this support away from simply increasing security within the PNA's territory and toward a full-fledged attempt to shore up one or another side in the conflict. The Presidential Guard, which was divided into different groups, was pitted against the Executive Force, which took its orders from Said Siyyam's ministry of the interior. Rashid Abu Shbak's Preventive Security Force, which was Mohammed Dahlan's operational arm, was pitted against the Izz al-Din al-Qassam Brigades. Yet even given all these factions, the help the West provided to the security organizations linked to the presidency between 2006 and 2007 was so openly known that many more than just Hamas supporters accused the president's security forces of being on the American payroll. No party explicitly claimed responsibility for the support provided to Hamas and the organizations to which it was linked, however, even when reports appeared in the international press about the flow of funds from Iran and Syria—even if there had been such funding, the Islamist movement would have steered well clear of advertising the fact. In any case, the support external powers gave to the security bodies on both sides could not at this point be stopped, and thus while the national unity government held together, the fragile executive coalition born from the Mecca Agreement attempted to forge a path between the Scylla and Charybdis of skepticism and outright sabotage. But the new government would not last even three months.

The Three-Month Adventure

Hamas wanted legitimization from Europe. Hamas leaders argued that European diplomacy had promised to recognize the Islamist movement if it could manage to form a national unity government. Mustapha Barghouthi, whose mediation was principally responsible for bringing the national unity government about, agreed with this. Barghouthi says that "Hamas signed the agreement because it wanted the embargo to be lifted, and I promised them as much because I was in turn promised this by many European Foreign Ministers, including Italy's Massimo D'Alema, who had been one of the best. But in Europe there is a system whereby two or three states can manage to block decisions."[23] This account is confirmed by those facilitators and consultants who during that period undertook the subtle work of talking to both parties on the sidelines, conveying each party's desires and demands. Hamas's leaders in Gaza, in the West Bank, and abroad all agree on this interpretation, and all also agree that the prospect of ending the international boycott the Quartet had put in place had been the turning point in the mediation that brought Hamas to share power with Fatah. Nasser al-Din al-Sha'er, the former deputy prime minister in the Hamas government of March 2006, said that "it was already common knowledge where Haniyeh would have traveled first as prime minister of a future national unity government of which Hamas would have been a part: London."[24] As the Sebastya-born Islamist leader recalled, the promise to recognize a Hamas-associated national unity government "had come from the offices of the prime ministers in European capitals." There were those who, requesting anonymity, were even more precise: the Norwegian foreign minister (although Norway is not a member of the European Union) and the Spanish, through a direct channel in the prime minister's office, as Javier Solana, "Mr. European Foreign Policy" himself, had told the Egyptians and the Saudis. The Germans also spoke about this possibility, while the Italians—then under Foreign Minister Massimo D'Alema[25]—promised nothing. At the official level, European diplomats deny ever having promised recognition to Hamas—which, during Italy's leadership of the EU in 2003, had been formally included in the list of terrorist organizations—unless the organization could meet the four conditions the Quartet had set out in spring 2006. European diplomacy itself had reacted quite ambiguously to the Mecca Agreement, with France appearing much more flexible than Germany, which held the EU presidency at the time and which under Chancellor Angela Merkel was gradually moving closer to Israel. For Hamas's part, the movement's openness toward Europe had been a precise strategic decision agreed on by all four of the movement's constituencies.[26]

Alastair Crooke, however, argues that at a certain point the European Commission became far more intransigent toward Hamas, placing before it not the Quartet's four conditions, but rather seven points that Hamas would have to fulfill.[27] In private, however, well-informed European diplomatic sources (who wished to remain anonymous) confirm that it is true that Hamas had been promised that the embargo would be lifted when the movement entered a national unity government, on the condition that it would then send a signal in the direction of recognizing Israel. "That signal was sent, and we found it to be a good starting point."

The signal was a statement Khaled Meshaal made to Reuters on January 10, 2007 (that is, before the Mecca Agreement and the national unity government). Meshaal did not recognize Israel directly, but did so indirectly in the context of his statement: "We in Hamas are with the general Palestinian and Arab position and we are with the consensus of the necessity of establishing a Palestinian state on the June 4 [1967] borders, including (East) Jerusalem, the right of return and the withdrawal of Israel to these borders."[28] When the journalist specifically asked whether accepting the 1967 borders implied the existence of Israel, Meshaal replied by again asking that Israel, in turn, recognize a Palestinian state. Meshaal stated that "the problem is not that there is an entity called Israel," adding, "there is a reality that Israel exists on Palestinian territory. The problem is that the Palestinian state does not exist. My concern as a Palestinian is to found this state. International relations are not based just on recognition."[29] As if that weren't enough, Meshaal had repeated this idea after the establishment of the national unity government, and it was no coincidence that he did so in Cairo, the home of Hosni Mubarak, who had notoriously been marginalized by the Saudi mediation. On February 22, Meshaal spoke again of a Palestinian state based on the borders of June 4, 1967, including Jerusalem and the right of return for all refugees, confirming that "before the conclusion of the Mecca Accord, we received promises from several European capitals suggesting that if a national unity government is brokered they would take steps to lift the sanctions imposed on our peoples in the wake of the election of Hamas [one year ago]."[30]

The signal that the Europeans had asked for behind the scenes had come, restated several times not just by Meshaal but also by Ismail Haniyeh, for example, in his inaugural speech as prime minister of the national unity government, as well as by a plethora of other leaders and spokespeople over the next few months. This signal, however, failed to overcome the remaining obstacles to a more incisive as well as gradual diplomatic intervention in recognition of the new Palestinian political reality.

From a formal point of view, something did indeed change with the advent of the national unity government. Although the movement itself remained listed among terrorist groups, the European Union could now bypass the prohibition on meeting Hamas members. Indeed, the EU organized meetings with independent members of the executive, from Ziad Abu Amr to Mustapha Barghouthi, who had been appointed minister for information, to Finance Minister Salam Fayyad, for whom many governments opened their previously closed doors. This stance should not be surprising. Fayyad was the most respected Palestinian abroad, as highly regarded as Abbas. The newly appointed finance minister knew the Western world very well, having earned a master's degree and a doctorate from the University of Texas, worked as an economist in the World Bank for eight years until 1995, and spent time in Jerusalem as a representative of the International Monetary Fund. Thus, as far as the West was concerned, he was reliable, and he permitted a loosening of the purse strings of international aid as well as of Arab support, which at last allowed the near-empty coffers of the PNA to be replenished.

The funds, however, could not resolve all problems. The question of the security organizations remained on the table. The Executive Force had not disbanded after Said Siyyam's resignation from the ministry of the interior. Hamas was not launching rockets, but was not preventing smaller factions from doing so, breaking the calm in Sderot and other Israeli cities in the Negev with the fear of Qassam rockets. The presidency was also making very few steps forward. The atmosphere became overheated when Abbas appointed Mohammed Dahlan to the post of national security advisor, illustrating all too vividly how important his role was within the presidency. Nonetheless, despite the tensions, the perception of the higher echelons of Palestinian institutions was still one of unity, so much so that both Hamas and Fatah were jointly present on the most important stage for regional politics: the Arab League summit that took place at the end of March in Riyadh. The Palestinian delegation was two-headed, but both Mahmoud Abbas and Ismail Haniyeh presented themselves as a symbol of a rediscovered Palestinian national unity: they shared the same plane to travel to Riyadh and were both received with a high-level welcome by the Saudis. Indeed, King Abdullah took advantage of the spotlight trained on the Palestinians to reiterate the old "Saudi Peace Plan" he had set out in 2002 at the Beirut summit, at a time when he was still regent and the throne belonged to King Fahd. At the time, Ariel Sharon had rejected Abdullah's plan, which included the idea of a Palestinian state within the 1967 borders, and Hamas responded ambiguously to the request that it accept it as a basis for negotiations. Israeli Prime Minister Ehud Olmert responded in an equally ambiguous but positive fashion. It did appear as though a new phase was dawning in the Middle East, with Hamas leaders carefully considering the Saudi plan, indicating on several occasions that they would be ready to talk about it. Disaster, however, was barely around the corner.

Mustapha Barghouthi again picks up the story. "The agreement lasted two months, then violations began on both sides until things deteriorated. It was the extremist wings in Hamas and Fatah who sabotaged the agreement. Dahlan and Abed Rabbo, on one side. Al-Zahhar and Siyyam on the other."[31] Hamas was of course divided into various factions, but Fatah itself also contained within it very different positions with respect to the national unity government. As Barghouthi says, "there were moderates like Abu Mazen, and extremists like Mohammed Dahlan and Yasser Abed Rabbo" who were against the agreement and who later played a very important role in weakening it. "Abu Mazen supported my effort; he wanted a solution; he did not want a confrontation." The hawks were themselves divided: among them, some were more closely linked to international circles, and some of them were inside the national unity government. Mustapha Barghouthi accuses them directly, albeit without mentioning names, saying it was precisely these individuals who, when they went abroad, would say, "'Wait, don't send the money, because the situation will change soon.' And that's precisely what happened."

Those working against an agreement, however, were not to be found exclusively in the ranks of Fatah and Hamas. As Barghouthi recalls, "What changed the situation was the power of the pressure exerted by Israel and the United States, and by the weakness of the European position, the inability of the EU and of the Arab states to counterbalance Israel and the United States. Ultimately, it was the Israelis who dictated the political line in order to continue to have a weak Palestinian counterpart, not a strong one, as would have happened with a national unity government. They did not want real negotiations with us. Palestinian democracy began to represent a threat, to Israel as to other states in the region. Hamas was not the target of the attacks against the national unity government: it was Palestinian democracy itself, because the executive represented 96 percent of voters." Barghouthi was irritated: "The government's program was progressive and secular, the part related to women was much better than under Salam Fayyad's executive, and the same can be said for other parts, from education to culture, which were very clear. It was a program which called for a total and reciprocal ceasefire."

The "Second Liberation"

June 2007. Rumors had been circulating for days. It was said that the men of the Preventive Security Force close to Fatah strongman Mohammed Dahlan were going to attempt to overthrow Hamas in Gaza. Even worse, the Preventive Security Force was going to carry out its attempt just after the *tawjihi,* the final examinations in high school. It is difficult to think of the *tawjihi* as an event that could so decisively distinguish a "before" from an "after." It is not so difficult to imagine within the Arab world, however, where the *tawjihi* is a rite of passage, a goal to reach to better one's future, and a mark of honor for a family. Students lose sleep and peace of mind for the *tawjihi,* fathers invest their money in private lessons, and the whole family supports the children to the utmost in order to celebrate them as though they had graduated with honors. For the school year 2006–2007, the PNA had set the starting date for the *tawjihi* as June 11. Some 50,000 students in the West Bank and Gaza, nearly half of them in the Strip, would have sat for that year's exam. But at least 200 did not manage this: nine of the *tawjihi* centers in Gaza City and three more in Khan Younis, not far from the Egyptian border, closed due to the battle raging in the streets. The first clashes between Fatah's and Hamas's armed men took place in the Strip the day before the eve of the exams, June 9, when minor scraps in the Tel al-Sultan district in Rafah acted as a detonator for seven days of armed confrontations. At the end of these seven days of fratricidal war on the streets of Gaza, the Islamist movement had taken total control.

Was the *tawjihi* chosen to be the watershed moment in the battle for Gaza? This was the most reliable version of events, according not just to those within Hamas's political wing, but also among the circle of experts and journalists who had most closely followed post-Arafat Palestinian politics. The most important pragmatists within Hamas, for example, had more than once stated that they knew nothing of the attempted coup, but that there were insistent rumors going around according to which armed groups linked to Dahlan "were planning to do something after the *tawjihi* examinations."[32] Ahmed Youssef, Ismail Haniyeh's main political advisor, told the International Crisis Group experts that "we knew they were training and smuggling weapons. We have seen the confessions and tapes. There is enough information to prove to the whole world those people were planning a civil war in which 10,000 would be killed. All the time we felt something was coming but we had no plan to take over Gaza."[33] This version of events was reiterated several times.

"The evening of the coup, we were in a car together, Ghazi and I." The Ghazi to whom Ahmed Youssef referred in November 2007 in his Gaza City office—his lights on in full daylight because the curtains were drawn for security reasons—is Ghazi Hamad, who until June 2007 had been Haniyeh's spokesman. He was one of the men of the "middle generation," considered to be the symbol of Hamas's wing that favored participation in government. "We were returning home to our families in Rafah," he continues. "Don't you think that if the coup had been planned a long time before, that the two of us, Ghazi and I, given our positions within the government, we would have stayed in Gaza City to follow events?"[34] From the West Bank, Hamas backed the same version. According to Farhat As'ad, "What happened in June was not prepared."[35] At the time, As'ad, who had spent many years in Israeli jails, was the movement's spokesperson, and before that had been one of Hamas's coordinators during the Second Intifada, as well as the overall coordinator of Hamas's electoral campaign in the 2006 general elections. In other words, he knew the movement intimately.

"If something *had* been decided," he adds—sitting in a chair in his Ramallah home, which faces the Israeli settlement of Psagot, barely a few weeks after having been released from jail in October 2008—"this was the response of the military wing [to] February 2007."[36] February 2007: that is to say, before the Mecca Agreement from which the short-lived national unity government would emerge. In February, before the agreement, Gaza had been plunged back into violence. Factions linked to Fatah targeted the Islamic University in Gaza City, Hamas's alma mater and one of the Muslim Brotherhood's bastions in the Strip. Buildings were hit, thousands of books were burned, and a communiqué was released to the press stating that an arms cache had allegedly been found in the university and that seven armed Iranian "advisors" had been arrested. There would never be any confirmation of the find or of the arrests. Hamas's response, however, was immediate. From reports at the time, it is known that armed groups linked to the Islamist movement effectively took control of the streets in Gaza. What Farhat As'ad refers to, however, is the way in which Hamas went well beyond the streets, taking control of around fifty buildings in which forces linked to Fatah were concentrated (which confirmed Osama Hamdan's explanation of Mohammed Dahlan's participation in the Mecca negotiations). The occupation lasted less than five hours, and was intended to send a precise military signal: if Hamas wanted to, it could take control of the Strip. But it didn't want to.

According to As'ad, the difference between what happened in February 2007 and what happened four months later lay in precisely this message. In June, the coup had not been prepared, as it had been in February. Instead, the clashes provoked a chain reaction from which there was no going back. Hamas had no military plan. This version is also confirmed by Salah al-Bardawil,[37] born 1959, professor of literature from Khan Younis, and a Hamas member ever since its inception. These different accounts strengthen the hypothesis that Hamas's military wing—both the Izz al-Din al-Qassam Brigades and the Executive Force linked to Said Siyyam's ministry of the interior—had in fact misled the political wing, and had decided to force its hand to the most extreme consequences, out of fear that time would favor Fatah. Or, more precisely, that it would favor the portion of Fatah that was pressing for a final confrontation with Hamas—the portion linked to Mohammed Dahlan, who at that time was considered even in some Western circles as the final bulwark against a Hamas-dominated Strip.

The unresolved tensions between security organizations—organizations that answered to their respective factions and not to the PNA's institutions—exploded a month before the showdown, in mid-May, in two nearly simultaneous episodes that marked the end of the brief truce between Gaza's armed factions. On May 14, a Hamas commando broke into a training base for Mahmoud Abbas's Presidential Guard near Karni, the commercial crossing that bridges Gaza and Israel. Eight men loyal to Abu Mazen were killed. During that period about 450 Fatah armed militants, who had been trained by the Egyptians, entered the Strip with Israeli consent through the crossing of Rafah, which had been closed for the majority of the previous year and a half. The entry of the Fatah men was perceived by Hamas not only as an unmitigated slap in the face by its partner in government, but also as a signal that the groups linked to Mohammed Dahlan were re-arming. An indirect confirmation that something dangerous was happening within the security institutions was provided by the resignation of the minister for the interior, also on May 14. Hani al-Qawasmeh, a political independent, used the resignation letter he presented to Ismail Haniyeh to make extremely harsh accusations to all parties concerned, including Haniyeh and Abbas, who had not given him the necessary power to reorganize security in Gaza and thus reduce the influence of individual armed factions.

Al-Qawasmeh's accusations were not leveled only at Hamas, but also at Fatah—and the accusations came complete with first and last names. Outstanding among the accused was Rashid Abu Shbak, head of the Preventive Security Force, director general of the ministry of the interior, and one of Mohammed Dahlan's lieutenants. On May 11, Abu Shbak had ordered thousands of Fatah's armed men to deploy on the Strip's roads without warning the Executive Force headed by Hamas and, most importantly, without asking for Qawasmeh's permission. This raised the general level of tension considerably, which had quieted down after the establishment of the national unity government. Abu Shbak's decision to deploy turned out to be crucial, however, and was criticized both by circles close to Abu Mazen and by Hamas, who perceived it as a full-blown provocation. Further raising the level of tension, Abu Shbak and Dahlan then opposed Qawasmeh's request for control over all of the armed groups (according to one of the best Israeli analysts, Danny Rubinstein). Thus Rashid Abu Shbak became the target to hit, as far as Hamas's military wing was concerned. On May 16, a commando broke into Abu Shbak's house and killed four bodyguards. Abu Shbak and his family were not hurt, but the message had been delivered. And thus the space for negotiation between Hamas and Fatah grew ever smaller as the two factions' military wings took over.

American envoy General Keith Dayton realized that the increased prominence of the military wings was the reason the situation was beginning to worsen. Dayton was in charge of a $59 million assistance program authorized by the US Congress intended to reinforce the Presidential Guard, the Karni crossing between Gaza and Israel, and Abu Mazen's national security office by re-arming Fatah and training the Presidential Guard. The "security assistance" goal, as Dayton himself told a subcommittee in the US House of Representatives twenty days before the coup in Gaza, was "to help create the conditions necessary to advance Israeli-Palestinian peace via the Roadmap" and, as a first step, to give the Presidential Guard "a 'security horizon', an assurance that they have support and have a future." Dayton argued that "the NSF [National Security Forces] and civil police, the forces tasked with the day-to-day responsibility for ensuring law and

order, do not have that assurance" because they had to "face a daunt-
ing challenge not only by HAMAS's Executive Force but also its military force, Izz al Din al Qassam Brigades, both of whom continue
to receive support from Iran and Syria."[38] Dayton, who served as the
US coordinator for security from November 2005 to October 2010,
had from the beginning adopted a purely military perception of the
Palestinian situation, one that focused on armed conflict between
factions and worked to ensure that Fatah would prevail in that conflict.[39] The signs that the United States was pursuing this objective
were clear, and Dayton had met Dahlan several times over the previous few months both in Jerusalem and in Ramallah. This American
strategy toward the PNA presidency pushed Quartet envoy Alvaro de
Soto to resign—and not quietly.

As time passed, rumors abounded in both the local and international press. They spoke of the arrival in the Gaza Strip of the Badr
Brigade, a Hashemite unit manned by Fatah-affiliated Palestinians
who lived in Jordan. EU and US officials had apparently paid this
unit several visits. In May, an internal American document was made
public, one that indicated that Mohammed Dahlan was the reference
point for a plan Dayton had drawn up to stop the launch of Qassam
rockets from border areas. The forces under Dahlan's command were
scheduled to deploy to the target areas by June 21. The 450 Fatah
fighters who crossed the border at Rafah in mid-May appeared to
confirm this scenario. The authorities in Cairo had given their blessing, as had the Israelis and the Europeans who had manned the crossing ever since November 2005 under the direction of a contingent of
Italian Carabinieri commanded by General Pietro Pistolese. According to calculations by the International Crisis Group, very little had
passed through the Rafah crossing, which had remained closed for
over two-thirds of the time during the year before the Hamas coup.[40]
Even members of the Palestinian government had problems reenter-
ing Gaza with suitcases of money. And yet 450 Fatah fighters passed
through the crossing without a hitch.

The Israelis also played a role in the confrontation between Fatah
and Hamas. On May 20, the Israeli air force attacked the home of
Khalil al-Hayyah. Al-Hayyah, the Hamas deputy who headed the

parliamentary wing, had been one of the most influential figures who secured truces between Hamas's and Fatah's armed militants over the previous few months, and had also been one of the most influential figures in the attempt to form a national unity government both before and after the Mecca Agreement. Moreover, he had been charged with the most delicate of assignments: the negotiations over the Islamist movement's entry into the PLO. The Israeli air force raid killed seven of al-Hayyah's family members, while he himself was at the Egyptian embassy putting the finishing touches on the agreement for the sixth truce with Fatah. From that point on, Gaza's streets began to fill with armed men affiliated with opposing factions. The principal factions were Rashid Abu Shbak's Preventive Security Force, who toward the end of May had decided to leave the Strip and take refuge in the West Bank, and groups loyal to Said Siyyam, who in the months ahead would be revealed as the link between Hamas's military and political wings. Thousands of tense, armed young men deployed throughout urban centers from Gaza City to Khan Younis, all the way north toward the border with Israel. Lighting a spark was all too easy, and in this context the ongoing attempts to provide mediation—such as the efforts of Egypt's powerful head of intelligence services, Omar Suleiman—proved of little use. At least seven truces, all broken within a few hours or days at the most, succeeded each other in the space of barely a month. Prime Minister Ismail Haniyeh even attempted to declare a ceasefire in order to allow the *tawjihi* to take place. All in vain—the 2007 *tawjihi* will be remembered as the *tawjihi* of Hamas's coup in Gaza.

The battle commenced on June 9 in the Tel al-Sultan district in the southern part of the Strip, then spread north to Gaza City, where it raged on the rooftops. In the run-up to the clashes, armed groups from Fatah and Hamas had taken control of strategic rooftops across the city, which they used to control the main arteries and important buildings. Because of the lack of space in Gaza City, it is full of tall buildings, up to and even beyond ten floors high. It was from these rooftops that the combatants targeted the centers of power, from the ministries to the compounds of security forces and important leaders. Opponents were thrown from rooftops. The first of these was

Mohammed Salama al-Swairki, twenty-seven, and a member of Abu Mazen's Presidential Guard; he was thrown off the fifteenth floor of the Ghefari Tower on June 10. Next came Hussam Mohammed Abu Qainas, a thirty-five-year-old Hamas militant who was thrown from the eleventh floor of the Muhanna Building in a district in southern Gaza during the evening of the same day. There was no place for pity on either side of the conflict during that bloody week in Gaza, not among Hamas's men, who riddled some of their most fearsome adversaries with bullets, and not among Fatah's, who did not spare imams or unarmed men. Armed clashes took place in the streets, among civilians, and inside hospitals, until, on June 14, the entire Strip was firmly in Hamas's hands, and Fatah's men were on the run, fleeing either toward the West Bank or toward Egypt in order to escape further retaliation by the Izz al-Din al-Qassam Brigades or the Executive Force. Hamas's hawks spoke of a "second liberation." The first liberation, in 2005, had been the unilateral withdrawal by Israeli armed forces and settlers from the boundaries of the Strip. Two years later, again in the summer, Hamas had "liberated" itself from those parts of Fatah's armed wing with which conflict had never really ended.

Governing the Strip

"A strategic error." This is what Ghazi Hamad calls it. The June 2007 coup "produced a thousand other political problems that Hamas could have done without." When the guns finally fell silent, politics again moved to center stage, albeit with far less weight than before. For Hamas's leadership, the *tawjihi* coup marked the beginning of a two-front struggle to administer power in Gaza. The first challenge of managing relations with Israel was in many ways simpler to deal with in terms of maintaining popular consensus. There was now, however, an entirely internal second challenge—managing relationships with the structures of the PNA itself as it distanced itself from Gaza and began to establish parallel institutions. In the immediate aftermath of Hamas taking power in Gaza, Mahmoud Abbas did not even attempt to mend the rift, but immediately dismissed Ismail

Haniyeh from his position as prime minister and installed Salam Fayyad in his place, as well as a new government in Ramallah, sealing the political break between the two geographically disparate centers of gravity in the Occupied Palestinian Territory. In the space of a few days, a two-headed Palestine had been created. On the one hand, there was Gaza, a small and internationally isolated territory now firmly under Hamas's control, in which the Israeli armed forces were not present. On the other hand, there was the West Bank, which did not suffer from international isolation and was the sole recipient of humanitarian and financial aid—but which saw Israeli soldiers deployed in the countryside, around the Israeli settlements, in the Palestinian villages, and even inside its very cities.

Over the following months, Mahmoud Abbas and Salam Fayyad, supported by the group of advisors around them and by Western countries, consolidated the separation of the West Bank from Gaza. Thus, by seizing power in Gaza, the Islamist leadership found itself forced to administer the Strip and its inhabitants through a system of institutions that they had barely begun to learn how to use. One got the impression that they felt like guests in their own homes, using the bureaucracies, the machineries, the photocopiers as though they were expecting the legitimate owners to return. The hope that the clash between Ramallah and Gaza might be overcome, however, dwindled as time passed, and the Hamas administration increasingly lost its feeling of transience, exhibiting the classic signs of an administration in the process of consolidating its ability to provide for people's basic necessities.

To start, Hamas attempted to establish a parallel bureaucracy. This was especially necessary due to the boycott organized in Ramallah, which continued to pay the PNA officials and employees who still worked in Gaza on the condition that they did not go to work in the offices now controlled by Hamas. This boycott blocked the machinery of government in Gaza. Not just clerks and judges, but also doctors, nurses, and teachers all stayed home, only to turn up in public standing in line at banks and cash machines in order to draw their Ramallah-deposited paychecks.

The Palestinian government's internal isolation thus pushed Ismail

Haniyeh's de facto government—the third, after the single-party administration of March 2006 and the national unity government which followed a year later—to begin performing the everyday functions of government through emergency measures. As one of the Hamas ministers commented, "We are managing a crisis, we aren't setting out a program for government."[41] There were two crucial elements in the administrative crisis, aside from the increasingly tight blockade to which the Strip was subjected: first, the lack of personnel as a result of the Fatah boycott, and second, the lack of a budget with which to meet the needs of Gaza's population. The personnel problem was overcome by means of a reduction in wages and through the employment of young people, often fresh out of college, who were less expensive to retain than their older counterparts. According to journalistic sources, the budgetary problem was assuaged by collecting municipal taxes and car registration fees, as well as by placing a tax on contraband cigarettes brought across the southern border with Egypt at Rafah. A similar "tax" was placed on those who ran the commercial tunnels that pass underneath the border, through which everything and anything that manages to pass into the Strip is smuggled to then be sold on to a population that lacks everything.

Thus, Hamas plugged the gap left by the PNA's effective departure. In the words of the International Crisis Group experts, "By boycotting the security, judicial and other government sectors, the PNA turned an intended punitive measure into an unintentional gift, creating a vacuum Hamas dutifully filled. From courts to municipalities, the Islamists asserted control of institutions on which the PNA pulled the plug."[42] As the months passed, Hamas's grip was consolidated through exemplary cases and symbolic gestures. Despite the economic blockade imposed by the international community and the Quartet, despite the lack of fuel and electricity provided by Israel, and despite the lack of basic goods like cement and spare parts, Gaza worked. Trash no longer piled up on the Strip's streets, but was collected thanks to a process by which each neighborhood, district, and refugee camp would take charge of providing its own services. The sense of uncertainty and of anarchy in the years before the coup also substantially quieted as the administration of security returned to the hands of a single organization, the Executive Force, leaving the Izz al-Din al-Qassam Brigades the job of facing the Israelis. As months went by, the Executive Force became Gaza's *police*. Indeed, the Executive Force had always wished to be regarded as a police force, as the 2007–2008 poster campaign that plastered the streets of the Strip's towns demonstrated through its request to change the name by which the group was known from *tanfisiyya* to police force, from a partisan armed faction to a security force serving all Gazans. Hundreds of women applied to this new police force, according to the account provided by Taghreed al-Khodary for the *New York Times*.[43]

From time to time, the Palestinian press as well as the Israelis published polls that spoke of a gradual loss of popular consensus for Hamas. Given the general suffering and immense daily difficulties that Gaza had faced in recent months, it was difficult to assess the value of these statistics as a measure of response to Hamas's actual policies. But one thing is certain: despite its internal conflict, Hamas's cohesiveness was never in question. The kidnapping of Gilad Shalit, the Israeli army corporal, at the end of June 2006 demonstrated as much: since then, no one had been able to obtain reliable information concerning the location where Shalit was being held, despite the fact that Gaza is a very small sliver of land within which Israel has built a network of informants over the years. Nothing had ever come to light about the young Israeli soldier, beyond the reports Hamas released on the state of his health, until he was freed after the deal between Israel and Hamas on the exchange of prisoners in October 2011.

In order to avoid scaring off the international community, Hamas leaders emphasized several times that the Islamist movement had no intention of establishing an emirate, a caliphate, or any entity in which the Islamist model of Hamas's old Charter would become reality. Salah al-Bardawil, for example, stated that Hamas wished to "create a honorable model."[44] In practice, the Hamas leadership attempted to manage daily life in Gaza without impacting existing power structures in the Strip more than was strictly necessary, while at the same time attempting to resolve the rupture with Ramallah and thus to overcome the uniquely dyarchic situation the Palestinian Territory found itself in. If the attempt to reach the first goal had objectively succeeded, despite the doubts and concerns raised by human rights associations (particularly with regard to the fate of the Fatah-led political opposition within the Strip), the second objective—mending relations with the PNA—had been problematic from its very inception: neither Hamas nor Fatah trusted each other anymore, and both feared losing even a single iota of their power.

Thus accusations flew between the West Bank and Gaza: all of the various groups that managed security in the Occupied Territory were at one time or another considered guilty of arbitrary arrests, torture, extrajudicial assassinations, and so on. The accusations, whether they came from partisan sources or independent bodies, were similar, with only the targets differing. Fatah accused the Executive Force of having carried out arbitrary arrests, harassment, and torture, as well as firing on demonstrators in the few protests that the nationalist movement had organized, interrupting wedding ceremonies, and making the Strip feel like a "regime." For its part, Hamas accused the security organizations loyal to Mahmoud Abbas of arresting hundreds of Islamist militants, of managing West Bank towns in which Palestinian military personnel were deployed—Nablus, Jenin, and Hebron—with an iron fist and with the none-too-hidden cooperation of the Israeli armed forces. In the West Bank, youth on the streets similarly spoke of a "regime atmosphere," one supported by those who were nicknamed "the Dayton guys," the men belonging to the security organizations trained by US General Keith Dayton's plan. The rupture became worse over time, ultimately reaching peaks never before witnessed in Palestinian history. Moderates were increasingly marginalized. Ahmed Youssef was no longer Haniyeh's most trusted advisor. A few months after Hamas's coup in Gaza, he asked: "If one is chased away from European airports, as has happened to some of our ministers, how can one think that our positions might be strengthened?"[45]

Ghazi Hamad resigned from his post as spokesperson immediately after the 2007 coup, and one has to ask whether it was merely a coincidence that at the same time a letter appeared on the Internet—a letter that Hamad never disowned—which described not only the reasons for his twenty-five-year-long membership in the Islamist movement, but also his view of where and how Hamas had made mistakes. Hamas, he wrote, ultimately lacked "a clear strategic vision that will combine resistance with political work and a flexible ability in tactics and political maneuvering."[46] Rigid positions, empty slogans, and the easy refuge in an ideology that stated that "resistance is our strategic position": according to the letter, all of these were mistakes that did not take into account the fact that "resistance is a tool, not a strategy."[47]

Time itself has shown just how much the situation was changing. For a full year after June 2007, Hamas kept behaving as though its administration of Gaza was only temporary. Sooner or later, an agreement would be reached with Fatah, and a unified PNA that would overcome geographical, political, and sectarian divisions would return to govern both Gaza and the West Bank. Yet in the summer of 2008, after a full year in power, the situation had patently changed. Hamas no longer merely administrated daily life, bureaucracy, and the constant emergencies that resulted from the total embargo that Israel continued to pursue. The change in the significance of the Islamist movement's role in power came from the June 19, 2008, truce brokered between Hamas and Israel itself. The agreement reached two objectives. First, it conferred upon Hamas de facto recognition by Israel, which bypassed Abu Mazen's PNA and allowed Israel and Hamas to negotiate directly. Second—in a phrase often heard among the people in Gaza—Hamas reinforced its power "only" within the Strip. Since administering the Strip meant having to deal on a daily basis with the desperation of over 1.5 million people trapped in a massive prison, the "calm" (*tahdiy'ah*) with Israel maintained a kind of paradoxical status quo. Yet combined with Hamas's clash with Fatah and the PNA in Ramallah, the *tahdiy'ah* crystallized the independence of that small slice of the planet, and thus also the independence of its Islamist administrators.

Although the de facto independence of Gaza since the coup had been obvious, this new singular de jure independence was exemplified by a change to the concrete corridor on the doorstep of the Strip, a change made in the fall of 2008, less than two months before the start of Operation Cast Lead in December. Beyond the long reinforced concrete corridor, half a mile past the yards upon yards of red dirt that lay among the skeletons of the buildings destroyed by Israeli artillery and the agricultural fields of Beit Hanoun that hug the border wall, a cargo container sat hidden from the view of Israeli soldiers. Inside the office were a desk, a computer, and an employee of the administration who presented the visitor with a form. Nothing much, the typical form one fills out upon crossing a border and entering a foreign state. Except that Gaza was not a state. Neither was the West Bank, and neither was Palestine within the borders of the 1949 armistice. Yet that office and those forms, which Hamas began to require over a year after the June 2007 coup, were the physical mark of changing times. The crisis had been set in stone.

Chapter 8

FROM RESISTANCE TO GOVERNMENT

War, Rubble, and Tunnels

"The truce is convenient only for Hamas's leaders," Ahmed said, here in Gaza City in front of the barracks that the military wing of the Islamist movement had taken over in June 2007 in a matter of hours. Ahmed, a young man of little more than twenty-five, was looking at a building painted a surprising turquoise, guarded by a few armed militants. Ahmed came from a *fatahwi* family through and through: his father had returned with the legendary Force 17 after the advent of the PNA and had stayed loyal to Yasser Arafat, but had then retired from politics, let down. In his life, Ahmed had known only Egypt, outside the borders of Gaza. It was the end of October 2008, weeks before Operation Cast Lead would turn the Gaza Strip into an inferno.

Since six in the morning on June 19, 2008, Gaza had been living in anticipation. The day before, June 18, the Gaza authorities and Israel had announced the six-month *tahdiy'ah*. There was no written agreement to seal the deal brokered by Egypt and negotiated with Tel Aviv. Nevertheless, the truce held: very few Qassam rockets had been fired on Israeli cities in the Negev, and the Israeli army's military operations had remained at their normal level of low-intensity conflict. And yet Gaza had been closed off from all sides: from the north, from the east, from the south (sealed by Gaza's Egyptian brothers), and from the sea, where, if one took a good look, one might see the Israeli navy blockading fishermen's boats in Gaza City's minuscule port. The truce did not have the expected result: the commercial crossings between Gaza and Israel remained closed.

What made it through—weapons, true, but more especially the

food, medicine, cows, sheep, mobile phones, and clothes that made it to the people on the street—passed through the hundreds of tunnels, the digging of which the Egyptians had not interfered with, in an effort to prevent the ongoing humanitarian crisis in Gaza from spilling over into Egypt. And yet it did spill over. On January 23, 2008, for example, when the iron wall at Rafah was blown up—by Hamas itself, in all likelihood—hundreds of thousands of Gazans poured onto the streets of the Egyptian town of Al-Arish in the Sinai to breathe a few hours of free air before returning to their open-air prison. It was the poorest of the poor who worked in the tunnels. For a few shekels they would go through the tunnel and back, risking their lives, one or two of them dying every single day. But those who survived the work would help their families get by. The shelves of Gaza's small shops held those goods that made it through: snacks, pasta, canned tuna, nuts, chips, cookies, detergent. For those who could afford them, of course. For those who couldn't—meaning the hundreds of thousands of people living in the refugee camps—even Rafah, which had become a large open-air market, remained an unattainable dream.

The truce is convenient for Hamas leaders, as Ahmed was saying. He is a secular young man, sporting the usual gelled hair, jeans, T-shirt, and V-neck pullover. "What do we get in exchange for the truce? We keep dying in here, in this prison, while Hamas's power grows." Indeed, ever since June 19, the Gaza Strip had remained isolated under the embargo, with the flows of international food aid and electricity constantly subject to hiccups. And beyond this, little had changed from the moment Hamas was elected democratically and transparently to the Palestinian parliament, much less at the start of the June 2007 coup when Hamas took control of the Strip and Israel declared Gaza to be an "enemy entity."

Hamas must have sensed the criticism coming from the likes of Ahmed the secularist and from the Gazan people when, in the autumn of 2008, it made the proverbial leap from the frying pan into the fire by entering into direct confrontation with the Israelis over the issue of renewing the truce.

Eyad al-Sarraj, the internationally known Palestinian psychiatrist, has a beautiful home in Gaza City, an Egyptian-influenced house bursting with secularist feeling. While the rain poured down outside and flooded the lush garden, and the truce held Gaza in limbo, Sarraj explained one of the major reasons behind Hamas's ultimate decision to break that truce: "They are closer to the people; they have a network of people who listen to what the community thinks."[1]

At the time, the community was thinking about the rain, which had the Strip's refugee camps on its knees. The fragile electrical network, already feeling the strain from a lack of maintenance after two and a half years of increasing isolation, had again gone offline during the morning, just as it had two days before, prompting Ahmed Youssef to say—from his spartan office adorned only with a photograph of Yasser Arafat, one of Abu Mazen, and a Palestinian flag—that he "would never have expected that his land could become like Somalia."[2] It was the fragmentation of the "social fabric," the increasingly clear-cut division between *fatahwi* and *hamsawi*, Fatah supporters and Hamas supporters, that worried Youssef, still one of Hamas's most moderate leaders. This division ran through cities, districts, individual streets, and even—indeed, especially—families. As Youssef put it, based on his direct experience barely a week before, "You don't even go to weddings or funerals anymore, if you belong to the opposite faction."[3]

This situation could not last. Hamas could not renew its truce with Israel without renegotiating its conditions. Cynically speaking, because so little had changed for Gaza's inhabitants after the truce, to maintain the status quo would have jeopardized Hamas's internal consensus. The *tahdiy'ah* hadn't saved Hamas or Islamic Jihad militants from death or prison—both continued to be struck down by Israeli targeted assassinations and Palestinian police roundups. Granted, the running battles on the streets between Hamas and Fatah militants had stopped, and indeed some clans, among them the largest and most powerful families in the territory, had been cut down to size, including the clan that had kidnapped British journalist Alan Johnston, who spent 114 days in captivity before being freed in a Hamas-driven operation after the movement had taken power in Gaza. One could walk the streets of Gaza freely, unlike the time when opposing factions would kidnap journalists to use as bargaining chips. But as for the rest—electricity, water, food, and children's clothes—not much had changed. It was true that fuel prices had dropped, mostly thanks to the tunnels through which Egyptian diesel oil would arrive. Prices had crumbled from three hundred shekels a gallon to roughly thirty (or from $80 to $8). For those few families who could afford it, the fuel could be used to cook, heat, wash, power the electric generator, and so on. But in terms of salaries in Gaza, those $8 remained, for many, an unattainable goal. So what about all these families, the masses of the unemployed who represented the majority of Gaza's Palestinians?

On November 4, the truce was broken. A month and a half before its "natural" term, Israeli tanks penetrated a few hundred meters into the Strip under cover of the Israeli air force. The official explanation was that the tanks were attempting to destroy a tunnel that Israel believed was being used in an attempt to capture Israeli soldiers. During the incursion, six Hamas militants were killed. The reaction from Hamas's military wing was not long in coming: dozens of rockets were fired against Israeli cities in the Negev. The Goldstone Report summarized the events: "The soldiers attacked a house in the Wadi al-Salqa village, east of Deir al-Balah, which was alleged to be the starting point of the tunnel, killing a member of the Qassam Brigades. Several Israeli soldiers were wounded. In response, the Qassam Brigades fired more than 30 Qassam rockets into Israel. Israel responded with an airstrike that left a further five members of the Qassam Brigades dead. Both sides blamed the other for the escalation of violence. Hamas also accused Israel of trying to disrupt talks between Hamas and Fatah that were scheduled for the following week in Cairo."[4]

Thus the drums of war had already begun beating well before the *tahdiy'ah* was due to expire on December 19 and well before Hamas formally refused to sign it again without renegotiation. Between November and December 2008, Israeli sources estimate, almost 200 rockets and more than 100 mortars had fallen across Gaza's border and onto the kibbutzim and towns in the Negev and north toward Ashkelon.

When Israel started its Operation Cast Lead against Gaza on

December 27, 2008, very few figures inside Hamas's political wing could say they had expected such an overwhelming show of strength by Tel Aviv. The Israel Defence Forces (IDF) launched the offensive at 11:30 a.m. on that Saturday with a surprise air strike campaign that targeted police stations and security premises. It was a devastating attack, not only due to the high number of victims among the policemen and young recruits, but also because of the timing, which coincided with school arrival and departure times, and so involved almost all of Gaza's students. At 11:30, the air strike sparked a state of panic among the hundreds of thousands of students in the streets of Gaza, several of whom were killed. It was only the starting point of a very short and very bloody military campaign, one which could be compared—for the timing and for the harshness of the bombardments—with the thirty-three-day Israel-Lebanon war in the summer of 2006. From December 27, 2008, to January 17, 2009, the entire Gaza Strip was pounded by airstrikes, artillery bombardments, and infantry attacks, many unreported or only distantly reported by the independent foreign journalists who were, for the entire duration of the Operation, forbidden entry to the Strip by the Israeli authorities. The casualty counts of the twenty-two-day Israeli military offensive were shocking, even considering the difference between the numbers collected by NGOs and those collected by international organizations. UNRWA states that "almost 1,400 Palestinians, including 347 children and 209 women, were killed and a further 5,300 persons were injured."[5] The attacks targeted military and civilian structures, as well. Around a quarter of all housing stock—more specifically, the homes of 59,779 families—was damaged or destroyed, affecting more than 300,000 individuals.[6]

The Goldstone Report's final conclusions were extremely severe regarding Israeli conduct during the war. "From the facts gathered, the Mission found that the following grave breaches of the Fourth Geneva Convention were committed by Israeli forces in Gaza: willful killing, torture or inhuman treatment, willfully causing great suffering or serious injury to body or health, and extensive destruction of property, not justified by military necessity and carried out unlawfully and wantonly. As grave breaches these acts give rise to individual criminal responsibility. The Mission notes that the use of human shields also constitutes a war crime under the Rome Statute of the International Criminal Court."[7]

But what happened to the Palestinian Islamist movement during Operation Cast Lead? More exactly, what happened to its security apparatus, both the Qassam Brigades and those thousands of armed militants absorbed by the Gazan police corps after the Executive Force's dissolution in October 2007? There is no doubt that Operation Cast Lead dealt a hard blow to Hamas's military wing, the extent of which is almost unknown due to the secrecy that covered both its security operations and its basic organizational structure. Even the Goldstone Report was unable to shed light on Hamas's military dimension, even to the extent of quantifying the losses suffered by the Qassam Brigades. The Goldstone Report merely presents the statistic that less than one-fifth of the total deaths were combatants rather than civilians, treating policemen in charge of internal security as distinct from actual combatants.[8] The casualty counts among the military during Operation Cast Lead triggered a battle of numbers between Israel and Hamas about the death-toll figures, a battle that immediately acquired an inescapable political significance. While the Israeli authorities, especially in early reports, described victims as belonging to Hamas, only providing statistics on the number of civilian dead when discussing the effects of bombings by the IDF, Hamas consistently focused on civilian casualties throughout its reporting on the war.

In retrospect, it is clear that Hamas was unprepared for a massive Israeli military campaign. The movement "had prepared for a two-week confrontation with limited Israeli incursions along the lines seen during the Second Intifada," as one the leading figures of Hamas acknowledged to the International Crisis Group's analysts.[9] The Hamas military wing—which, during the Operation, was in charge of other armed groups in the Gaza Strip, including Islamic Jihad and the PFLP—therefore had to change its strategy on the run. Their strategic goal became bringing the Israeli infantry on its soil and forcing a direct confrontation in the streets of Gaza. The IDF avoided this kind of direct combat, however, wishing to minimize its losses. This strategy took into account the political climate, with the Israeli public increasingly reluctant to bear the weight of high military casualties. After the 121 soldiers who had died in the 2006 war with Lebanon, the Israeli public had already made its strong opinion known to its leaders.

Hamas's reaction to this unexpected show of strength by the IDF was to implement a "conservative military strategy."[10] The military wings began to send only a few men at a time on the ground while continuing to fire rockets from Gaza into the Negev towns and to Ashkelon, in order to show that the powerful Israeli military machine did not affect the ability of the Qassam Brigades and other armed groups to strike beyond the borders of Gaza. The political repercussions of this attempt to contain Gaza's human costs were complex and developed over a long period of time.

Two ceasefires, announced simultaneously by Israel and by Hamas, came into force on January 18, 2009. Soon after, Hamas had to face the postwar period by juggling different roles. First, it had to bear the role of a government in full administrative control of Gaza. Second, Hamas was still a movement that, since its origins in the Muslim Brotherhood, had built its influence and popular consensus on its continuous social presence in the refugee camps and in the streets of Jabalia, Deir al-Balah, Khan Younis, and Gaza City. Thus as soon as the guns and rockets fell silent, domestic policies became totally consumed with assessing the amount of destruction and managing the humanitarian crisis. In order to forestall protests against the government's performance and to satisfy the needs of its strongest constituency, Hamas had to respond immediately to the needs of the Gazan people. It did this through giving direct aid, often in dollar reimbursements, to those who had their houses destroyed or damaged in the fighting.

But a more complex issue remained to be tackled in the aftermath of the Operation, namely, the relationship between the government—and not least of all its bureaucracy—and the international organizations that had managed the impressive machine of emergency aid and support by which the majority of the Gazan population had survived for dozens of years. (These international organizations had also been affected by Operation Cast Lead; to take one example, Israel had to compensate the UN for the damages suffered by UNRWA buildings in the Gaza Strip due to IDF artillery strikes.) The task of these organizations had been to channel the massive amount of international aid other nations offered for the purpose of repairing the widespread damage to the Gaza Strip—and the organizations had to do this despite explicit restrictions against putting any of this aid money into the hands of the de facto government. This was a difficult and paradoxical play, one that had many different actors on its stage: the international organizations, Hamas, Israel, the PNA in Ramallah, and Egypt. Even after the major defeat in terms of public opinion it had suffered after Operation Cast Lead, Israel still held on tightly to the keys of the Gaza crossings. The Abu Mazen and Salam Fayyad–led PNA remained the sole point of reference in the Palestinian spectrum, as far as the United States and Europe were concerned. And finally, Egypt was not only the mediator on several negotiating tables, but also the guardian of the door at Rafah along the southern border of Gaza.

Right after the war, both Hamas and the Haniyeh government in Gaza did not dispute the notion that the aid would be managed and distributed by the international organizations, mostly through the UN agencies that worked in Gaza. However, they rather strenuously objected to the idea that the PNA in Ramallah would be placed in charge of the aid and the money; relations between Hamas and the Abbas-Fayyad duo had never improved, even during the worst days of Operation Cast Lead. In fact, soon after the Operation, lingering doubts arose inside Hamas's leadership and in the streets of Palestine as to exactly how the PNA stood with respect to its brother Palestinians in Gaza. Had the PNA done its best to help Gazans? Immediately after the war started, rumors spread that Ramallah and even Cairo had known well in advance about Israel's decision to attack the Gaza Strip. Direct confirmation of this rumor arrived through US diplomatic documents released through WikiLeaks. During a meeting with two important delegations of US senators and congressmen in June 2009—one from the Senate Foreign Relations Committee led by Senator Robert Casey and the other from the House Com-

mittee on Foreign Affairs led by Congressman Gary Ackerman—
Ehud Barak, defense minister during the war in Gaza and in the
Netanyahu cabinet that followed it, confirmed the rumors. Barak
"explained that the GOI [government of Israel] had consulted with
Egypt and Fatah prior to Operation Cast Lead, asking if they were
willing to assume control of Gaza once Israel defeated Hamas. Not
surprisingly, Barak said, the GOI received negative answers from
both."[11]

Therefore, Hamas had reasons to mistrust the Ramallah-based
PNA. But it did trust the UN aid machine, well tested after dozens
of years inside the refugee camps, and well known to be efficient at
distributing emergency aid (an efficiency tested more in the Gaza
Strip than in the West Bank). Even given that, the consequences of
Operation Cast Lead revealed the political shift in Gaza that complicated its relationship with the UN: Hamas was no longer confining
its role to a mere presence in the camps, as it had before the 2007
coup, but was now formally holding power there.

The friction that occurred between the UN and the Hamas government, especially in the early weeks after the war, was a result of this
new political situation. The international community also rendered
the situation even more confusing, due to the fact that it had again
been "forced" to deal with Gaza during and after the Israeli military campaign,[12] after having avoided the issue for the previous few
years. At the beginning, the international community exerted only
light diplomatic pressure on the Israeli military operation, fueling
the widely popular idea in the Arab world that the West had secretly
endorsed the campaign. As the death toll rose to an unprecedented
level, an increasingly embarrassed international community decided
to intervene. Almost two months after the ceasefire, in March 2009,
it hurriedly launched through the Sharm el Sheykh conference a
humanitarian appeal for donations, with the ambitious goal of raising $3 billion for the reconstruction of Gaza. The collection exceeded
even this goal, raising $4.5 billion among the 80 countries gathered
at Sharm. Money poured in like rain, and all of it was supposedly
headed for Gaza. Widespread confusion, however, reigned then and
afterward as to the means by which the aid would be collected and

sent to the Strip. The West's problem had not been resolved: Hamas was a political entity. Consequently, the international community had to deal with the fact that it had no existing relationship with the government that had controlled Gaza since 2007. Formally and materially, who would receive the aid funds? Who would handle them? In her first entry on the Middle East stage as the new US secretary of state, Hillary Clinton showed continuity with the previous administration by publicly supporting the PNA run by Mahmoud Abbas and Salam Fayyad, never naming Hamas.

However, the situation on the ground made it impossible to channel funds and aid to the Ramallah-based PNA in order to avoid contact with Hamas and to preserve the Islamist movement's isolation. The people of Gaza needed immediate help, for one, and for another, Operation Cast Lead had affected the image of Hamas both inside and outside the Palestinian territories in a paradoxical way. The day after the Sharm el Sheykh conference, Rami Khouri, one of the most acute Middle East analysts, signed a blunt comment in the Lebanese newspaper *Daily Star*: "Using billions of dollars in international aid to maintain much of the Israeli siege of Gaza while trying again to prop up the Abbas government and ignoring the role of Hamas will not move anyone closer to genuine peace or security."[13]

Rami Khouri's severe assessment underlines the international community's constant lack of preparation in dealing with the Israel-Palestine situation generally, and Gaza in particular. Western governments and their Arab allies could not overcome the impasse that had invalidated their strategy on the conflict since Hamas had entered the PNA as a democratically elected government in 2006. Nevertheless, Operation Cast Lead was a turning point in the recent history of the Middle East. Through the war, Hamas came back on stage as one of the main actors. Israel didn't succeed in its goal of overthrowing the Hamas government in Gaza. On the contrary, Israel had to negotiate a ceasefire with Hamas before the new Obama administration took power. Indeed, the ceasefire negotiations mediated by Egypt indicate the new and even more complicated situation more than any other event since December 27, 2008. The result of Operation Cast Lead was exactly the opposite of the one most expected: war put Hamas back on track.

Don't Talk with Hamas, but Negotiate

In the middle of the war—more precisely, on January 9, 2008—some Hamas leaders crossed Rafah to negotiate the ceasefire. Among them were Jamal Abu Hashem, Salah al-Bardawil, and Ayman Taha. Each of them represented a different generation inside the Harakat al-Muqawwama al-Islamiyya: the founders, the middle generation, and the youth, this last represented by Ayman Taha, then thirty-eight and himself the son of the highly profiled Muslim Brotherhood in Gaza. Hamas chose its envoys among the officials known widely for their capabilities as mediators. One of the leading figures inside the elder generation, Jamal Abu Hashem, had been the mediator between Hamas and Fatah, a role also played by Salah al-Bardawil from the middle generation. Over the course of a week, meetings followed upon meetings in Cairo with Egyptian government officials, Hamas leaders from Gaza, and movement members from the political bureau all in attendance. The Damascus-based office sent the second-in-command in the political chain, Moussa Abu Marzouq, as well as Mohammed Nasr, considered the man nearest to Khaled Meshaal. "That week was the most difficult one," said Salah al-Bardawil two years later in a conversation in his Gaza office, bringing to mind those dense talks.[14]

After a tough negotiation with Egyptian officials, Hamas accepted a truce, provided that Israel would commit itself to withdraw its troops from the Gaza Strip in a week's time. Both parties verbally agreed to the ceasefire, and Moussa Abu Marzouq announced it publicly at noon on January 18. Israel withdrew its troops well before the deadline. In less than two days—before dawn on January 21, when Barack Obama was sworn in as the forty-fourth president of the United States of America—soldiers had redeployed along the border between Israel and Gaza. Due to the timing, many consider the Israeli move an attempt to ease tensions with the new US administration. In fact, rumors spread that the president-elect's transition team had "also helped persuade Israel to end the bombing of Gaza and to withdraw its ground troops before the Inauguration."[15] Objectively, Operation Cast Lead embarrassed the Obama administration, and the new president took steps to let the parties know his stand on the issue soon after he became the White House's new inhabitant. Prominent among these steps was that rather than calling Israeli President Shimon Peres or Prime Minister Ehud Olmert, the first call the newly appointed US president made to a foreign leader was to PNA President Mahmoud Abbas on January 21.

Meanwhile, Israel was once again experiencing a heated electoral atmosphere, with early elections slated for February 10. The political campaign was in full swing, and most of it was focused on Gaza. On December 26, 2008, the Ehud Olmert government had approved Operation Cast Lead "unanimously,"[16] with the strong support of the Labor defense minister Ehud Barak and Kadima member Tzipi Livni. In the war's aftermath, Livni held not only the role of minister of foreign affairs, but was also the Kadima Party's candidate for the premiership in the upcoming elections. In addition, she carried on her shoulders direct responsibility for the war's disappointing results. Therefore, the miniscule electoral returns for Kadima can be directly attributed to the defeat in Gaza, which paved the way for opposition candidate Binyamin Netanyahu. The Likud's leader was able to build an alliance throughout the spectrum of the Israeli Right, which had increasingly been seized by the settlers' lobby and the ultra-Orthodox sectors of the population. After Netanyahu had been entrusted with the task of forming the new government, Labor joined the coalition as its weakest member. Monopolized by Ehud Barak's leadership, it was riddled with divisions and splits and had recently shifted to a center-oriented policy.

It was not only Israel that found itself in a very delicate position after Operation Cast Lead. The United States was also passing through its most dramatic political transformation in a decade, transitioning from the Bush administration and its aggressive Middle East policy to Barack Obama, the protagonist of the Democrats' political redemption. Obama won the presidential elections by a substantial margin just a few weeks before the largest Israeli military campaign against the Palestinians in the Occupied Territory since 1967.

After the war in Gaza, too many variables had changed in the Middle East situation. The death toll caused by the bombardments was high and the humanitarian crisis was self-evident. The Gaza Strip was on its knees, its already miserable economic system (factories, greenhouses, farms) devastated and destroyed. Even Israel experienced a dramatically weakened position due to the strong accusations made by an increasingly broad sector of the international community that Israel had used disproportionate force. Gradually, the idea materialized that the Israeli military high command should be referred to international justice—up to and including the International Criminal Court—and the UN easily approved the establishment of a fact-finding mission headed by South African judge Richard Goldstone.

Thus Operation Cast Lead was a political failure for Israel with respect to the international community, but also one with respect to its own relationship with the dual leadership of Palestine. During the operation, Israel had performed targeted assassination attempts against senior Hamas ministers, notably the powerful Minister of the Interior Said Siyyam, but the flexibility of the Hamas movement's structure had already survived similar assassinations, and it was not greatly affected by the new attempts. Additionally, Israel had failed to do any serious damage to the foundations of Hamas's infrastructure by repeatedly bombing the movement's offices, which the Israelis considered important in the organization of the Harakat al-Muqawwama al-Islamiyya. The air raids and artillery actions designed to target those offices, however, overwhelmingly involved civilians to the degree laid out in the Goldstone Report, a result that succeeded only in terrorizing the population rather than driving it to rebel against Hamas.

The Gazan people did not revolt against Hamas, although in the months and years following the war a growing dissatisfaction toward the regime would become palpable. This dissatisfaction had little to do with the way that Hamas had underestimated the Israeli military reaction in December 2008. Rather, the people criticized the way Hamas managed its power in Gaza using a patronage system similar to Fatah's. Hamas's system of patronage was less outright cronyism, as it sought to strengthen the movement over any one individual within it, but it was equally inclined to favor its own side. And all the while, Gaza's borders remained closed, just as they had been since before the war.

In this situation of nearly total isolation, which endured into 2009 and 2010, the issue of reconstruction took on heightened political significance. The international community had raised a great deal of funds, but what would it do with them? Would the West continue in maintaining the isolation of Hamas, or would it at last try to open a channel with the Islamic leaders? In the first weeks after the war, the international community pursued efforts toward the latter course, as diplomacy ran parallel to the redundant speeches of the donor's conference at Sharm el Sheykh. Signs of this diplomatic approach toward Hamas were particularly evident in the tours of Gaza that many international celebrities began to make. Among the visitors were US Senator John Kerry; Quartet envoy Tony Blair; Norway's Foreign Minister Jonas Gahr Stoere; Douglas Alexander, the UK minister for international cooperation; and Javier Solana, head of European Union foreign policy. Even Gerry Adams, Sinn Fein's historic leader in Northern Ireland, paid a visit. Adams was a politician with no specific agenda on the Israeli-Palestinian conflict, but his presence after Operation Cast Lead assumed a more symbolic meaning. It testified to the opinion shared by intellectual circles and think tanks, especially in Europe, that Northern Ireland could be usefully compared to Gaza in order to better understand (and maybe even facilitate) Hamas's possible transition from a violent resistance movement to a group that could work stably within Palestinian representative institutions.

Thus, while diplomats still formally refused to talk to Hamas, internationally renowned public figures visited postwar Gaza to ascertain with their eyes the amount of destruction the Israeli bombs had caused. In essence, they were trying to understand whether there could be any opportunity to open a channel to talk to Hamas, without making any changes to the pillar of the Israeli and Western strategy on Gaza (that is, continued isolation of the Strip). As this was happening, some Western countries stepped up their contact with the Hamas leadership outside the West Bank and Gaza. They did this through diplomats, but also through the experts, politicians, and parliamentarians of various European nations who traveled to Damascus to meet with Khaled Meshaal. The video conference between Khaled Meshaal and British parliamentarians marked one striking example of the diplomatic climate. The conference happened in Westminster in April 2009 and triggered a strong controversy in London. The controversy was not solely because of the video conference itself, but in part because of the organizer, Clare Short, who had previously been the secretary of state for international development in the Blair government for six years and who had made a visit to Damascus along with three other MPs. Unlike many other meetings with Hamas in Damascus, the UK delegation's visit was given mainstream media coverage.

Aside from the UK visit, which was the exception to the general rule of media silence regarding these meetings, public opinion and analysts knew very little about the talks and contacts established with Hamas leadership, especially since, strictly speaking, the EU has been disallowed from having any contact with Hamas since the movement was blacklisted as a terrorist organization in 2003. Governments and intelligence officials had to use channels outside of Europe and the United States in order to assess the possibility of using diplomacy to move beyond the impasse on Hamas. One of the few public cases of such nontraditional channels being used was the visit Mahmoud al-Zahhar paid to Switzerland in June 2009, where he met Federal Minister of Foreign Affairs Micheline Calmy-Rey. Switzerland, due to its traditional neutrality and its role as a host country for the UN, seemed to have assumed the role of a facilitator. "Hamas is an important political actor and must not be left out in discussions over a solution to the Middle East conflict," said Minister Calmy-Rey over Swiss public radio, specifying that Switzerland, "unlike the European Union, did not consider Hamas a 'terrorist organisation', but condemned any terrorist activities."[17] The comments drew irritation from the Israeli government.

Mahmoud al-Zahhar, who went to Switzerland together with the Hamas government's Minister of Health Bassam Na'im, also met with two other figures: former US Undersecretary of State Thomas Pickering and Robert Malley, one of the talking heads of the International Crisis Group and former US President Bill Clinton's special assistant for Arab-Israeli affairs during the Camp David summit in 2000. It is almost impossible to know more detailed contents of the meetings between these US figures and Hamas, but it is no accident that this intense activity—which included efforts by former US President Jimmy Carter—began right after Operation Cast Lead and Barack Obama's inauguration, then continued throughout 2010. No change in strategy was on the horizon for Washington, but contacts indicated that the new administration needed a better understanding of the state of affairs in the Palestinian house, including a better understanding of Hamas.

In fact, the Israel-Palestine issue became one of the main points in the speech Barack Obama made at Cairo University on June 4, 2009, a speech that showed a dramatic discontinuity with the Bush administration regarding the Muslim world and the Middle East. To the Palestinians, Obama's speech represented a critical step: the recognition of the legitimate aspirations of the Palestinian people, counted as equal to "the aspiration for a Jewish homeland . . . rooted in a tragic history that cannot be denied. . . . On the other hand," as Obama affirmed in Cairo, "it is also undeniable that the Palestinian people—Muslims and Christians—have suffered in pursuit of a homeland. For more than 60 years they've endured the pain of dislocation. Many wait in refugee camps in the West Bank, Gaza, and neighboring lands for a life of peace and security that they have never been able to lead. They endure the daily humiliations—large and small—that come with occupation. So let there be no doubt: The situation for the Palestinian people is intolerable. And America will not turn our backs on the legitimate Palestinian aspiration for dignity, opportunity, and a state of their own."[18] It was enough for the Palestinians, for all the Palestinians, to believe that there had been a major change in US policy, and this change was contained in a sentence: "Israelis must acknowledge that just as Israel's right to exist cannot be denied, neither can Palestine's."[19]

Then there were the unspoken words in Obama's speech. The US president never pronounced the word "terrorism," a word he also left unsaid when speaking on the Afghanistan and Pakistan scenario and on the years that had followed September 11, 2001. Obama used other words, such as "violent extremism" or "violent extremists," to define the complexity of political violence in the Muslim world, and to again signal discontinuity with the US foreign policy of the previous eight years. But why was this linguistic change of pace so important? Despite the new vocabulary, Obama did not evade the issue, namely Hamas's presence in the Palestinian political landscape. Indeed, he recognized the mandate Hamas had gained through its 2006 electoral success. It is only after having acknowledged this political legitimacy that Obama called on Hamas to respect the Quartet's conditions. The drift of Obama's speech was clear: "Hamas does have support among some Palestinians, but they also have to recognize that they have responsibilities. To play a role in fulfilling Palestinian aspirations, to unify the Palestinian people, Hamas must put an end to violence, recognize past agreements, recognize Israel's right to exist." Palestinians, Obama said, "must abandon violence" and "focus on what they can build."[20]

The US president's message was sharp and clear in calling on Hamas to abandon violence. However, due to the obvious change in the language the United States used toward the Muslim world, the speech was greeted with genuine openness by the Islamist movement. Khaled Meshaal confirmed this interpretation in a televised speech from Damascus given twenty days after Obama's and two weeks after the speech Binyamin Netanyahu made at Bar Ilan University in response to the new US administration. Meshaal said: "We sense a change in the American tone and rhetoric towards the region and the Islamic world, as was evident from President Obama's speech in Cairo. We welcome this with great courage. We evaluate any change in an objective manner." He provided, however, only a temporary opening to Obama. "We are not entranced by speeches. Speeches do not win us over. The effect of rhetoric is temporary. We are looking for change in the policies on the ground."[21]

The changes on the ground that Meshaal referred to, however, would not come from the new US democratic administration during the following years. The signals the United States gave regarding the Middle East were almost schizophrenically different depending on who was speaking from within the complex machinery of American foreign policy. For its part, Hamas continued to follow its policy of ambiguity about the demands that it comply with the peace agreements signed by the PLO and that it recognize Israel, making it difficult, if not impossible, for the Obama administration to reconsider its traditional positions on the Islamist movement. Hamas's response to the disputed results of the mid-June Iranian presidential elections also precluded any softening in the Obama administration's strategy. In line with the attitude its leadership had consistently followed for more than twenty years, Hamas took a hands-off approach to the internal politics of its allies and of any country with which it maintained relations. Therefore Hamas neither stigmatized the Muslim Brotherhood's continuous repression in Syria and Egypt nor attacked the Iranian regime over the issue of elections. In fact, the Hamas leadership congratulated Mahmoud Ahmadinejad on his reelection as president of Iran, despite the Iranian opposition's protests and accusations of vote rigging and harsh repression carried out by the Tehran regime. "No doubt what is happening in Iran concerns and worries us, but we consider it to be an internal affair," Meshaal affirmed in August 2009 in an interview for Qatari newspaper *Al Watan*. "But we are definitely not worried about the relationship with Iran or the support that Iran offers us."[22]

This apparent alliance with Tehran negatively impacted the Western attitude toward Hamas. The timid openings European and American diplomats had been making toward Hamas immediately tightened up. At the same time, Hamas became a source of friction between Riyadh and Tehran, as described by Saudi King Abdullah during a meeting in spring 2009 with the White House advisor on counterterrorism, John Brennan: "The King described his conversation with FM Mottaki [the foreign minister of Iran at the time] as a heated exchange, frankly discussing Iran's interference in Arab affairs." When challenged by the King on Iranian meddling in Hamas affairs, Mottaki apparently protested that "these are Muslims." "No, Arabs," countered the King. "You as Persians have no business meddling in Arab matters."[23]

Hamas continued to send signals to the Obama administration, most prominently with a series of letters. The letters always had similar content, always came from Gaza, and were always written by Ahmed Youssef, deputy foreign minister and Hamas pragmatist. Youssef's long experience in the United States had given him direct knowledge of how to work within the American bureaucratic system. For example, a few weeks after the truce between Israel and Hamas in February 2009, Senator John Kerry paid a visit to Gaza to see the destruction. Karen Abu Zayd, high commissioner of UNRWA, was directed to give Kerry a letter Ahmed Youssef had written. Without opening it, Kerry gave the letter to the American consul in Jerusalem, Jacob Walles. In this way, US officials and politicians could, technically speaking, be free of the stigma of communicating with Hamas. But Youssef's devices for breaking through the isolation Hamas was subjected to by the international community still allowed the movement's message to be delivered to Obama, and the message was once again the same: "There can be no peace without Hamas." In other words, it was impossible, in the aftermath of Operation Cast Lead, to exclude the Islamist movement from any solution to the conflict.

In a subsequent letter in Arabic that was delivered through a group of American women visiting Gaza, Ahmed Youssef went further and called on Obama to visit the Gaza Strip on the eve of the US president's speech in Cairo. At the same time, the South African judge Richard Goldstone made a visit to Gaza as the special envoy appointed by the United Nations in order to compile the report that the international community had requested on the legality of the war. Youssef used the letter to Obama to point out that Hamas considered its behavior to be within the parameters set by the UN. "We are, in the Hamas government, committed to a just solution to the conflict in keeping with international law and the rulings of the International Court of Justice and the [UN] General Assembly and human rights organizations. We are ready to continue with all parties on the basis of mutual respect, without any prior requirements or conditions," wrote the vice foreign minister.[24]

But Hamas's attempts to open a channel with the new American president who had raised so many expectations in the Arab and Muslim world did not succeed in changing US Middle East policy. Washington's attitude toward Hamas remained the same, even though many signals from within the Obama administration seemed, especially in 2010, to push for involving Hamas in attempts to negotiate a lasting solution. Just as the United States was opening itself to possible negotiation with the Taliban in Afghanistan, experts, influential media figures, and even analysts within the Obama administration's bureaucracy drew the obvious parallel: Peace in the Middle East could not be achieved without the participation of Hamas.[25] But what seemed possible in Kabul remained much less possible in the Middle East, despite the experts' recommendations.

The official line the United States followed in the Middle East was not shared by everyone in charge of US defense and foreign policy. In the summer of 2010, a confidential report sent by the so-called Red Team to the US Central Command (CENTCOM) was published by Mark Perry in *Foreign Policy*. The report that senior US intelligence officials had prepared for its recipient, General David Petraeus, provided a perspective that was different from the one envisioned in the Obama administration's official statements. It indicated a solution to the conflicts in the Middle East that went beyond the Israeli-Palestinian crisis and that included the whole Levant. "The U.S. role of assistance to an *integrated* Lebanese defense force that includes Hizballah; and the continued training of Palestinian security forces in a Palestinian entity that *includes* Hamas in its government, would be more effective than providing assistance to entities—the government of Lebanon and Fatah—that represent only a part of the Lebanese and Palestinian populace respectively," concluded the Red Team report. In fact, although Hezbollah and Hamas "embrace staunch anti-Israel rejectionist policies," both the Lebanese and the Palestinian Islamist movements are "pragmatic and opportunistic."[26]

The Red Team thus decided to embrace a realistic approach. They had this in common with former US President Jimmy Carter, who since the the 2006 Hamas electoral victory had tried to keep a channel with the Islamist movement open and to involve it both in the Palestinian internal political transition process and in negotiations with the Israelis. Despite American officials repeatedly stressing that Carter had no role in the Obama administration, the State Department publicly confirmed that they were aware that between 2006 and 2010, Carter had met on different occasions with all the leading members of Hamas in Gaza, the West Bank, and especially in Damascus.[27] Jimmy Carter's shuttle diplomacy was not part of official US diplomacy. Nevertheless, it was an open channel between Hamas and the United States, and one that Washington found necessary for collecting news and getting direct responses from the Palestinian movement.

Gaza, however, is not Kabul. The privileged relationship between the United States and Israel and Tel Aviv's strong opposition to involving Hamas without preconditions meant that US Middle East policy could not depart from its traditional track, even with Barack Obama installed as president. And despite the change in government and what changes there were in the diplomatic situation, Israel maintained its traditional attitude toward Hamas and toward the siege on Gaza.

In short, nothing changed—that is, until the arrival of a regional player that muddied the Middle East conflict. Turkey's involvement in the Freedom Flotilla affair finally disrupted the diplomatic impasse on Gaza and forced Israel to alter, significantly, the restrictions it placed on the goods entering the Strip. The latent conflict between Israel and Turkey that led to its involvement in the Gaza situation exploded with the Israeli navy's bloody attack against the Turkish vessel *Mavi Marmara* on May 31, 2010—an attack that once again showed the extent to which Israel was still the cornerstone for the American strategy in the Middle East. Even an ally like Turkey—crucial in terms of the US military position in the region—could not undermine the relationship between Washington and Tel Aviv. In response, Turkey, after the dispute with Israel over attack on the Freedom Flotilla, moved strategically toward the East.

The Shifting Sands of Reconciliation

The attack took place live on television. It was half past four in the morning, and the dawn had yet to rise on the eastern Mediterranean when the boats of the Israeli navy's special operations unit Shayetet 13, along with a helicopter, started the attack against the *Mavi Marmara*. The *Mavi Marmara* had sailed from Istanbul under the Turkish flag ten days earlier, and was the largest in a convoy of six ships, called the Freedom Flotilla, that intended to break the blockade Israel had imposed on the Gaza Strip by bringing 10,000 tons of humanitarian aid. The whole operation was recorded by the journalists on board. The Shayetet 13 men were fully armed as they attached their ropes to the ship and climbed aboard. Then shots—injuries—blood. These live broadcasts, ending at 5:08 a.m. on May 31, were the last news from *Mavi Marmara* until official Israeli sources later provided their report. And thus a blanket of silence descended over the fate of over 700 peace activists from all around the world. The nine dead in the attack of the *Mavi Marmara* were all Turks.[28]

Meanwhile, the small port in Gaza was still colored by red Turkish flags with the crescent and star. In the days before the attack, the miserable marina had become a destination for small families who hoped to sight the peace flotilla. Hamas's leaders were always there, ready to be photographed by the cameras on the pier or on the police boats that patrolled the waters. Their rhetoric focused on the "liberators" who were coming to break the blockade around the Strip. But the horizon of Gaza City remained empty. Even so, Turkey acquired significance in the minds of the people: it was the only power that had not bent to Israel and that had defied the blockade around Gaza. They paid a high price: the lives of nine men, for whom the *gazawi* population organized funerals in absentia and after whom they named streets. The Turkish flag became almost as important as the Palestinian national flag, as Turkey overnight became a regional player in the Israeli-Palestinian conflict. The Islamist movement was already looking at the Turkish Prime Minister Recep Tayyip Erdogan as a model for what could have happened after the 2006 elections. And once again, after the *Mavi Marmara* affair, Hamas saw Ankara as an important ally at the various negotiating tables where it was involved, or where it wanted to be involved. Most importantly, the Islamist movement saw Turkey as a diplomatic ally that, unlike Iran or Syria, could open a channel with the West.

Indeed, Turkey had been the staunchest defender of Gaza, especially after Operation Cast Lead. Despite being one of the pillars of NATO in the Mediterranean, the country was crying out to break the blockade. The war in Gaza marked the tombstone of the mediation efforts that Ankara had performed between Israel and Syria in 2008, but gave Erdogan's government a new route to becoming a regional power. In an attempt to undermine the role Jordan and Egypt had played for decades, therefore, Ankara tried to be called on to intervene with its good offices in the Israeli-Palestinian conflict. This same motivation was behind Turkey's request at the end of July 2009 to enter negotiations between Fatah and Hamas.

Since the beginning of the reconciliation process between Fatah and Hamas, Egypt had functioned less as a neutral mediator and more as one of the parties. A long-standing supporter of Fatah, Cairo had since 2005 undergone a difficult and delicate transition to democracy linked to the question of who would succeed President Hosni Mubarak, a crisis that led to the January 25, 2011, revolution. This internal political instability made Egypt even more sensitive to what happened in the region, however, especially when political Islam entered the institutional game through Hamas. Hamas stemmed from the same predecessor group as the Egyptian Muslim Brotherhood, the only real competitor of the then-ruling party, the National Democratic Party. Thus the reconciliation between Fatah (the party Egypt had always supported) and Hamas (an Islamist movement strengthened by both an electoral victory and by the complete control of Gaza) was almost a matter of national policy to Cairo. "Egypt's delicate domestic situation cannot withstand the emergence of a successful or partly successful Muslim Brotherhood-inspired experiment anywhere in the Arab world, and certainly not on its very doorstep," commented Khaled Hroub in his analysis of one of the most muddled chapters in the reconciliation process.[29] The US diplomatic documents released by WikiLeaks during autumn 2010 make Egypt's ambiguous role in the talks more clear. Omar Suleyman adamantly explained Cairo's priorities regarding the Palestinian question: "Egypt's three primary objectives with the Palestinians were to maintain calm in Gaza, undermine Hamas, and build popular support for Palestinian President Mahmoud Abbas."[30]

Turkey's offer to enter the mediation process thus seriously worried Egypt. Ankara represented more of a competitor for Egypt than an ally. It is not surprising, therefore, to hear the comments that Hamas leaders made regarding what happened behind the scenes of the mediation process. "Turkey was not able to play a role, because Egypt vetoed it in order to monopolise the talks, and . . . US officials at the time backed Egypt up."[31]

However, Ankara's inability to join the Hamas-Fatah negotiations and to thus become part of the Middle Eastern diplomatic milieu did not succeed in curtailing Turkey's role as a regional power. The solution Turkey found has been erroneously defined as neo-Ottomanism. In real terms, however, the Freedom Flotilla affair was a legitimately modern way to wield regional influence, and it became an integral part of Turkey's new strategy of interventionism in the Israel-Palestine conflict. Turkey became known as the only regional power that used its political strength in an attempt to break the blockade of Gaza. But Ankara activism failed to achieve its goal. Egypt remained the only power managing the main negotiating table after the 2008–2009 war in Gaza until the revolution whisked away the Mubarak regime in 2011. From the very day after the dismissal of Hosni Mubarak, and especially after Nabil al Arabi became the new Egyptian foreign minister, the whole Middle East changed, the relationship between Turkey and Egypt included.

But in 2009 all the negotiating tables to which Hamas was invited were under the mediating authority of the Egyptian security services under Omar Suleyman. There were three such negotiations: the first on a renewed and longer-lasting truce between Israel and Hamas, the second on a prisoner exchange between Israeli corporal Gilad Shalit and the over one thousand Palestinian prisoners in Israeli jails, and the third on brokering a reconciliation between Fatah and Hamas. The points to be negotiated were to be managed according to "domino" logic: one would have to be settled before the next could be reached.

At the start of the negotiating process, Israel and the Islamist movement discussed a very different truce from the one that had brought about the 2008 ceasefire. Hamas wanted the crossings to be reopened, allowing Gaza to break out of its isolation. The intersection and overlap of these three separate Cairo negotiations, however, made it impossible for the diplomatic process to proceed in an orderly and linear fashion over the years. There were surprising moments of acceleration, in which the results appeared to be close at hand, that were followed between 2009 and 2010 by impasses, continuous delays, extensions, and unending changes to the same points on the agenda.

Still, in mid-February 2009, Hamas and Israel seemed to be on the verge of coming to an agreement on a new truce. Israeli domestic politics was the main factor that pushed Hamas to accept the agreement, given the possibility that Binyamin Netanyahu might be asked by President Shimon Peres to form a new government. In Cairo, contacts were put in place with a mid-level Hamas delegation from Gaza, at which point Mahmoud al-Zahhar and Nizar Awadallah joined the talks (there is little information on Awadallah, but it seemed he played a role in the military wing's organization during the 1980s and 1990s). Al-Zahhar, who had both Palestinian and Egyptian blood in his veins, went directly to Damascus to discuss the Egyptian offer with Hamas's political bureau. He returned accompanied by Moussa Abu Marzouq and Mohammed Nasr, considered at the time to be Khaled Meshaal's right hand. At the end of this round of negotiations, Moussa Abu Marzouq said that the truce was possible. The second-in-command of the political wing of Hamas then released to the Egyptian news agency MENA the news that the agreement's first phase had been accepted. There would be a ceasefire between Hamas and Israel for a period of a year and a half, in exchange for the opening of the crossings between the Strip and the Israeli territory—even if the question of which goods would receive permission to enter Gaza remained uncertain.

The issue of the border crossings intersected with the issue of reconciliation between Fatah and Hamas. Hamas sources in Gaza said, in fact, that the Palestinian Islamist movement had no desire to bring complications to the reopening of Rafah, and would thus be willing to allow Mahmoud Abbas's Presidential Guard to manage the border crossings. It was obvious, according to the Hamas sources, that the agreement would involve the border being patrolled by Egyptian forces, the PNA's, and Hamas's own. At this point in the negotiations, however, Israel decided to change the order in which the negotiations would proceed and called for the release of Gilad Shalit before a final decision could be made on the ceasefire agreement and the opening of Gaza crossings.

In the face of this, Egypt decided to put aside the first two issues and begin with the topic of reconciliation between Fatah and Hamas. This was an issue that for many years had been stalled due to both the stubbornness of both the PNA and Hamas, but also because of pressure from different international actors. Israel, for example, had worked against the reconciliation because it was interested in negotiating with only one part of the total Palestinian political representation. The divide between Fatah and Hamas meant, for Israel, that the PNA in Ramallah would be weaker, and that there would be no end to Hamas's isolation. Additionally, the United States and Egypt did their part to maintain the impasse between the two "heads" of the Palestinian government.

February 26, 2009, marked the first negotiation on the topic of the Hamas and Fatah split after the war in Gaza. Five committees were formed to overcome the obstacles, starting with the task of reorganizing the security forces and releasing the Hamas members that the PNA had detained in the West Bank and the Fatah members imprisoned in Gaza. The "stone guest" at this feast, however, was once again the question of reforming the PLO, reforms that still had not been implemented. The contenders knew all too well the underlying problem: the entry of Hamas into the PLO would mean that Hamas could potentially hold legitimate authority over the territory administered by the PNA. Khaled Meshaal had originally placed such reform as the sine qua non condition for Hamas's participation in the national unity government before the Mecca Agreement in February 2007, after which he softened his position. Hamas's entry into the PLO was also the cornerstone of the March 2005 agreement among all Palestinian factions, an agreement initiated, mediated, and concluded by Mahmoud Abbas. The 2005 agreement gave the go to

Hamas's participation in the parliamentary elections for the PNA and was intended to pave the way for the Islamist movement's entry into a reformed PLO, but this latter part of the agreement was never implemented.

After the war on Gaza, Khaled Meshaal put pressure on the Ramallah-based PNA, threatening to create an alternative national platform for those groups that were not represented in the PLO. A parallel PLO, in short. This "solution" was ultimately just a trial balloon launched by Meshaal, but it indicated that the sticking point of the negotiations remained the same: the issue of reforming the PLO had never been truly addressed in negotiations. To address it would mean undermining the established powers within the Palestinian society. In particular, it weakened Abu Mazen's position, already fragile after the end of his term as PNA president on January 9, 2009, while weapons still thundered in Gaza. Abu Mazen, however, maintained the position of PLO chairman, the PLO being the legitimate representative of the entire Palestinian people. To reform the PLO, then, would mean going deep into the heart of the issue of representation of the different Palestinian political forces.

But this phase of the Cairo negotiations still lay ahead, to be mediated as always by Omar Suleyman, who went to Washington in March to moderate the American position on Hamas and to allow the establishment of a national unity government. Expectations, however, were soon dashed. On March 19, the talks—which would have called for presidential and parliamentary elections to be scheduled for January 25, 2010—were postponed until after the Arab League summit. On April 2, there was a meeting with the participation of some of the most important representatives of both factions: Nabil Shaath and Ahmed Qureia for Fatah, and Moussa Abu Marzouq for Hamas. The negotiations became even more complicated when the possibility arose that Salam Fayyad might be installed as a transitional unity government's prime minister in a reunited PNA. Fayyad had submitted a sort of preventive resignation to Abbas. Hamas did not say outright that it would veto Fayyad as a transitional prime minister, but it was evident that he would not be capable of mending the differences between Fatah and

Hamas. Far from being just a technocrat, after nearly two years of leading the Ramallah-based Palestinian government, Salam Fayyad had already developed his own political stature and come out of the shadow of Abu Mazen and entrenched Fatah power. In addition, the strong support he received from the West precluded his being a neutral figure in the eyes of Hamas.

There were other matters that made it complicated to accept Fayyad as a potential prime minister. The bureaucratic institutions in Ramallah and Gaza also had their own agendas that made reconciliation difficult. Given that Palestine is not recognized as a state, the day-to-day administration of both Gaza and the West Bank fell mainly to the parallel bureaucracies in each territory. As the PNA in Ramallah is the only one recognized by the international community, and thus the only one that received and administered the massive economic aid that allows Palestine to survive, Salam Fayyad—as someone who had taken steps to maintain very centralized executive power over the Ramallah bureaucracy—was poised to play a political game of his own. Even Israeli President Shimon Peres described Fayyad in February 2010 as a sort of Palestinian Ben-Gurion. The remarks came after Fayyad's government launched an ambitious program to strengthen Palestinian institutions in preparation for supporting a Palestinian state with full sovereignty over the 1967 Territory, with East Jerusalem as its capital. The program was to be completed by August 2011,[32] a date that coincided impressively with the PNA's request that the United Nations recognize the State of Palestine in September 2011. The thirty-seven page program meant to accomplish this administrative overhaul, however, is essentially devoted to practical and logistical matters, without any larger economic, social, or cultural vision for the nature of the new potential state. Despite this exclusion, Salam Fayyad and the program he initiated had given him a much stronger political role.

Fayyad's presence as the PNA prime minister was based on his control of the West Bank cities defined in the Oslo Accords as Area A, which were formally under the authority of PNA security forces. Thus the Palestinian prime minister was credited increasingly in Europe and the United States—but also in a part of the Israeli establishment—as the figure on which Western ambitions and support should focus, often at the expense of attempts to reconcile the divided Palestinian political scene. The utmost expression of such ambitions was the "West Bank first" scenario, widely discussed in Western diplomatic circles, in which a viable Palestinian state would be established—but only in the West Bank. According to the Western diplomats, this goal would have to be accomplished before there could be any reconciliation between Hamas and Fatah.

This was the context as the regular meetings in Cairo reached the end of May 2009, with the main points of disagreement remaining the same—again, the makeup and political objectives of the national unity government, the reform of the security forces, and reform of electoral law. The script was always the same: representatives for Hamas and Fatah traded accusations that the other side was uninterested in reaching a real agreement. And as had happened before, the situation on the ground began to play its own part in stalling the talks. In Qalqilya, in the northern West Bank, PNA security forces and members of the Hamas military wing clashed once on May 31 and again on June 4. There were eight deaths, among them Islamist militants, policemen, and civilians. In response, Hamas arrested Fatah members in Gaza. The Palestinian Center for Human Rights released its opinion that each side had adopted repressive policies toward the other by condemning the arrests in Gaza while at the same time speaking of the hundreds of Hamas activists in Fatah jails.[33] Everyone was afraid that 2006 would repeat itself, and that the West Bank would experience what Gaza had experienced in the earlier clash between the factions. The PNA in Ramallah, however, used the clash to strengthen the security apparatus around Abu Mazen, supported by the United States through the presence of General Keith Dayton. To control the West Bank, starting from the north, would mean meeting the demands of Israel's security forces, a goal that Hamas could not support. Thus the Islamist movement considered Fatah's decision to work with Israel to be one of the reasons reconciliation would not be possible. "Among the Palestinian brothers in Hamas and Israel, Fatah chose Israel. He decided to side with the occupant," was the comment Hamas deputy Mushir al Masri, youngest among the Hamas members elected in 2006, made a year and a half after the clashes in Qalqilya.[34] Even after Keith Dayton was replaced in October 2010 by Michael Moeller, this relationship between the PNA security apparatus in the West Bank and US advisors indeed remained one of the obstacles to reconciliation, and Hamas immediately called for Moeller's resignation, stating that reforming the security forces also required reforming the "ethics which prohibit security coordination and integration with the enemy."[35]

However, even if the negotiations between Hamas and Fatah were often held hostage by members of the international community, it is equally true that the failure of dialogue between Hamas and Fatah was the result of a division in Palestinian society that time has increasingly deepened. "Reconciliation remains elusive . . . as neither Hamas nor Fatah really want an agreement," said Omar Suleyman to US General Petraeus.[36] Both sides have consistently used the repeated impasse in the negotiations to strengthen their own positions, widening the fracture between the West Bank and Gaza and essentially abandoning East Jerusalem to its fate.

A typical example is what happened at Fatah's sixth general conference, which in the summer of 2009 represented yet another obstacle placed in the path of reconciliation. Postponed again and again, the phoenix of the sixth congress marked for exactly twenty years the deep divisions within the nationalist party. In particular, the long delay highlighted the clash between the leadership that returned from exile to Palestine together with Yasser Arafat in the aftermath of the Oslo Accords, and the younger elite who grew up in the Occupied Territory during the First Intifada. The internal battle became even more acute after the bitter electoral defeat in January 2006 and the seizure of power by Hamas in Gaza. But the conference, which opened on August 4, 2009, at the Terrasanta School in Bethlehem, followed a different logic than that of the Fatah internal reform, which many party cadres had requested during the entire period between the 1989 fifth congress and the sixth. The goal of the sixth congress was primarily based on Abu Mazen's need to gather support from the delegates so that he might function effectively as the new head of Fatah and the true successor to Arafat. Abu Mazen had to be the man, who—through the congress's broad vote—could be said to have a real consensus among the Palestinians.

Since the eve of the conference, Mahmoud Abbas succeeded in maximizing his domestic support. First, he urged that the congress take place in Bethlehem, and not abroad, as was traditional. This insistence on a location within the West Bank was a tool used to reinforce the centrality of the territory under the PNA's control and to diminish the significance of the groups within Fatah that were strong in the refugee camps (in particular Farouk Qaddoumi's wing). Abu Mazen succeeded in setting the congress location in Bethlehem and further managed to strengthen his leadership in the final vote, at the same time containing the support of the leader in absentia, Marwan Barghouthi, and his supporters. In this case, however, the "stone guest" was Gaza. Hamas prevented the Fatah delegates from the Strip from traveling to the conference, owing to the failure of the PNA to release many of Hamas's West Bank leaders. For a moment, there was speculation that the absence of Gaza delegates could jeopardize the entire conference. "Without Gaza there is no conference," said Nabil Shaath, who had tried unsuccessfully to facilitate an agreement because, according to him, Gaza was "the catalyst of our failures, the result of our problems."[37] But the conference had gone ahead, despite everything, giving Abu Mazen, seventy-four, the legitimacy he had hoped to secure through the congress. Mahmoud Abbas was formally designated Arafat's successor and the leader of Fatah. But Fatah did not reform itself.

Given his strengthened position, Abu Mazen was ready to reopen the question of reconciliation at Cairo. Rumors were beginning to spread that Germany was acting as the mediator in the negotiations between Israel and Hamas for the release of Gilad Shalit in exchange for the release of the Palestinian prisoners in Israeli jails, a situation that caused the Egyptians to suddenly be concerned about the time the negotiations were taking. The unusual visit that Khaled Meshaal paid to Cairo in early September confirmed that there were two negotiations in the making. Even Mahmoud Abbas was in the Egyptian capital, but the leaders of the two factions did not meet; the fracture was too deep. But the simultaneous presence of high-ranking Hamas and Fatah leaders meant that the negotiations had reached an important point. Thus, with time running out on the Egyptians, they pushed for an immediate end to the rift by preparing a reconciliation document to which they would not accept any changes or amendments. One of the amendments involved the procedure used to determine elections. The Egyptians proposed a mixed system, but that the share devoted to proportional votes be increased to 80 percent of the seats, compared to the 50 percent used in the 2006 elections. Fatah accepted. Hamas had yet to decide. Their positions in this case were not so far away from each other, but Hamas still made repeated requests for changes to the agreement. The Egyptian response was take it or leave it.

Yet agreement on reconciliation seemed within reach thanks to what was happening on the other negotiating table with Israel on the prisoner exchange. A two-minute video in which Corporal Shalit appears was handed to the Israelis on October 2, in conjunction with the release of twenty Palestinian prisoners, all women. It was the first time since Shalit was captured in late June 2006 that anyone had seen the Israeli soldier, who reads a letter in the video. This first (and only) tangible result between 2006 and 2010 on the Shalit file happened through the efforts of the Bundesnachrichtendienst (BND), the German intelligence services, which since 2005 had been led by Ernst Uhrlau. In his capacity as mediator, Uhrlau had achieved a major success in 2003 by getting the Israeli government led by Ariel Sharon to agree to a prisoner exchange with Hezbollah. Among the prisoners released by Israel, there were also Jordanian and Palestinian nationals. Uhrlau achieved another success in 2008, again through mediation between Israel and Hezbollah, on the exchange of bodies of soldiers from previous conflicts. Two hundred bodies of Hezbollah fighters were exchanged for the bodies of the two Israeli soldiers whose murder in an ambush two years earlier had sparked off the thirty-three-day war between Tel Aviv and Beirut. In addition, Israel released Samir Kuntar, the man responsible for one of the most heinous terrorist attacks against Israel. The exchange broker in this 2008 deal was Gerhard Conrad, a BND official about whom little is known, except that he studied in Syria and knows Arabic well.

Rumors spread that Conrad was the man chosen in 2009 to assist the Egyptians in the negotiations between Israel and Hamas.

At the Cairo table, the agreement on reconciliation was almost complete when it was suddenly postponed. The cause was the mid-September 2009 release of the UN fact-finding mission's report on the Gaza Conflict, known as the Goldstone Report. The Richard Goldstone–led report was harsh and accused Israel of having carried out serious violations of human rights and humanitarian law, to the point of suspecting openly that Israel had committed war crimes and crimes against humanity. Although Hamas also took the blame for firing rockets on Israeli towns and other human rights issues, the Goldstone Report was indeed a *j'accuse* against Israeli conduct in the Gaza War, as well as an unequivocal condemnation of the occupation of the West Bank and the blockade of Gaza. But the PNA did not take advantage of the opportunity to discuss Israel's responsibilities to the occupied territory in a public debate at the UN Human Rights Council. On the contrary, it stalled for at least two weeks, as it would later be discovered by the Palestinian committee set up to investigate the PNA's behavior with respect to the Goldstone Report. On October 1, in a last-minute decision, the Palestinian ambassador in Geneva, Ibrahim Khreishe, accepted that the debate on the Goldstone Report in the UN Human Rights Council be postponed until March 2010.

It was an unexpected decision, and one that unleashed a storm on the presidency of Mahmoud Abbas. And the first victim of the postponement of the Goldstone Report was the reconciliation agreement. Hamas now refused to sign the take-it-or-leave-it Egyptian agreement, considering the PNA's action not only an attack on Hamas, but also an insult to the victims of Operation Cast Lead and to the suffering of the people of Gaza. In a few days, the wave of indignation mounted, causing Abu Mazen's closest advisers to try to repair the damage they had done in Geneva. From Amman, the chief Palestinian negotiator Saeb Erekat made it known that Abbas was seriously considering presenting the Goldstone Report to the UN General Assembly and the Security Council. But this disclosure did not stop the attacks, which came from all sectors of Palestinian society, as well as from the whole Arab world. A committee of inquiry assigned to investigate the PNA's postponement of discussions on the Goldstone Report reached the unavoidable conclusion: Mahmoud Abbas had given in to American pressure to delay the debate.[38]

The suspension of the negotiations on reconciliation affected also the other negotiating table on prisoner exchange, where silence quickly enveloped the difficult and secret talks. Reports surfaced in early 2010 that Gerhard Conrad had resigned as a mediator due to Hamas's insistence on including certain controversial Palestinian prisoners on the list of those to be released, an insistence Hamas arrived at through one of its characteristic decisions made among its four constituencies. In short, negotiations on the prisoner exchange were once again frozen. The sophisticated 3D video produced by the Qassam Brigades, which surprisingly was made public in April 2010, did not help unfreeze the talks. The video depicts Gilad's father, Noam Shalit, waiting for the release of his son. Finally, he is released, but in this nightmarish vision of the future, he arrives at the Erez crossing in a coffin.[39] The political wing of Hamas immediately denied— in the words of Mahmoud al-Zahhar—that the Qassam Brigades had represented Hamas's position. But it is evident that this attempt to wage psychological war on Israel through the movement's military wing showed that the Qassam Brigades clearly desired their own political input on the prisoner negotiations.

On the Israeli side of the table, the Netanyahu government found it impossible to overcome two objections to the exchange. First, Israel wanted to prevent certain detainees from returning to their places of origin in the West Bank and insisted that they instead be deported to Gaza or outside of Palestine altogether, as happened in 1992 at Marj al-Zuhour. Second, the Netanyahu government refused to release the most controversial names on Hamas's list, which included prisoners that belonged to all factions. Marwan Barghouthi would not be released and neither would Ahmed Saadat, secretary general of the Popular Front for the Liberation of Palestine. Israel also said no to the release of some Hamas militants: Abbas Al-Sayyed, Hassan Salameh, Ahlam al-Tamimi, and Qahera al-Sa'di. Netanyahu repeatedly insisted on these two conditions, even after Noam Shalit increased pressure on the government to negotiate with Hamas for his son's release, even to the point of leading a march throughout Israel in June and July 2010 to force Israel to reopen negotiations after a complete six-month freeze. Then, in early October 2010, Gerhard Conrad returned to Gaza to pick up the thread of a speech he had left interrupted many months earlier. It is hardly a coincidence that the reopening of the prisoner exchange negotiations came at the same time as Netanyahu and Abbas reopened the peace process between Israel and Palestine—a process that soon closed again after Israel refused to put a stop to the settlements springing up in the West Bank and East Jerusalem.

But whatever the state of the prisoner negotiations, Israel's policy toward Hamas during 2009 and 2010 did not change. The Netanyahu government continued the blockade of Gaza, refused to open any regular diplomatic channel to Hamas, and exerted strong pressure on Western countries to ensure that they continued isolating the Islamist movement. There was, however, one important change in the Netanyahu government's handling of Hamas: it did not oppose the Islamist movement with a massive attack. Instead, it took actions against individuals. This was consistent with Netanyahu's previous handling of the Hamas situation, in particular the approval he gave during his term as prime minister in 1997 to the assassination attempt against Khaled Meshaal (an attempt that became known as one of the worst Mossad failures). In January 2010, then, the Israeli prime minister gave the green light to another strike, this time against Mahmoud al-Mabhouh in Dubai. A member of the Muslim Brotherhood in Gaza, a Hamas militant since the movement's beginning, and a member of the Hamas military wing linked to Salah al-Shehadeh, al-Mabhouh had spent many years in exile in Damascus. His military actions—as he recounted in detail in a 2009 interview with Al Jazeera, during which the Hamas militant wore a hood—were all confined to the early years of Hamas and all directed against Israeli soldiers.[40]

Al-Mabhouh, fifty-eight, was not a notorious figure, even among Israelis. His name became widely known only when he was killed in the elegant Al Bustan Rotana hotel in Dubai, where he was found dead on January 20 in the room he had checked into the day before. He had been suffocated with a pillow. Mossad's hand in the assassination was possible, as was the interpretation of Dubai's police chief, Lt. Gen. Dahi Khalfan Tamim. After very quick investigations, the police chief was able to publish the pictures of the dozens of men and women involved in the murder. Video footage showed the commandos who had followed al-Mabhouh, the passport photos, and all the different images that immortalized the faces of the potential Mossad agents. The pictures were shown on television around the world and collected by the Dubai investigators, who were able to go through tens of thousands of hours of footage recorded by cameras throughout the Emirate in order to confirm the identities of a group of at least thirty-five people who were involved. Fingerprints and DNA findings were then sent to Interpol, together with an arrest warrant. Dahi Khalfan Tamim was unwavering: Mossad had killed al-Mabhouh. Israel—as always happens in these cases—neither confirmed nor denied the operation.

Whatever the Israeli government's purpose, however, al-Mabhouh's assassination boomeranged on Tel Aviv. If the faces Tamim had broadcast really did belong to Israeli intelligence agents, their career was irreparably exposed; in espionage jargon, they were "burned." In addition, the investigations discovered that the passports the suspected Mossad agents had used to enter Dubai had been cloned from authentic travel documents belonging to different European countries and to Australia. Thus the al-Mabhouh assassination became a scandal that put a strain on the relations between Israel and major Western countries, some of which were considered close friends of Tel Aviv. Britain, France, Germany, Ireland, Australia—all countries involved in the passport cloning—reacted in various ways to Dubaigate, ranging from complaints presented to the Israeli ambassador in each country to the expulsion of diplomats and officials from Britain, Ireland, and Australia, all the way up to the arrest of an Israeli citizen in an unidentified country in the summer of 2010.

Al-Mabhouh's assassination in January 2010 also shed a different light on an episode that had happened just three weeks before, one that had been given much less emphasis in the media. Two bodyguards of Osama Hamdan, the Hamas representative in Lebanon, were killed by an explosion at the end of December 2009 in the Haret Hreik area in southern Beirut. The Haret Hreik neighborhood was totally under the control of Hezbollah and was thus considered immune to attacks by Israeli intelligence. There were different interpretations of the attack: were explosives mailed to one of the Hamas offices in the region, or was the "attack" an accident caused by Hamas's clumsy handling of its own weapons materials? The curtain of mystery around the incident has never been lifted, even by Hamas, which admitted immediately after the attack through its spokesman, Ayman Taha, that the "circumstances of the explosion are unclear and it is too early to name the [responsible] party."[41] Whether or not it was an attack, the odd blast of Haret Hreik combined with the assassination of al-Mabhouh in raising the question of the use of targeted killings of Hamas members by Israel.

But in terms of the reconciliation talks, stalled in October 2009, there was nothing to speak of; Ramallah and Gaza were consolidating their own separate powers. Both sides made the usual redundant statements, recriminations, and accusations of repressing, arresting, or torturing opponents. Nabil Shaath's visit to his native Gaza in February 2010, the first of a senior Fatah member since the coup three years earlier, could only open a crack in the armor of mistrust, despite the importance the media devoted to the event. Shaath and members of Hamas were shown smiling and embracing in photos, and later, far from television cameras, Nabil Shaath tried to act as peacemaker by meeting with some Hamas leaders in the West Bank. But his attempt had little success.[42]

It was not until late spring that something changed. According to sources inside Hamas, the negotiations on Hamas and Fatah's reconciliations opened again due to a substantial "nonintervention" by the American administration, which decided not to oppose the dialogue between Hamas and Fatah. Mahmoud Abbas relied on a committee made up of four important figures in the Palestinian political and intellectual landscape—Munib al Masri, Hanan Ashrawi, Hanna Nasser, and Nasr Eddin al Shaer—to try and reopen the talks. The committee's mandate was short, with only a few weeks remaining until June. Nevertheless, Abbas's committee organized four or five meetings, as well as came to the conclusion that the document drafted by the Egyptians—on which the factions had almost reached an agreement in October 2009—was not sufficient. The committee did not discuss specific points, but only their general strategy: they would seek an agreement between all the Palestinian factions on the disputed points, then go with this compromise in hand to Cairo. The committee's idea of a parallel document drafted by the Palestinians that would be combined with the unamendable Egyptian agreement was behind the push to return to active negotiations. Surprisingly, Omar Suleyman was behind the push.

At the beginning of September 2010, however, Fatah and Hamas were even more at odds after negotiations between the PNA and Israel resumed at the request of Barack Obama. In Washington on September 2, Mahmoud Abbas and Binyamin Netanyahu began bilateral talks under the supervision of Secretary of State Hillary Clinton and the White House envoy for the Middle East, George Mitchell. It was not a relaxed diplomatic atmosphere, and not only because of the controversial issues on the agenda. First and foremost, the number of Israeli settlements in the West Bank and in East Jerusalem continued to grow rapidly. The day before, Israel had buried the four victims of an attack for which Hamas had claimed responsibility. The attack had been chosen for its symbolic value: the Palestinian village of Bani Naim, in the outskirts of Hebron, just behind some of the more radical Israeli settlements in the West Bank. The most important of those settlements was Kiryat Arba, in whose cemetery is buried Baruch Goldstein, the infamous settler who massacred twenty-nine faithful in the Ibrahimi Mosque in Hebron in February 1994.

The four settlers had been killed in an ambush. The Hamas military wing immediately, yet ambiguously, claimed responsibility. From Gaza, the spokesman of the Izz al-din al-Qassam Brigades, Abu Obeida, stated that the attack had occurred "in the Palestinian land occupied in 1967."[43] Not in Israel, therefore, but to the east of the Green Line. What did this mean? That Hamas continued in its own way to "respect" the unilateral ceasefire declared in early 2005 that had ended the suicide bombings inside Israel? This seems the most plausible reading of Abu Obeida's message. Together with a confirmation—so to speak—of the territorial limitation of violence, the Hamas military wing also launched a warning directed exclusively to the PNA. Hamas had attacked Hebron, which was still considered the West Bank's Islamist stronghold. As such, Hebron had been subjected to tough and thorough restrictions administered by the PNA security apparatus. Yet Palestinian security forces and intelligence services had failed to stop the Qassam Brigades member prior to the attack, though they did subsequently perform hundreds of arrests directed at the Islamist militancy. But this was too little, too late: Hamas had shown that its military ability to harm the West Bank had not been reduced, as had been generally believed before the attack. The tragic episode not only affected relations between Ramallah and Gaza, but also between Palestinians and Egyptians. In Cairo, the attack seemed to show that the increasing radicalization in Gaza might no longer be manageable. The talks had been stalled intermittently since February 2009, during which time the borders of Gaza remained closed, an intolerable situation that was slowly but certainly radicalizing the population. The growing Salafi and Jihadist sectors in the Strip could, in Cairo's view, easily bind together with the growing dissatisfaction of the Sinai population. For dozens of years, this Sinai population had represented a thorn in the side of the security services led by Omar Suleyman, but the threat was considered even more dangerous in September 2010, on the eve of the Egyptian parliamentary elections in October.

Thus Omar Suleyman again revived the talks between Hamas and Fatah in September, in the face of this growing threat and while Israel and the United States were committed to the negotiations in Washington. As Ramadan drew to a close, Suleyman and Khaled Meshaal took advantage of the Muslim holy month's last days to meet in Mecca. The powerful Egyptian intelligence chief was formally in Saudi Arabia to report to the authorities in Riyadh on the face-to-face meeting between Abu Mazen and Netanyahu in Washington. The September 8 meeting between Suleyman and Meshaal took place over the two hours before the prayer of *fajr*, the dawn, as the pan-Arab newspaper *Al Hayat* discovered. After the talks, Suleyman called Mahmoud Abbas.

Beyond the issue of the Sinai and the succession, however, there were reasons of timing behind Suleyman's push to reopen the negotiations on Palestinian reconciliation during the peace process. Suleyman's efforts were made in the context of a comprehensive American push to restart the diplomatic engine of the entire Middle East. In mid-September, during the second meeting between Netanyahu and Abbas, Senator George Mitchell left Hillary Clinton to mediate between the two leaders and flew to Damascus. This visit, as well as the next stop in Beirut to meet with the highest authorities in Lebanon, was a part of the new White House's Middle East strategy. Since its inception, the Obama administration had always insisted that any lasting peace in the Middle East had to go beyond agreements between Israelis and Palestinians. Thus Mitchell went to Syria and to Lebanon in search of a comprehensive regional solution to the problem. First, there was the September 19 news that Hamas had sent a letter to the Obama administration seeking an open diplomatic channel. Hamas had sent such letters before, but this one distinctly stated that Hamas would not oppose the creation of a Palestinian state on the 1967 borders, with Jerusalem as its capital. The Palestinian security forces, concerned by the possibility that the letter might result in a change in Washington's strategy, indirectly confirmed the new interest that Europeans and Americans had toward the idea of Hamas involvement in the Israeli-Palestinian negotiation process. "The Palestinian leadership has learned that the US officials are now studying the situation of Hamas the same way they studied the situation of the PLO in 1990," General Adnan Damiri told the *Jerusalem Post*.[44] Damiri was the spokesman for the security forces in the West Bank that had been trained through Keith Dayton's programs. If Damiri was right, then the possibility of the West opening a channel to Hamas might be on the table.

It was in the context of these events that a few days later, on September 24, an important meeting was held between Fatah and Hamas in Damascus. The three-hour-long talks boasted a small army of important figures from the political and security wings of Fatah and

Hamas. In the Fatah delegation there was Azzam al Ahmad, General Nasser Youssef, and Sahar Basiso, the nationalist party's intelligence chief. For Hamas, there was Khaled Meshaal, Moussa Abu Marzouq, the head of intelligence, Izzat al Resheq, and Mohammed Nasr, this last still considered the man nearest to Meshaal. Thus the reconciliation process started again, this time with the explicit intent of dealing with the crucial points left unanswered and unresolved in previous meetings. As Abbas's committee had decided, the 2009 Egyptian-authored text of the agreement was not touched, but the process by which it would be implemented would be changed, requiring Fatah and Hamas to prepare a parallel agreement. After the minisummit in Damascus, each party returned to its traditional script: high-toned and optimistic declarations, followed by complaints and postponements. What was different this time, however, were the signals coming from Hamas, echoing what the letter to Obama had said: the Islamist movement could possibly accept the establishment of a Palestinian state on 1967 borders, with East Jerusalem as its capital and with the guaranteed right of return for refugees. Hamas's four constituencies had already accepted this formula years before and had announced it in the international media more than once since 2006. But now, in September and October 2010, Khaled Meshaal repeated this stance over and over in numerous interviews in a clear media offensive that Hamas leadership launched through several American and European newspapers.

The novelty of this situation related to the organization's internal balance and to what was happening in Gaza under the Israeli embargo. The blockade, now in its third year, had two politically relevant results: first, Gaza, as a constituency, had become more important to Hamas since the 2007 coup, and second, Gaza had become increasingly radical. At that time, few people could imagine or even dream that Gaza's isolation would be broken only a few months later in 2011, after a revolution that would oust Hosni Mubarak from the presidency in only eighteen days.

We Understood Better Than They Did

A fisherman casts nets by hand, plunged into the sea up to his waist. The sea is dark, its pollution obvious to the naked eye. An acrid and unhealthy smell wafts up to the beach to level ground not far from a large outdoor coffee shop: four old tables and a few blue plastic chairs. This is al-Shati, which started its life as a refugee camp and later became the northern outskirts of Gaza City. But even if this is one of the most neglected places of the world, it does not take much to enjoy the sea—even if the sea in Gaza is fouled by the sewage that washes up on shore, while the chimneys of Ashkelon in Israel, only a handful of miles away, puff white smoke into the air. Only two hundred meters from the shore, small fishing boats drag the water, which at this distance becomes blue and clear—as the sea should be. There are very few fish this close to shore, but to go any farther out means challenging the Israeli naval blockade. Under the Oslo Accords, the limit was twenty nautical miles from shore. Since Operation Cast Lead, Israel has restricted Gazan boats to three.

In many ways the coastal road in al-Shati is no different than any other road in the world. There are men jogging, occasional cars, buses with old and rusted carburetors, scooters, Egyptian motorcycles, and tuk-tuks—motorcycles with carts attached. Thousands of Chinese-made tuk-tuks have been smuggled into Gaza through the Rafah tunnels from Egypt, just as the motorcycles and the scooters have been. The Gaza Train completes the false picture of normality in the Strip: a red and white train for children that travels on wheels from somewhere to the miserable coastal road in al-Shati.

Only here, in the largest refugee camp in Gaza City, can this false normality hold. There are no shanties left, as there were between 1948 and 1951, when the refugees arrived from the north. Now there are only buildings two or three floors high, many houses built literally on top of each other, all the way to the edge of the beach. The buildings often have no plaster on their exposed gray bricks. After Operation Cast Lead, the Gazans took the concrete rubble left after the Israeli bombardments, crushed it, and kneaded it into new gray bricks. They are weaker and less durable than bricks made of real concrete, useful only to expand existing apartments.

The poverty of the refugee camps is obvious. It is constantly before your eyes: in the shops that sell made-in-China trinkets, in the battered streets, in the cheaply dressed inhabitants, in the people wearing black slippers. It is in the Egyptian-flavored marriage processions. The band plays drums to celebrate the couple, riding in a bright yellow truck. And then the guests arrive, all on a bus rented for the occasion, because cars and fuel are an unattainable luxury. After the marriage and the party, even the furniture for the new house (or more probably for the room where the couple will live) will arrive on that yellow truck.

The home of Abul Abed (as al-Shati's residents continue to call Prime Minister Ismail Haniyeh) is there, close to the waterfront. Abul Abed has not abandoned the refugee camp where he was born. The only changes in Haniyeh's life after being appointed prime minister are the safety measures next to the house. Armed police are stationed in a booth on the waterfront, a bar closes the access road to the house, and what seems to be a bullet-proof metal covering protects the front door. "The fact that Abul Abed remained here in Shati really matters to me," says a young man named Mahmoud. "The more the leaders are close to us, the more they are part of us, part of the population. It means also that they have remained modest." Mahmoud has no hesitation. He is thirty-three, with prematurely graying hair, a pair of small and fairly elegant eyeglasses, and a soft-colored striped polo shirt, identical to the many polo shirts that one can find along the Mediterranean coasts. "As prime minister, he can live wherever he wants. Among his duties, Abul Abed needs also to receive the government's guests. But the fact that he did not want to live elsewhere really matters to me." Mahmoud calls himself a Hamas activist, one of those who believed (and still believe) in the 2005–2006 decision to participate in elections in the PNA. "We always see Abul Abed; we meet him during Ramadan; he is still the imam in our mosque."[45]

Mahmoud is not the only one to speak in these terms about the Harakat al-Muqawwama al-Islamiyya leaders. The description is always as follows: They are not corrupt, and even the last three years in power in Gaza do not seem to have changed their habits. Abul Abed lives in his house inside the al-Shati refugee camp, near the great mosque with the green Hamas flag on top of it, and he is only one among the many Hamas leaders who decided to remain in his house, among the people.

Something, however, has changed in the very simple picture drawn by the Hamas activists, as the power of the Palestinian Islamist movement consolidated in the Strip. Probably there is no individual corruption of the kind that began to afflict Fatah, according to countless critics in Palestinian society. However, Hamas's militants would use every possible tool to strengthen their movement. Even if the leaders have not fundamentally changed their lives after entering power, it does not mean that the popular consensus that elected Hamas remains the same in Gaza. Indeed, the years after the 2007 coup have shown a far more complex, gray-toned picture of the movement. On the one hand, the population recognizes that Hamas as a government and as a bureaucracy has been able to administer a territory despite a lack of literally everything that one would seem to require: no financial resources, no productive infrastructure worthy of the name, no commercial network able to trade with the external world, no freedom of movement. And yet daily life in Gaza, closed like a prison, somehow functioned. The trash was collected. The ministries functioned, and there was working Internet available for public use. The traffic laws were upheld, and penalties and fines were assessed. Incredibly, the so-called black market of the tunnels was even properly taxed.

What was missing was freedom. The only link with the outside world beyond the concrete walls was the tunnels. As time elapsed, the people began to make more and more accusations, not only against the Haniyeh government, but also against the judiciary and the police department. The accusation was always the same: the authorities want to Islamicize the Gaza Strip. Indeed, the territory, already known for its conservative mores, became even more restrictive after the closure. Both activists and Hamas leaders were among the first to recognize that Gaza was gradually radicalizing, though there were different explanations as to why. "It is the society which became more conservative than our movement, because the enduring occupation affected the mentality," according to one of the "middle generation" Hamas leaders. "The occupation," he continued, "transformed the behaviors into pathological ones. Only when there is freedom, arts and culture can develop and flourish. The most obvious example is what happened during Al Andalus era, in the heyday of Muslim renaissance. Now, even those who love art and cultivate it, they prefer to do it on their family's walls."[46] In other words, away from the inquisitive eyes of conservative Gazan society.

There were many among the middle-generation leaders in the West Bank and Gaza who stigmatized the radicalization, which affected the Islamist youth in particular. Hamas activists provided two different explanations. In Gaza, radicalization derived from isolation. In the West Bank, it derived from repression by the PNA security forces. One of the sources of the radicalization of most serious concern, highlighted by the members of that generation who had studied abroad or who still managed to cross the borders of the Occupied Palestinian Territory, is the heavy Internet use among young activists. This older generation has no ideological preconception against Internet use—quite the contrary. Their concern is regarding what the young are reading online: not Western ideas, but rather extremist Jihadist or Salafist information. "For example, forcing young Hamas activists into hiding," said one of the movement's leaders in the West Bank, "means forcing them into solitude and blocking them from building social relationships. They were left alone with a computer and what radical information passed in front of them, without any mediation."[47] This kind of analysis—an Islamist leader worried about the extremist trend on the rise in a movement that he himself considers moderate— is completely opposed to the stereotypical Western way of reading Hamas. The same interpretation also came from younger members, especially regarding the situation inside Gaza. "Boys prefer to go into the Qassam Brigades rather than engaging in politics," said Mushir al Masri. "In short, boys support the military option, because the international community no longer has much appeal for them. They believe that the international community supports only those who hold the power, those who have strength, and that it does not bear those who made democratic choices. Participating in the 2006 elections and voting Hamas was a democratic choice,"[48] said al Masri, who had in 2006, when he was only twenty-nine years old, become the youngest PLC member in the Hamas parliamentary wing. Mushir al Masri's political career inside Hamas differentiates him from his peers, not only for his academic credentials in political science, but especially because he was well known in leadership circles, meeting assiduously with Sheikh Ahmed Yassin, Abdel Aziz al-Rantisi, and Ismail Haniyeh. In sum, Masri had represented a bridge between the old and the new generation since the time he led the university student council.

The generation now in their fifties, who had been raised by the stones of the First Intifada in 1987, had endured terrorist attacks inside the Israeli cities, cafés, and buses, but had then abandoned suicide attacks unilaterally in March 2005. This exit strategy from the Second Intifada was that generation's great political success, albeit a short-lived one. The younger generations' experience was very different: they had passed through the Al-Aqsa Intifada's extreme violence, had lived through the electoral process, but had become immediately disillusioned. Soon after the 2006 elections, in fact, Gaza lost any hope for its future, not only politically, but also economically and socially. It could be interpreted as a paradox, since the Israelis left Gaza after the 2005 unilateral disengagement, leaving behind them empty settlements and land. Nevertheless, from the perspective of the Islamist younger generation's activism, their "elder brothers" had failed to achieve any of the objectives they had in mind. By entering the PNA institutions, Hamas's middle generation cadres had wanted to achieve recognition both in Palestinian politics and from the international community. Hamas's youth saw only the negative results of this strategy: the isolation of Gaza and the war. Therefore, they felt a profound disappointment and one focused especially on Europe, which even in the Gaza Strip was considered the cradle and the model of democracy. Called to cast their vote in democratic, fair, and free elections, the Palestinians had been punished for choosing Hamas. This is the phrase heard all throughout the Palestinian Territory, especially in Gaza.

Thus some youth groups in the Gazan social fabric reacted vehemently by shifting toward the fringes of Islamism represented by Salafism. The Salafi threat became clear the afternoon of August 14, 2009, when the Hamas government's police forces attacked the stronghold of Jund Ansar Allah at the Ibn Taymiya mosque in Rafah. Earlier, the preacher Moussa Abdul Latif, also known as Abu Al Nour al Maqdisi and a medical graduate in the Egyptian university of Alexandria, proclaimed the establishment of an "Islamic emirate." The violent fighting between the police force and the Jund Ansar Allah militants lasted until the day after and resulted in a bloody death toll: twenty-five dead, including three children, three civilians, and six members of the Hamas police. There were more than one hundred injured, and more than ninety people were arrested. Among the victims was the acknowledged leader of Jund Ansar Allah, Moussa Abdul Latif, who—according to the ministry of the interior spokesman, Ihab al Ghussein—had detonated the explosive belt he was wearing when the police went to arrest him the morning of August 15. In the case of Jund Ansar Allah's sedition, Hamas decided to violently suppress the growth of a radical *jihadi* wing inside the Gaza Strip. The extremists represented for Hamas not only a dangerous competitor, but also a thorn in the side of the security apparatus. This deep concern was palpable, for example, in a letter that Ahmed al-Ja'bari, the strong man of the Qassam Brigades, addressed to Khaled Meshaal, warning against divisions within the military structure of Hamas.[49]

Paradoxically, however, it was the political influence of Salafism that most concerned Hamas. For all its ideological foundations, Hamas is very far from the Salafi literalist interpretation of Islam. The theology of Hamas is rooted clearly in the reformist interpretation of the Muslim Brotherhood, which broke with the traditional reading of the Muslim faith. The Ikhwan proposed, on the contrary, a reading that brought together religious and political beliefs, adherence to the faith's confident vision combined with a strong engagement in society and politics. Yet it should not be forgotten that Hamas sees itself as a moderate Islamic party, and that the Salafi movement in Gaza shared the same view of itself. For these radical Islamist fringes, Hamas and the Muslim Brotherhood departed from the right path (that is, a very narrow and literal Salafi interpretation of Islam). Omar al-Ansari, leader of Jaish al-Islam, a Gaza-based Salafist movement, described in his own way the profoundly different religious and ideological interpretation that divides the literalist groups from Hamas. "The problem is that Hamas has decided to deal with modernity, and they chose the path of democracy; thus dealing with the western world. Thus creates a gap between us and them,"[50] he explained in mid-2010, exactly a year after the Hamas-led crackdown against Jund Ansar Allah.

The Salafists were born in 2001, explained another leader, but they grew after 2005–2006 and Hamas's decision to participate in elections. "Hamas' participation in elections and [its joining] the 'atheist' Palestinian Legislative Council was the spark that ignited Salafi thought, gradually appearing and spreading among young men," said Abu al-Hareth, a leader of Jund Ansar Allah, which—according to this description—constitutes the backbone of the Jaljalat, the Salafi social world within Gaza, together with Omar al-Ansari's group and two other Salafist organizations. In 2010, according to al-Hareth's description, Jaljalat had 11,000 men, including some members of the Qassam Brigades.[51] Beyond the fog that still surrounds the structure of Salafism in Gaza, the political problem for Hamas was to address two issues. First, it had to mediate between the description of its movement as the representation of a moderate and political Islam and as a resistance group and a nationalist movement that fights against the occupation of the Palestinian land.

Representing their movement as the moderate political Islam in Palestine, however, did not provide Hamas leaders with the tangible results they expected in terms of international recognition. Therefore, in the total isolation of Gaza, Hamas's political failure could not but strengthen the most radical and uncompromising groups in society. It is no coincidence that all the local Hamas activists and leaders gave the same interpretation of the battle against Jund Ansar Allah. They all emphasized that Salafism was popular especially among young people, who preferred the military option and armed struggle as a reaction to a situation that has not improved substantially for years. The drift toward the *jihadi* trend and the groups inspired by Al Qaeda (albeit presumably from an ideological point of view rather than due to actual links with the bin Laden network) is therefore the result of Hamas's choice to turn to politics and the isolationist strategy the international community had decided to pursue toward the Islamist movement.

Beyond active repression, Hamas also reacted to the growth of Salafism by yielding to Salafism's radical tendencies and "homogenizing"[52] some of its positions on social mores and moving closer to a substantial Islamization of Gazan society. Even if pursued in a gradual way, this kind of soft Islamization implied in any case a shift by Hamas toward a more conservative position compared to the one expressed in the electoral program of the 2005–2006 Change and Reform list. It is likely that the shift to more conservative positions by the Hamas wing in Gaza affected the internal balance of the Islamist movement as a whole, in all its constituencies. It was the head of the political bureau, Khaled Meshaal, who differentiated the 2010 Hamas position from the Salafist position on Islamization and the role of women in social and political spheres. In an interview with *Al Sabeel*, Meshaal said that Hamas would not allow "'the ages of backwardness or the weight of social norms and traditions that stem from the environment rather than the religious text'" to distort Islamic concepts, 'especially since the environment of Palestine is not a closed one but a historically civilized one, enjoying plurality and openness to all religions, civilizations and cultures.'"[53]

From the point of view of Hamas's internal political balance, Meshaal's clarification said something more than this. It said clearly that the leaders of Hamas were actively concerned with the radical views gaining ground within some areas of the movement in Gaza. The decision to enter politics was the first target of the radicalization that affected the younger generation after 2007—the generation from which the future leaders of Hamas would arise. If this is true— if the turn to politics decided on by the "fifties" generation no longer appeals to the "thirties" generation—then the possibility of Hamas becoming involved in the PNA and in the peace negotiation process between Israel and Palestine is endangered.

Al sha'b yurid . . .

March 15, 2011, was not a classic "Day of Rage." It was not as it was in other Arab countries, shaken in the same months by the perfect storm of the Arab Spring. And yet March 15 was the day when the Palestinian youth took to the streets of Ramallah and Gaza City in protest against the divisions inside the Palestinian house.

As had happened in Cairo, Tunis, Manama, Tripoli, and Damascus, the protest grew by means of that postmodern "market square," the Internet, both through blogs and through social networks like Facebook and Twitter. And as in the other Arab cities, the protesters in Palestine were all young people in their twenties and thirties, young people who had, during the previous months, drawn up documents listing their political demands. These included not only the obvious demand to end the division between Fatah and Hamas, but also to reshape radically the concept of Palestinian identity. No longer should Palestine-as-nation be thought of exclusively in terms of the West Bank, Gaza, and East Jerusalem; in the view of the young protesters, it must include the Palestinians of Israel, the Palestinians in the refugee camps outside the West Bank and Gaza, and the Palestinians in the Diaspora. Given the young people's view of an ideal Palestinian national identity, it is no coincidence that another of the demands requested a new PLO parliament (the PNC) through new elections. At the same time that Hamas was offering its ambiguous acceptance of a Palestinian state on the 1967 borders, the "March 15" youth asked all the factions to call new elections that would bring to power those who would represent Palestine beyond the borders of the PNA. This request was by no means simple to answer.

There were not as many people in Ramallah and Gaza City on March 15 as there were in Tahrir Square. Still, the protestors in Manara Square in Ramallah filled the center of the West Bank city. Around them, however, there were too many brand new flags—flags carried by Fatah's young militants, indicating that Fatah and the PNA were attempting to "piggyback" on the youth protests in order to lower to some extent the pressure the Palestinian street was placing on them. Hamas did the same in Gaza, where the situation was even more acute. It was clear that Gaza's youth, far more than the protestors in the West Bank, belonged to the same generation that was revolting against the authoritarian Arab regimes. The Gazans even borrowed slogans from the Arab revolutions, especially the most powerful one: *al sha'b yurid*, the people are demanding. But here, people were not demanding the "fall of the regime" as they were in Cairo and in Tunis, in Sana and in Homs. Instead, the Palestinians demanded "the end of the division"—a unity that would lead naturally to a new government and new administrative rules to replace the two cabinets in Ramallah and Gaza City. The people were demanding; they were once again revealing themselves to be the source of legitimacy for power, and the Palestinian factions were forced to listen. This was especially true given the scandal that struck some leading Palestinian political figures during the Egyptian revolution, when Al Jazeera published the Palestine Papers, nearly 1,700 internal and confidential PNA documents that covered more than a decade of the Israeli-Palestinian conflict.

Hamas's reaction to the March 15 protest was to signal its immediate openness to a compromise with Fatah. On the same day, Ismail Haniyeh's government invited Mahmoud Abbas to Gaza via a live television broadcast. "I call on the brother, President Abu Mazen, and on Fatah to meet us right now here in Gaza or anywhere else, to begin the national dialogue in order to achieve reconciliation," said Haniyeh.[54] Abbas instantly accepted. The timing of Haniyeh's invitation and Abu Mazen's prompt reaction showed the efficacy of the youth protests, which finally broke the impasse toward reconciliation and led directly to the agreement that Fatah, Hamas, and all the other factions formally signed on May 4, 2011, in Cairo.

Understandably, given the sudden and unpredictable fall of Zine al Abidine Ben Ali and Hosni Mubarak, both Hamas and Fatah dreaded the possibility of being overwhelmed by a wave of unrest in the West Bank and Gaza. Although the numbers were certainly smaller than those of the revolutions in Tunisia and Egypt, both Palestinian political organizations were and are fully aware of the lack of consensus they had suffered ever since the Hamas coup in Gaza in June 2007 and the crystallized division between the two governments. Reconciliation, therefore, was a strange but unsurprising result of the Second Arab Awakening.

Given its history, it is unsurprising that Hamas was the first to reach out to Fatah in response to the protests. Born and bred within Palestinian society, Hamas has always been incredibly sensitive to the reactions of the street to its political strategies, as well as pragmatic enough to adjust those strategies in response. It is very likely that even during the first months of the Second Arab Awakening, the Palestinian Islamist movement was recording the popular reactions to the uprisings and formulating potential political responses to them. And clearly the many ears of Hamas knew about the reactions to the Arab Spring in Gaza and the West Bank, in the world of refugees, and in the other countries involved in the Israel-Palestine conflict. Fatigue, frustration, and disaffection toward both Hamas and Fatah had been manifest in Palestinian society for years. The Second Arab Awakening gave the necessary push to that nascent frustration, which culminated in a request for reconciliation that, had it not been granted, could have easily have detonated as a new Intifada against the Israelis as well as an uprising against the elites in power in the West Bank and Gaza.

Equally as important as internal Palestinian politics was the influence of the upheaval throughout the region. On that same day, March 15, Syria's opposition forces also began a revolution, albeit a much more difficult and bloody one. Syria's instability represented danger for Hamas, many of whose leadership had lived in Damascus for over a decade. Faithful to the strategic choice that had guided it even before the movement was formally founded in 1987, Hamas never meddled in the internal affairs of the states it had relationships with. This policy was in sharp contrast to the actions of Fatah and other PLO factions, as is evident in the PLO's expulsion from Beirut by the Israeli army in 1982. Even Hamas's long season of terrorism never ventured beyond the borders of Israel.

Thus, despite the fact that the Muslim Brotherhood was illegal and was harshly repressed under Bashar al Assad's regime, Hamas maintained a neutral position in the first phase of the 2011 revolt, and allowed Syria to play a full part in the reconciliation process between

Hamas and Fatah that produced the May 4 agreement. At the same time, however, Hamas's embarrassment toward the Syrian regime began to be increasingly evident, and rumors spread that the Hamas political leadership might move its headquarters to other countries. The most credible of the rumors to this effect was that the Hamas leadership abroad would be divided into three sections, which would eventually be located in Cairo, Doha, and Ankara. After a certain time, the rumor fell through due to the embarrassment those governments felt at the idea that they might play host to Hamas.

Regardless of the rumored transfer of the political bureau out of Damascus, however, the most interesting aspect of the Arab Spring, as far as Hamas is concerned, remains the "strategic posture" Hamas took relative to the revolutions.[55] In Gaza, Ismail Haniyeh's government had repeatedly used its security forces to prevent opposition demonstrations and dissenting voices. Hamas itself was the regime, since it held power and controlled a territory (albeit an embargoed one.) But externally, Hamas was encircled by the upheavals that confronted the Syrian and Egyptian regimes in Damascus and Cairo. If Damascus's instability put the relationship of patronage between the regime of Bashar el Assad and Hamas at risk, the fall of Hosni Mubarak completely changed Egypt's role in the Israeli-Palestinian conflict. Post-revolution Cairo looked at Gaza from a role far different from the perspective the Mubarak regime had taken, a position that in recent years had been seen as a sop to US strategy in the Middle East (especially regarding Egypt's faithful alliance with Israel). Although Gaza still remained a major internal and security problem on the Sinai border, Egypt's role in the conflict had changed.

The Islamist movement's political bureau recognized the powerful meaning of the Arab revolutions. Moussa Abu Marzouq considered both the March 15 movement and the Egyptian revolution the root causes of the Palestinian reconciliation. He went even further in a commentary published in *The Guardian* twenty days after the reconciliation accords, asserting that political Islam was one of the key components of the Arab revolutions: "The winds of historic peaceful change sweeping the Middle East will, sooner or later, reach the shores of the west. Its governments can no longer marginalize, disparage or ignore the democratic popular Islamic movements in the region; and that includes Hamas."[56] Even Khaled Meshaal recognized the role of the youth in the Arab Awakening by paying a visit to the different organizations that made up the Egyptian revolutionary movement that had overthrown Hosni Mubarak. By meeting the "Tahrir youth," Meshaal clearly signaled that Hamas recognized them as a key political force in the changed regional landscape.

And yet the reconciliation agreement signed on May 4 in Cairo was not a product of the Tahrir revolutionary spirit, despite the fact that one of the facilitators, Munib al Masri, told Robert Fisk that "both sides realised they might miss the boat of the Arab Spring."[57] The negotiations were first and foremost a diplomatic success of Egyptian intelligence, which wanted to rebuild its perceived stature after Omar Suleyman had disappeared from the scene. Suleyman was second in the Mubarak regime's chain of command, and was well known for his prominent role in the Cairo negotiations on reconciliation. However, thanks to the diplomatic American and Palestinian documents released through WikiLeaks, as well as the Palestine Papers, analysts know that Suleyman's aim was not to bring about a reconciliation between Fatah and Hamas, but instead to exercise a tough control on the Palestinian leadership, especially Hamas. This was evident from the fact that Fatah had signed the nonnegotiable Egyptian-authored reconciliation agreement of October 2009. One of the key reasons that Ramallah signed was its certainty that Hamas would never do the same, a fact Suleyman must have been aware of.[58]

But after the Egyptian revolution, Cairo intelligence and the new government of Prime Minister Essam Sharaf wanted an immediate success as proof of a successful transition from the era of Mubarak and Suleyman. In particular, the transitional minister of foreign affairs, Nabil el Arabi, pushed for the reconciliation between Fatah and Hamas to go forward. Nabil el Arabi personified the shift in Egypt's Middle East policy after Mubarak. A staunch opposer of the Camp David peace agreement, el Arabi brokered meetings between Egyptian intelligence and a small team of Palestinian independent figures who had worked unsparingly during the previous years to accomplish reconciliation. Only after these meetings did the independent team meet also with Amr Moussa, at the time still the Arab League's secretary general. One remarkable detail stands out from the meeting between the independents and el Arabi. During the meeting, Nabil el Arabi asked the participants if they would accept another party in the negotiations. Upon their agreement, he asked Turkish Foreign Affairs Minister Ahmet Davetoglu to join the meeting.[59] It was a turning point in the relations between Cairo and Ankara, especially considering how assiduously the Mubarak regime had prevented Turkey from playing any part in the Palestine negotiations.

With both Palestinian factions weakened by the fast changing scenario in the Middle East, Hamas and Fatah agreed to reopen the negotiations on reconciliation, knowing full well that this time it would be quite impossible to use delaying tactics, as had been done during the previous rounds of talks. The October 2009 Egyptian document, signed only by Fatah, remained the stumbling block, but the agreement by both factions to draft a parallel document still stood, and they finally accomplished this goal with the "New Understandings Paper" that they signed on April 27, 2011. Purposely ambiguous to leave room for political maneuvering, the new document still managed to resolve important political issues while raising new and important ones. For example, the "New Understandings Paper" remained deliberately ambiguous on security and on the question of PLO reform. At the same time, the factions agreed that the national unity government had to be formed "in consensus between them" regarding the appointment of ministers, including the prime minister position. The most important addendum related to the issue of representation. There would be three elections one year after the signing of the "New Understandings Paper," all conducted simultaneously, to elect the president, the parliamentarians, and the Palestinian National Council. This was a vital change—one that put the issue of providing representation to Palestinians outside of the PNA back on track.[60]

The reconciliation ceremony—held in Cairo on May 4 in the presence of all the factions and the Egyptian leadership—was a true achievement. However, the following months witnessed the same delaying tactics that had always sapped the force of reconciliation efforts. Nothing happened: there was no new national unity government, nor were the procedures needed to hold elections performed. The reconciliation agreement also became the hostage of the bid the PNA was making in September 2011 for statehood at the UN, a bid that asked that the State of Palestine be recognized as a full member of the UN. Thus, still crystallized in their quasi-states of the West Bank and Gaza, Fatah and Hamas again avoided tackling the political problem. They still could not share power, which meant no reunification of the Palestinian territory under an institutional umbrella, no independence from patronage, and no representation for the Palestinian people outside of the PNA.

The events of September and October 2011 signaled that the various Palestinian negotiations (formally led by the Mubarak-era Egyptian intelligence services) were profoundly linked to each other, as if they were parts of a chain. Only few months after the May 4 agreement on reconciliation, the Middle East's paradoxical impasse was broken by an unexpected event. On October 11, Israel and Hamas suddenly announced that they had reached the long-awaited deal to swap Gilad Shalit with 1,027 Palestinian security prisoners detained in the Israeli jails. The deal between Israel and Hamas on the so-called "prisoners' file" followed the agreement on reconciliation. One after the other, one because of the other: it was the direct confirmation that the dossiers were closely linked, and that their solution relied on the negotiators' good will.

The swap took place exactly one week later, on the morning of October 18, following a complicated and delicate procedure that allowed the newly appointed Sergeant Gilad Shalit to be freed and handed over by the Hamas military wing to the Egyptian mediators at Rafah crossing, who would transfer him to IDF officials inside the Sinai peninsula. Meanwhile, 477 security prisoners—many of them Hamas militants carrying heavy sentences or life terms—were transferred to the West Bank, Gaza, Israel, and Egypt. The deal provided for a second phase in which another 550 Palestinian security prisoners would be liberated from Israeli jails.

Put in the cone of shadow by the PLO bid for statehood, Hamas regained its place on the political stage with full strength through the prisoner swap. It was undoubtedly a success for the movement inside the Palestinian society. Regarding Hamas's internal balance, however, it confirmed the increased political role of the military wing, whose participation was essential to reaching the deal on Gilad Shalit, as Ahmed al Jaabari's presence during the last phase of the negotiations in Cairo testifies. The list of freed prisoners incuded not only Palestinians from the West Bank and Gaza, but also, and symbolically more important, from Jerusalem and from Israel. Top figures, such as Marwan Barghouthi and Ahmed al Saadat, were not freed by the exchange. The national success for Hamas, however, was beyond doubt.

The prisoner swap was not only a consequence of the reconciliation agreement, but also of the changes caused by the Arab Spring, especially in Egypt. Additionally, it put Mahmoud Abbas and Khaled Meshaal again on the same level in international perception, underlining once again that the Palestinian politics continued to be two-headed, and as a consequence divided. Still, in Ramallah and in Gaza City, flags from all the factions waved again together on October 18, 2011, to celebrate the prisoners.

EPILOGUE

War of Flags

Once upon a time, the flags that flew in Gaza seemed to prove that the Strip could never be controlled entirely by a single force, neither Fatah nor Hamas. The flags flew not only on military maps, but from rooftops, from balconies, or from the roofs of ramshackle huts along the seafront. On one roof, a yellow Fatah flag near a satellite dish. On a neighboring building, a PFLP flag. A little farther along, the black banner of Islamic Jihad, and then the green of Hamas. And then, in 2008, Hamas consolidated its grip on power, and the flags grew increasingly worn. Even the material for flags was in short supply. The only exception was the green of Hamas's own banners.

Then there came a time during which flags became banners for the militants of only one or another movement, utterly excluding all others—all adversaries—even at private events such as weddings or funerals. And then the flags flew together once more during the Israeli bombardments of Operation Cast Lead. Flags flew beside one another at the funeral processions; they covered the bodies of the victims lined up next to each other, large adult bodies and the small bodies of children. Hamas's green banners next to Fatah's yellow.

But this was perhaps merely a reconciliation that occurred in grief, a reconciliation whose roots were more in the societal behavior than in politics, as it was when—exceptionally—the flags flew beside one another to celebrate the liberation of hundreds of Palestinian prisoners under the deal between Israel and Hamas in October 2011. However, with time politics divided Palestinian society as it had throughout the post-Arafat transitional period, and the flags returned to the territory under each faction's political control, as in a macabre game of Risk. Green in the Gaza Strip. Mostly yellow in the West Bank. Whatever the color, the flags generally flew with the Palestinian national banner; Hamas and Fatah wanted to show their constituencies and the people that each of them was the sole legitimate government of the PNA. This is the reason, especially in the last seven years, that flags epitomized the core issue of the post-Arafat era in Palestine: the inability to share power. The Fatah versus Hamas conflict typified the endless and incomplete political transition, marred by the incapacity to effectively participate in the Palestinian National Authority, an institution that was certainly bound up by the strings of the Oslo agreements and the necessary limitations of its sovereignty, but nevertheless the only national institution where Palestinians could exercise power. It was this inability to share power that led to the war of flags.

It is impossible to deeply understand the roots of this war of flags without questioning the mainstream interpretation of Hamas's history, from its formal birth in 1987 as an Islamist resistance group in Palestine through its different stages: the Revolt of the Stones, the fight against the Oslo process, the violent phase of terrorism, Yasser Arafat's death and Israel's assassination of Sheikh Ahmed Yassin, and finally Hamas's decision to take part in the political process through its participation in the 2006 general elections. From pebbles to power, one might say, from terrorist attacks to ministries: this is the history that I have attempted to trace, without forgetting that these two decades took place within the context of the history of political Islam and the Muslim Brotherhood in Palestine. The roots of that history do not go back merely two and a half decades to 1987, nor even only to the 1970s and the establishment of Ahmed Yassin's Mujamma al-Islami. The roots of Hamas are deep, dating back to the late 1920s with the establishment of Hassan al-Banna's Ikhwan al-Muslimun in 1928.

These dates acquire meaning only if they indicate a historical trajectory. The historical trajectory of the Muslim Brotherhood, now the most important Islamist movement in the Middle East and North Africa, begins precisely when Egypt was undergoing the most interesting and vibrant period in the construction of its modernity. It evolved side by side with the sea changes that the Arab world has witnessed over the last eighty years: colonialism and decolonization, nationalism and pan-Arabism, the establishment of Israel and the origins of the Palestinian Question, the failure of Nasserism and the exponential growth of Islamism, the return of Western (military) power to Arab lands, and the (endogenous) transition toward democracy.

Along this path there must be a special chapter for the Palestinian Muslim Brotherhood, special not least because Islamists themselves consider it to be special, a *sonderweg* which derives its specificity from the Israeli-Palestinian conflict. The Ikhwan that the followers of Hassan al-Banna spread to Gaza, Jerusalem, and Hebron was not the product of the Israeli-Palestinian conflict, but that conflict set it apart from all the other national incarnations of the Brotherhood. In 2007, one of the Egyptian Muslim Brotherhood's most prominent leaders, Abdel Moneim Abul Futouh, explained Hamas's specificity to me in terms as simple as they were disarming: "Hamas is the only movement that traces its roots to the Ikhwan that has used violence. Nor could it be otherwise: Hamas must face an occupation. All the other national movements of the Muslim Brotherhood chose non-violence decades ago."[1]

It is precisely this inescapable genealogy, the ideological and programmatic link between Hamas and the Muslim Brotherhood, that makes it a simplistic generalization to say that the Palestinian Islamist movement is nothing but a terrorist group. This is the perspective taken by a sizable slice of published works on Hamas. And yet a fuller reading of history—one that includes Hamas, the Mujamma al-Islami, and the Palestinian Muslim Brotherhood—tells a much broader story.

This story tells us, for example, that the terrorist period—the one marked by suicide attacks within Israel's borders—was not born along with Hamas in 1987, but at a very specific moment in the history of the fundamentalist movement. Before 1994 and after 2005, the political and strategic behavior of the Islamic Resistance Movement was different. Before this period, Hamas had to scramble to establish its nationalist credentials and its credibility with respect to other factions such as Fatah or the PFLP, who had for years committed themselves to armed struggle against the Israelis as a way to fight against the occupation. The social and religious movement of which Hamas is a splinter had different priorities. Not politics as a means to maintain power, or as resistance to the occupation, but rather something more radical still: the construction of the good Palestinian Muslim. The pillar of the Mujamma al-Islami—the result of the initiative Sheikh Ahmed Yassin took in the same year as the Yom Kippur War—was the need for Palestinian society to return to Islam. In this view, it was the abandonment of the straight path of a conscious and rigorous adherence to the faith in daily life that had been the cause of Palestine's desperate status as an occupied land. It was necessary to build a new society, as well as its ethical foundations, religious creed, and traditional and conservative values. And in order to do this, it was necessary to tackle the questions central to social stability: family, health, emancipation from poverty, care of the young, and the reestablishment of the traditional role of women.

The Palestinian Muslim Brotherhood's fundamentalist message thus reached the heart of Gazan society without initially referring to the occupation. At different times and to different extents, this also happened in the West Bank. This despite the fact that it was precisely the occupation that ultimately determined who the Brotherhood's constituencies would be, as well as ultimately the Mujamma's and Hamas's: the refugee camps, which changed the face of the Gaza Strip, tripling its population in the space of a few days, and the poor West Bank villages that no longer had any connection with pre-1948 Palestinian cities. Paradoxically, it was Israel that would give the Ikhwan the possibility to grow and develop by following a strategy similar to the one Sadat had used in Egypt against the socialists: Israel would pit Islamists against nationalists.

It is in this context that the Islamist movement's leadership was born, took shape, and was strengthened. Its leaders today are between forty-five and fifty-five, and have been at the forefront of the last seven years of Palestinian history. This generation reflects the history and lifework of one man—Sheikh Ahmed Yassin—but it also reflects the cultural context in which these leaders were brought up.

In particular, there were the universities. On the one hand, there were the Palestinian universities established after 1967, which became the first terrain in which the middle-aged leaders of today had matured into an entirely homegrown elite. On the other hand, there were also the Arab universities in Cairo and Alexandria, Damascus and Beirut, all in ferment throughout the 1970s and driven by the campus clashes between secularists and Islamists. Thus, although the leadership of these "professors" is therefore the result of a political and cultural history that goes beyond the confines of Palestine and is in this sense fully Arab, at the same time the political commitments of the Islamist leadership that emerged in the West Bank and in Gaza have always been resolutely national rather than pan-Islamic. The Palestinian Muslim Brotherhood was certainly far from the tradition of guerrilla warfare and from the fedayeen when for years they concentrated their efforts on a social network, using the licenses they obtained from the Israeli authorities to operate schools, universities, and hospitals. And yet all of this was done within a Palestinian framework. This national focus and the deep social roots that went with it explain why Hamas has become a part of contemporary Palestinian history, rather than simply part of the conflict with Israel. Even given the relevance of Hamas beyond the conflict, its role in that conflict can be inferred from Israel's own military-style campaigns aimed at eradicating the Islamist movement, from the deportations between the 1980s and 1990s to the long line of targeted assassinations after 9/11. The snake, however, did not die after it was decapitated. Indeed, it rose from the ashes yet again, demonstrating not only an unexpected organizational vitality, but also a pragmatic ability to change its strategy.

After Yasser Arafat's death, Hamas decided upon a clean break in its political direction, just as it had in 1987, when the youngest among the Palestinian Muslim Brotherhood's leadership had forced the previous generation to accept the birth of an operational organization such as Hamas. In 2005, Hamas decided upon a unilateral suspension of suicide attacks inside Israel and committed itself to entering the political mainstream. Notwithstanding the extremely harsh blows dealt to its leadership—the assassination first of its spiritual leader Sheikh Ahmed Yassin and then of his political heir Abdel Aziz al-Rantisi—Hamas demonstrated yet again an ability to interpret the mood of its constituencies that was far superior to that shown by other political movements such as Fatah. This was confirmed by the historical record itself: namely, from the majority consensus Hamas received at the municipal elections that took place in the Occupied Palestinian Territory between 2004 and 2005, as well as in the general elections of January 25, 2006—a consensus that was not the result of the terrorist attacks it had carried out over previous years, but rather the reward for its social engagement and for a different kind of national political presence.

Far from bringing the international community a measure of relief, Hamas's shift from using political violence to participating in traditional politics placed a conundrum before Western governments. Should they accept a more mainstream Hamas in the hope of moderating its political views? Or should they isolate it and bet yet again on Fatah, the adversary to Israel that they had consistently chosen to negotiate with for two decades? After a timid attempt to open up to Hamas, Israel, the United States, and Europe decided on the second option. In so doing, they contributed to the worsening conditions within the Occupied Palestinian Territory with the birth of two governments and two Palestines, one controlled by Hamas and the other by Fatah. The first phase of Hamas's history drew to a close with its coup in June 2007. In the space of twenty years, the movement had gone from the founding charter of 1988 that called for the destruction of Israel to the "Hamas in a suit" of Ismail Haniyeh, the student and right-hand man to Sheikh Yassin who between 2006 and 2008 repeatedly stated the proposal for a long-term truce with Israel and for the recognition of a Palestinian state within the 1967 borders, a de facto recognition of the state of Israel within the Green Line.

Exercising its power on the specific territory of the Strip, Hamas, after its coup in Gaza in June 2007, became not only a de facto institutional actor, but also opened up a new chapter in the shaping of its internal structure. This profound change has been epitomized by the military wing's role in the negotiations for the prisoners' exchange, finalized in October 2011 with the liberation of the Israeli soldier Gilad Shalit and of 477 out of 1,027 Palestinian prisoners involved in the deal. The military wing imposed its weight on Hamas's political structure, as the Gaza constituency also began to play a larger role in the movement's internal balance of power.

There are two diametrically opposite ways of interpreting these changes in Hamas's strategy, including its participation in the PNA institutions. The first—and certainly the most popular—views the decision to take part in elections as just another instrument Hamas had adopted in order to reach its unchanging objective of destroying Israel. This is a wholly unscientific and wholly political Manichean reading of the last two decades of Palestinian history, one that fails to take into account the evident pragmatism of Hamas in responding to events, and one that demands that a "side" be chosen in the conflict. The second approach instead sees Hamas as a movement that has used terrorism, but that cannot be thought of as simply a terrorist organization. Behind the dark façade of suicide attacks, of their instigators, and of their "wicked teachers,"[2] Hamas has also maintained a complex welfare network and political strategy, a moral rigor, and an ongoing political analysis of concepts such as citizenship, common good, and public interest. Just as in other movements, which hark back to their religious roots—for example, European ecclesiastical communities and parties that take their cue from Christianity—there is a continuous reflection upon the relationship between religion and politics, between faith and collective morality, between the government of public affairs and the necessity to respond to the needs of citizens.

Even within Israeli historiography itself, scholars of the caliber of Hamas expert Shaul Mishal encounter considerable difficulties when attempting to portray the Islamist movement as a rigid organization. "Despite the horrifying toll claimed by Hamas's violence, it is essentially a social and political movement, providing extensive community services and responding constantly to political reality through bargaining and power brokering. Along this line, it has been reluctant to adhere to its religious dogma at any price and so has tended to adopt political strategies that minimize the danger of rigidly adhering to principle, doctrine, or ideology, ready to respond or adjust to fluid conditions without losing sight of ultimate objectives."[3] Henry Siegman goes even further. An expert in Middle Eastern politics,

Siegman was born in Germany in 1930, escaped anti-Jewish persecu-
tion in 1933 first in the Netherlands and then in the United States,
and served as president of the American Jewish Congress for sixteen
years. In an article published in the *London Review of Books* in late
January 2009, Siegman states that "it is too easy to describe Hamas
simply as a 'terror organization'. It is a religious nationalist movement that resorts to terrorism, as the Zionist movement did during
its struggle for statehood, in the mistaken belief that it is the only
way to end an oppressive occupation and bring about a Palestinian state. While Hamas's ideology formally calls for that state to be
established on the ruins of the state of Israel, this doesn't determine
Hamas's actual policies today any more than the same declaration in
the PLO charter determined Fatah's actions."[4] One of the hallmarks
of the Israel-Palestine conflict is its paradoxes. Thus it is possible to
talk of political choices, strategies, and electoral manifestos within
the Palestinian Territory as though one were speaking of the domestic politics of a state rather than of an entity that lacks form and borders. Putting the conflict aside for a moment, it is possible to study
Hamas as a political movement made not just of structures, but of
ideas, programs, and perspectives. Taking such an approach provides a three-dimensional picture of an important piece of Palestinian history and implicitly rejects the all-too-often one-dimensional
representation of events in the Middle East. Such a view allows us
to understand the two events that marked Hamas's history between
2007 and 2009: the coup, and the showdown between Hamas and
Israel that followed a year later.

An Aborted Final Jump?

Why did the Islamist movement not make the final jump from "resistance" to "politics"? This is the basic question of Hamas's recent history, and given that Hamas is still involved in a conflict with Israel,
the question is on its face difficult to answer. Since its inception, the
very name of the movement has contained the word "resistance,"
and it is difficult to erase this component entirely—especially if the
initial conditions that prompted that resistance remain. The West

Bank remains occupied, and the military fence still isolates the Gaza Strip that Ariel Sharon "liberated" in Israel's unilateral withdrawal in 2005.

Between 1995 and 1996 the first window of opportunity opened with Al Khalas experiment, which attempted to resolve the debate between resistance and politics by distinguishing Hamas as a movement from the political party Al Khalas. But this experiment lasted barely more than three years and was ultimately aborted because the mother ship, so to speak, did not manage to give its satellite the autonomy it needed. Distinguishing between Hamas, the movement, and Al Khalas, the political party, would have forced politicians to undertake a different path within the embryonic Palestinian national institutions. Ghazi Hamad, who took part in the experiment, has said that Hamas was not yet mature enough to function with such differentiated responsibility. And history certainly isn't built on ifs and buts. It was necessary to pass through the most violent and bloody chapter in the recent history of the conflict—the Second Intifada—before Hamas was ready to discuss again the passage from resistance to politics.

The decision to enter national politics after the Second Intifada is extensively documented by witnesses within the movement. The decision to enter the PNA formally is equally well documented. There are no records, however, of political debates concerning the suicide attacks, which ended after the unilateral truce in January 2005, with the exception of the isolated case of an attack in Dimona, inside Israel, in February 2008. The topic of suicide attacks is considered taboo among Islamists, at least in their interactions with outside interlocutors. But there are, indeed, ambiguous answers that I collected from some Hamas leaders that clearly lead to the following hypothesis: the political wing invariably consulted its four constituencies in order to decide whether or not to continue with suicide attacks. One leader in Gaza told me about having consulted the four constituencies in order to decide whether to "increase or decrease the resistance"—a euphemism for the suicide attacks. But we must infer the existence of a specific political decision on the matter to explain why the military wing has not launched a single suicide attack in the six years since the unilateral truce. Of course, this does not mean that there were no more indiscriminate attacks targeting civilians, as indeed happened through the launch of thousands of homemade Qassam rockets from the Gaza Strip. But these rocket-launches differed from suicide attacks in two key respects. First, they thankfully did not have the devastating firepower of the kamikaze attacks that spread fear and death into the very hearts of Israeli cities. Second, suicide attacks are closer to a conception of armed confrontation that is typical of guerrilla warfare. In a way, then, the choice to abandon suicide attacks in favor of rocket launches appears to suggest that the political wing of Hamas militarized, so to speak. And it is precisely this militarization that holds back the transition from resistance to politics, leaving the confusion that surrounds Hamas unresolved and encouraging the international community to subsume armed factions and political wings, Qassams and participation in government under a single roof.

Yet it is certain that the positions the international community adopted since 2006 affected Hamas's (in)ability to complete the process of "de-radicalization" that had been demanded of it. The intransigence, the isolation, the embargo, the marginalization, the preconditions required before any contact whatsoever with the international community was possible—all these were crucial in reducing the influence of moderates, or at least of pragmatists, within the Palestinian Islamist movement. In this sense, a highly debatable page of the history of diplomacy, of media information, and of politics—and not just Middle Eastern politics, but European, Western, and American politics as well—has been written. The West avoided real opportunities to moderate Hamas positions by enclosing them within a diplomatic framework that would place armed radicals in a position from which they could no longer damage the process. The result has been that the moderate voices within Hamas have been silenced in favor of the hawks. Especially after Operation Cast Lead, the new generation of Hamas's activists have been less and less inclined to pragmatism and more and more attracted to a renewed "military option."

The condition in which Palestinian politics as a whole finds itself today—namely an existence with a very limited degree of sovereignty—cannot be explained without understanding the role of the complex corridors of power in Ramallah and in Gaza City. The movement's intention in standing for election in 2006 was to partake of legislative power by entering parliament but not sully its hands with executive power. This half measure was immediately swept away by the result of the elections, which forced Hamas to put itself completely on the line—yet, in a decision for which Hamas bears full responsibility, not commit completely to participating in the PNA. Palestinian Islamists' proverbial lack of flexibility was the root cause of the failure of a possible coalition government in the spring of 2006, resulting in the Hamas-only government led by Ismail Haniyeh. Hamas's slow decision-making process and its inability to negotiate politics' inevitable compromises, however, could not save Fatah from its own culpability. Fatah's equally inflexible inability to share power, its inability to reform itself, and to address the problems that had led to its electoral defeat represent the other root cause of the darkest chapter in Palestinian politics: the civil war that exploded onto the streets of Gaza in the spring and summer of 2007. In the aftermath, Palestinian politics submitted to the will of its international patrons, and while Hamas—despite being supported by Syria and Iran—maintained a national perspective, in the perception of Palestinians on the streets Fatah slowly but surely came to echo the political objectives of others. This perception weakened not just Fatah, but most importantly the very institutions of the PNA, first and foremost Mahmoud Abbas's presidency.

The split between Fatah and Hamas, between the West Bank and Gaza, has without a doubt diminished the national dimension of the Palestinian Question. There are plans on the desks of certain administrations for the establishment of two separate entities—Gaza and the West Bank—that are increasingly thought of in terms of their links to would-be patrons such as Egypt and Jordan. These plans are the result of the split. Yet that split is not only a result of internal Palestinian politics; it has been stoked and sustained from the outside. The strong role the international community has taken in Palestinian internal affairs has only made existing problems worse. In particular, military intervention by Israel has failed to produce any definitive result. On the contrary, even an operation on the scale of Operation Cast Lead has failed to destroy Hamas, either from the outside through bombardments or from the inside by inciting the population to revolt. The Qassam rocket launches continued up until a few hours before the January 18 truce; Egypt has reiterated that it has no intention of absorbing Gaza as a protectorate; and Mahmoud Abbas remains only half a president, with the war having rendered his international image even more fragile.

What happened to Hamas after the twenty-two terrible days of war between 2008 and 2009? The Islamist movement lost one of its hawks, Said Siyyam, killed in one of the last bombardments on Gaza City—a bombardment very similar in style to the one that killed Salah Shehadeh, who had founded the movement's military wing. Hamas, however, has already demonstrated throughout its history of targeted assassinations that it manages to replace its leaders very quickly.

Instead, the two crucial questions about the effects of the war on Hamas are about the movement's internal equilibria and about its popular consensus. On its knees as a consequence of the thousands of militants arrested in the West Bank by both the Israelis and the security forces loyal to Abu Mazen's PNA, Hamas has increasingly made Gaza its stronghold. And it is Hamas's political and military control of Gaza, as well as its ability to keep the Strip running despite the miserable landscape of destruction created by Operation Cast Lead, that have kept Hamas active as a major player in Palestinian politics. However, according to recent polls and independent sources, Hamas's total political and military control of the Strip has distanced it from the people, who are already profoundly tired of the isolation, Israel's grip, and the division between the two Palestinian governments. A question arises, and louder than it has before: is Hamas "serving the people," as it has claimed for over two decades, or is Hamas starting to "serve itself"? This is the kind of accusation that is now spreading among the people: the assertion that Hamas has become like Fatah. Although it is too simplistic to equate the experience of the two parties, power has changed Hamas, as it changed Fatah during the first twelve years of the PNA.

Another consequence of Hamas's focus on Gaza has been the diminishment of the movement's West Bank constituency, which was in the spotlight during the 2005–2006 elections and in the early months of the Hamas-led government. The West Bank constituency has paid the price for its distance from Gaza (not only a geographical distance), a price that takes the form of arrests and pressures exerted by the PNA organs in Ramallah. Given that pressure, and given the inability to move freely through the Occupied Territory, both the political and military wings of the West Bank constituency have had difficulty maintaining its identity as a movement "on probation." There is, rather, a tendency to view Hamas in the West Bank as a more moderate, pragmatic, and political constituency, despite the militancy it showed during the street fighting with Fatah.

Yet Hamas's struggle to maintain its identity and representation in the West Bank clearly indicates that Hamas does not mean just Gaza. The movement is present in all of its four constituencies and in the popular consensus, and while the leadership inside the Strip is crucial to maintaining the Islamist movement's internal equilibria and to managing its negotiations with international actors, the real question concerns the movement's ability to retain popular support. There are two possible answers. The first is that Hamas has been weakened because a part of the population—and not just in Gaza—considers it partly responsible for the humanitarian disaster. The second is that Hamas has in fact been strengthened, given that in the Arab world, the Gaza War resulted in a favorable outcome for Hamas. Historically, Hezbollah's profile in Lebanon and in Arab public opinion was not diminished after the destruction of the 2006 war with Israel, an outcome that might occur with Hamas.

Despite the war's seeming proof that Hamas, counter to its identity as a servant of the people, was unable to defend its people, the war brought Hamas back to center stage in Middle East politics after a year and a half of nearly total isolation. In particular, the Arab states had been isolating Hamas prior to the war, an isolation broken by Khaled Meshaal's turning up in Doha to take part in an alternative meeting of Arab states hosted by Qatar. The Gaza War resulted in Egypt seriously losing status in the Arab world for having essentially given the Israeli government the go-ahead for the operation.[5] At the same time, Turkey emerged as a newly strengthened regional power with ambitions, as the Freedom Flotilla clearly stated.

Hamas's renewed presence on the Middle East's political and diplomatic scene reinforces the hypothesis that the Islamist movement cannot go back on the choices it has made over the past seven years since the elections, choices that shifted the movement's internal center of gravity inescapably toward politics.

If on the one hand the events of 2010 and 2011 have shown that Operation Cast Lead strengthened the more militant and radical fringes of political Islam, it is equally possible that this direction might shift in the long term. The seeds of this more moderate political trajectory could already be detected immediately after the unilateral truces that put an end to the Israeli military operation in Gaza. Hamas was quick to adhere to the ceasefire decided upon by Israel on the eve of the swearing in of Barack Obama as the American president because fighting militarily would have done nothing but weaken the Palestinian Islamist movement's popular support. This is the reason why barely a few days after the ceasefire had entered into force, Hamas began again to provide welfare services and to distribute compensation to those whose houses had been destroyed or damaged.

There are two possible trajectories for Hamas going forward. One is to continue on the path of politics, pragmatism, and moderation. The other is to pursue a return to arms and to the opposition of armed groups within the Strip to any possibility of negotiations. This latter path is indicated by the desperate choice of so many among the young Palestinians who answered the question of what they would do when the bombing of Gaza stopped with a single word: *muqaw-wama*, resistance. And yet, if radicalization is an unfortunately foregone conclusion of each and every new spark in the close-quarter struggle of the Israeli-Palestinian conflict, one cannot therefore conclude that the Islamist movement will be involved in—or overwhelmed by—that same knee-jerk reaction.

In sum, there are those who argue that radical movements in crisis zones, movements that have built into their very birth this dual logic of resistance and politics, cannot but enter—whether sooner or later—the framework of negotiations, in the context of a sustainable dialogue with institutions. It happened in Northern Ireland with the complete transition of Sinn Fein and the IRA into politics—a transition that, like the one Hamas is currently undergoing, was not wholly free of obstacles that at the time seemed insurmountable. The transition from resistance to politics also happened in Africa, from the pathway to power traced by the ANC in South Africa to the co-optation of the Mozambique resistance movement RENAMO by the Vatican-backed Community of Sant'Egidio, at a time when the question of recognizing RENAMO was taboo for some governments.

The transition toward politics of a movement that uses violence and resorts to terrorism never follows a straight line, nor is it without phases of returning to armed struggle. The definitive jump across the chasm is the responsibility first and foremost of those who make the choice to use violence, but the context within which that choice is made is never irrelevant. In the case of Hamas, the context is the conflict itself. Nor is the influence of those who are already present at the scene of the conflict inconsequential. Different approaches to the issue of Hamas have been taken within the Arab world, within the broader Middle East, within the European Union (which to this day remains ambiguous about its ability to act independently within Mediterranean politics), and finally within the United States, which at the beginning of the Obama administration seemed to be taking a new and more open look at the Muslim world.

The last few years of Hamas's life have shown that the debate over the transition to politics has been far too intense and protracted to be considered merely a passing phase. Access to power has changed something within Hamas, although it is not yet possible to determine exactly how much has changed, in what terms, or for how long.

One cannot separate this transition from the larger transition in Palestinian politics from the pre-Arafat era to the post-Arafat one. The world of post-Arafat Palestine and the new elites, distinct from those who had administered the Oslo process, is a Palestine focused on a wholly national horizon: Palestine within the Green Line—in other words, including the West Bank, Gaza, and East Jerusalem—as epitomized by the request the PLO made of the UN in September

2011 to recognize the State of Palestine. This national focus might appear at odds with the Hamas structure and its leadership based in Damascus, deeply connected as it is with the world of those refugees who fled in 1948 and in 1967. And yet even that leadership abroad bases its national perspective on the Palestine carved out by the PNA. It is this Palestine, the PNA Palestine, that Hamas's leadership can neither do without nor disregard.

It is no coincidence that Hamas's leadership has often reiterated its acceptance of a Palestinian state on 1967 borders, with Jerusalem as capital and with the refugees' right of return. Sheikh Yassin proposed it in his long-term *hudna* of 1997; the Hamas government proposed it in 2006; Khaled Meshaal proposed it over and over in the media blitz of 2010. Agreeing to a Palestinian state on the 1967 borders means, for Hamas, narrowing the "space" prescribed by the Mithaq. It does not mean the acceptance of Israel, but it does mean that Hamas has put effort into the goal of joining the PLO as a political actor and thereby gaining total and indisputable national legitimacy. It is this policy that has characterized the last chapter of Hamas's history, especially throughout the negotiation on reconciliation led by Egypt in 2009 and 2010 and achieved after the Mubarak regime's fall with the May 4, 2011 agreement in Cairo among all the Palestinian factions. Politically speaking, the core issue in the reconciliation process was not security. Instead, it was the PLO reform and the subsequent admission of Hamas as a full-fledged member of the PLO, the only Palestinian institution considered to be the source of legitimacy, even among the refugees who are so vital to Hamas's support. The importance that Hamas attaches to its PLO admission does not undermine its struggle for power inside the PNA. On the contrary, admission to the PLO would give to Hamas's role inside the PNA the national legitimacy it needs.

Erdogan, not Taliban

"Aren't we thinking about how the Taliban might be brought into the fold, or at least admitting that they are part of Afghanistan's social fabric?" US Colonel (ret.) Philip J. Dermer "traveled and worked continuously throughout the [Middle East] since the late 1970s" until his retirement, as he explains in his "trip notes on a return to Israel and the West Bank."[6] A reading of his "notes," published in 2010, reveals him to be neither naïve nor cynical, but rather a Realpolitiker with a strong field background. Colonel Dermer is only the latest in the elite circles of Middle Eastern affairs to affirm that Hamas simply cannot be ignored, if the goal is to be a just and long-lasting peace between Israel and Palestine.

"For the Palestinians," says Colonel Dermer, "if concrete progress is to be made in dealing with the Israelis, Hamas cannot be ignored or wished away—they exist and they *are* Palestinian. How many years was it before we came to the overdue conclusion that Arafat and his PLO were not going to go away and took steps to deal with that reality?"[7] Hamas is part of the Palestinian social fabric, and one that takes a less radically fundamentalist approach to religion and politics, compared to the Taliban. On the contrary, most of the Hamas's leadership and cadres perceive themselves as moderates, centrists, or moderate conservatives. In post–World War II Western European historical and provocative terms, they can be thought of as an Islamic version of the Christian Democrats. Thus they say *Erdogan, not Taliban*, hoping that this association with the moderate Islamism of Turkey might help them overcome the obstacles in the contemporary Western perception of Islamism.

The participation in the elections was Hamas's first major push to be accepted in its new guise as a political movement, following the course of the Muslim Brotherhood in Egypt. The international community as a whole rejected this offer by the movement, considering it ambiguous and untrustworthy. Yet as time passed, marred by the blood and suffering of Operation Cast Lead and an idiosyncratic peace process, more and more of those in diplomatic and military circles understood the depth of the strategic mistake committed in 2006. That was *the* moment, *the* occasion, *the* possibility for the West to have put a political bridle on Hamas and dragged it into a democratic institutional framework.

Now that moment has passed. The fifties generation of leaders are feeling the pressure of a new brood of young leaders bred by the "prison syndrome" in Gaza and by the dangerous seeds of Hamas's failure to be incorporated smoothly into the PNA. Involving Hamas is now a bitter and inescapable necessity, but it is not as feasible as it was in 2006, in part due to the divide between Hamas and Fatah that Western diplomats helped cultivate. Thus both Hamas and Fatah have failed and continue to fail to solve the core issue of sharing power, institutions, and responsibility. Consequently, Palestine is sabotaging its future and losing its best chance at statehood on its terms.

However, the Second Arab Awakening suddenly offered a second window of opportunity, as underlined by the reconciliation agreement signed in Cairo in May 2011, the prisoners' exchange between Israel and Hamas in October 2011, and the summit between Mahmoud Abbas and Khaled Meshaal in Cairo at the end of November 2011 to decide the parliamentary election date. Something changed also inside the Palestinian arena, just as it changed in the rest of the Arab world.

Despite this window of hope, the time that remains—to adopt the title of last masterpiece of Palestinian film director Elia Suleiman—is the most difficult, yet the political elite of Palestine must maintain its identity in order to guide its destiny and promote the dignity of its people.

DRAMATIS PERSONAE

In addition to personal accounts provided by interviewees and official sources, much information was gleaned from *Palestinian Personalities—A Biographical Dictionary*, edited by Mahdi Abdul Hadi (Jerusalem: Palestinian Academy Society for the Study of International Affairs, 2006).

MAHMOUD ABBAS, NOM DE GUERRE ABU MAZEN (SAFED, 1935)

The president of the PNA since January 9, 2005, he did not resign at the end of his four-year mandate and retained his position as head of the PNA in addition to his position as leader of the PLO. Having become a refugee in 1948 in Syria, he was one of Fatah's founders and has been a member of its Central Committee since 1964. He holds a doctorate in history from Moscow University and has since 1977 been a strong supporter of the "two-state solution" (one Palestinian, one Israeli). Among the protagonists of the Madrid conference, he led the Palestinian delegation in the secret Oslo negotiations and on September 13, 1993, signed, on behalf of the PLO, the Declaration of Principles along with Shimon Peres. Having returned to Palestine in 1995, after forty-seven years in exile, he has remained one of the central figures in the PNA ever since. In 2003, he became prime minister for barely ten months. He negotiated the first *hudna* in 2003 and the second in 2005 in an attempt to co-opt Hamas into the PNA. He headed Fatah's sixth congress in Bethlehem in August 2009, where he was elected head of Fatah and of its Central Committee.

OMAR ABDEL RAZEQ (SALFIT, 1958)

Abdel Razeq was elected to parliament on the Change and Reform list in January 2006 while under administrative detention in an Israeli jail. He took up the post of minister of finance during the

341

first Hamas government of March 2006, just after his release. He holds a PhD in international economics from the University of Iowa and taught in the United States before being appointed at Al-Najah University in Nablus. He was arrested by Israeli authorities along with other Hamas ministers and deputies after the kidnapping of the Israeli soldier Gilad Shalit. Freed in August 2008, he handed himself in to Israeli authorities the following December 15 after receiving an injunction to return to prison for a further four months of detention.

YASSER ABED RABBO (JAFFA, 1945)

Cofounder of the DFLP (Democratic Front for the Liberation of Palestine) in 1968, he was expelled from the organization in 1991. He has been head of the PLO's Department of Information and Culture since 1973. As one of Arafat's closest advisors, he was part of the Palestinian delegation at the Madrid conference of 1991, as well as of the secret negotiations that led to the Oslo process. A minister in various PNA governments, Abed Rabbo was, along with Israeli politician Yossi Beilin, the originator of the idea for the 2003 Geneva peace initiative. An advocate of taking a hard line vis-à-vis Hamas, he became one of current PNA President Mahmoud Abbas's closest advisors.

ZIAD ABU AMR (GAZA CITY, 1950)

A university professor with a strong grounding in philosophy and political science, Abu Amr holds a doctorate from Georgetown University and has a long list of positions, professorships, and publications to his credit. He is also a specialist in political Islam and in international relations. He served as minister of culture in Mahmoud Abbas's 2003 government and is a member of the PLO's Central Committee. He was elected as an independent member of parliament in the January 2006 general elections and was appointed foreign minister in the short-lived 2007 national unity government.

SAMIR ABU EISHEH (NABLUS, 1960)

An engineer with a doctorate from the University of Pennsylvania, Abu Eisheh became president of the Engineering College at Al-Najah

University in Nablus and was later appointed minister for planning in the first Hamas government of 2006. On June 29, 2006, he was arrested along with other Islamist PLC members and ministers, but released after two weeks. He also became interim finance minister following the arrest of Omar Abdel Razeq and in this role signed an agreement for the supply of fuel to the West Bank and Gaza in October 2006 with the Israeli private company Paz, despite the economic isolation to which the Haniyeh government had been subjected. He was reappointed minister for planning under the national unity government of spring 2007.

MOUSSA ABU MARZOUQ (RAFAH, 1951)

Abu Marzouq headed Hamas's politburo between 1991 and 1995, until his arrest at the hands of US authorities. He remained in a New York jail until May 1997, when Israel dropped its extradition request, whereupon he temporarily returned to Jordan. He studied engineering in Egypt, worked in the Gulf, and later immigrated to the United States, where he obtained a doctorate in engineering. He currently lives in Damascus, where he is Khaled Meshaal's deputy in Hamas's politburo. He took part in many negotiations, including the 2002 talks with Fatah and other Palestinian factions and the truce reached with Israel in June 2008, which ended six months later. During 2009 and 2010, he was one of the chief figures in the reconciliation process between Fatah and Hamas. Since 2003, the US government has included him on its list of Specially Designated Global Terrorists.

SAYYED ABU MUSAMEH (1948)

Having become a member of the Muslim Brotherhood at the start of the 1970s, Abu Musameh studied at the University of Damascus. He is among the earliest members of Hamas and in 1989 rose to fill the post of head of the politburo for a year and a half after the arrests of Ahmed Yassin and of Ismail Abu Shanab. He was himself arrested in 1992, sentenced to twelve years in prison, and freed three and a half years later in a prisoner exchange. A journalist and the head of the *Al-Watan* newspaper, he was arrested by PNA security forces in

1995 and later released. He is regarded as one of Hamas's moderates in Gaza.

JAMAL ABU SAMHADANA (AL-MAGHAZI, 1963–2006)

A Fatah militant ever since he was a young man, Abu Samhadana undertook a journey in exile beginning in the 1980s that would take him to Egypt, Syria, Morocco, Tunisia, and later Germany to attend a military college, finally ending with journeys to Algeria and Iraq. He returned to the Occupied Palestinian Territory upon the installment of the PNA. Representing a critical voice against the PNA's repression of Hamas and Islamic Jihad militants, he left Fatah and established the Popular Resistance Committees during the Second Intifada. Hamas Minister of the Interior Said Siyyam appointed him in April 2006 to the post of the inspector general of the ministry of the interior. He was killed a few months later on June 8, 2006, during an Israeli raid on Rafah. He was second on the list of those sought by the authorities in Tel Aviv during the raid.

ISMAIL ABU SHANAB (NUSEIRAT, 1950–2003)

A professional engineer, Abu Shanab earned a degree in Egypt in 1975 and later took on several posts within academia and civil society. Ever since Hamas's establishment, he was among its leaders, and for a year and a half until his arrest by Israeli authorities in 1989 he filled the post of head of the politburo. Released in 1997, he was considered Hamas's most pragmatic leader and the bridge between the Islamist movement and the PLO. He was one of the central figures in the internal Palestinian negotiations in 2002, as well as of the 2003 *hudna*. He was killed by the Israelis in a targeted assassination on August 21, 2003, in Gaza City's Al-Rimal district.

RASHID ABU SHBAK (JABALIA, 1954)

One of the most important figures in the landscape of Palestinian security institutions, Abu Shbak became a Fatah member in 1971 and was arrested by the Israelis for the first time in 1972. He remained in Israeli jails from 1973 until 1987. Before leaving for Tunis, where Yasser Arafat was based at the time, he rose to leadership of Fatah's military wing, the so-called Hawks. He returned in 1994 upon the installment of the PNA and became Mohammed Dahlan's deputy in the Gaza Preventive Security Force, of which he took charge in 2002. In April 2005, he began his rise to the very top of the security services when Abu Mazen appointed him head of the Preventive Security Force in the West Bank and Gaza. On February 20, 2006, he was appointed head of the security services; later, on April 6, 2006, he was made director general of internal security at the ministry of the interior. Along with his strongest rival, Mohammed Dahlan, Hamas considers him responsible for the repression against it since the mid-1990s and for the clashes between Fatah and Hamas in 2006 and 2007.

AHMED (HAJ ALI) AHMED (QASIRIYYA-HAIFA, 1940)

Haj Ali received a religious education in Damascus and Nablus, residing in the nearby refugee camp of Ain Beit al-Ma'. Later, he was among those deported to Marj al-Zuhour in Lebanon, and he has been arrested several times by the Israelis. He was in jail when elected to parliament on the Change and Reform list in January 2006, receiving a high number of votes. He left prison in February 2006 but was re-arrested and released several times between 2006 and 2007.

YASSER ARAFAT, NOM DE GUERRE ABU AMMAR (CAIRO, 1929–2004)

Arafat spent most of his childhood and adolescence in Cairo, where he was born. He was cofounder of Fatah in 1957 along with Khalil al-Wazir (also known as Abu Jihad) after having established the Union of Palestinian Students in 1956. Fatah spokesperson until 1968, he became the president of the PLO's Executive Committee the following year. Ever since his speech to the PNC's assembly in Algiers on November 15, 1988, he undertook the path that would lead to the Oslo process, to the Declaration of Principles of 1993, and to the birth of the PNA the following year, an organization of which he then became the first president. Also in 1994, Arafat—together with Rabin and Peres—received the Nobel Peace Prize, and he remained the absolute protagonist of the PNA until his death in 2004. After the failure of the Camp David negotiations with Ehud Barak in July 2000 and the start of the Second Intifada two months later, he was increasingly isolated by the Israeli government, to the point that under Ariel Sharon's premiership, his Ramallah residence, the Muqata'a, was placed under siege. He died in a military hospital on the outskirts of Paris, having been transported there via Amman. His funeral, attended by several world leaders, took place in Cairo, after which his body was taken via Egyptian helicopter back to the Muqata'a in Ramallah, where it currently rests.

FARHAT AS'AD (A-TIRA, RAMALLAH, 1968)

As'ad became a member of the Muslim Brotherhood in his teens while in secondary school at A-Tira, in Ramallah. Between 1995 and 1996, he was Hamas's coordinator for all university campuses, preparing and managing elections to student councils. Between 2000 and 2003 he was Hamas's West Bank coordinator for the Second Intifada. Arrested several times by Israel, he spent one hundred months in administrative detention in Israeli jails. He was the coordinator for Hamas's electoral campaign in the run-up to the January 2006 general elections.

YOUNIS AL-ASTAL (KHAN YOUNIS, 1956)

Having earned a degree in Saudi Arabia and then a first doctorate in *fiqh* in Jordan and a second in Shariía jurisprudence in the Sudan, he headed the Shariía Faculty of the Islamic University in Gaza City for two years. He was elected to parliament on the Change and Reform list in the January 2006 general elections with nearly forty thousand votes and is one of the best-known preachers for Al-Aqsa, Hamas's television channel in the Gaza Strip.

YAHYA AYYASH (RAFAT-NABLUS, 1966–BEIT LAHYA, 1996)

After studying for an engineering degree at Birzeit University in Ramallah, he became a member of Hamas in the early 1990s, just as the Izz al-Din al-Qassam Brigades were being established. He was quickly nicknamed *al-Muhandis*, "the Engineer" or "Engineer of Death," because he had prepared the explosives used in many suicide attacks in 1994 and 1995. Wanted by the Israeli authorities, he was assassinated in the Gaza Strip on January 5, 1996.

AHMED BAHER (KHAN YOUNIS, 1950)

Baher was elected to parliament on the Change and Reform list during the January 2006 general elections, then voted first deputy speaker by his peers. A member of the Muslim Brotherhood since the 1970s, he was active within Sheikh Ahmed Yassin's Mujamma al-Islami and in several other charitable organizations. Having received a religious education, he took on several roles, among them that of *khatib* and of imam of the famous Palestine Mosque in Gaza City. He was a member of Al Khalas party in the mid-1990s. He was also a leader of Hizb al Khalas.

SALAH AL-BARDAWIL (KHAN YOUNIS, 1959)

A literary critic and a specialist in Palestinian literature, al-Bardawil earned a doctorate from Cairo University and for over fifteen years taught at the Islamic University in Gaza City. He founded the weekly *Al-Risala* and was spokesperson for Al Khalas party from 1996 to 2000. Considered one of Hamas's moderates, Bardawil was elected to parliament on the Change and Reform list during the January 2006 general elections, and later became spokesperson for the parliamentary wing. He headed the Hamas delegation to Cairo in January 2009 to take part in negotiations for a truce with Israel both during and after Operation Cast Lead.

SHEIKH MAJID BARGHOUTHI (KOBAR, 1964–RAMALLAH, 2008)

Barghouthi held the post of imam in Kobar, a village near Ramallah. Arrested by the Israelis, he spent four years in jail before being released in 2005 in a prisoner exchange. Very well known in the area, Barghouthi toured surrounding villages as a preacher on behalf of the Ministry of Waqf. In February 2008, he was arrested by Palestinian intelligence and interrogated in order to extract information on what were thought to be arms caches. According to an independent commission of inquiry, he was subjected to torture and died of a "heart attack."

MARWAN BARGHOUTHI (KOBAR, 1959)

A Fatah member since his youth, Barghouthi was cofounder of the movement's youth branch, the Shabiba. His first arrest was in 1978, following which he was imprisoned for five years. Upon his release, he became active in the student movement at Birzeit University in Ramallah. Deported to Jordan, he played a fundamental role during the First Intifada as a link with the leaders inside the Territory. He became a member of the PLO Central Committee and returned to the West Bank in 1994. He was elected to the first PLC in 1996. As Fatah's secretary general in the West Bank, he became the best-known leader of the Second Intifada. He was arrested in Ramallah in April 2002 and sentenced to five life sentences plus another forty years, accused of having ordered attacks carried out by Al-Aqsa Martyrs' Brigades. He was elected to parliament for a second time in the 2006 general elections while still in jail. He was one of the first to sign the so-called Prisoners' Document of May 2006 that aimed at Palestinian reconciliation.

MOHAMMED BARGHOUTHI (KOBAR, 1968)

Labor minister under the first Haniyeh government in March 2006, Mohammed Barghouthi later took on the position of minister for local government in the brief national unity government of March 2007. He has been arrested several times, accused of being a member of Hamas and has spent five years in Israeli jails.

MUSTAPHA BARGHOUTHI (JERUSALEM, 1954)

Mustapha Barghouthi graduated from medical school in Moscow and undertook medical practice in Jerusalem. He was a member of the Palestinian Communist Party and later established the Union of Palestinian Medical Relief Committees based in Ramallah. After further studies in the United States, he became one of the main activists in Palestinian civil society and in NGOs. Along with Haidar Abdel Shafi and Edward Said, he cofounded the Palestinian National Initiative (Al-Mubadara) in 2002, during the Second Intifada. He ran as a candidate in the Palestinian presidential elections in January 2005 after Arafat's death. He was elected to parliament on an independent ticket in the general elections of January 25, 2006, and served as a mediator during the formation of the national unity government, which lasted between March and June of 2007, for which he acted as minister for information.

SHEIKH HAMED BITAWI (BITA, 1944)

Bitawi studied Shariía at Amman University and has been a Shariía court judge for forty years, as well as a *khatib* in mosques across the West Bank and at the Al-Aqsa Mosque in Jerusalem and a professor at Al-Najah University and at Al-Rawda College. Considered one of the most conservative leaders of Hamas in the West Bank, he serves as president of the Union of the Palestinian Ulama, as well as heading several other groups, including the organization in charge of collecting *zakat* (charity tax) in Nablus. Since 1990, Bitawi has been arrested several times by the Israelis and was among the deportees at Marj al-Zuhour in Lebanon. He was a member of the Muslim Brotherhood before joining Hamas and was elected to parliament on the Change and Reform list in the January 2006 general elections.

MOHAMMED DAHLAN (KHAN YOUNIS, 1961)

Dahlan began his political activity in Fatah's youth organization, the Shabiba. Arrested several times during the first half of the 1980s, he later became a key figure in the First Intifada in Gaza. He was expelled from the Occupied Palestinian Territory by the Israeli authorities and remained in the PLO's headquarters in Tunis until 1994, when he returned to Gaza with Yasser Arafat. Until 2002, he headed the Preventive Security Force, masterminding the arrests of Hamas leaders and militants in the mid-1990s. He became Arafat's national security counselor in 2002 and the following year was promoted to minister for security affairs in Mahmoud Abbas's government. He was later appointed minister for civilian affairs in Ahmed Qureia's government between 2005 and 2006. He was elected to parliament as a Fatah candidate in the general elections of January 25, 2006, and selected to act as national security counselor by president Mahmoud Abbas.

MOHAMMED AL-DEIF (KHAN YOUNIS, 1965)

Al-Deif is believed to have been the commander of the Izz al-Din al-Qassam Brigades, a position he supposedly took around the time of the killing of Salah Shehadeh in 2002. Having become a member of the Muslim Brotherhood in the 1980s and later joining Hamas, he was arrested by the Israeli authorities in the first massive wave of arrests in 1989. After his release, he took part in the establishment of the Izz al-Din al-Qassam Brigades alongside Yahya Ayyash. He was arrested in 2000 by the Preventive Security Force and later freed. He currently tops the Israeli authorities' most-wanted list and has been the target of several assassination attempts by the Israelis. He is believed to have been injured, but independent sources of information regarding him are very scarce.

ABDEL FATTAH AL-DUKHAN (ARAK AL-SWEIDAN, 1936)

Al-Dukhan is a member of the Muslim Brotherhood and heads the largest charitable organization in Gaza, Al-Salah. He was one of those in attendance at the meeting at which Hamas was established on December 9, 1987. Al-Dukhan is a teacher and is considered to have written the Hamas Charter published in August 1988. He was one of those deported to Marj al-Zuhour in Lebanon and had two sons killed by the Israeli army: the first during the Second Intifada and the second while—according to Israeli armed forces—he was placing a bomb along the border with the Gaza Strip. He was elected to parliament on the Change and Reform list in the January 2006 general elections and is the oldest member of the second Palestinian legislature.

AZIZ DWEIK (NABLUS, 1948)

A trained geographer, Dweik holds three master's degrees and a doctorate from the University of Pennsylvania. He founded and directed Al-Najah University's Geography Department. He has been a Hamas member ever since its establishment and was among the 415 deportees at Marj al-Zuhour in Lebanon. Given his family roots in Hebron, he was elected to parliament on the Change and Reform list in January 2006 in the southern district of the West Bank, and he was later elected PLC speaker. He was arrested by Israeli authorities on August 5, 2006, and was imprisoned between Ramallah and Jerusalem until June 2009.

QADDURA FARES (SILWAD, 1962)

Fares is one of the most prominent among the current so-called young guards within Fatah. After having spent fourteen years in Israeli prisons, he was elected to the first PLC in 1996. He was a minister without any special role in Ahmed Qureia's administration between 2003 and 2005, and is among the signatories of the Geneva peace initiative. Defeated in the January 2006 elections, he heads the Palestinian Prisoners Society. He is considered one of the Fatah politicians closest to Marwan Barghouthi.

MARYAM (UMM NIDAL) FARHAT (GAZA, 1949)

Farhat was elected to parliament on the Change and Reform ticket in January 2006. Known in Gaza as the "Mother of Martyrs," she has six children and became the subject of international headlines when she appeared beside her seventeen-year-old son in a video in which he claimed responsibility for a suicide bombing he would soon carry out against an Israeli settlement in the Gaza Strip. Two more of her sons were killed during the Second Intifada. In 2008, Hamas asked Egypt to allow her to pass through the Rafah crossing in order for her to receive medical attention after suffering a heart attack.

SALAM FAYYAD (DEIR AL-GHUSSUN, TULKAREM, 1952)

Fayyad holds a degree in engineering from the American University in Beirut, as well as a master's degree and a doctorate from the University of Texas. He worked for the World Bank between 1987 and 1995 and from 1995 to 2001 as the International Monetary Fund representative in Jerusalem. After a brief period in the Arab Bank, he became finance minister in the Palestinian government in 2002 and began the process of reforming the PNA's financial infrastructure. He held the same post again under Mahmoud Abbas's government in 2003, as well as in later governments between then and 2005. He was elected to parliament on the Third Way ticket in the 2006 general elections and was also finance minister in the brief national unity government of March 2007. In July of that year, he was designated prime minister in the emergency government established in Ramallah by President Mahmoud Abbas after Hamas had taken control of the Gaza Strip in June and the national unity government had been dissolved.

MOHAMMED GHAZAL (NABLUS, 1957)

Ghazal is a professor of mechanical engineering at Al-Najah University in Nablus, holding a doctorate from the University of Pennsylvania. A Hamas member since the end of the 1980s, he is the Islamist movement's spokesperson in the West Bank. It was he who in March 2005 announced Hamas's decision to take part in the elections for the second Palestinian legislature. He was arrested a few months later, in September, by the Israeli authorities and remains in administrative detention.

IBRAHIM GHOSHEH (JERUSALEM, 1936)

Ghosheh is an Egyptian-educated engineer and as a student became an activist in the Islamist sector of the Student League. Beginning in 1961, he worked on several projects in Jordan and in Kuwait, becoming director of the Jordanian King Talal Dam until 1978. He became a member of Hamas in 1989, and during the 1990s he was Hamas's spokesperson in Amman and a member of its politburo. He was arrested by Jordanian authorities in 1999 and later expelled from the country. After spending two years in Qatar, the Hashemite Kingdom allowed him to return to Jordan on the proviso that he would no longer take an active part in Hamas's politics from Jordan.

SAMIRA HALAIKA (HEBRON, 1964)

A journalist writing for *Al-Risala* and *Sawt al-Haq*, Halaika was elected to parliament on the Change and Reform list on January 25, 2006. Her husband and one of her sons have been arrested several times by the Israeli authorities for their affiliation with Hamas.

GHAZI HAMAD (RAFAH, 1964)

Hamad joined the Muslim Brotherhood in 1982 at the age of eighteen. He spent five years in the Sudan studying toward a degree in veterinary medicine. Upon his return to Gaza, he took part in the First Intifada. In 1989, he was arrested by Israeli authorities and imprisoned for five years. In jail he became Hamas's spokesman. As a journalist, he wrote for the weekly *Al-Risala* and emerged as one of Hamas's moderates. He took part in Al Khalas experiment between 1996 and 2000 and became the spokesman for the Haniyeh government of 2006–2007 and later for the national unity government. He resigned from his post after Hamas's coup in June 2007.

JAMIL HAMAMI (MA'AN, 1952)

Hamami is among the founders of Hamas in the West Bank. He studied Shariía and law at the prestigious Al-Azhar University in Cairo, and he has a great deal of experience within Palestinian religious institutions, including the Waqf. A member of the Muslim Brotherhood, he was arrested three times by the Israelis: in 1988 for over a year and a half, in 1990 for a further twenty months, and yet again in 1995. In 1996, he left Hamas after the movement's decision not to take part in the first parliamentary elections for the PNA.

OSAMA HAMDAN (AL-BUREJ, 1964)

A Hamas representative in Lebanon since 1998, Osama Hamdan received his secondary education in Kuwait and later studied chemistry in Jordan. Upon returning to Kuwait, he worked in the oil industry for three and a half years. He joined the Muslim Brotherhood at the beginning of the 1980s and was, along with Khaled Meshaal, among those who planned the birth of Hamas. He moved to Iran, where he worked first as assistant to Imad al-Alami, Hamas's representative in Tehran, and then took his place in 1994. Since 2003, he has been listed as one of the Specially Designated Global Terrorists by George W. Bush's administration.

FATHI HAMMAD (BEIT LAHYA, 1961)

Hammad became a member of the Muslim Brotherhood in 1983,

and was also a member of several charitable organizations in the Gaza Strip. He was elected to parliament on the Change and Reform list in the January 2006 elections and achieved notoriety as director of Al-Aqsa, the television channel established by Hamas in Gaza. He assumed the role of minister of the interior after the assassination of Said Siyyam during Operation Cast Lead.

ISMAIL HANIYEH (AL-SHATI, 1962)

In March 2006, Haniyeh was the first Hamas leader to become prime minister in a PNA government. He joined the Muslim Brotherhood in the early 1980s while studying pedagogy and Arabic. He led the Islamist student bloc in Gaza and took part in the First Intifada. In 1988, he was arrested for the first time and again in 1989. In 1992, he was deported to Marj al-Zuhour in Lebanon. He was an assistant to Hamas founder Ahmed Yassin from 1997 until Yassin's assassination in 2003. He was also prime minister of the 2007 national unity government, and after Hamas's June 2007 coup he acted as head of the executive branch that administered the Gaza Strip on a de facto basis.

KHALIL AL-HAYYAH (GAZA CITY, 1960)

Al-Hayyah has an education in religious studies culminating in a doctorate obtained in the Sudan and a career entirely within the Islamic University in Gaza City. He is a member of the Union of Palestinian Ulama and was elected to parliament in January 2006. He is considered one of Hamas's pragmatists and was among the main mediators of the various truces between Fatah and Hamas during the violent clashes that took place in 2006 and 2007. On May 20, 2007, his house was struck in an Israeli air raid, killing seven members of his family.

BASSAM JARRAR (JENIN, 1948)

Jarrar was considered one of the most important and charismatic Islamist thinkers in the West Bank during the 1990s and directed the Al-Nun Center for Qur'anic Studies in Al-Bireh, Ramallah. He was deported to Marj al-Zuhour in Lebanon in 1992.

JAMAL MANSOUR (BALATA, 1960–2001)

Mansour was a student leader at Al-Najah University in Nablus during the early 1980s and later became one of the highest-profile members of Hamas in the West Bank. He was among the prisoners deported to Marj al-Zuhour in Lebanon and was arrested several times afterward both by the Israelis and by the PNA, spending a total of five years in Israeli prisons. He became the Hamas spokesperson for the West Bank until he was killed in an Israeli targeted assassination on July 31, 2001, during the Second Intifada.

MONA MANSOUR (NABLUS, 1961)

Widow of Jamal Mansour and a physics teacher, Mansour is one of the six women deputies elected in the January 25, 2006, general elections on the Change and Reform list.

KHALED MESHAAL (SILWAD, 1956)

Meshaal became a refugee in 1967 and immigrated to Kuwait, where he attended secondary school and later college. He obtained a degree in physics and was very active in the Islamist student movement. He worked in Kuwait until the Gulf War in 1990 and then moved to Jordan until 1999, when he was expelled to Qatar before moving to Damascus. For years he was Moussa Abu Marzouq's deputy until the latter's arrest in 1995, whereupon Meshaal became head of the politburo abroad until 2004. After Ahmed Yassin's death, he became the top leader of Hamas. In 1997, he survived a poisoning attempt by Mossad, the Israeli secret service. He took part in intra-Palestinian negotiations between 2005 and 2011. Along with Mahmoud Abbas, he was the major force behind the Mecca Agreement to establish a national unity government in February 2007.

BASSAM NA'IM (BEIT HANOUN, 1963)

Na'im was health minister in the first government presided over by Ismail Haniyeh between 2006 and 2007, and later the minister for sports and youth in the national unity government installed in March 2007. He returned to the ministry of health in the de facto government presided over by Ismail Haniyeh after Hamas's coup in Gaza in June 2007. Having obtained a doctorate and a degree in medicine in Germany, he worked as a doctor at the Shifa Hospital in Gaza City.

His first son, Naim, a member of the Izz al-Din al-Qassam Brigades, was killed at the age of seventeen during an Israeli incursion in the Shujaya district of Gaza City.

ABDEL KHALEQ AL-NATSHEH (HEBRON, 1954)

Al-Natsheh, a religious authority in Hebron from one of the most notable clans in the city, obtained a degree from the Saudi University of Medina. He was arrested several times by Israeli authorities for his militancy in Hamas. In 2000, he became the movement's spokesperson for the Hebron area. He was one of the 415 deportees to Marj al-Zuhour in Lebanon. In 1996, he took part in the attempts to establish a dialogue between Hamas and the PNA. As Hamas's most eminent representative in jail, he was one of the first to sign the Prisoners' Document in 2006, along with Fatah's Marwan Barghouthi. He has been arrested by the Israelis with the accusation of directing funds intended for charitable organizations toward the Izz al-Din al-Qassam Brigades.

MOHAMMED JAMAL AL-NATSHEH (HEBRON, 1959)

Mohammed al-Natsheh is one of Hamas's leading members in the Hebron area and has been arrested eight times by the Israelis, most recently in July 2002, an arrest that carried a sentence of eight years (later extended under administrative detention). He is one of the signatories of the Prisoners' Document in 2006 and was elected on the Change and Reform list in January 2006 while in prison. A teacher by profession, he was released from detention on September 12, 2010.

SHEIKH IZZ AL-DIN AL-QASSAM (JEBLA, 1882–1935)

Al-Qassam was a religious man of Syrian origins who became Haifa's most famous preacher. Based in the Al-Istiqlal (Independence) Mosque, he worked with the marginalized and the workers of the port area, and worked in the countryside around Haifa, as well. He established the Young Men's Muslim Association, which became one of the city's most important labor organizations. He later moved from political activism to armed struggle against the British Mandate and the Zionists. He was killed in an ambush set by British soldiers at Ya'bad in 1935.

AHMED QUREIA, NOM DE GUERRE ABU ALA (ABU DIS, JERUSALEM, 1937)

Qureia is one of Fatah's oldest leaders, having been a member since 1968. He became a member of the Fatah Central Committee, later of the PLO Central Council, as well as of the PNC. He followed Arafat into exile and took part in all stages of the Oslo process. He was the speaker of the first Palestinian parliament between 1996 and 2003, and later headed PNA governments as prime minister until 2006.

JIBRIL RAJOUB (AL-DOURA, HEBRON, 1953)

Jibril Rajoub was for many years considered the strongman of the PNA security forces in the West Bank. At the age of only fifteen, he had been sentenced to life in prison for having thrown a grenade against an Israeli army convoy. He spent seventeen years in prison, until 1985 when he was released in a prisoner exchange. A member of Fatah since 1970, he took part in the First Intifada, was expelled from the West Bank, and became a close advisor to Yasser Arafat, first in Tunis and later in Ramallah after the establishment of the PNA. He was head of the Preventive Security Force in the West Bank and national security counselor to Arafat in 2003 and later to Mahmoud Abbas in 2005. He is the brother of Nayef Rajoub, a Hamas leader in Hebron.

NAYEF RAJOUB (AL-DOURA, HEBRON, 1958)

Nayef Rajoub, younger brother of Jibril Rajoub, is a well-known imam and religious leader in Hebron. Since 1989, he has been arrested several times by the Israeli authorities. In 1992, he was among the 415 deportees to Marj al-Zuhour in Lebanon. He was elected to parliament on the Change and Reform list in January 2006, and was later appointed minister for religious affairs in Ismail Haniyeh's first government. He was arrested after the kidnapping of the Israeli soldier Gilad Shalit at the end of June 2006, along with several other ministers and Hamas deputies.

MAHMOUD AL-RAMAHI (RAMALLAH, 1963)

An anesthesiologist in Ramallah hospitals, al-Ramahi graduated in medicine from the University of Rome. During his years in Italy, he was involved in the Muslim community and served as the president of the Union of Muslim Students. One of the leaders of Hamas in the West Bank, he was in charge of the politburo of the Hamas movement in central areas such as Ramallah, Jerusalem, Bethlehem, and Jericho until the end of 1992. Later arrested and detained in Israeli jails, he continued to be involved in the Hamas leadership. He was elected to parliament on the Change and Reform list in January 2006 and was later elected the parliament's secretary general. He was arrested by Israeli authorities on August 20, 2006, from his home in Al-Bireh (where his wife was elected municipal counselor in 2005) and released in March 2009. He was rearrested in November 2010

ABDEL AZIZ AL-RANTISI (YIBNA, 1947–2004)

Al-Rantisi became a refugee in 1948, settling in Gaza, and spent his infancy and adolescence in the Khan Younis refugee camp. During the early 1970s, he studied medicine at the University of Alexandria, where he moved closer to political Islam. He returned to Gaza for his internship and later to Alexandria to pursue a specialization as a pediatrician. He joined the Muslim Brotherhood in 1976 and was one of the participants in the meeting that established Hamas on December 9, 1987. He was also the author of Hamas's first communiqué. In Marj al-Zuhour, he became the spokesperson for the 415 Islamists the Israeli authorities had deported. Between 1995 and 1997 he was detained in an Israeli jail, and between 1998 and 2000 he was incarcerated by the PNA. He was wounded in an attempted targeted assassination by the Israelis in Gaza City in June 2003. He was considered to be among Hamas's "hawks" and took over from Sheikh Ahmed Yassin after the latter's assassination on March 22, 2004. On April 17, less than one month later, he was himself killed in an Israeli raid. He was among the six Hamas leaders included on the Specially Designated Global Terrorists list by George W. Bush's government.

AHMED SAADAT (AL-BIREH, RAMALLAH, 1953)

Saadat became a PFLP member in 1969 and was immediately arrested by the Israeli authorities. Between 1970 and 1992, he spent eleven years in jail in several stints. A member of the PFLP leadership since 1981, he became the party's head in 2001 after Israel assassinated then Secretary General Abu Ali Mustapha. He was arrested in 2002 by the PNA after the killing of Israeli Minister Revaham Ze'evi, an act carried out by PFLP militants in revenge for the killing of Abu Ali Mustapha. In the context of an agreement mediated by the United States, Saadat was taken to the Palestinian prison in Jericho, where he was kidnapped by Israeli forces in March 2006. Since then, he has been detained in an Israeli jail. He was nevertheless elected to parliament in the January 2006 general elections on the Abu Ali Mustapha list.

MARYAM SALEH (DEIR AL-AMAR, 1952)

Saleh received an education wholly centered on Islam, earning a doctorate in Shariía from a Saudi university and becoming a professor at the Al-Quds University in Jerusalem. She was elected to parliament on the Change and Reform list in the January 2006 general elections and was appointed, two months later, as minister for women's affairs in the first Hamas government.

NASSER AL-DIN AL-SHA'ER (SEBASTYA, NABLUS, 1961)

Al-Sha'er, from a poor family in Sebastya, is one of the best-known and most appreciated intellectuals of the West Bank, specialized in Islamic and Middle Eastern studies. He was president of the Student Council of Al-Najah University in Nablus between 1980 and 1981. After obtaining a doctorate from Manchester University in the UK, he directed the Shariía Faculty at Al-Najah University for five years. He has been arrested several times by the Israeli authorities, including once during the electoral campaign of 2005–2006. The deputy prime minister in the first Haniyeh government of March 2006, he considers himself a moderate Islamist and has always denied being a member of Hamas. He was arrested in August 2006, along with other ministers and deputies, but was freed after a few months. He became education minister in the national unity government of March 2007. He was then re-arrested in 2009 and later freed on September 18, 2009, after six months in jail under administrative detention.

SALAH SHEHADEH (AL-SHATI, 1952–2002)

Shehadeh was a social worker who joined the Muslim Brotherhood while a student in Alexandria, Egypt, in the early 1970s. He worked particularly in Beit Hanoun, not just as a social worker but also as a preacher, later becoming head of the Department of Student Affairs at the Islamic University. Among those closest to Ahmed Yassin, he took part in the establishment of the first armed Islamist groups, as well as in the establishment of Hamas on December 9, 1987. Considered the leader of the Izz al-Din al-Qassam Brigades, he spent twelve years in Israeli prisons until his release in 2000. Accused by the Israelis of being the mastermind behind suicide attacks and the production of Qassam rockets, he escaped several assassination attempts before dying in a targeted killing on July 23, 2002, along with fourteen other people.

SAID SIYYAM (AL-SHATI, 1959–2009)

Siyyam earned a doctorate in Shariía studies and taught science and mathematics. He took part in the First Intifada and was a member of Hamas ever since its inception. He was among the 415 prisoners deported to Marj al-Zuhour in 1992. Three years later, he was arrested by the PNA's security forces. In 2006, he was elected on the Change and Reform list. During the first Hamas government, as minister of the interior, he established the Support Force in April 2006, later renamed the Executive Force. He also designated Jamal Abu Samhadana director general of the ministry of the interior. Considered one of the "hawks" in the Hamas leadership in Gaza, he was killed, along with nine other people, in an Israeli raid during Operation Cast Lead on January 15, 2009, by means of a one-ton bomb dropped on his brother Iyad's house, where he was attending a meeting.

SHEIKH AHMED YASSIN (AL-JOURA, 1938–2004)

Sheikh Ahmed Yassin joined the Muslim Brotherhood in the 1950s and later became the founder of Hamas. After an accident in his adolescence, he was struck by a serious form of quadriplegia, which would worsen over time. He received his education in Egypt and taught in Gaza until his retirement. In 1973, he established the Mujamma al-Islami, the core around which Hamas would later be established. Well before the birth of Hamas, he was already working toward the establishment of an operational branch of the Muslim Brotherhood, for which he was sentenced by Israel for the first time in 1984 to thirteen years in prison, but was released the following year in a prisoner exchange. The meeting at which Hamas was established took place in his home on December 9, 1987. He was again arrested in 1989 and remained in prison until 1997, when he was released following Mossad's failed attempt to kill Khaled Meshaal in Amman. He was believed to be Hamas's spiritual and charismatic leader, even though political responsibilities were shared among a number of leaders. At dawn on March 22, 2004, he was killed in a targeted assassination ordered by Israeli Prime Minister Ariel Sharon just outside the mosque near his home in the Al-Sabra district of Gaza City.

AHMED YOUSSEF (RAFAH, 1950)

Youssef left the Gaza Strip and moved to Cairo in 1973. After earning a degree in engineering from Al-Azhar University, he worked in the Gulf and later immigrated to the United States, where he obtained two master's degrees and a doctorate in political science. He replaced Moussa Abu Marzouq as the director of a Virginia-based Islamist think-tank, the United Association for Studies and Research (UASR), which he led for fifteen years, also directing the UASR's *Middle East Affairs Journal*. A well-known journalist in the Arab world, he's the author of a dozen books on political Islam. He returned to Gaza to become Ismail Haniyeh's closest advisor during the first Hamas government and the national unity government. He is considered one of the Islamist movement's most moderate voices.

SHEIKH HASSAN YOUSSEF (AL-JANIYA, RAMALLAH, 1955)

Youssef is considered Hamas's most important religious figure in the West Bank. He holds several positions in Muslim religious institutions in Ramallah, where he also works in the famous Market Mosque. He is a member of Hamas's politburo in Ramallah and has been arrested many times by Israelis authorities. He was among the 415 deportees to Marj al-Zuhour in December 1992 and was detained several times for short periods over the following decade until his arrest in 2002. He has been under administrative detention since September 2005. He was elected to parliament as a member of the Change and Reform list in the 2006 general elections.

MAHMOUD AL-ZAHHAR (GAZA CITY, 1945)

Al-Zahhar spent much of his childhood, between 1947 and 1958, in Ismailiyya, Egypt. He returned to Gaza in 1965 but then went back to Egypt to study medicine in Cairo. He experienced the Six Day War from Egypt, and only in 1972 did he manage to return to Palestine. He began working as a surgeon in the Shifa Hospital of Gaza City, later moving to Khan Younis. He was among the founders of the Islamic University in Gaza City and among the earliest members of Hamas. He was arrested in 1989 and incarcerated for a few months. He was later among the 415 deportees to Marj al-Zuhour in Lebanon, where he became one of the camp's spokesmen. Arrested by the PNA police in 1995, his beard was shaved as a sign of mockery. After the assassinations of Ahmed Yassin and Abdel Aziz al-Rantisi in 2004, he was one of the three leaders of Hamas in the Gaza Strip. He was appointed foreign minister in the first Haniyeh government of March 2006. He is considered one of the Islamist movement's "hawks," although he has always rejected this characterization. In 2003, he was the target of an assassination attempt in which his son Khaled was killed. On January 15, 2008, his youngest son was killed in an armed clash with Israeli soldiers during a raid in Gaza City.

NOTES

EMOTIONAL PROLOGUE

1. Tom Segev, "Trying to 'Teach Hamas a Lesson' Is Fundamentally Wrong," *Ha'aretz*, December 29, 2008.
2. The Israeli Ministry for Foreign Affairs reports statistics updated to June 2008 that indicate 542 victims of suicide attacks carried out between 2000 and 2007 (http://www.mfa.gov.il/MFA/Terrorism-%20Obstacle%20to%20Peace/Palestinian%20terror%20since%202000/Victims%20of%20Palestinian%20Violence%20and%20Terrorism%20sinc). Suicide attacks, however, began at least six years earlier, in 1994. According to numbers reported by the same ministry, 250 Israelis were killed in terrorist attacks between 1994 and 1999. "Terrorist attacks" is a broad term that also includes suicide attacks carried out inside Israel, the borders of which are defined as the armistice lines of 1949—in other words, the borders of the Green Line.
3. I chose not to engage the long-standing debate on the settlement/colonies definition, and in this book have preferred the terms "settler/settlement" over "colonist/colony."

CHAPTER 1: BETWEEN WELFARE AND RESISTANCE

1. Of those hours, the pages written by Amira Hass, who was then the *Ha'aretz* correspondent from Gaza, remain the best; see Amira Hass, *Drinking the Sea at Gaza* (New York: Henry Holt & Co., 1996), pp. 13–30.
2. Beverley Milton-Edwards, *Islamic Politics in Palestine* (London: I. B. Tauris, 1996), p. 95.
3. Benny Morris, *The Birth of the Palestinian Refugee Problem Revisited*, 2nd ed. (1988; Cambridge, UK: Cambridge University Press, 2004), pp. 528–29. For Moshe Dayan, "it was necessary to build a port city for the Negev in Majdal." Meron Rapoport, "History Erased: The IDF and the Post-1948 Destruction of Palestinian Monuments," *Journal of Palestine Studies* 37, no. 2 (2008): p. 82; see also Orna Cohen, "Transferred to Gaza of Their Own Accord" in *The Arabs of Majdal in Ashkelon and Their Evacuation to the Gaza Strip in* 1950 (Jerusalem: Harry S. Truman Research Institute for the Advancement of Peace, Hebrew University of Jerusalem, 2007), p. 27.

4. Eitan Bronstein, "The Nakba in Hebrew: Israeli-Jewish Awareness of the Palestinian Catastrophe and Internal Refugees" in *Catastrophe Remembered. Israel and the Internal Refugees: Essays in Memory of Edward W. Said (1935–2003)*, ed. Nur Masalha, (London: Zed Books, 2005), p. 223.

5. Sara Roy, *Failing Peace: Gaza and the Palestinian-Israeli Conflict* (London and Ann Arbor: Pluto Press, 2007), p. 55.

6. See *Gaza dans l'antiqué tardive: archeologie, rhetorique et histoire*, ed. Catherine Saliou, Actes du Colloque International de Poitiers, May 6–7, 2004 (Salerno, Italy: Helios, 2005); Carol A. M. Glucker, *The City of Gaza in the Roman and Byzantine Periods*, BAR International Series, no. 325 (Oxford: Bar Archaeological Reports, 1987).

7. Khaled Hroub, *Hamas: Political Thought and Practice* (Washington, DC: Institute for Palestine Studies, 2000), pp. 13–15.

8. Ziad Abu Amr, *Islamic Fundamentalism in the West Bank and Gaza: Muslim Brotherhood and Islamic Jihad* (Bloomington and Indianapolis: Indiana University Press, 1994), pp. 2–3. Abu Amr argues that the first branch of the Muslim Brotherhood that was opened in 1948 by 'Aysh 'Amira, and that Egyptian influence—particularly that of officials in Cairo's army such as Abdel Moneim Abdel Raouf—was very important.

9. Milton-Edwards, *Islamic Politics in Palestine*, p. 43.

10. Ibid.

11. Ibid.

12. Ibid., pp. 43–44.

13. I chose the definition of Occupied Palestinian Territory (OPT), as officially used by the United Nations, instead of Palestinian Occupied Territories, because the first definition better describes not only the aspirations of the Palestinian population, but also the elites' political discourse.

14. Amnon Cohen, *Political Parties in the West Bank under the Jordanian Regime, 1949–67* (Ithaca, NY: Cornell University Press, 1982), p. 145.

15. Abu Amr, *Islamic Fundamentalism*, p. 5.

16. Ibid.

17. Sayyed Abu Musameh, interview by the author, Gaza City, October 26, 2008.

18. Ibid.

19. Ibid.

20. For example, one of Hamas's leading spiritual authorities in the West Bank—and one of the most conservative—Sheikh Hamed Bitawi, states: "If it is true that Hamas was born in Gaza, it is equally true that the debates were taking place in the West Bank as well." Sheikh Hamed Bitawi, interview by the author, Nablus, November 2, 2008.

21. Osama Hamdan, interview by the author, Beirut, November 15, 2008.
22. Ibid.
23. Jamila Abdallah al Taha Shanti, interview by the author, Gaza City, September 21, 2010.
24. Shaul Mishal and Avraham Sela, *The Palestinian Hamas: Vision, Violence, and Coexistence* (New York: Columbia University Press, 2000), p. 20; Abu Amr, *Islamic Fundamentalism*, p. 16.
25. The registration request for the Jamiyyat Jawrat al-Shams al-Islamiyya, the Mujamma's official name, was presented on August 4, 1977, signed by Ya'cub Othman Qwaik, and addressed to the Israeli military authorities. See Mishal and Sela, *Palestinian Hamas*, p. 204.
26. Milton-Edwards, *Islamic Politics in Palestine*, p. 128n42.
27. Ibid, p. 104.
28. Glenn E. Robinson, *Building a Palestinian State: The Incomplete Revolution* (Bloomington and Indianapolis: Indiana University Press, 1997), p. 138.
29. Farhat As'ad, interview by the author, Ramallah, October 15, 2008.
30. Ibid.
31. Emile Sahliyeh, *In Search of Leadership: West Bank Politics since 1967* (Washington, DC: Brookings Institution Press, 1988), p. 145.
32. Abu Amr, *Islamic Fundamentalism*, p. 140.
33. Milton-Edwards, *Islamic Politics in Palestine*, pp. 108–14.
34. Abu Amr, *Islamic Fundamentalism*, p. 33.
35. "Khalid Mishal: The Making of a Palestinian Islamic Leader," interview by Mouin Rabbani, *Journal of Palestine Studies* 37, no. 3 (Spring 2008): pp. 59–73.
36. Azzam Tamimi indicates the country in which the 1983 conference took place, whereas the Hamas leaders do not specify the location. Azzam Tamimi, *Hamas: Unwritten Chapters* (London: Hurst & Co., 2007), p. 45.
37. Osama Hamdan, interview by the author, Beirut, November 15, 2008.
38. "Khalid Mishal," interview by Mouin Rabbani.
39. Osama Hamdan, interview by the author, Beirut, November 15, 2008.
40. International Crisis Group, "Dealing with Hamas," *ICG Middle East Report*, no. 21 (January 26, 2004): p. 6.
41. Osama Hamdan, interview by the author, Beirut, November 15, 2008.
42. See Eyal Weizman, *Hollow Land: Israel's Architecture of Occupation* (London: Verso, 2007), p. 70, on the "five fingers" strategy.
43. Roy, *Failing Peace*, p. 33.
44. Hass, *Drinking the Sea at Gaza*, pp. 34ff.
45. Azzam Tamimi, interview by the author, London, July 12, 2008.
46. Hamas Charter, quoted in Hroub, *Hamas*, p. 269.

47. Amal Jamal, *The Palestinian National Movement: Politics of Contention, 1967–2005* (Bloomington: Indiana University Press, 2005), pp. 106–10. Jamal also provides a table with the sociological provenance and educational level of Hamas leaders.

48. Al-Ahram Center for Strategic and Political Studies, *The Spectrum of Islamist Movements*, ed. Dia'a Rashwan (Berlin: Verlag Hans Schiler, 2007), p. 110.

49. Abu Amr, *Islamic Fundamentalism*, p. 6. Cohen, *Political Parties in the West Bank*, pp. 162–64.

50. Flier republished in Hroub, *Hamas*, p. 265. The precise chronology of Hamas communiqués is still subject to debate among historians. According to Jean-François Legrain, a scholar who has catalogued fliers, communiqués, and documents on the First Intifada in general, Hamas's true organizational phase begins with its fourth communiqué, dated February 11, 1988, while the use of the acronym HAMAS, meaning "zeal," begins during May–June 1988. See Jean-François Legrain, "The Islamic Movement and the Intifada," in *Intifada: Palestine at the Crossroads*, ed. Jamal R. Nassar and Roger Heacock (New York: Birzeit University and Praeger, 1991), p. 182.

51. Tamimi, *Hamas*, p. 11.

52. The full text of the first communiqué can be found in English in Hroub, *Hamas*, pp. 265–66. All subsequent citations are drawn from this text.

53. Ibid.

54. Osama Hamdan, interview by the author, Beirut, November 15, 2008.

55. Mishal and Sela, *Palestinian Hamas*, p. 128.

56. Bassam Na'im, interview by the author, Gaza City, November 6, 2007.

CHAPTER 2: SNAPSHOTS FROM HAMAS'S WORLD

1. International Crisis Group, "Islamic Social Welfare Activism in the Occupied Palestinian Territory," *ICG Middle East Report* (April 2, 2003): p. 7. On Islamic NGOs in the Gaza Strip, see Roy's *Failing Peace*.

2. Salwa (Al-Salah employee), interview by the author, Deir al-Balah (Gaza), December 6, 2007.

3. Ibid.

4. See International Crisis Group, "Squaring the Circle: Palestinian Security Reform Under Occupation," *ICG Middle East Report*, no. 98 (September 7, 2010): p. 28. Anonymous Hamas leader, interview by the author, Ramallah, September, 28, 2010.

5. US Treasury Department in "Additional Background Information on Charities Designated under Executive Order 13224," available at http://www.treasury.gov/resource-center/terrorist-illicit-finance/Pages/protecting-charities_execorder_13224-a.aspx.

6. As quoted in Kim Murphy, "Hamas Victory Built on Social Work," *Los Angeles Times*, March 2, 2006.

7. US Treasury Department press communiqué available at http://www.treasury.gov/press-center/press-releases/Pages/hp531.aspx.

8. Author's interview with representatives of the Jamia'a al-Khairiyya al-Islamiyya, Hebron, May 11th, 2008.

9. Maysoun Darwish, interview by the author, Hebron, May 11, 2008.

10. Carrie Rosefsky Wickham, *Mobilizing Islam: Religion, Activism, and Political Change in Egypt* (New York: Columbia University Press, 2002), p. 102.

11. Hamas Charter in Hroub, *Hamas*, p. 280.

12. Glenn E. Robinson, "Hamas as Social Movement," in *Islamic Activism: A Social Movement Theory Approach*, ed. Quintan Wictorowicz (Bloomington: Indiana University Press, 2004), pp. 126–29.

13. UNESCO/OCHA, "Food and Cash Assistance Programs, October 2000–August 2001: A Brief Overview," p. 18.

14. Conal Urquhart, "Hamas Uses Charity to Lure Support," *The Observer*, August 31, 2002, http://www.observer.co.uk/international/story/0,6903,784146,00.html.

15. Roy, *Failing Peace*, p. 130.

16. Milton-Edwards, *Islamic Politics in Palestine*, pp. 106–8.

17. Eyad al-Sarraj, interview by the author, Gaza City, October 28, 2008.

18. Osama Hamdan, interview by the author, Beirut, November 15, 2008.

19. Eyad al-Sarraj, interview by the author, Gaza City, October 28, 2008.

20. Anonymous activist, interview by the author, Hebron, February 4, 2008.

21. Vivian Salama, "Hamas TV: Palestinian Media in Transition," *Transnational Broadcasting Journal* 16 (2006). Accessed online at http://www.tbsjournal.com/Salama.html.

22. Agence France Presse, "Palestinian prosecutor moves to shut down Hamas TV," *The Daily Star*, January 23, 2006, http://www.dailystar.com.lb/News/Middle-East/Jan/23/Palestinian-prosecutor-moves-to-shut-down-Hamas-TV.ashx#axzz1jMWxpVfi.

23. Fathi Hammad, as quoted in Eric Westervelt, "Hamas Launches Television Network," *Morning Edition*, US National Public Radio, February 3, 2006, http://www.npr.org/templates/transcript/transcript.php?storyId=5186883.

24. Ibid.

25. Hamas activists, interview by the author, Gaza City, September 20, 2010.

26. Hamed Bitawi, interview by the author, Nablus, November 2, 2008.

27. Reema Hammami, "From Immodesty to Collaboration: Hamas, the Women's Movement, and National Identity in the Intifada," in *Politi-*

cal Islam: Essays from Middle East Report, ed. Joel Beinin and Joe Stork (London and New York: I. B. Tauris, 1997), pp. 194–210.

28. Omar Barghouthi, interview by the author, Ramallah, October 15, 2008.
29. A. (Hamas militant), interview by the author, West Bank, March 2008.
30. Samira Halaika, interview by the author, Hebron, February 4, 2008.
31. Ibid.
32. Jamila al Shanti, interview by the author, Gaza City, September 21, 2010.
33. Islah Jad, "Between Religion and Secularism: Islamist Women of Hamas," in *On Shifting Ground: Muslim Women in the Global Era*, ed. Fereshteh Nouraie Simone (New York: The Feminist Press, 2005), p. 185.
34. Jamila al Shanti, interview by the author, Gaza City, September 21, 2010.

CHAPTER 3: CONSOLIDATION

1. Anonymous source, interview by the author, November 2008.
2. Legrain, "The Islamic Movement," p. 182.
3. Quoted in Hroub, *Hamas*, p. 274.
4. Ibid., p. 267.
5. Ibid., p. 273.
6. Ibid.
7. Yasser Arafat announced the changes to the National Charter to then–US President Bill Clinton in a letter sent from Nablus on January 13, 1998, which confirmed that the extraordinary PNC session of April 1996 had already undertaken the appropriate changes to those parts of the Charter that were not in line with UN Security Council Resolutions and with the Oslo Accords. Formally, however, the changes would be made only in 1998.
8. Nasser al-Din al-Sha'er, interview by the author, Nablus, November 2, 2008.
9. Azzam Tamimi, interview by the author, London, July 12, 2008.
10. Mahmoud al-Zahhar, interview by the author, Gaza City, December 6, 2007.
11. Sayyed Abu Musameh, interview by the author, Gaza City, October 26, 2008.
12. Moussa Abu Marzouq, "Hamas' Stand," *Los Angeles Times*, July 10, 2007, http://www.latimes.com/news/opinion/commentary/la-oe-marzook10jul10,0,777568.story.
13. Ibid.
14. Ibid.
15. Hamas leaders, interview by the author, Gaza City, September 21, 2010.

16. "Hamas Leader Says Charter Is Not the Koran," Reuters, September 2005.

17. Hamed Bitawi, interview by the author, Nablus, November 2, 2008.

18. Khalid Amayreh, "Hamas Debates the Future: Palestine's Islamic Resistance Movement Attempts to Reconcile Ideological Purity and Political Realism," Conflicts Forum Monograph, November 2007, p. 5 n. 2, http://conflictsforum.org/briefings/Hamas-Debates-the-Future-monograph.pdf.

19. Ahmed Youssef, interview by the author, Gaza City, November 6, 2007.

20. Osama Hamdan, interview by the author, Beirut, November 15, 2008.

21. Mahmous al-Zahhar, interview by the author, Gaza City, December 6, 2007.

22. Mahmoud al-Zahhar, interview by the author, Gaza City, December 6, 2007. Al-Zahhar also recalls meetings with Israeli political and military leaders in an autobiographical piece included in *Beyond Intifada: Narratives of Freedom Fighters in the Gaza Strip*, ed. Haim Gordon, Rivca Gordon, and Taher Shriteh (Westport, CT, and London: Praeger, 2003), p. 116. See also Hroub, *Hamas*, p. 74.

23. Mahmoud al-Zahhar, interview by the author, Gaza City, December 6, 2007.

24. Ibid.

25. Sayyed Abu Musameh, interview by the author, Gaza City, October 26, 2008.

26. Tamimi, *Hamas*, pp. 60–61.

27. Ibid., p. 61.

28. Azzam Tamimi, interview by the author, London, July 12, 2008.

29. On Israeli pacifist organization B'Tselem's appeals to the Supreme Court, see Tami Bash, Yuval Ginbar, and Eitan Felner, "Deportation of Palestinians from the Occupied Territory and the Mass Deportation of December 1992," Jerusalem, June 1993, available at http://www.btselem.org/Download/199306_Deportation_Eng.doc.

30. Mohammad Nimer, *The Structural Development of an Islamist Society*, available at http://www.islamonline.net/iol-english/qadaya/qpolitico.asp.

31. Ayman Taha, one of the youngest former Marj al-Zuhour deportees, interview by the author, Gaza City, September 21, 2010.

32. Abdel Moneim Abul Futuh, interview by the author, Cairo, November 28, 2007.

33. Hamas leaders, interview by the author, Gaza City, September 21, 2010.

34. Ahmed Attoun, Mohammed Totah, and Khaled Abu Arafeh, interview by the author, Jerusalem, International Red Cross compound, September 10, 2010.

35. Mishal and Sela, *Palestinian Hamas*, pp. 91–93.
36. Osama Hamdan, interview by the author, Beirut, November 15, 2008. See also Hroub, *Hamas*, pp. 103–9.
37. "Hamas made very minor changes to the curriculum when it held the unified Ministry of Education from March 2006 until June 2007, most significantly increasing the number of hours devoted to religion as a subject. That change has not been reversed by the Fayyad cabinet" (Nathan J. Brown, "Are Palestinians Building a State?" Carnegie Commentary, June 2010, p. 8, http://carnegieendowment.org/files/palestinian_state1.pdf).
38. See al-Zahhar, *Beyond Intifada*, pp. 120–21.
39. Mishal and Sela, *Palestinian Hamas*, pp. 122–30. The full 1992 document is included here.
40. The Egyptian Muslim Brotherhood would undertake an identical approach in deciding to create a specific political party, the Freedom and Justice Party, after the fall of Hosni Mubarak in February 2011. In both cases the electoral party was separate from the Muslim Brotherhood's structure.
41. Ibid.
42. Ghazi Hamad, interview by the author, Gaza City, October 26, 2008. All subsequent citations are drawn from this interview.
43. Mahmoud al-Ramahi, interview by the author, Ramallah, September 28, 2010.
44. Salah al-Bardawil, interview by the author, Gaza City, September 20, 2010. Jamila al Shanti, a member of the first political bureau of Al Khalas, doesn't agree with Salah al-Bardawil on the party's legacy inherited by Hamas (Jamila al Shanti, interview by the author, Gaza City, September 21, 2010).
45. Ghazi Hamad, interview by the author, Gaza City, October 26, 2008.
46. Salah al-Bardawil, interview by the author, Gaza City, September 20, 2010.
47. Ghazi Hamad, interview with the author, Gaza City, October 26, 2008.
48. Osama Hamdan, interview by the author, Beirut, November 15, 2008.
49. Hamed Bitawi, interview by the author, Nablus, November 2, 2008.
50. Osama Hamdan, interview by the author, Beirut, November 15, 2008.
51. Nigel Parsons, *The Politics of Palestinian Authority: From Oslo to Al-Aqsa* (New York and London: Routledge, 2005), p. 193.
52. Andreas Tai, "Widerstand im Namens Allahs. Hamas als politischer Faktor im Friedensprozess," in *Der Friedensprozess im Nahen-Osten: Eine Revision*, ed. Ferhad Ibrahim and Abraham Ashkenasi (Berlin, Hamburg, and Muenster: LIT, 1998), p. 157.

53. Khaled Amayreh, "Hamas Says No," *Middle East International,* December 15, 1995, p. 8.

54. Parsons, *Politics of Palestinian Authority,* p. 193.

55. Osama Hamdan, interview by the author, Beirut, November 15, 2008.

56. Mohammed Muslih, "Hamas: Strategy and Tactics," in *Ethnic Conflict and International Politics in the Middle East,* ed. by Leonard Binder (Miami: University of Florida Press, 999), p. 325.

57. Avi Shlaim, *Lion of Jordan: The Life of King Hussein in War and Peace* (London: Penguin, 2007), p. 571.

58. Graham Usher, "Hamas Suspicious of Hamas-Jordan Links," in *Middle East International* 561 (October 24, 1997): p. 3.

CHAPTER 4: FROM THE "UNDERGROUND" SHEIKH TO HUMAN BOMBS

1. Shabtai Teveth, *Ben-Gurion: The Burning Ground, 1886–1948* (Boston: Houghton Mifflin Company, 1987), p. 512.

2. See Rashid Khalidi, "The Palestinians and 1948: The Underlying Causes of Failure," in *The War for Palestine: Re-writing the History of 1948,* ed. Avi Shlain and Eugene L. Rogan (Cambridge University Press, 2001); and Abdallah Schleifer, "The Life and Thought of 'Izz-Id-Din Al-Qassam," *Islamic Quarterly* 23, no. 2 (1979).

3. Joel Beinin, *Workers and Peasants in the Modern Middle East* (Cambridge, UK: Cambridge University Press, 2001), p. 94.

4. Shai Lachman, "Arab Rebellion and Terrorism in Palestine, 1929–39: The Case of Sheikh Izz al-Din al-Qassam and His Movement," in *Zionism and Arabism in Palestine and Israel,* ed. Elie Kedourie and Sylvia G. Haim (London: Frank Cass, 1982), p. 67; and Walter Laqueur, *A History of Zionism* (New York: Schocken, 2003), pp. 505–11.

5. Weldon C. Matthews, *Confronting an Empire, Constructing a Nation* (London: I. B. Tauris, 2006), p. 237.

6. Ted Swedenburg, *Memories of Revolt: The 1936–39 Rebellion and the Palestinian National Past* (Minneapolis and London: University of Minnesota Press, 1995), p. 33. On the Arab Great Revolt, also see Tom Segev, *One Palestine, Complete: Jews and Arabs under the British Mandate* (New York: Henry Holt & Co., 2000), pp. 361–74.

7. Joel Beinin and Zachary Lockman, eds., *Intifada: The Palestinian Uprising Against Israeli Occupation* (Cambridge, Mass.: South End Press, 1989), p. 329.

8. Elias Sanbar, "Izz al Din al Qassam, un homme d'humanitè. Remarques preliminaires à une recherche sur le mouvement de Sheikh Izz al Din al Qassam," in *Studia Palestina: Studies in Honour of Constantine K. Zurayk,* ed. Hisham Nashashe (Beirut: Institute for Palestine Studies, 1988), pp. 52–68.

9. Hamas Charter in Hroub, *Hamas*, p. 271.

10. It was no coincidence that during Ramadan 2001 the Hezbollah Lebanese Islamist movement's television station produced and broadcast a period drama based on Izz al-Din al-Qassam, addressing it to its Palestinian audience. The four-part series was entitled *Izz al-Din al-Qassam: Qisit al-jihad wa al-muqawam* (Izz al-Din al-Qassam: A Story of Jihad and of Resistance). Cf. Olfa Lamloud, "Le Hezbollah au miroir de ses medias," in *Le Hezbollah: Ètat des lieux*, ed. Sabrina Mervin (Arles: Actes Sud, 2008), p. 39.

11. Abd el-Fattah Mohammed al-Azaisi, *The Muslim Brothers and the Palestine Question, 1928–1947* (London: I. B. Tauris, 1998), p. 120.

12. Ibid., p. 117.

13. Alastair Crooke, "From Rebel Movement to Political Party: The Case of the Islamic Resistance Movement," Conflict Forum Briefing Paper, no. 3, 2007, p. 3, http://conflictsforum.org/briefings/Hamas-From-rebel-movement-to-political-party.pdf.

14. The name "strategy of tension" indicates the period roughly from 1969 to the beginning of the 1980s, when Italy was hit by a series of terrorist bombings, many of them carried out by right-wing extremists in connection with some elements from the Italian intelligence services. Some of the terrorist bombings—from the attack in Banca dell'Agricoltura in Milan, in 1969, to the bombing of the Bologna train station in 1980—caused large numbers of civilian deaths.

15. Swedenburg, *Memories of Revolt*, p. 201.

16. For a description of Baruch Goldstein by the more radical Israeli fringes, see http://www.jonathan5742.com/Right_Wing_Zionist_Homepage/Kahane.htm.

17. Moussa Abu Marzouq, interview by George Baghdadi, "Defining Terrorism," *Time Magazine*, April 8, 2002.

18. International Crisis Group, "Enter Hamas: The Challenges of Political Integration," *ICG Middle East Report*, n. 49 (January 18, 2006), p. 2.

19. Abdel Aziz al-Rantisi, quoted in *Kul al-Arab*, January 9, 1998.

20. Osama Hamdan, interview by the author, Beirut, November 15, 2008.

21. Ahmed Youssef, interview by the author, Gaza City, October 26, 2008.

22. International Crisis Group, "Dealing with Hamas," *ICG Middle East Report*, no. 21, January 26, 2004, p. 16.

23. Beverley Milton-Edwards, "Factors behind Hamas Bombings," *Middle East International*, August 1995, pp. 18–19.

24. Ibid.

25. As quoted in ibid.

26. Marzouq, "Defining Terrorism."

27. Ahmed Youssef, interview by the author, Gaza City, October 26, 2008.

28. Shaul Mishal, "The Pragmatic Dimension of the Palestinian Hamas," *Armed Forces & Society* 29, no. 4 (Summer 2003): p. 583.

29. Hamas leader, interview by the author, Gaza City, September 21, 2010.

30. Mushir al Masri, interview by the author, Gaza City, September 21, 2010.

31. As Mohammed Dahlan himself said in an interview with investigative journalist David Rose, author of the most significant inquiry into the Bush administration's plans to trigger a civil war among Palestinians after the Hamas electoral victory of 2006: "Arafat had decided to arrest Hamas military leaders, because they were working against his interests, against the peace process, against the Israeli withdrawal, against everything.... He asked the security services to do their job, and I have done that job," admitting that it was not "popular work." For many years, Hamas said that the forces led by Dahlan routinely tortured detainees. David Rose, "The Gaza Bombshell," *Vanity Fair*, April 2008, http://www.vanityfair.com/politics/features/2008/04/gaza200804.

32. See Rashwan, *Spectrum of Islamist Movements*; and Helga Baumgarten, *Hamas: Der politische Islam in Palästina* (Berlin: Diederichs Verlag, 2006), p. 129.

33. Graham Usher, "The New Hamas: Between Resistance and Participation," in *Middle East Report*, August 21, 2005, http://www.merip.org/mero/mero082105.

34. Ibid.

35. Farhat As'ad, interview by the author, Ramallah, October 15, 2008.

36. Ibid.

37. Ibid.

38. Osama Hamdan, interview by the author, Beirut, November 15, 2008.

39. Ibid.

40. Karin Laub and Dan Perry, "Hamas Leader: Arafat Urged Attacks on Israel," *Associated Press*, October 1, 2010.

41. Sahar Khalifeh, *The End of Spring* (Northampton, Mass.: Interlink Books, 2007).

42. Quoted in Mustafa Abu Sway, "The Concept of Hudna (Truce) in Islamic Sources," PASSIA, Religious Studies Unit article, August 6, 2006, http://www.passia.org/meetings/2006/Hudna.htm.

43. Alastair Crooke, "From Rebel Movement to Political Party," p. 6.

44. Quoted in Hroub, *Hamas*, p. 75. The interview is dated April 21, 1995.

45. Shaul Mishal, *Pragmatic Dimension of the Palestinian Hamas*.

46. Ibid..

47. Ibid.

48. Quoted in Robert Plotkin, "Hamas Would Accept Saudi Peace Plan, Spokesman Says. Group Would Stop Attacks on Israelis If Occupation

Ends," *San Francisco Chronicle*, April 28, 2002, http://www.sfgate.com/cgi-bin/article.cgi?f=/c/a/2002/04/28/MN222422.DTL.

49. Ibid.
50. Parts of these conversations are published by Aaron Klein on WorldNet-Daily, an American information website with clearly conservative ideological sympathies ("EU shocker: Hamas are 'freedom fighters'. Official blamed terrorism on 'Israeli occupation' in secret meeting," April 14, 2005). Klein cites phrases taken from the meeting minutes of the PNA's Preventive Security Forces in Gaza during an Israeli army operation. Available online at http://www.wnd.com/?pageId=29833.
51. Israeli armed forces communiqué, August 2, 2002, available online at http://www.mfa.gov.il/MFA/Government/Communiques/2002/Findings%20of%20the%20inquiry%20into%20the%20death%20of%20Salah%20Sh.
52. Ibid.
53. Ibid.
54. Hosni Mubarak launched his verbal attack in Paris, after a meeting with French President Jacques Chirac. Various sources reported the statement, including *The Independent* in the UK. See http://www.commondreams.org/headlines02/0726-07.htm.
55. Palestinian Center for Policy and Survey Research (PCPSR), Public Opinion Poll no. 5, August 18–21, 2002, http://www.pcpsr.org/survey/polls/2002/p5a.html#elections.
56. Crooke, "From Rebel Movement to Political Party," p. 5.
57. Ahmed Youssef, interview by the author, Gaza City, October 26, 2008.
58. Osama Hamdan, interview by the author, Beirut, November 15, 2008.
59. Ibid.
60. As recounted by Hamdan in ibid.
61. Ibid.

CHAPTER 5: THE MARCH WATERSHED

1. Osama Hamdan, interview by the author, Beirut, November 15, 2008.
2. Ghazi Hamad, interview by the author, Gaza City, October 26, 2008.
3. Ibid.
4. Mohammed Jamal al-Natsheh, interview by the author, Be'er Sheva, Eischel Detention Center, January 12, 2005. Al-Natsheh would later be elected to the PLC in the January 25, 2006, general elections on the Change and Reform ticket while in prison. A teacher by profession, he was released from detention on September 12, 2010, after more than eight years of imprisonment.

5. The full text of the Cairo Declaration is accessible on the United Nations Information System on the Question of Palestine at http://www.miftah. org/PrinterF.cfm?DocID=6938.

6. Mishal and Sela, *Palestinian Hamas*, pp. 98–99.

7. Ghazi Hamad, interview by the author, Gaza City, October 26, 2008.

8. Cairo Declaration, http://www.miftah.org/PrinterF.cfm?DocID=6938.

9. Azzam Tamimi, interview by the author, London, July 12, 2008.

10. In its conclusions, the manifesto of the Change and Reform list through which Hamas took part in the general elections of January 2006 states that Al-Aqsa Intifada "created new facts on the ground that have rendered the Oslo program a thing of the past, and different parties, including the Zionist occupation, have already spoken of 'burying Oslo.'" Text reprinted in Tamimi, *Hamas*, pp. 274–94.

11. Farhat As'ad, interview by the author, Ramallah, October 15, 2008.

12. International Crisis Group, "Enter Hamas: The Challenges of Political Integration," *ICG Middle East Report*, no. 49 (January 18, 2006): p. 5.

13. Crooke, "From Rebel Movement to Political Party," p. 1.

14. Bassam Na'im, interview by the author, Gaza City, November 6, 2007.

15. Ghazi Hamad, "Elections Are Vital," January 2, 2006, *bitterlemons*, http://www.bitterlemons.org/previous/bl020106ed01.html#pal2. From the same article: "Elections might serve to create a common strategy for how to confront Israel. Hamas believes there must be a mix between armed resistance and political negotiations. It is a belief rooted in the fact that after ten years of PA [sic] negotiations with Israel, little or nothing has been achieved. It is around such a strategy that Hamas is hoping to find national consensus. Such national consensus is important not only for internal strength but for external credibility. If Palestinians speak with one voice, the message is more likely to be heard and respected by Israel."

16. Hamas leaders, interviews by the author, West Bank and Gaza Strip, September 2010.

17. Ahmed Youssef, interview by the author, Gaza City, October 26, 2008.

18. Ayman Taha, interview by the author, Gaza City, September 21, 2010.

19. Anonymous Islamist militant, interview by the author, West Bank, October 2008.

20. Ghazi Hamad, interview by the author, Gaza City, October 26, 2008.

21. Anonymous Islamist militant, interview by the author, September 2008.

22. Osama Hamdan, interview by the author, Beirut, November 15, 2008.

23. Rose, "Gaza Bombshell," http://www.vanityfair.com/politics/features/2008/04/gaza200804.

24. Ibid.

25. International Crisis Group, "Enter Hamas: The Challenges of Political Integration," *ICG Middle East Report*, no. 49 (January 18, 2006): p. 7.

26. Graham Usher, "Hard Rain," *Al-Ahram Weekly*, no. 763, October 6–12, 2005.
27. Qaddura Fares, interview by the author, Ramallah, February 27, 2008.
28. Chrystie Flournoy Swiney, "Ideological and Behavioral Metamorphoses: A New Charter for Hamas" (master's thesis, University of Oxford, 2007), 33, http://users.ox.ac.uk/~metheses/FlournoyThesis.pdf.
29. Nasser al-Din al-Sha'er, interview by the author, Nablus, November 2, 2008.
30. The full text of the manifesto is reprinted in Tamimi, *Hamas*, pp. 274–94.
31. Ibid., p. 281.
32. Ibid., p. 286.
33. International Crisis Group, "Enter Hamas: The Challenges of Political Integration," *ICG Middle East Report*, no. 49, January 18, 2006, 1.
34. Farhat As'ad, interview by the author, Ramallah, October 15, 2008.
35. Ibid.

CHAPTER 6: ABUL ABED'S DOUBLE-BREASTED SUIT

1. "Double-breasted suit" is the literal translation of the Italian expression *doppiopetto*. In Italian political terms, the *doppiopetto* means a reassurance regarding the intentions, the programs, and the behavior of a party or a political organization, especially if the party or the organization has armed factions or radical programs. It was used especially after World War II to describe the participation of the Italian Communist Party (PCI) in the birth of the Italian Republic, a reference to the *doppiopetto* that the PCI's leader Palmiro Togliatti used to wear.
2. Alvaro de Soto, "End of Mission Report—Confidential," May 2007, pp. 15–16, http://image.guardian.co.uk/sys-files/Guardian/documents/2007/06/12/DeSotoReport.pdf.
3. Alvaro de Soto, written interview by the author, September 16, 2010.
4. Citations are from a letter supposedly written by Ghazi Hamad after he stepped down from his post as the spokesperson of the national unity government, due to his opposition to Hamas's coup in Gaza. The letter was widely circulated at the time on different websites. For example, http://media.mcclatchydc.com/smedia/2007/10/30/17/hamadletter-English.source.prod_affiliate.91.pdf.
5. Ibid.
6. Ghazi Hamad, interview by the author, Gaza City, October 26, 2008.
7. Salah al-Bardawil, interview by the author, Gaza City, September 20, 2010.
8. Ibid.
9. Reprinted in Hroub, *Hamas*, p. 280.

10. Moussa Abu Marzouq, "What Hamas Is Seeking," *Washington Post*, January 31, 2006.

11. Ibid.

12. Nathan J. Brown, *Palestinian Politics After the Oslo Accords: Resuming Arab Palestine* (Berkeley: University of California Press, 2003), p. 144.

13. "Justice Cheshin: PA Is a De Facto Enemy State," *Jerusalem Post*, February, 14, 2006, http://www.jpost.com/Israel/Article.aspx?id=13282.

14. International Crisis Group, "Palestinians, Israel and the Quartet: Pulling Back from the Brink," *ICG Middle East Report*, no. 54 (June 13, 2006): p. 2.

15. "Statement by Middle East Quartet," January, 30, 2006, http://unispal.un.org/UNISPAL.NSF/0/354568CCE5E38E5585257106007A0834.

16. De Soto, "End of Mission Report," p. 18.

17. Author's email exchange with Alvaro de Soto, September 16, 2010: "During my time there was never any request by the Quartet to the UN to open a channel to Hamas leaders."

18. Since Hamas's electoral victory, news started to spread about the role of the US administration in reshuffling the PNA security establishment and in strengthening the security forces around the presidency. A former adviser of the United States Security Coordinators team (USSC) in Israel and the Occupied Palestinian Territory, who preferred to remain anonymous, revealed in 2010 that USSC coordinator General Keith Dayton "was involved in discussions after the 2006 elections about which security forces would be under President Abbas's control and which would be under the government's." See International Crisis Group, "Squaring the Circle: Palestinian Security Reform under Occupation," *ICG Middle East Report*, no. 98 (September 7, 2010): p. 12.

19. Associated Press, "Hamas' Down-Home Prime Minister Most Popular Palestinian Politician Despite Strife-Ridden Year," *USA Today*, February 23, 2007, http://www.usatoday.com/news/world/2007-02-23-hamas-leader_x.htm.

20. Ghazi Hamad, interview by the author, Gaza City, October 26, 2008.

21. Osama Hamdan, interview by the author, Beirut, November 15, 2008.

22. De Soto, "End of Mission Report," p. 21.

23. Ibid.

24. Khaled Hroub, "A 'New Hamas' through Its New Documents," *Journal of Palestine Studies* 140 (Summer 2006): pp. 6–27.

25. Quoted in Wendy Kristianasen, "Palestine: Hamas Besieged," *Le Monde Diplomatique*, June 2006, http://mondediplo.com/2006/06/03hamas.

26. Article 9 states that the "government will deal with the signed agreements [between the PLO/PNA and Israel] with high responsibility and in accordance with preserving the ultimate interests of our people and

maintaining its rights without compromising its immutable preroga-tives." Article 10 states that "the government will deal with the interna-tional resolutions [on the Palestine issue] with national responsibility and in accordance with protecting the immutable rights of our people." Quoted in Hroub, "A 'New Hamas.'"

27. Ibid.

28. Mohammed Barghouthi, Kobar (Ramallah), February 26, 2008, and Nasser al-Din al-Sha'er, Nablus, November 2, 2008, interviews by the author.

29. Ibid.

30. Moussa Abu Marzouq, "What Hamas Is Seeking," *Washington Post*, January 31, 2006, http://www.washingtonpost.com/wp-dyn/content/article/2006/01/30/AR2006013001209.html.

31. International Crisis Group, "Palestinians, Israel and the Quartet," p. 3.

32. Salah al-Bardawil, interview by the author, Gaza City, September 20, 2010.

33. Quoted in Kristianasen, "Palestine," http://mondediplo.com/2006/06/03hamas.

34. International Crisis Group, "After Mecca: Engaging Hamas," *ICG Mid-dle East Report*, no. 62 (February 28, 2007): p. 6.

35. Ibid., p. 25.

36. *Ria Novosti*, March 3, 2006.

CHAPTER 7: HAMAS VERSUS FATAH

1. *Entry-Points to Palestinian Security Sector Reform*, ed. Roland Friedrich and Arnold Luethold (Geneva: DCAF, 2007), p. 22.

2. "The Full Text of the National Conciliation Document of the Prisoners," May 26, 2006, http://unispal.un.org/UNISPAL.NSF/0/CE3ABE1B2E 1502B58525717A006194CD.

3. Author's meeting with activists from Fatah, Hamas, Islamic Jihad, and PFLP at the Be'er Sheva prison, January 12, 2005. Representing Hamas at the meeting was Mohammed Jamal al-Natsheh himself. Israeli authorities would later transfer him to the Ketziot prison.

4. Abdel Khaleq al-Natsheh would later temporarily withdraw his signa-ture of the document when the clash between Haniyeh and Abbas over the possibility of a referendum became more strident, in June 2006.

5. De Soto, "End of Mission Report," pp. 21–22.

6. US Consulate in Jerusalem, "Fayyad and Abed Rabbo on National Dia-logue and Civil Society Proposals," May 6, 2006, available at http://wikileaks.org/cable/2006/05/06JERUSALEM2058.html

7. Mustapha Barghouthi, interview by the author, Ramallah, August 16, 2007.

8. "National Conciliation Document of the Prisoners," June 28, 2006. Text accessible on the website of the United Nations Information Sys-

tem on the Question of Palestine (UNISPAL), http://unispal.un.org/ UNISPAL.NSF/o/7CCBF1FC97FE8BB98525719B005EFCF2.

9. In January 2009, there were still forty-five members of parliament held in Israeli jails. Most of these were affiliated with the Change and Reform list, including detainees whose preventive incarceration terms had been lengthened despite the fact that they had completed their sentence.

10. Quoted in Rose, "Gaza Bombshell," http://www.vanityfair.com/politics/ features/2008/04/gaza200804.

11. De Soto, "End of Mission Report," p. 22.

12. Quoted in Rose, "Gaza Bombshell," http://www.vanityfair.com/politics/ features/2008/04/gaza200804.

13. Mustapha Barghouthi, interview by the author, Ramallah, August 16, 2007.

14. Ibid.

15. Ibid.

16. Ibid.

17. De Soto, "End of Mission Report," p. 21. In his investigation, David Rose adds that Condoleezza Rice had telephoned Arab allies toward the end of 2006 so that they would train armed groups linked to Fatah. A consignment of weapons destined for Fatah was then moved into Gaza at the end of December through an Israeli-controlled crossing.

18. Osama Hamdan, interview by the author, Beirut, November 15, 2008.

19. Ibid.

20. "Text of the Mecca Accord for the PA Coalition Government," *Jerusalem Post*, February 8, 2007, http://www.jpost.com/LandedPages/Print-Article.aspx?id=50948.

21. Quoted in International Crisis Group, "After Mecca," p. 18. Abu Marzouq pronounced these words two weeks before the Mecca agreement.

22. Mustapha Barghouthi, interview by the author, Ramallah, August 16, 2007.

23. Ibid.

24. Nasser al-Din Al-Sha'er, interview with the author, Nablus, November 2, 2008.

25. Massimo D'Alema confirmed that no promise had been made to end Hamas's isolation. Massimo D'Alema, interview by the author, Jerusalem, September 5, 2007.

26. Jamal Abu Hashem, interview by the author, Gaza City, September 21, 2010.

27. Alastair Crooke, interview by the author, London, July 12, 2008.

28. "Q&A with Hamas leader Khaled Meshaal," Reuters, January 10, 2007, http://www.reuters.com/article/newsOne/idUSL1046412720070110.

29. Ibid.

30. Quoted in Dina Ezzat, "Resistance Wears New Look," *Al-Ahram Weekly*, no. 834 (March 1–7, 2007).

31. Mustapha Barghouthi, interview by the author, Ramallah, August 16, 2007. All quotations in this and the following paragraph are from this interview.

32. International Crisis Group, "After Gaza," *ICG Middle East Report*, no. 68 (August 2, 2007): p. 13.

33. Ibid., p. 14.

34. Ahmed Youssef, interview by the author, Gaza City, November 6, 2007.

35. Farhat As'ad, interview by the author, Ramallah, October 15, 2008.

36. Ibid.

37. On the first anniversary of the *tawjihi* coup, Bardawil, Hamas's parliamentary spokesperson, confirmed that the taking of Gaza "had never been part of Hamas' plans" (Agence France Press, "Hamas Rule in Gaza Enters Second Year Unchallenged," June 15, 2008). And yet, during those very same days, Bardawil had used extremely harsh words toward Fatah, arguing that Hamas "would fight to the end" in order to "eliminate those elements within Fatah which have tortured and killed our men. . . . This is our final decision and we will not go back on it" (quoted in Khaled Abu Toameh, "Abbas Accuses Hamas of Staging a 'Bloody Coup,'" *Jerusalem Post*, June 12, 2007).

38. "Remarks by U.S. Security Coordinator LTG Keith Dayton, Update on the Israeli-Palestinian Situation and Palestinian Assistance Programs," House Foreign Affairs Middle East and South Asia Sub-Committee, May 23, 2007, http://www.internationalrelations.house.gov/110/day052307.htm.

39. For an updated and detailed analysis of Keyth Dayton's role in the trasformation of PNA military apparatuses, see Nathan Thrall, "Our Man in Palestine," *New York Review of Books* 57, no. 15 (October 14, 2010), http://www.nybooks.com/articles/archives/2010/oct/14/our-man-palestine/. See also a conversation between Dayton and Israel Security Agency chief Yuval Diskin on Palestinian security forces, which contains a severe description of Mohammed Dahlan: US Embassy in Tel Aviv, "Ussc Dayton Raises Rafah, Ama And Badr Brigade With Isa Diskin," October 12, 2006, available at http://wikileaks.org/cable/2006/10/06TELAVIV4032.html.

40. International Crisis Group, "Ruling Palestine I: Gaza under Hamas," *ICG Middle East Report*, no. 73 (March 19, 2008): p. 4.

41. International Crisis Group, "Ruling Palestine I," p. 14.

42. Ibid., p. 6.

43. Taghreed el Khodary, "Hamas Police Force Recruits Women," *New York Times*, January, 18, 2008, http://www.nytimes.com/2008/01/18/world/middleeast/18gaza.html.

44. Quoted in International Crisis Group, "Ruling Palestine I," p. 15.
45. Ahmed Youssef, interview by the author, Gaza City, November 6, 2007.
46. Letter of resignation supposedly written by Ghazi Hamad, after he stepped down from his post as the spokesperson of the national unity government, due to his opposition to the Hamas coup in Gaza. The letter was widely circulated at the time on different websites.
47. Ibid.

CHAPTER 8: FROM RESISTANCE TO GOVERNMENT

1. Eyad al-Sarraj, interview by the author, Gaza City, October 28, 2008.
2. Ahmed Youssef, interview by the author, Gaza City, October 26, 2008.
3. Ibid.
4. "Human Rights in Palestine and Other Occupied Arab Territories. Report of the United Nations Fact Finding Mission on the Gaza Conflict," also known as the Goldstone Report (after Richard Goldstone, head of the UN fact-finding mission), September 15, 2009, p. 78, http://www2.ohchr.org/english/bodies/hrcouncil/specialsession/9/docs/UNFFMGC_Report.pdf.
5. UNRWA, "36th Emergency Appeal Progress Report, January–June 2009," p. 2, http://unispal.un.org/pdfs/UNRWA-EmerAppealProgRpt-Jan-June09.pdf.
6. Ibid.
7. Goldstone Report, http://www2.ohchr.org/english/bodies/hrcouncil/specialsession/9/docs/UNFFMGC_Report.pdf, p. 537.
8. Ibid., p. 108. "The Mission notes that the statistics from non-governmental sources are generally consistent. Statistics alleging that fewer than one out of five persons killed in an armed conflict was a combatant, such as those provided by PCHR and Al Mezan as a result of months of field research, raise very serious concerns about the way Israel conducted the military operations in Gaza."
9. International Crisis Group, "Gaza's Unfinished Business," *ICG Middle East Report*, no. 85 (April 23, 2009): p. 2.
10. Ibid., p. 3.
11. US Tel Aviv Embassy to State Department, "Codels Casey and Ackerman Meet with Defense Minister Barak," WikiLeaks, June 2, 2009, http://www.wikileaks.ch/cable/2009/06/09TELAVIV1177.html.
12. At the beginning of February, two thefts from a convoy and a warehouse belonging to UNRWA worsened the tension between the UN agency and the Hamas de facto government. In response, UNRWA suspended delivery of humanitarian aid to the Gaza Strip. On February 9, the stolen aid supplies were returned to UNRWA, and the agency resumed its routine activities. It was a very short arm-wrestling match, the ten-

sion between Hamas authorities and John Ging, at that time director of UNRWA operations in Gaza, esteemed and experienced official.

13. Rami G. Khouri, "The Monumental Folly at Sharm el-Sheikh," *Daily Star* (Lebanon), March 4, 2009, http://www.dailystar.com.lb/article. asp?edition_id=1&categ_id=5&article_id=99817#axzz12LGlVQdo.

14. Salah al-Bardawil, interview by the author, Gaza City, September 20, 2010.

15. Seymour M. Hersh, "Syria Calling: The Obama Administration's Chance to Engage in a Middle East Peace," *New Yorker*, April 6, 2009, http:// www.newyorker.com/reporting/2009/04/06/090406fa_fact_hersh.

16. Israel Ministry of Foreign Affairs, "PM Olmert Press Briefing on IDF Operation in the Gaza Strip," December 27, 2008, http://www.mfa.gov. il/MFA/Government/Speeches+by+Israeli+leaders/2008/PM_Olmert_ press_briefing_IDF_operation_Gaza_Strip_27-Dec-2008.htm.

17. "Swiss Defend Hamas Visa after Israeli Protest," *Swissinfo.ch*, July 15, 2009, http://www.swissinfo.ch/eng/politics/Swiss_defend_Hamas_visa_after _Israeli_protest.html?cid=7509778.

18. "Remarks by the President on a New Beginning," Cairo University, Egypt, June 4, 2009, http://www.whitehouse.gov/the_press_office/ Remarks-by-the-President-at-Cairo-University-6-04-09.

19. Ibid.

20. Ibid.

21. Khalid Meshaal, "Meshaal Delivers Speech on Obama's Position on Peace Process," *Conflicts Forum*, June 25, 2009, http://conflictsforum.org/ 2009/meshaal-delivers-speech-on-obamas-position-on-peace-process/.

22. "Hamas says Iran's support for group not in danger," Associated Press, August 17, 2009, available at http://webmail.iranian.com/main/news/ 2009/08/17/hamas-says-iran-s-support-group-not-danger.

23. US Riyadh Embassy to State Department, "Counterterrorism Adviser Brennan's Meeting with Saudi King Abdullah," WikiLeaks, March 22, 2009. Because of ongoing legal issues with Wikileaks, there are no stable URLs for this document at the time of this book's publication. Currently, the cable can be accessed through the WikiLeaks website at http://wikileaks.org/cablegate.html, which provides a mirrored download of all the released diplomatic cables. The original URL accessed was http://cablegate.wikileaks.org/cable/2009/03/09RIYADH447.html. The citations of WikiLeaks documents that follow will all give the original URL accessed at the time of writing, with the understanding that there is not likely to be a stable URL for these documents for some time.

24. "Exclusive: Hamas Invites Obama to Gaza in Letter," Ma'an News Agency, June 3, 2009, http://www.maannews.net/eng/ViewDetails. aspx?ID=210985.

25. There were many comments on the issue. One example is Babak Deh-ghanpisheh's comment, "A Place for Mr. Meshaal," *Newsweek*, October 18, 2010, http://www.newsweek.com/2010/10/18/is-hamas-ready-for-peace-with-israel.html. See also Henry Siegman, "US Hamas Policy Blocks Middle East Peace," *Noref Report*, no. 8, September 2010.

26. Mark Perry, "Red Team: CENTCOM Thinks Outside the Box on Hamas and Hezbollah," *Foreign Policy*, June 30, 2010, http://www.foreignpolicy.com/articles/2010/06/29/red_team.

27. Before meeting Khaled Meshaal in Damascus and Ismail Haniyeh in Gaza in June 2009, Carter met Near Eastern Affairs Bureau Deputy Assistant Secretary David Hale and National Security officials, as confirmed by the Department of State.

28. In the years to follow, Israel obstinately refused to formally apologize for the deaths it has provoked. In September 2011, this refusal led to a deep diplomatic crisis between Tel Aviv and Ankara, to the point that Turkey suspended its commercial cooperation with Israel and expelled the Israeli ambassador.

29. Khaled Hroub, "Pressures on Hamas in Reconciliation Talks," *Sada* (formerly *Arab Reform Bulletin*), Carnegie Endowment for Peace, April 2, 2009, http://carnegieendowment.org/arb/?fa=show&article=22929.

30. US Cairo Embassy to Department of State, "General Petraeus' Meeting with Egis Chief Soliman," WikiLeaks, July 9, 2009, http://cablegate.wikileaks.org/cable/2009/07/09CAIRO1349.html. See note 23, above.

31. International Crisis Group, "Turkey and the Middle East," *ICG Europe Report*, no. 203, (April 7, 2010): p. 18.

32. Palestinian National Authority, *Palestine: Ending the Occupation, Establishing the State. Program of the Thirteenth Government*, August 2009, http://www.mop-gov.ps/web_files/issues_file/090825%20Ending%20 Occupation,%20Establishing%20the%20State%20-%20Program%20 of%20the%2013%20government.pdf.

33. Palestinian Center for Human Rights (PCHR), "PCHR Is Concerned Over Arrest Campaigns against Fatah Activists in Gaza and against Hamas Activists in the West Bank," June 8, 2009, http://www.pchrgaza. org/portal/en/index.php?option=com_content&view=article&id=1 116:pchr-is-concerned-over-arrest-campaigns-against-fatah-activists-in-gaza-and-against-hamas-activists-in-the-west-bank-&catid=36:pchr pressreleases&Itemid=194.

34. Mushir al Masri, interview by the author, Gaza City, September 21, 2010.

35. "Hamas Calls for Dismissal of US Security Coordinator," in Ma'an News Agency, October 16, 2010, http://www.maannews.net/eng/View-Details.aspx?ID=324422.

36. US Cairo Embassy to Department of State, "General Petraeus' Meeting with Egis Chief Soliman," WikiLeaks, July 9, 2009, http://cablegate. wikileaks.org/cable/2009/07/09CAIRO1349.html. (See note 23.) Suleyman also forecasted that the reconciliation talks would be suspended for a while, supposedly due to the Fatah sixth congress: "Soliman also doubted that a reconciliation agreement would be reached by July 7 as Egypt previously announced, and anticipated that talks would be suspended for one-two months."

37. Nabil Shaath, interview by the author, Ramallah, July 25, 2009.

38. "Abbas Takes Blame for Goldstone Delay, Commission Says," Ma'an News Agency, January 9, 2010, http://www.maannews.net/eng/View Details.aspx?ID=253025.

39. The video is available on YouTube, at http://www.youtube.com/ watch?v=tbqLBlO3AaU.

40. "To Israel I Am Stained with Blood," Al Jazeera, February 7, 2010, http://english.aljazeera.net/focus/2010/02/2010271441269105.html.

41. "Hamas Refuses to Accuse Any Party for Killing Its Members in Beirut," *People's Daily Online*, December 28, 2009, http://english.peopledaily.com.cn/90001/90777/90854/6853825.html.

42. Hamas members in the West Bank, interviews by the author, various dates.

43. "Al-Qassam Brigades: Al-Khalil Operation Response to Settlers' Crimes," Palestinian Information Center, September 1, 2010, http:// www.palestine-info.co.uk/En/default.aspx?xyz=U6Qq7k%2bcOd87M DI46m9rUxJEpMO%2bi1s7e32WrfoAxvEL%2boRg3g56ykp4%2fZj2i 6Q2DMQVCnwnKYvNRnNrrbLA66%2bzzSY%2bWjJWAXfRbw9x p%2fnP24eOEyfjUhpGH6Goc3Gir5buE7e%2fISQ%3d.

44. Khaled Abu Toameh, "PA Wary over US, EU Efforts to Draw Hamas into the Peace Process," *Jerusalem Post*, October 28, 2010.

45. Interview with Hamas militants, Gaza City, September 2010.

46. Ibid.

47. Ibid.

48. Mushir al Masri, interview by the author, Gaza City, September 21, 2010.

49. "A complex power play may be at work here. A letter purportedly written by Qassam commander Ahmad al-Ja'bari in early March accused Minister of Interior Fathi Hammad, whom it described as close to the Da'wa arm of Hamas, of losing control over internal security, and of building a personal 'executive force' by co-opting Qassam members in northern Gaza. Northern Gaza was also the main area of activity of radical cleric and university professor Nizar Rayyan, a senior Hamas decision-maker who doubled as liaison officer with the Qassam Bri-

gades and as Jaljalat's mentor until his death in Operation Cast Lead. The suggestion that Jaljalat was at least partly a power base used for internal struggle within Hamas is clear, as is the threat to the unity of both Hamas and the Qassam Brigades" (Yezid Sayigh, "Hamas Rule in Gaza: Three Years On," *Middle East Brief*, Brandeis University Crown Center for Middle East Studies, no. 41 [March 2010]: p. 4).

50. Ibrahim Qannan, "Exclusive Interview with Gaza's Salafi Leader," Ma'an News Agency, May 21, 2010, http://www.maannews.net/eng/ViewDetails.aspx?ID=285562.

51. Ibrahim Qannan, "Exclusive: New Gaza Salafist Faction Numbers 11,000," Ma'an News Agency, April 23, 2010, http://www.maannews.net/eng/ViewDetails.aspx?ID=277513.

52. Hassan Mneimneh, "Convergence? The Homogenization of Islamist Doctrines in Gaza," *Current Trends in Islamist Ideology* 9 (December 16, 2009): pp. 5–17, http://www.currenttrends.org/research/detail/convergence-the-homogenization-of-islamist-doctrines-in-gaza.

53. Quoted in Henry Siegman, "US Hamas Policy Blocks Middle East Peace," *NOREF Report*, no.8 (September 2010): p. 5, http://www.peacebuilding.no/var/ezflow_site/storage/original/application/c4154e8f5a6c4e0dbc761f9ce335bf60.pdf.

54. "Abbas Calls for Vote, Haniyeh Wants Emergency Talks," *Maan News*, March, 15, 2011, http://www.maannews.net/eng/ViewDetails.aspx?ID=368944.

55. International Crisis Group, "Palestinian Reconciliation: Plus Ça Change . . . ," *ICG Middle East Report*, no. 110 (July 20, 2011): p. 3.

56. Moussa Abu Marzouq, "Welcome Hamas's Conciliation with Fatah," *Guardian*, May 23, 2011, http://www.guardian.co.uk/commentisfree/2011/may/24/fatah-hamas-palestinian-musa-abumarzuq.

57. Quoted in Robert Fisk, "Revealed: The Untold Story of the Deal that Shocked the Middle East," *Independent*, June 7, 2011, http://www.independent.co.uk/news/world/middle-east/revealed-the-untold-story-of-the-deal-that-shocked-the-middle-east-2293879.html.   Palestinian billionaire Munib al Masri recounted to Robert Fisk the details of the reconciliation efforts, citing also the other three independent Palestinian figures who took part in the meetings and tours: Hanna Nasser, Mahdi Abdul Hadi, and Hani al Masri.

58. During 2011, many documents were leaked on the reconciliation issue, both by WikiLeaks and through the Palestine Papers. There are at least three important documents precisely on the Egyptian reconciliation document, formally known as "Palestinian National Conciliation Accord." The first interesting document, released through WikiLeaks, originated from the US consulate in Jerusalem after a conversation with

the head of the Fatah team on reconciliation, Azzam al Ahmad, who said that "he delayed providing Egyptian General Intelligence Service (EGIS) officials the signed draft until just before a midnight [October 15, 2009] deadline, to minimize the risk that Hamas would also sign before the deadline and a deal would be reached. Al Ahmad claimed that Fatah knew in advance that Hamas would not sign, due to strong objections from Gaza-based Hamas military wing commander Ahmed Ja'bari, as well as opposition from Syria and Iran. When Hamas did not come forward by the midnight deadline, al Ahmed said, Fatah's approval of the reconciliation text became null and void" ("Fatah Negotiator on Palestinian Reconciliation," WikiLeaks, November 2, 2009, http://wikileaks.org/cable/2009/11/09JERUSALEM1970.html). Then there are two conversations during the month of October 2009 between Saeb Erekat and former US Senator George Mitchell (Palestine Papers, Meeting Minutes: Dr. Saeb Erekat—Sen. George Mitchell, State Department, October 2, 2009, http://transparency.aljazeera.net/files/4844.pdf), and with Marc Otte, EU special representative for the Middle East Process (Palestine Papers, Meeting Minutes: Dr. Saeb Erekat—Marc Otte, Ramallah, October 12, 2009, at http://thepalestinepapers.com/en/document/4868).

59. Fisk, "Revealed," http://www.independent.co.uk/news/world/middleeast/revealed-the-untold-story-of-the-deal-that-shocked-the-middleeast-2293879.html. See also author's interview with one of the meeting's participants, Jerusalem, September 20, 2011.

60. Fatah and Hamas Reconciliation Agreement, May 4, 2011. An English version of the agreement is available at http://www.jmcc.org/Documentsandmaps.aspx?id=828.

EPILOGUE

1. Abdel Moneim Abul Futouh, interview by the author, Cairo, November 28, 2007.

2. *Translator's note*: The Italian term "wicked teachers" (*cattivi maestri*) was used to describe university professors such as Toni Negri (author, with Michael Hardt, of the best-selling *Empire*) who were accused in the 1970s of stoking radicalism in left-wing Italian youth, as well as of being the intellectuals who provided the ideological legitimization for left-wing terrorism.

3. Shaul Mishal, "The Pragmatic Dimension of the Palestinian Hamas," *Armed Forces & Society* 29, no. 4 (Summer 2003): p. 570.

4. Henry Siegman, "Israel's Lies," *London Review of Books* 31, no. 2 (January 29, 2009): pp. 3–5, http://www.lrb.co.uk/v31/n02/sieg01_.html.

5. The Mubarak regime's stand on the Gaza War weakened it, which was one of the factors that led to the Egyptian revolution in January 2011.

6. US Colonel (ret.) Philip J. Dermer, "Trip Notes on a Return to Israel and the West Bank: Reflections on U.S. Peacemaking, the Security Mission, and What Should Be Done," *Journal of Palestine Studies* 39, no. 3 (Spring 2010): pp. 81, 68, and 1, respectively, http://palestine-studies.org/files/pdf/jps/10706.pdf.

7. Ibid., p. 81.

INDEX